Jackfruit: A Bicycle Quest Through Latin America

David E.X.N. Nghiem

Booklocker.com, Inc. 2009
Cover photographs © David E.X.N. Nghiem
Book design by David E.X.N. Nghiem.
Coral reef photograph from the Isla de Pescado by Anthony Khan.
Maps are public domain courtesy of the University of Texas Perry-Castañeda
Library Map Collection
All photographs, unless otherwise noted, are © David E.X.N. Nghiem

ISBN 978-1-60145-922-0

Printed in the United States of America.

10 9 8 7 6 5 4 3 2 1

First Edition

For Tito

To Stephanie!
Carpe Diem!
Live life fully! And
sometimes adventure is
best experienced vicariously!

All the best,

Preface

I lay sweating on my back in the tent, naked, my diving knife clutched in my right hand, and a can of pepper spray in the other. The strong wind rattled my tent, shaking the flaps, poles and ropes so violently the nylon fabric popped, sounding like sporadic gunfire. I stared at the dark, domed ceiling and shook with terror as a high beam from a vehicle slowly lit, and then left my tent. Could it be a bandito, a murderous ex-contra prowling the hills and valleys that lay in the shadow of a live volcano in the distance? Or was it a land squatter searching for a quiet place for a home and hearth? I didn't know. I didn't care. In the depth of my fear, I was ready to stab anyone who entered my tent.

I closed my eyes in the dark, only to confront an even deeper darkness. Why was I doing this? What sort of thing drove me to commit this mad, lonely act, to ride a bicycle across Latin America? It seemed so simple at first. It was supposed to be a leisurely three-month joyride across South America from Lima, Peru to Buenos Aires, Argentina. Instead, I was on the side of a road in an desolate stretch of north western Costa Rica, hiding from vagrants and highwaymen, perched on a cliff in front of a volcano, worn from my inability to sleep, and scared out of my mind.

I put the cold, steel blade on my bare chest, and wiped away a tear. I was thousands of miles from home, in an alien, hostile place, alone, exhausted, and overwhelmed from seven months of intense trials through three third-world countries.

A confluence of unforeseen events had forced me to extend the length of my trip several times. And then there were the three mysteries that entrapped me: my strange intuitive desire to come to Latin America, a visit to a forbidden, sacred, symbol-laden site that almost killed me, and a new personal interest – borne from September 11th - in the geopolitical interaction between the USA and Latin America. These three subjects became my inexorable obsessions, and as with any irrational desire, my path was dangerously full of pitfalls and obstacles.

I held the cool, slim tube of the pepper spray, and checked the nozzle. I looked at the door of my tent as it shook. I glanced back at my watch, as the hour hands glowed a dim green. It was three in the morning, and I hadn't slept at all. I had just two more hours to endure before I could greet the sun, and the security and relief that it represented. I covered my eyes with my knife arm, and touched the cold metal tubes of my bicycle frame. I reminded myself that survival wasn't just enduring the elements, it was also about enduring my own emotional obstacles.

And it would be two more months before I would find the link in El Salvador that would help me resolve the mystery of the symbols.

Contents

North America

Chapter 1

The Fortune Teller

I rode my bicycle down Mt. Auburn St. into Harvard Square. The day was warm enough for a green tank-top and shorts, but the leaves were already changing color to warm browns and reds. Piles of leaves whipped around the streets as cars drove by. I sniffed the air, and smelled the aroma of hot dogs, fried dough, and pizza, as the crowds slowly meandered through the street next to the Wordsworth bookstore. It was Oktoberfest 1999, and I'd taken a break from my engineering homework to relax in the party. I locked up my bike at the bus stop, put on a blue bandanna, and walked around.

I was a part time biomedical engineering student at Boston University, recently laid off from my job as a systems analyst in the Genetics Institute. I used that time to finish my degree as quickly as possible.

As I walked through the square, a distinctive sound caught my attention. It was a pan flute of a Peruvian band, Inca Son, and they played music that I'd never heard before. I went to the crowd around them, and listened. It was an exotic sound, yet as I listened to them play, I felt an odd feeling inside, as if I'd known that music for my entire life. I dismissed the feeling, and bought a CD from them.

"Peru, that's in South America, right?" I asked one of the band members. Their faces were painted, and their skin was reddish brown. They wore rainbow colored outfits that reminded me of Native Americans.

"Si, it is in South America," said the man as I gave him the fifteen dollars, "have you ever been there?"

"No."

"You should go one day. It is beautiful. Have you ever heard of Macchu Picchu?"

"Yes! I've read about it."

"Good. I know you will go soon."

"Sure, sure, hey, thanks for the CD."

I will go to Peru soon? It wasn't a bad idea, but I had no desire to go to Peru. I was too caught up in finishing my diploma, my NASA rocket project, and I was dating Ann, a pretty, athletic, Cuban Jewish girl I met in the gym. Go to Peru? No. What I wanted was to become an astronaut. It was the reason I went to work on the project in the first place. In fact, my identity and existence morphed into my participation in the NASA rocket project.

In 1996, I, a junior, and four freshmen, with plenty of guidance from Dr. Chakrabarti, founded the SPECTRE project, which stood for the Student-run Program for Exo-atmospheric Collecting Technologies and Rocket Experimentation. We were one of the few groups to get the NASA grant as a bunch naive, undergraduate students. Naturally, it was my pride, joy, passion, suffering, and it was my identity.

I lost my scholarship to work on the project, and I fought with my parents to stay in Boston, when they tried to persuade me to go home and recuperate my GPA at another university. Because of that, I refused to acknowledge them for years afterward. I hated them for their stereotypically Asian parental response. SPECTRE was my dream, and I was willing to do whatever it took to stay in Boston to continue the project. At one point, after several months of looking for a job, I applied as a waiter in a restaurant, just to have money to stay in town. Luckily, through a friend, the Genetics Institute hired me as an analyst. I built and administered computer systems to sort genetic sequences for protein discovery. The Genetics Institute helped pay for my degree, and they even gave me time to continue with SPECTRE. It was the best possible solution for me, but my resentment towards my parents would fester for years afterwards.

As of October, SPECTRE had run her course, and would soon launch. I was laid off with just two more courses to go for my diploma, and I had enough of a stipend to focus my energies on my school work, and my relationship with Ann. All I wanted was to finish my degree, launch, and go to NASA.

As I walked through the fair, I sampled some jewelry, a jade colored

4

neck choker, when I heard a female voice call out to me, "hey you! Hey handsome!"

I looked to my right, where a pretty woman in her twenties, held a smoking cigarette in her hand. She sat behind a table with some tarot cards laid on it, and she wore a black bandanna. We were in front of Wordsworth, and she looked at me with a beckoning smile.

"Want a palm reading?" I winked at her and smiled.

"No, I'm kind of skeptical. But thanks for the offer."

"You'll come back. Think about it." She winked at me.

I went through the square to Au Bon Pain, a café and sandwich bistro, and watched a German group perform their traditional dances, complete with green hats and knickers. The day was winding down, and it was late afternoon as people started to close up shop. As I headed toward my bicycle, something inside me propelled me to the fortune teller. It was near the end of the day, so I decided I could use some entertainment. I walked back to the fortune teller's table.

"I knew you'd be back."

"Well, I feel like being a sucker today." I said as I sat down.

She looked at me haughtily, smiled, took a drag on her cigarette, and then took the cigarette out of her mouth. She offered her hand, and I extended my hand into it. She held my hand for a few seconds, softly massaged it, and then she spoke.

"You're the kind of guy who can do anything he puts his mind to."

"That was generic." I thought to myself.

"Your friends are not your friends, be careful of them, but you do make friends very easily." She paused, and then said, "I see you going far. I see much travel."

Then she asked me a question. "Do you have a girlfriend?"

"No." I lied. She immediately squeezed my hand, and fiercely applied a discomforting pressure on the palm.

"The one you're with now, you just met her a month ago?"

"Yes!" I said in astonishment. I did meet Ann a month ago.

"She's not the one. Next year, you'll meet someone... someone very important. She's your lifetime companion." As she said that, the hairs on my back stood on end, as an electric current went up my spine. I didn't know why, but my eyes started to tear. I looked into her eyes, and her gaze never wavered. She had a sly smile on her face, as I unconsciously took out my wallet, and gave her the ten dollars for the reading. As I stood up, she said,

"Still a skeptic?"

"Uh, no. I think." I stammered.

"Bye handsome. Remember what I said."

****

I was miserable, and I felt awful, as I sat in the Amtrak train in 30th Street station, Philadelphia. I was on the northeast corridor train, headed for Boston, and it hadn't departed. I looked at my watch. It was still ten minutes till departure, and I looked out onto the other train platforms in the station. The shiny steel hulls of the trains reflected the harsh glare of the fluorescent lights overhead in the tunnel bay. I sat back in the seat, and lowered it as I closed my eyes.

I spent the Thanksgiving holiday with my parents. We didn't talk much, but they didn't insist either. I almost completed my degree, and since I paid for half my tuition by working full time, my father didn't try to say anything to me. His only dream was for his four sons to complete their degrees. My mother insisted that I look into medical school, and be a doctor. I failed a course when we won the project, and for me, my dream was space, NASA, and the stars. I had no desire to torture myself any longer doing premedical courses, which I faired poorly in, and had a strong distaste for. She stopped when I told her to leave me alone and to let me live.

But that wasn't the reason I was miserable. Three weeks earlier, I had a bad break up with Ann. We broke up in the Student Union that night, when I went to see her hip hop dance performance. She told me that I had issues. I was so angry after the break up that I went to the Boston Common, and I railed in anger at Fate. My tears came out as I cried out in fury.

"You fucker! You've been fucking with me my entire goddamn life! From elementary school till now, you just don't quit! Huh?! You goddamn fucker!" I screamed as nine years of pent up frustration and anger boiled into an explosion. Several dogs came barking at me, and I roared at them. They turned around and ran, yelping back to their owners. As I walked out of the Common, a police car pulled up next to me, its lights flashing, as I heard the intercom blare through the static, "there's a disturbance in the park... unidentified male, race unknown, is there causing a disturbance."

I didn't bother to look at them. I didn't care if they arrested me. I didn't give a damn, and I kept walking to the harbor, where I laid down on the water's edge, and looked up at the stars.

When we broke up, I felt like all of white American society was driving a wedge between us, even though nothing substantial had happened. I felt like all the crap I dealt with as a minority, of Vietnamese descent, growing up and going from lower to middle class in a white, Jewish suburb in southern New Jersey, outside of Philadelphia was about to spill out. I felt like we were taboo together, and there was a subconscious reaction from white, Boston society to us. It was ironic, because in New Jersey, most of the Asian guys I grew up with eventually married non Asian women. But this was Boston, a "progressive" town, where I heard a racist slur every two to three weeks, and a white taxi cab driver intentionally rammed his car into my body, while I crossed the street when the signal indicated to cross. He waited until I was right in front of him, revved his engine and hit me. This was on my second day at the University. When I was out with Ann, white men stared at us in disgust. Ann never noticed it, but I did. Unfortunately, by acknowledging them, I internalized my anger, their anger, and I was erupting inside. It was my fault for permitting those assholes and society to control me, and I knew it.

I looked out the window. The train started moving. A middle aged white man sat down beside me. We introduced ourselves, and he also was a Philadelphian. We talked about the differences between Boston and Philadelphia. I was born in, and I grew up in, until I was seven, a ghetto in West Philadelphia. Up till then, I never encountered any problems with the other kids. My playmates were white, black, and a few Hispanic. It wasn't until my father's job moved to the suburb of New Jersey that I became hyper aware of my race. Because I was a native of Philadelphia, the gentleman and I got along well. We weren't fond of the cold rudeness of the Bostonians. I didn't talk about race with him.

I sat back in my chair, and my mind drifted to the incident in Oktoberfest, to the soothsayer's words, *"next year, you'll meet someone important. She's your lifetime companion."*

I always carried a drawing pad with me when I traveled, and I drew cartoons, comic book characters, and body builders. It was a hobby I did maybe once or twice a year. I also drew portraits, but I could never do them

7

without a photo. I couldn't even do them with a person in front of me. I was an amateur and self taught. "A lifetime companion." I thought to myself. What would she look like? What would she feel like?

I put the pad on the fold out table, and held the pencil in my hand. I closed my eyes, and cleared my mind. I went inside myself, and I felt myself sink, deep into my heart. I settled into a dark and warm space. Slowly, a wave of electricity coursed through my veins. It grew, until it crested through my body. Then, my eyes half opened in a trance, barely conscious, my hand and pencil started to move across the pad. First, an oval appeared. Soon, the eyes revealed themselves, and later, a nose. Lips and ears came to life, as well as eyebrows, a neck, and cheekbones. Soon hair grew, and my pencil worked across the board, faster, and faster. Then, my fingers touched the face, and worked, adding shade, tone, and dimension. I licked my index finger, and outlined depth as I smudged grays and blacks into place. Finally, with the tip of the pencil, I gave her eyes life.

I opened my eyes fully, and was shocked at what I saw. For the first time, and the last time, I drew a face that jumped out from the page with life. It looked so real and alive.

"How did I do that?" I asked myself. Every attempt I ever made at drawing a person's face, a human face with no reference, no photo, or even an appearance, always looked like a cartoon. Yet, on my pad, was a person who could possibly exist. The gentleman next to me looked at the picture, smiled at me, and said, "Is that your girlfriend?" I looked at him, stunned.

"She's... a friend." I stammered back.

No she wasn't. It was just a picture, and a hand made drawing. That was all. How could she be a friend, let alone a lover, when I never met, saw, or encountered anyone with the likeness of the picture? I closed the pad, and went back to ruminating about Ann and the breakup, as the train raced through the Northeast, among forests of trees bare of their leaves.

Chapter 2

SPECTRE

"10... 9... 8... 7... 6..."

"Five!" We said, as we started chanting with the flight tower announcer.

"4... 3... 2... 1..."

"Ignition."

A loud electronic beep came from inside the gray, block control house. A spark came from under the twenty five foot, two stage rocket, a Nike Orion missile, which pointed at an angle into the clouds of the overcast sky over the Middle Atlantic.

"Boom!", "Fwooosh!" A blue flame erupted underneath, as a thick ring of dust spread out in a shock wave, which hit us, eight hundred meters away in the outdoor observation platform. I felt the sonic wave enter and pass through my body, and suddenly, the rocket slowly rose, and then shot like a bullet into the sky.

"Woo hoo hoo!!" I whooped as I hugged Terry, a Greek American kid who was one of the founders of the project, and Julia, another founder and a fellow Philadelphian. We were reunited to finally see the rocket fly. Terry whooped in glee, and Julia jumped and clapped her hands in delight. In the sky, we heard the sonic boom reach us, as the rocket broke the sound barrier. In the horizon of the ocean outside Wallop's Island, Virginia, we saw a tiny object hit the water with a thunderous boom, and a giant crest of a splash. The second stage was off, and the final stage was close to sub-orbit.

We screamed in delight, and four years of passion, suffering, long nights, dreaming, effort, the team work of many electrical engineering students in

Dr. Ruane's project class, with Dr. Chakrabarti's assistance, of George, the Hungarian programmer from Thailand, Jack, the genius from Wisconsin on the subsystems, John, the 40'ish college dropout who came back to master-mind the computer system and finally get his electrical engineering degree, Rick, the Alabaman whiz kid on the electronics, Jenny, the southern speaking mechanical engineer who built the hull, and of countless other BU and NASA staff, it all finally culminated in a beautiful, glorious moment where our dreams, our teamwork, and our efforts, took off into space.

For me, the project was my redemption for almost failing out of school. I sat back on the bench of the viewing platform, under the overcast sky. A calm ocean wind blew our hair as we walked down to greet and shake hands with Dr. Ruane and Dr. Chakrabarti in congratulations. We took pictures, and celebrated at a restaurant in Chincoteague Island later that afternoon, and then in the evening, we went swimming off the island's waters. All through it, as we talked and cheered the finish, I felt hollow inside. For four years, my identity and my life, was carried in the aluminum hull of the rocket, and the project was done.

Earlier that year, I graduated on January, 2000, which fulfilled my father's dream. The rocket took off on June 13th, the day before my birthday. It was the perfect birthday gift, and a month earlier, I was hired by a medical school on Longwood medical campus in the center of Boston as a systems analyst. I needed to pay my bills, as my stipend had run out. I had nothing to look forward to anymore. All the long nights, the daily dreaming, was done. My dream was done, and my role as the project coordinator was over. My identity was gone.

****

I was home for the weekend, one warm August afternoon, and I had lunch with my family. "You're depressed, David." Said my father as we ate phó the traditional Vietnamese noodle soup.

"You truly are depressed with the way you sound." He said. I looked into my bowl, and fished in the rice noodles with my chopsticks. The smell of cumin, anise seed, hoisin sauce, and cinnamon filled my nostrils as I ate. I looked out the dining room window at the two eighty year old maple trees, and a large oak tree, in the backyard. I called the trees the "Three Brothers", since they were so close to each other.

10

Depressed? I was depressed? I looked at my father. His gray beard and mustache were stubble, and my mother sat down with us. They talked to each other in Vietnamese, as I listened to the familiar, yet foreign phrases. I understood a little, since I grew up speaking it until I was six. After that, I went to school, where I had to speak English. They got up and left the table to go upstairs.

I looked outside at the trees. The leaves hadn't fallen yet, but they were starting to change color. I took a bite into the fried, textured soy protein that my mother flavored to taste like beef. It's meaty taste spread over my tongue. I looked across the table at the statue of a Quan Yin Bodhisattva on top of the dark, worn, cherry wood bureau. I wanted to leave, and I was tired. The next day, I took the train back to Boston.

Nothing meant anything to me anymore. I was finally getting over a bad break up with Jenny, an Italian girl I met during a Spring Break trip to the Dominican Republic back in February. In addition, without SPECTRE, I became aimless. My days consisted of getting up, bicycling to work, handling computer problems and user issues, biking to the gym, working out on the weights, and then home. It was mind numbing.

Later, in October, I became disillusioned with the Space movement and with NASA in general, after going to a conference in Los Angeles, California. I discovered just how disconnected the people were with the needs of society. My friend, Navroop, a Punjabi American, and I presented a business idea to a board of directors, with the hope that we'd be able to pitch to venture capitalists later on. They shot us down, citing that we were too young and inexperienced.

Later that month, I broke Sonja's heart, a German exchange student I'd started seeing in August. During our time together, I felt that maybe she wasn't interested in dating anymore, and wanted to be friends. I misread her feelings, and one night, I made the mistake of showing up at her friend's house with an ex to go dancing for the night. Sonja, suddenly showed up, saw the two of us, and said with a shaking voice, "Zu are still friend with your ex?" She quickly left for Germany after that. I felt worse when I learned from a mutual friend that the reason she left Germany was to get away from a broken relationship, only to meet me.

At work, I got into fights with the M.D. Ph D's whose egos couldn't fit through the door of my office. I didn't work for them, but their demands on me were straining me and my boss. Everything was wearing down on me.

Still, I did what I could to keep a level head. My friends Tracey and Laura hung out with me at restaurants and cafes, where we ate, and they listened to my relationship crashes. Tasnim, a Bahraini girl who I met in the local ballroom dance club, frequently listened to me bitch about my relationship troubles. Mistrani, an Indian Muslim doctoral student, who was like my older brother, took me out to the movies, and events around town. Maria, a Salvadorian girl would scold me and lift my spirits up about how relationships weren't always all that. I kept going to the gym, and the guys there were like family. We worked out, and sometimes commiserated. I practiced and taught kick boxing at the University Kung Fu club, and they too were like family. They all helped me keep some semblance of sanity in a world that was steadily dulling, and dying in monotony.

I kept my mind active, reading books about lost cities and cultures, and ancient, strange mysteries. I spent many Sunday evenings in the tea shop in Harvard Square, reading magazines. But it wasn't enough. The year 2000 was wrapping up, and it was the end of the Millennium. I knew something wasn't right with me. Intuitively, something inside of me was screaming to emerge, but I couldn't figure out what it was.

Everyday, I read reports about earthquakes, global warming, and solar system events. It felt like everything was building up to something unprecedented. Each day, there was another earthquake in an odd place off the US Geological Survey, or a new climate temperature record being set. As I continued my daily life, I tried to ignore the feeling. I tried to ignore the feeling that inside of me was another being, struggling to emerge. I closed myself off inside with walls of rationality, skepticism, and logic. I shielded myself in my ignorance, but the feelings couldn't be denied.

Everyday, they grew stronger, and they entwined my heart and gut. I couldn't escape it, and I threw myself into more activities to get away from it. I did ballroom dance, Argentine tango, went to nude drawing classes, rode with friends into the woods, and climbed rock walls with Aleks, an Olympic class rower who I befriended in engineering. I dated more women, and read trashy novels, but to no avail. Whatever it was, it wouldn't be ignored. It was emerging, and I couldn't do anything about it.

Chapter 3

Kendra

"Dave! Are you alright?!" Asked Mistrani, as I lay on his futon, writhing in pain, in his tiny studio in Brookline.

"No." I moaned as I clutched my right rib cage.

"What happened?"

I pulled up my shirt, and revealed a dark, protruding lump between the bones of my ribs.

"That's gotta hurt! Let me get some ointment for you." Mistrani grabbed a bottle with Urdu writing on it, and slathered the stuff on my skin. It stung as he touched it.

"Ow!" I yelped.

"Man! You took that one pretty hard! What did you do?"

"Fell on the handle bars of my bike. I don't know how I managed to do that." I groaned. Mistrani sat down. I laid on the futon as my rib cage throbbed, and tried to remember what happened. I rubbed the lump on my head, and felt it throbbing with blood.

Earlier that evening, I went with the club to see a martial arts exhibition, in a theater in the heart of Boston. When the show was over, I walked outside to join my group, as crowds of people exited. There was a woman standing in front of me, and she was dressed in a long, dark skirt, which wrapped around her legs. She was elegantly dressed, and she had a dark red top on. She was slim, and her long dark hair was in a bun, with two sticks holding it together. Her eyes were dark, and they didn't reflect the light. Her face seemed familiar, which startled me at first, since I'd never met her before. I looked at her, and she quickly looked away from me.

"How odd." I thought. I didn't think much of her, since she was just another pretty face, and I was going out with another woman. Our club went to a restaurant in China Town for dinner. I sat down opposite of her, and decided to play with her eyes again, just to see if she would repeat her same reaction. I looked into her eyes, and she quickly looked down to the right, away from me.

"What an odd character." I thought to myself. We ordered dinner, and ate. Later, she asked the group,

"Anyone want to try my dish?" No one answered.

"Is it vegetarian?" I finally asked.

"Yes."

"OK, I'll try some."

I passed my dish to her. I didn't bother to ask the rest of the group, since they knew my diet. As we ate, I glanced at her. I knew I never met her before, but for some odd reason, she looked familiar. I brushed off the thought, and joked with my friends. After dinner, we walked to the subway station.

"So what's your name?" I asked.

"Kendra."

"Kendra? Nice to meet you. I'm David."

"Pleased to meet you."

She was a freshman, and recently joined the club. Her father put her in a karate class when she was younger, and she hated it. So, he put her in a Kung Fu class, and she loved it. Her best friend's violin teacher taught her about vegetarianism, which resonated deeply with her values. She was the only one in her family to practice it, and it was difficult for her, since they were Italian. But she managed to persevere for herself. For a woman from the South, she had a quick tongue, like a New Yorker. We departed at the subway station, and I had to get back, since I was expecting a call from Mia, the half Norwegian half Syrian woman I was dating.

As I biked back, I smugly said to myself, "The year two thousand is almost over. Just one more month and a half and I will win." For all of that year, I was at war with the fortune teller. I was determined not to meet anyone who qualified for her prophecy. I didn't mind dating someone, but in my heart, I kept it inconsequential. Even though I sometimes got emotionally involved, in the inevitable break up, I used that as an excuse to recover quickly. I met Mia in 1999, so she didn't count. All I had to do was get to January 1st, 2001, without any substantial relationships, and I would win. As I biked through the Boston University campus, an errant thought appeared in my mind.

"Do you suppose it's Kendra?"

Abruptly, I crashed into a high curb, and uncharacteristically, I flew up and slammed into my handlebars. The round metal punched in between my ribs, and I came down in a heap on the bar. It was a miracle that nothing broke. My head slammed into a concrete block on the sidewalk, and I was stunned. I looked up, dazed, and saw stars. I closed my eyes, looked up again, and a blurry image of the Warren Towers student dormitory came into view. The pain was numbing, and my eyes kept flashing.

"Oh fuck." I thought. The pain was excruciating as I regained my feeling. Did I break something? I felt my ribs. I didn't break anything. Well, I couldn't tell, and some students who saw the accident helped me up. I managed to hobble to Mistrani's apartment, where he helped to alleviate some of the pain.

Later that night, after a painful bike ride to my apartment, I checked my voice messages. An irate Mia left a message about not calling her. I decided not to call her back, and collapsed in my futon. My side ached, it was late, and I was in pain.

Mia decided to give me one more chance, and I saw her once more at a Bhangra competition. Bhangra is a style of Indian dance from the Punjabi region of India, and I was a dancer in Navroop's bhangra squad as a heavy lifter. I squatted and lifted three men on my shoulders, and danced. The night of the competition aggravated my injury, and an argument with Navroop kept me from seeing Mia. I never saw her again after that.

But, it was 2001, and I also didn't see Kendra, so I was thrilled. I'd won against the fortune teller. My destiny, my Fate, was once again in my own hands. My world was whole, and it was the way I wanted it to be.

Chapter 4

Omens

There was very little snow that winter of 2001, which was strange. Boston typically received a lot of snow, but for the last few years, due to global warming, it was scant. I walked into my apartment in Watertown, after a heavy routine in the gym. I sat down, and on a whim, decided to draw something. It'd been over a year since I last drew anything. I grabbed my drawing pad out of the book shelf, and flipped through the pages. There were pages of body builders, fitness women, cartoons, comic book characters, and portraits. I flipped to the last one, the one I did on November 27th, 1999. I looked at the picture, and I thought to myself, "I remember how I drew that. I didn't have a photo, a person, nothing. I did a good job."

I looked at the drawing, and noted the shining of the eyes. The face was beautiful, and the gaze was one of intense focus, but the softness of the eyes showed a deep undercurrent of compassion and caring. As I looked at the picture, some questions come to my mind.

"I wonder why she looks so... familiar. Wait. It's familiar because I drew it. That's why." I looked at the picture and studied it. I drew that picture on the train, and it came from nowhere. How can a picture from nowhere be familiar? As I studied the drawing, in my mind was a list of names and faces, which it began to match with, and, slowly, I began to realize who it was.

"No. It's not. It can't be. That can't possibly happen. That's impossible." I slowly said to myself. I knew where I saw that face. I knew why the picture looked so familiar. I knew who it was, and I did not like it at all.

"This didn't happen." I said as I put the pad away.

When I realized what the picture was, and who it could possibly be, and most importantly, what it could mean, it became a key which unlocked a door in my psyche. Immediately, I stopped the door from opening, and slammed it shut, fearful at what the greater meaning was. The force behind the door, pounded into my psyche, into my mind, and I kept trying to deny it. The pressure was ready to blow, and there was nothing I could do to stop it.

I hadn't seen Kendra in months, since she rarely showed up to the club's practice sessions. She did show up once, and we worked out together, but she kept glancing away from me. Yet when my back was turned, I could feel her eyes pierce into me.

In March, I woke up on a Wednesday, with a powerful, almost over-whelming urge to go as far south as possible. I couldn't understand it, and I didn't understand why. I packed up my bags, called in sick, and left on a train for Miami. I had a layover in Philadelphia, so I stayed at my parents. My mother asked if I was off to rescue someone. In Miami, I immediately went to the airport, to find a ticket to South America. I was going mad. Why was I doing this? What was calling me? Who was calling me? I just knew I had to somehow, touch down in South America. The feeling was powerful, and I was undeterred, until I saw the ticket prices.

I took a return flight back to Boston on Sunday. All during that time, I couldn't stop the feelings. Something was going to happen.

In April, I went to visit my parents for the weekend. I sat down to brunch with my father. My mother was preparing phó in the kitchen, and the smell of soup filled the air with an aromatic spice. Ginger sizzled in the blue flame of the range. My father was reading one of his engineering technical reports, and I was reading a science fiction novel, when we suddenly heard a "tap tap tap" on the sky light. We looked above our heads, and a dark bird outside, tapped on the glass. It tapped once. Then twice. And then on the third tap, the bird flew through the glass. It flew into the dining room, then back to the skylight, tapped it with its beak, and then flew into the kitchen, where it landed on some hanging herbs and chirped. The skylight was intact.

"Dave's friend is here." My father calmly said. I practically leaped out of my skin.

"My God! Did you see that?! It flew through the freaking window!"

"David! You always make such a big deal out of these things." Said my

18

mother.

"Dad! You saw it! You saw it fly through the window!" He shrugged his arms, and laughed with a smile.

"Mom! I swear to God, We saw that bird fly through the goddamn window!"

"David! Watch your language!"

"Dad! You saw it too!"

"Don't worry about it." He said.

"It flew through a solid glass window like it wasn't even there, and you guys are acting like this?!"

My brother Jeff opened the kitchen window, and let the bird fly out. "It's a blue bird, and not a black bird, so it isn't bad luck." He said, as he tried to reassure me. I ran around the house to check all the windows, to make sure I wasn't seeing things. They were all closed. The bird came in through the sky light, and nowhere else. I was going mad. I knew what I saw, and my Dad saw it with me. I went back to Boston the next day, feeling disturbed. I walked into my apartment, and on the floor, was the drawing pad. It fell out of the bookcase, but no one was there.

"How did this get out here?" I mumbled as I walked to it. I picked up the pad, and opened it. It opened right to the picture. I tore the picture out, and looked at it again. I contemplated throwing it out, but the voice inside said not to. Then, it took over me, and I rolled it up, and went to a framing shop. I had the picture framed in a dark, exquisitely carved, wooden frame. I put the picture back on the shelf, and looked at it.

"Impossible." I said. Little did I know, the door that I closed inside of me, had been blown wide open by the bird's entry. Everyday, for the next few months, I looked at the picture. It became a curse to me. It was a window to a possibility that I refused to consider. It was a window which destroyed the foundations that I built my world out of, a world where everything happened logically.

In April, the club had a party and she was there. Mistrani, I, and my roommate went, and we watched a B Kung Fu movie for entertainment. Afterwards, my instructor, who observed Kendra and I in practice, "volunteered" me to walk her back to the campus. We walked and had a light conversation. I didn't mention the picture, since I wanted Mistrani to confirm if there was or wasn't a match. Kendra had her glasses on, and I learned that she was a biology major. Also, she was interested in Buddhism, and a lover of animals. I saw her try to woo our friend's pet rabbit. The next day, Mistrani came over to look at the picture. I put my glasses over the eyes.

"Holy schmoly." He said in awe.

"Please no," I replied.

"I'm sorry. No, I'm not kidding you, man. The drawing matches her."

In May, I saw Kendra one more time. I was getting tired of being aggravated with the picture. We talked some more, and agreed to write to each other. I still didn't say anything about the picture, but I had a plan. I had one more shot at beating Fate, and I figured it would be the Ace in my hand.

I had a difficult time in my work place. One M.D. PhD, Dr. Rodentsky, came in one morning yelling at me for no reason. I considered it harassment, and threw him out of my office. I then called the cops on him. My boss was on my side, but his superiors pressured him to force my resignation. It was just as well. The urgency inside of me to go to South America was overwhelming. The door inside was wide open, but I couldn't see beyond it. All I knew, was I had to walk through. So, I made a plan.

I bought a ticket to Lima, Peru, and a return ticket three months later from Buenos Aires, Argentina. I bought panniers for my bicycle, and with the help of my friend and fellow engineering major, Aleks, we prepared my bike. I bought survival equipment, and a tent. I closed my lease on the apartment, donated some of my things, and stored the rest. I figured on returning in three months. That would be enough time for me to discover the hidden reasons for going to South America. I had enough money saved up, by living thriftily to last for at least eight months of living expenses if I needed to return to Boston.

Everyone thought my plan was insane. What kind of a maniac bikes across a continent? I looked at a road map of South America. It didn't look too big, and three months would be plenty of time to get to Buenos Aires. Everyone was against it. I argued bitterly with my mother over the phone. She tried to have my brothers convince me not to do it. They said it was cool what I was doing, but probably insane. Tasnim, and her boyfriend questioned what could possibly compel me to do such a thing. Her Colombian friend, Lina said I would be kidnapped, robbed, and probably raped. She thought I was insane. No one believed I was serious about it. Maria, a Salvadorian friend from the club called me up one day to question me, and to see if I was serious.

"So you're definitely doing this, Dave?"

"Yes."

"Why?"

"I don't know why. I just know that something big is going to happen. Something that's going to affect all of us, and change everything. All I know is that I have to get out of here, quickly, and that there's something, and someone I have to find in South America." She was silent on the phone for a moment.

"Wow. So you are serious."

"Why wouldn't I be?"

"Well, stay alive and send me an email."

"OK."

The conflict inside and outside of me created an internal war. One side of me, my rational part, said I was insane to follow my intuition on this mad plan. My other side, my intuition, calmly said I had to go, that it was imperative that I went, and that I had to find something, and meet someone down there. I was on the cusp, and I would have to decide soon.

In July, I submitted my resignation letter and my two week notice. My roommate of four years, Nate, an Armenian friend, helped me move my stuff into storage. On the last day, I had lunch with Walid in his restaurant, Sepal, where he and his wife wished me good luck, and to be careful not to destabilize the planet. We laughed about it. His wife said that my trip would be a spiritual one. After lunch, I put my panniers on, loaded my bicycle, and biked to South Station, where I took the Amtrak train home. I also took the picture with me. When I arrived home, I mailed the picture to Kendra, as well as a letter explaining the story.

When I came home, I was a festering boil of conflict. My brother, Jeff, said that I brought a war home. I knew I was in for a fight. At the dinner table, I argued with my parents again, and the argument turned into a shouting match, when suddenly my nose started to bleed. My mother stopped in frustration. The next day, we fought again, as I loaded my things into the car.

"I'm not driving you to the airport. Go find someone else." She said.

"What the hell?! I don't believe this. Look, there's nothing you can do that will stop me, mom. It's my goddamn life! It's mine!"

I watched her stare ahead. A minute passed. Finally, she turned on the ignition. At the airport, I got out of the car, and unloaded my things. "Bye mom." She didn't say anything. She didn't look at me and drove off.

I breathed a sigh of relief, and went into the airport where the check in representative greeted me with a smile. He helped me put the bicycle in a box, and gave me the passage for the bike for free. I checked in my bags, and went to the departure area. It was the afternoon of July 31st, 2001, and I would arrive in Lima Peru, on August 1st.

I didn't know why I had to go. I just had to, but at the same time, I could use it to defeat the prophecy. My hope regarding Kendra was for the picture and story to shock her. In my eyes, I considered most American women to be paranoid of anything that resembled stalking or obsession. I figured I could use that trait to my advantage; hopefully she would throw the things away, and my victory over Fate would be assured. Whatever the case, it didn't matter, the picture was in her hands now, and I was leaving the country for a while. Three months would give me enough time to accomplish my crazy plan, give me time to think, have some fun, and see another part of the world. After three months, I would be back in Boston, I will have beaten Fate, and if everything went well, I'd be working as an analyst again in my logical and rational world.

South America - Peru

Chapter 5

Bewildered in the Nazca Desert

"Welcome to Lima International Airport." Said the stewardess's voice over the intercom, as the plane taxied into the terminal. My flight was finally over. For several hours into the night, I flew over the inky black ocean of the Carribean, and then over land where I didn't see any lights. A cluster of lights was an island, and then there were stretches of darkness. A single light was a ship. Over the darkness of the Amazon, a cluster of lights was a village. I arrived into an unknown with a language where I knew at most, fifty words, thirty of which were for flirting with women, thanks to Maria's lessons. The rest I gleaned from a cram session on the plane, and I memorized a routine conversation for getting a taxi, and finding a hotel.

During the plane flight, I thought about what I'd do when I arrived. I had a road map of Peru, and all of Southern South America. While analyzing the map, I noticed my lonely light in a dark, slumbering cabin. Nervous, and hyper, I drank five cups of coffee. Then I went to the bathroom four times, and smiled at the stewardesses each time.

"Too much coffee?" She asked me.

"Yes."

When the plane landed, I was anxious to get off. After customs, I washed up in the bathroom, and smiled to myself in the mirror. "I did it!" I said to myself. I hurried to the baggage claim, and grabbed my bags, but my bicycle box wasn't there. Thirty minutes later, a reddish brown man came in with a cart, and a big box. I picked up my bicycle, and carted everything to the tariff zone.

"*How much is the bicycle?*" Asked the officer. I looked at her, then the box, and then back at her again.

"*Fifty dollars.*"

The custom's officer looked at me curiously and said, "*that's it?*"

"*Yes. It's an old bike.*"

"*OK.*"

I walked through the exit gate, and looked around. I was surrounded by a large crowd of brown people looking at me as I walked through. Some held signs, that said, "Satori", or "Yamaguchi". They looked at me in anticipation, but when I didn't say anything, they returned to scanning the passengers leaving the gate. As soon as I walked out the door, eight cab drivers approached. One man, a short man with a baseball cap, stood next to a station wagon. It was big enough to carry the bicycle. He asked me, "*how are you buddy! Need a cab?*"

"*Hello! Good hostel, know where?*"

"*Yes. Let's get your things in the car first.*" I got in the car as he loaded my things into the bay, and we drove into Lima.

"*Is this your first time in Peru?*"

"*Yes.*"

"*Are you Japanese?*" I looked at him funny, and felt a bit annoyed.

"*No. I'm not Japanese. I'm north American.*"

"*What? You look Japanese.*"

"*No, no, Vietnam.*"

"*Vietnam?*"

"*My parents are. I am American.*"

"Well, now that you're talking, you do sound like a gringo."

We drove through San Miguel, one of the many neighborhoods of Lima. Bright lights of neon signs lit up the road way, as people hurried to strip malls, shops, and cafes. Motorcycles outfitted to look like tiny cabs whizzed by, and the traffic clogged the streets. Small, Japanese minivans equipped with extra seats, stuffed full of people, called "micros", honked and aggressively pushed for space near the sidewalks to pick people up.

"*Ahh, here we are!*" He said as we pulled into a small building on a quiet road. We unloaded my things, and Edgar, the hostel's assistant, helped carry my equipment into my room. After tipping the driver, and registering in the hostel, I collapsed on my things.

I woke up midmorning, left to eat, and after lunch, I wandered in circles around the city of Lima for the next two hours, asking people if they knew where Hostal Franchia was. No one knew. Trying to recover my bearings, I wandered through the city blocks, into a small plaza nearby a university, where a crowd of people gathered around a sign in a protest. A sign in the center showed the face of Alberto Fujimori, the recent president of Peru, in a gorilla suit. They chanted anti-Fujimori slogans. I walked up to a lady in the crowd, and asked, *"what's this about?"*

She suddenly leaped up in excitement, grabbed my arm, and started dragging me into the crowd. Bewildered, I tried to say, *"what are you doing!"*, but she didn't hear me, because she was yelling out, *"make way for this Japanese guy! You see! Even the Japanese know that Fujimori is a criminal! Make way for the Japanese guy! It's important that he sign the petition!"*

She planted me in front of the crowd, and pointed proudly to the pad as the crowd enclosed in on me. Her smile was bright; I looked to my left, and then my right, and saw many eager eyes in anticipation.

"Will he sign in kanji?" Asked a man next to me. At that moment, it dawned on me what was going on.

"Uh, I'm north American." I said.

"What? You're not Japanese?"

"No. My family is from Vietnam."

"Ah crap, a damn gringo." Said the man who was looking for the kanji script. The crowd, as quickly as they came, departed as I added my signature.

"So your signature is worthless." Said the woman.

She sighed as I asked her where the hostel was. She didn't know, so I asked her directions to the central Plaza. Since I was lost, I made the most of it. At the plaza, I asked a girl for directions to a good vegetarian restaurant. Luckily, she knew one that was nearby, "Restaurante Natur Vegetariano." When I found it, the owner, Mark, greeted me warmly, and he spoke English, so we conversed as I ate his "ceviche de soya". I recounted the incident at the protest, as he laughed.

"Well Dave, you do look Japanese."

"I don't like that! I'm not Japanese!"

"Is that so bad? My brother in law is Japanese. My great grandfather was Japanese."

"I didn't mean to insult you, I mean I'm being called something that I'm not."

He laughed, and patted me on the back, as he said, "welcome to Peru, my friend. Here, people have many ancestries, and we appreciate our bloodlines. When we call each other "Japanese", or "Chinese", it's meant to affectionately. Not insultingly. We are an affectionate people."

"Oh. I didn't know that. Thank you for the information."

"It's not a problem. Remember, many Peruvians are of Japanese and Chinese descent, so when they call you Japanese, most likely they will think of you first as a Peruvian."

"That's not how that lady reacted."

"There are a few like her, but she is a minority."

"Ah, I didn't know that."

I asked him if he knew where my hostel was. He didn't know, so we found the hostel in the Yellow Pages, and called the owner. Speaking in Spanish, Mark wrote down the directions.

When I got back to the hostel, the owner smiled at me, and said, "so you lost?"

"Yes."

"We have map." He held it up with a smile.

The next day, I went to the South American Explorer's Clubhouse, an organization dedicated to the exploration of the unknown areas of South America, and a gathering place for explorers and travelers. I walked in, and while signing up for a membership, someone tapped my shoulder. I turned around to see a short, stout, blond haired woman with a big grin on her face.

"I knew I recognized this gringo!" She said with a grin.

"Marie!" I exclaimed. We hugged each other. Marie was the past president of the Boston University Kung Fu Club. Marie was an archeology major, and she worked in the south of Peru, near Tacna, in an excavation dig. I sent her an email before I left, telling her that I'd show up, but I had no idea she was in town.

"This is Jamie." She said as she introduced me to a taller girl, who had native American cheekbones and eyes. She had blond, brown hair, and stood nearly a head taller then Marie.

"So what's your plan Dave?" Asked Marie.

"You know some of the details. I'm biking to Buenos Aires."

"Damn! That's a long way. Have you looked a the map?"

"Yeah, it looks doable in three months."

"I think you need to look at one of these maps, Dave."

We went to the map room, and Marie pulled out a large map. It was much bigger then the road map that I had. And the scale was much more accurate.

"Are you going to Cuzco?" Asked Marie.

"Cuzco?"

"In the Andes. You're going to Macchu Picchu, right?"

"Yes."

"Good, because we bought you a plane ticket."

"What? I was going to bike there! I was planning to meet you there."

"Are you insane, Dave? Oh wait, this is you we're talking about." She shrugged.

"What do you mean?"

"Dave, look at the map. It's 4000 meters in altitude in some places! That's 13,000 feet high, and you haven't even acclimatized yet. You're going to do that in seven days? We gotta get this guy some coca tea."

"You're kidding me." I said as I looked at the map.

"You want to die?" Marie said.

"Not really."

"Then you're coming with us."

Marie had a good point. I didn't know what I'd encounter, and it was best to familiarize myself first with the local terrain. Later that day, Marie and Jamie took off for Iquitos, a city deep in the Amazon Region of Northeastern Peru. We arranged to meet back in Lima in a few days. I took a bus to Ica to see the Nazca lines. Nazca intrigued me; I read about the gigantic petroglyph's that could only be seen in the air, and I wanted to get some sand boarding in. I was an avid snow boarder, and sand boarding appealed to my desire for a variation on the theme.

The bus dropped me off at night in the quiet desert town of Ica; in the floodlights of the empty bus lot, I reassembled my bike, put the panniers on, and biked eighteen kilometers into Huancachina, an oasis resort amongst the giant sand dunes of the Nazca desert. At the center of Huancachina was a large pond full of fish. Most of the hostels were filled, but the last one had a bed available, and I shared a quarter with Michael and Jenny, a British couple.

In the morning, I took a micro, to the Nazca lines. I rode the bus with the locals, and noted their reddish brown skin, almond shaped eyes, and strong cheekbones. When I got on board, they looked at me, smiled, and said hello. I smiled and greeted them in turn. Every person who boarded, was greeted with a hello, and I was not used to it, but I enjoyed the custom. Still, never before in my life was I amongst a group of people whose skin was so red. I grew up amongst Asians, blacks, Indians, white, and Hispanics. The Hispanics were from Puerto Rico, or the Caribbean; I knew the tones of yellow, black, brown, and white. Red was new for me. Their eyes and faces made me think of my sun burnt cousins in the summer, when we surfed the waves at the New Jersey Shore.

We didn't talk much, but with my limited vocabulary, and some sign language, I managed to communicate traveling. We smiled at each other when he understood. Then he tried English.

"Go Nazca?"

"Yes, see lines."

"Oh! Beautiful! Mystery. Many sand storms. No cover."

The Nazca lines were still a mystery, one of many in South America. Made famous by Erich Von Daniken, who linked Extra-terrestrials with the lines, the lines themselves were an enigma. The lines were a few inches deep in the desert, and sand storms often covered the area. Yet, somehow the lines were never buried. If someone was cleaning up the lines, they deserved commendations, especially regarding their secrecy.

In a small, poorly maintained Cessna single propeller plane, I took off above the lines to 5000 feet, where I saw the designs in their full glory. We flew over several square kilometers of designs, and between the choking of the engine, and me choking on my own stomach upheavals, I saw giant glyphs of whales, spiders, the world famous "owl man", which didn't even look like an owl's head, and a monkey with a perfectly formed spiral tail. The owl man was the definite give away for why Von Daniken thought of extraterrestrials. It looked like a large gray alien that was so famously propagated in the media. But that wasn't interesting to me. The monkey and the spiral caught my attention. I looked at the spiral, and felt a shiver go through me. Finally, after looking at the giant spider glyph, my stomach had enough. We landed, and when I recovered, the pilot educated me on the poor maintenance of the planes.

"So what do you do?" He asked.

"I'm an engineer."

"You are? We need help here! Can you get service manuals for our planes? We need them!"

****

Over the pits of the ancient Nazca necropolis, I stood in the harsh sunlight, staring into the empty eye sockets of a five year old kid. His, or her brightly polished skull reflected the harsh sun light. It had a crooked smile, and the rest of the body was wrapped in a lama cloth bag. It looked like a skull and neck bone stuck into a sack. As I wandered the desert site, I looked at the other, open air mummies, some with hair still attached, and they sat in the same position as they were buried. The aridness of the desert lent itself to natural mummification, and the mummies were thousands of years old.

My tour group went to a cistern, fed by an enormous aqueduct system in the Andes. In the high Andean mountains, the Nazca built a network of spiraling cisterns, and each one had a spiral like stair case that went down the hole. The cisterns were lined with stone, and like capillaries to veins, they fed a network into a large main duct, lined with stone, which extended for kilometers from the high Andes all the way into the Nazca desert. The entire aqueduct was amazingly, underground. The pipes fed an enormous underground reservoir system, which supplied water into the city of Nazca.

The fields were a unique synthesis of sustainable agriculture and hydrological technology. A combination of rain water and field water filtered through the soil during crop irrigation, and fed the cisterns. Around the cisterns, fine soil and sand removed impurities, and even microorganisms. The cisterns formed a network connected to the main pipe. The system was at least a thousand years old, and of the 40 conduits discovered, 29 were still in use by the city of Nazca.

If this tiny remnant of the Nazca civilization was capable enough to serve the needs of thousands of residents in a modern city, what other hidden treasures of technology did they have to offer? What other secrets were there? Water is central to life, and modern civilization doesn't provide a way to reuse and renew resources; it mainly consumes and disposes. This isn't sustainable in the long term. In addition, to even build a system like the Nazca aquifers, required hundreds of years of expertise, insight, research, design, quantum leaps, and accumulated knowledge. There wasn't a doubt in my mind that the hydrological engineering, and the Nazca lines which defied the elements were just the tip of the iceberg of an enormous reservoir of highly advanced, lost civilizations. We drank some of the water straight from the cisterns without filtering or adding iodine. I didn't get sick afterwards, and I praised the ancient engineers, scientists, and laborers who built the system.

After a tour of Ica, I went sand boarding. I walked out of my room with my sandals, board, and hooded baseball cap for sun protection. I stepped out the door, went around the corner of the hostel, and I stopped in my tracks. In front of me, were people, no bigger than ants, climbing up the monstrous dune. It was eighteen stories high, and half a kilometer long. At the top, the wind gently blew the sand and made a golden mist in the air.

"You've got to be kidding me." I said.

"Come on Dave!" Said Karen, an Israeli girl. I met her and Anita, a British South Indian girl in Ica when we went out for lunch.

"How do you surf that thing?" I asked her.

"I don't know, but we'll do this together." She replied.

I watched Karen's slim figure, dressed in a sweat shirt and short shorts hike up the dune in the afternoon sun. She had a board in one hand, and a lit cigarette in the other. I followed behind. At the top, she got on her board, stomach first.

"That one's for my army friends!" she laughed as she slid down the slope. As she slid down, she hit a bump, fell off the board, and rolled down the dune. When she stopped, she burst out laughing.

"Your turn Dave!" She called out.

I didn't fare much better. I went down, surfer style, hit a bump, and then I went down head over heels into the soft sand, and tumbled down after Karen. For the rest of the afternoon, we went up, and surfed down the giant dunes. It wasn't as fast as snow, but it had its rewards. I ate sand instead of ice, and the sand was easier to fall in, as opposed to the packed ice on the slopes in Vermont.

Later that evening, I went out for dinner with Anita. We dined in a chifa, a Chinese restaurant. Chifa is the Peruvian term for Chinese food. With 150 years of immigration into Peru from China, about 15% of the population had Chinese blood or were of Chinese descent. Most of the immigrants were male laborers from southern China, and historically, they worked the railroads and plantations. With time, Chinese cuisine fused with the Incan, and pre Incan to form a totally new Peruvian cuisine.

As we ate, we talked about the events which led up to our journeys.

"Did you notice how everything just led up to making the trip easier?" She said.

"Well, except for the opposition from my parents, yes."

"That's obvious. Most parents are like that anyway. But look at the other things, like your job you resigned from, or how the airline staff helped you with the bike, and how quick and easy it was to get everything together. Do you know all the things that came together to get you here?"

"What are you getting at?" I asked.

"You were meant to come here."

"Aw come on, that was my decision to go."

"Are you sure? Things could've been much harder. You wouldn't be able to go if it wasn't your Fate."

"I don't believe in Fate." I retorted.

"You don't?"

"I believe that nothing is written unless I choose to write it."

"Ah," she said as she mysteriously leaned closer, smiled, and said, "you'll learn." Abruptly, she winced as she grabbed her neck. "Ow!"

"What's up?"

"Oh bother, my neck is cramped. I slept without a pillow last night."

"Turn around and let me take a look." I said. She moved her seat closer to me, and turned around. I started massaging her neck muscles, when I felt something stiff.

"You definitely got something cramped back there." I said as I worked the spot.

"Mmm, that's better."

"So what got you to travel down here?"

"I wanted to travel to Peru, Chile, and Bolivia. I'm working my way up to Venezuela."

"Do you speak Spanish?"

"Yes, and you?"

"Just eighty words now. I picked up some more since I got here, but half of them are flirting phrases from my Salvadorian friend. She said to be careful of the locals though."

"Oh come on! Sample the local delicacies."

"Ha ha! And you? What was your cuisine?"

"I've had a Canadian and an Israeli."

"What, no local?"

"No. I think you will have it better than us women. Your selection here is better. Go to a club, my god, watching Peruvian women dance is such eye candy."

"Really? I used to do ball room dancing."

"Oh, it's much better here."

We went back to the hostel, where Anita decided to help the bar tender mix drinks. I sat down next to Oad, a bearded Israeli, who was fresh out of special forces. We introduced ourselves.

"So what do you do, David?"

"I'm an engineer. Well, I used to be one. And you?"

"I was an army commando. Not anymore though, I don't want to have anything to do with them."

"Where have you been?"

"I was part of the wave. At anytime, a half million Israelis are traveling the globe. We start in Brazil, and then we go through the continent. I've been to Bolivia, Colombia, and here. I didn't like Bolivia. It reminded me of the Palestinian refugee camps." He looked off into the distance with a haunted look in his eyes. I didn't pry further into it.

"Commando huh? I trained with an army guy in Kung Fu." I commented.

"You know Kung Fu?" He asked.

"I was an instructor."

"I can get you a job in Colombia."

"Really?"

"Yes. We need a guy like you. Great pay, you get a beautiful house, lots of beautiful women, and lots of drugs, if you want. We can get that for you."

"I can do without the drugs. Beautiful women, now we're talking. What's the job position?"

"Hand to hand combat training for body guards and mercenaries."

"How much is the pay?"

"How much do you want? I can get you up to fifty thousand dollars. My friend and I are starting a personal guard company. We can use a guy like you. Here's my card."

"I'll think about it." I replied as I took the card.

"You know how to get in touch with me. Call me when you come to Cali."

I started talking to Karen, and she finally convinced me that extending the trip was a very good idea. She saved up as a waitress and a bartender after her army service in Israel, before traveling for the past four months.

"Dave, three months is very short you know."

"Yeah, but everyone in the states said that was a long time."

"Pah! You Americans are all wimps! What is wrong with your people? Most of you don't even leave your home town. At any time there are a half million Israelis traveling around the world long term. It is so important to travel!"

"Well, that's why I'm here. To meet beautiful and charming women like you." I replied with a smile.

"Well," she smiled, "you are brave, and crazy to go on a bicycle. Three months is very short though. What can you see in three months? What can you do? You can't change yourself in three months. You need at least six months to change."

I heard a commotion to my right, and turned to see a Peruvian guy pleading with Anita. "You are so beautiful. Will you come with me on a date?" He asked her.

"No thank you." She replied. I looked at Anita and grinned. "Got yourself a fan?" She rolled her eyes.

"Hey, what's wrong with having an admirer?"

"I think he's too much." She said.

The Peruvian, after a few more attempts, left her alone. Karen went to sleep, and I played poker with Oad, as he tried to sell me on the benefits of being a mercenary defense instructor, when I felt a tap on my shoulder. Anita was rubbing her neck.

"Dave, could you massage that again?"

"Sure. Let's go to your room."

"OK."

We closed the door behind us, and Anita didn't lock it. She got on the bed. "Lay on your stomach, and put the pillow under you." I said, as she followed the instructions. I started massaging her neck, and found the kink. While working the kink out, Anita moaned quietly.

35

"Mmmm, god that feels good. Can you get my shoulders?"

"I can, but your shirt is in the way." She took off her shirt, and I worked her shoulders, squeezing then releasing the tender, smooth, and supple flesh as I worked my hands into her muscles.

"Lower please." She gently requested, and I moved my hands down her back; I moved my hands in cup motions, pulling and squeezing the skin and back.

"Lower." She said, softer than the first, and I moved my hands lower - suddenly, the door burst open, and Michael looked in. Startled, both Anita and I jumped up; she grabbed my hands, which were on her shoulders. Her bra sagged, and I pulled the strap up to keep it in place.

"Oh! Sorry! I didn't mean to interrupt!" Said Michael, smiling with an open mouth.

"Uh… no problem. I'm just, ah, giving Anita a massage." I said.

Anita glared at Michael in complete shock.

He looked at us, grinned broadly, and said, "cheerio David! Carry on!" as he closed the door. Anita looked at me.

"Oh god, we must have looked so dodgy."

"You're telling me." I let go of the strap.

"My bra!"

"It was coming off."

"Thanks for holding it up." She said as she put the clasp back on.

"No problem."

We walked out of the room, with big grins and laughed about what had happened. I sat down with Oad, Michael, and Jenny, while Anita went to the bathroom. The Peruvian guy gave me a sour look.

"So the two of you were doing a little… chatting?" Michael joked.

"We had verbal intercourse." I said.

"That's a load of bullocks! Oh my god, verbal intercourse? You pulled, didn't you?" Laughed Jenny.

"So, Daveed, how was it?" Asked the bar keep as she smiled knowingly.

"How was what?"

"You were in there for 30 minutes. We timed the two of you. How was it?"

"Why do you want to know?"

"Look, we told Michael to check on the two of you, and he came in, and her bra was off. And the two of you were in the bed! Poor Pablo over there is broken hearted." She said as she pointed at Pablo. The Peruvian gave me an angry stare.

"So tell me! Did you kiss her?" She asked.

"No, no, no." I said as I shook my head, and then smiled.

"Liar! Come on, what did you say to her?" She demanded.

"I told her a sweet phrase." I said as I decided to play along.

"What?"

"You really want to know?"

"Yes!"

I said with a sweeping flourish, *"your eyes are beautiful, and your lips are precious. And your face is prettier than the full moon."*

"Agh!" The bar keep screamed as she grabbed her hair. "You are just like my ex boyfriend, that Chinese son of a bitch!"

"What?" I said in surprise.

She pointed a finger at me, and seethed, "You. You men."

"Hey, hey! I'm not trying to pick you up!" I said defensively.

"It doesn't matter. You men are all alike." She said as she stared at me warily, and added, *"womanizers!"*

Oad sat next to me, and wanted to play a drinking game. I declined since I didn't drink. "But we need one more person." He whined.

"Let me get Karen." I replied. I went to a dark room, number 107. "Was it 106, or 107?" I thought to myself. I couldn't remember. I knocked on 107, and the door was slightly ajar. It opened gently, and I didn't hear a thing inside, no snoring or even a breath. It was utterly silent. I turned back and walked to Oad.

"I guess she's not there." The bar keep stared at me in shock.

"You... you know what you just did?"

"No. Why?"

"You interrupted my brother while he was fucking his woman!"

"Huh?"

"Room 107 is his room! You just walked into them having sex!"

"No way."

Beside me, walked up a Peruvian man, with brown skin, about my height, with a bowl shaped hair cut. A lighter skinned woman accompanied him.

They didn't look at me, and sat down next to me. They weren't smiling, and the woman lit up a cigarette.

"One pisco sour, please." Said the man. He sighed.

"Did I just..." I started to ask.

"Jes."

"I'm so sorry." I quickly apologized, and added, "I was trying to find my friend."

He smiled, "it's not a problem. I was doing this," he said as he stood up, and thrust his pelvis rhythmically, "and when I heard the door, I went, huh?" He said as he suddenly stopped his pelvis inwards, and made a bewildered look.

"Oh man! I would never interrupt anyone having sex. I'm really sorry."

"It's OK." Said the woman.

"Well, I'm David by the way," I said as I extended my hand to the man. He shook it.

"Jose. It is no problem. There is always tomorrow." He said as he drank the sour. Karen came up to the table, and was rubbing her eyes when she said, "What's going on?"

"I think the Benny Hill show." I said, and then we started laughing.

As I went to bed that night, I felt the need to go. I made one person jealous, and I interrupted a couple's amorous night. That didn't make for good vibrations, and I didn't want to overstay my welcome. So, early the next morning, I took off for Ica. I had to catch up with Marie and Jamie. We were going to the source of my feelings, the place where the secrets inside of me would unfold, into the heart of the mythical, sumptuous, and legendary Incan Empire.

Figure 5.1: A baby mummy in the Nazcan necropolis sits in the pit.

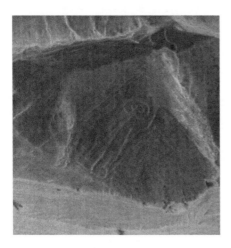

Figure 5.2: One of the famous Nazca lines that I flew over, the "Owl Man", who waves from the desert.

Chapter 6

Cuzco

Cuzco is the navel of the Incan Empire, and it's referred to as the navel by the Quechua, the Inca's descendants. The empire of the Inca is known as Tawantinsuyo, or the four corners of the world, as it's translated from Quechua. Quechua is the Spanish transliteration of Qheshwa. The four corners consists of Chinchinsuya to the north, Antisuya to the East, Contisuya to the west, and Collasuya to the South. It's one of the oldest continuous major cities in the Americas, and it still functions as a center of commerce and culture for much of the Quechua. At 3120 meters in thin air, it's also a high city.

When we arrived in Cuzco, I noticed immediately that my head felt like it was swelling. We took a taxi to a hostel; at the hostel, I sat down on the bench, while waiting for Marie and Jamie to fill out the room forms. I held my head in my hands, as I felt the dull ache in my head. I imagined there must've been a vise grip around my temples, as the throbbing squeezed on my head. My sinuses felt full, and the feeling was like a sinus infection, without the infection.

"What's going on with me?" I groaned.

"Uh oh, Dave's got soroche. That's high altitude sickness." Said Marie.

"Do you have any coca tea?" She asked the hostel owner, Carlos, who was a short and kind man. His face was wrinkled, with a large gray beard and mustache. *"Yes, come this way."*

We unloaded our things into our room. I struggled with my bags and the bike. What happened to my strength?

41

"You haven't adjusted to the oxygen levels here yet. Give yourself a few days, you'll be producing a lot more red blood cells." Replied Jamie. In the hostel kitchen Carlos poured me a cup of coca tea.

"Poor guy." He said as he looked at me. My head was in my arms resting on the table, half dazed, as I sat.

"You will need a few days to get used to the height." He said.

I grabbed the sugar bowl, and started eating large clumps of brown sugar. They were sweet, but they tasted metallic against my tongue. "Drink this." Said the owner as he handed me a steaming cup with green coca leaves inside. The coca leaves steeped a greenish tint in the water, and I breathed in the steam. It was thirty five degrees outside, and the high mountain air was dry and cold. I took the cup in my hands, and took a sip. It tasted like spinach with sugar. In a few minutes, I felt my hand warm up, and the dull ache in my head began to release its clamp.

"That feels better." I said, as I felt my body slowly stir awake.

"Coca tea really helps with the soroche." Said Marie.

"Yeah, make sure you drink the coca tea. Up here, you need to be careful of what your body is doing. You don't want to have AMS." Said Jamie.

"AMS?"

"Acute mountain sickness. It can disable or kill you. The moment you start showing signs of it, we're going to have to carry you down to the Sacred Valley in a stretcher."

"What are the signs?"

"Well, it looks like you have some of the signs right now, but the moment you start vomiting is when we start carrying you down."

"That's comforting."

"How do you feel Dave?"

"I feel like someone stuck a clamp around my head, and everything feels loopy."

"You're fine then. We had it for a few days too. Wait till the third day, then you'll feel like taking on the world. Your body adjusts really quick."

I drank the cup, and ate another spoonful of sugar. "Why do I keep eating sugar?" I asked as I poured another spoonful.

"It looks like your body is adjusting instinctively to the level." Said Marie.

I went to bed and slept for the next thirty six hours. When I woke up, I felt my body almost vibrate with energy. "Whooh! What the hell happened?" I said to myself as I got out of bed. I looked at myself in the mirror. I definitely felt better, the throbbing was gone, my sinuses felt clear, and I was anxious to get out and have a look around Cuzco. Jamie and Marie weren't around. They were touring the Sacred Valley of the Incas.

"Ah! You look much better today!" Said the hostel owner as he waved at me. I walked out of the hostel, as a small, KIA taxi rumbled down the cobblestone road in front of me. The entire street was lined with a large and ancient Incan wall. The sun was bright as it cast harsh shadows on the ground. The air was crisp, dry, and mild. It felt warm at forty two degrees. I looked at the gray stones, and noted that not one stone was exactly the same length as the other, as I walked down the hill into the city. I gazed at the red roof tops of roofing tile, and it was a city unlike any I'd ever seen in my life. Nothing in the US, Europe, Africa, or Asia came close to its appearance. I'd never seen anything like it in any photo, documentary, or report.

Cuzco is a magical blend of the ancient and the colonial. Most of the Incan empire's structures formed the foundations of the Spanish imperial constructions. There's a certain poetic justice about the Incan construction. The Incans, the world's premier masonry engineers, took stone masonry to a level unmatched anywhere else in the world. No stone was the same size, yet as I walked by the walls, the stones were perfectly fit in polygonal shapes. The fit was so tight, and they didn't use cement, mud, or any other adhesive to hold the walls together. A benefit of the polygonal construction was their uniquely earthquake proof characteristics. Cuzco and the surrounding areas typically had earthquakes that could level San Francisco several times over. When the Spanish came, as a symbol of their might and the Catholic religion, they destroyed as much of the Incan constructions as they could, and then they built churches and cathedrals on the rocks they couldn't topple. The city gets periodic earthquakes, and sometimes they get one or two that really levels things. Every time that happened, the Spanish churches and structures were destroyed, while the Incan structures stood in silent vindication for centuries.

I walked through the central plaza. The local people greeted me with good mornings, or a merchant came up to me hawking wares for tourists. I continued down the cobblestone road for several blocks, as I passed by the giant, ancient walls, and the temple of Coricancha, known as the temple of the Sun and the Moon. A church was built on its foundations, but much of the ancient temple was preserved for the tourists. I headed for the South American Explorer's Club branch in Cuzco, to get some information, and to get some bearings on where I was in South America. I knew I was here for a reason, and that I was supposed to meet someone. I didn't know how I knew, or why, but there was something I had to learn here. I had set aside three to four weeks to explore Cuzco and Macchu Picchu. As I walked, I reminded myself to cancel my plane ticket, and to extend my trip for another 3 months. I pulled out a slip of paper, where I wrote down the office address from the Lima branch. "1458, 1459, 1460. Here it is!" I said as I passed down the numbers in front of the homes.

I walked inside, into a living room with walls full of books. It was shady and bright, from the harsh glare of the sun through the glass blocks and windows, and a brown haired British lady greeted me at the desk. She gave me a tour of the facilities. We walked through the library, map room, outdoor area, kitchen, and the explorer library. Marie was in the library.

"Dave! You're OK! Are you feeling better? You got through the soroche really quick." Said Marie.

"Yeah, I'm feeling a lot better. How was the sacred valley?"

"Gorgeous, we're going to the Pikallactay ruins today. Want to come?"

"Sure! Let me grab some breakfast first."

We walked out and went toward the hostel to Café Haylilly, where a pleasant woman, Luisa, served us hot fried potatoes, fruit salad, avocados, bread and butter. Afterwards, we took a taxi down to the ruin. The ruins were far lower in elevation than the city, and it was much warmer. I got out of the car, and stepped on the dry red soil. There were shrubs with giant thorns, and cacti. The air was warm and dry, and the sun was strong. I put my sun cap on.

"Be careful of the thorns. They can puncture a thick boot." Said Marie. We walked around the ruin, which looked like a burned down village. All that was left were the adobe brick walls of homes and a village center that once bustled with a large population.

"This is pre Incan?"

"Yes. The Incans are just the name of the empire, but the people who built the empire, they were once a republic, or a group of nations long before the Incans ever came here. The Incans were only an empire for a few hundred years."

The brick walls were red like the soil. There were strange holes in the walls, and they didn't always match up with a hole opposite of it. Afterwards, we went to an ancient Incan wall further up the road. The wall was enormous, and it seemed to extend for miles off into the horizon into another mountain. It was partially buried by dirt, but the parts that were excavated impressed the engineer inside of me. Some of the stones were the size of a small car, and like the walls in Cuzco, they were polygonal, and they precisely fit within each other. Part of the wall seemed to be cut, and faced with stone, as if it was a kind of an entrance. I imagined that there were once guards here, patrolling the wall as the gatekeepers. We walked up the wall to look at the top. The wall seemed to also function as an aqueduct, but I had some reservations, since the distance in between the sides of the opening was large enough for an eighteen wheeler truck.

Marie, Jamie, and I had an argument that started my conflict with the western archaeologists and anthropologist's. Their theories regarding the structures and peoples I met during my journey were colored with Western bias. I felt that something important was missing, and as I continued my journey, I found that I had allies, who were the local red and brown skinned people.

"Where's the rest of the aqueduct?" I asked.

"What do you mean?" Asked Marie.

"It looks like they just stopped on the two sides. Are you sure this is an aqueduct?"

"Yes."

"I don't know, it's starting to look structural to me. Wouldn't they at least finish the job?"

"They probably used something organic in between."

"What? After all that work with stone, and then they'd use something organic to bridge the gap? That doesn't make sense. That's like a half ass job."

"Why wouldn't it?"

"OK, they obviously are able to cut out this huge slab of stone," I said as I pointed to the big stone next to me, "fit it in, without mortar, so tight that my knife can't fit in it, and then you're going to tell me that they just left the top off without finishing it?"

"See, that's the difference between you engineers and us archaeologists."

"What's that?"

"You always try to see what the practical use of something is."

"Well, to build this thing, you'd have to think like an engineer. It takes engineers to build things. If you're going to spend that much energy to build something, you'd want to do it well, and you'd want to complete it. I would think the emperor would've thought the same way."

"Well, archaeologists try to find the why behind something."

"The why behind what?"

"Why did they build this?"

"It's a wall. The reasons are pretty obvious. But they wouldn't just leave an aqueduct incomplete."

After touring the ruins, we went back to Cuzco, and hung out in Mama Africa, a restaurant bar in the Central Plaza. We started talking about love, our past relationships, and about how most men were horrible at making a commitment. She wanted a house and kids. I wasn't too sure about what I wanted, but I knew that I wanted someone along the lines of a lifetime adventure and travel companion. Wait a minute, Marie with a house and kids?

"And a white picket fence. Well, it doesn't have to be white." She added.

This was the same woman who traveled and worked in Morocco, Spain, and now Peru. Marie could slap a man around like a rubber doll. She was a former president of the Kung Fu Club. Marie had a soft side? This was new. We started discussing men's phobias to commitment.

I said, "if you think about it, if that person seriously was committed to anything, than he would either be planning the trip with the full intent of doing it, or already be there. He can't even commit to the most important person in his life. Himself. Face it. You can't ever lose your independence unless you choose to. All that crap about losing independence is an excuse for why they're not able to make their own lives worthwhile. I think it's important to be happy first. Making a commitment to yourself is most important, that's my opinion. Besides, if you decide that you need someone to be happy, you'll often just end up being miserable. Neediness isn't happiness."

"And what about you Dave?" She asked after I got off my soapbox.

"What about me?"

"How come you've never been in a long term relationship?"

"I have a bad habit of unconsciously breaking people's hearts."

"Oh. You're one of those kinds of guys."

"Yes, I'm a totally uncommitted bastard. But, right now I'm fulfilling a commitment to myself."

"Well, I want a boyfriend. I just don't want to see him." Said Jamie.

"How can you have a boyfriend and not see him?" I asked.

"There's the internet, video conferencing, and the phone."

"You sound jaded." I said.

"Well, what's so great about a relationship anyway? Nothing special ever happens when people meet, and all the guy wants is sex." She retorted.

"I dunno about the nothing special part when you meet someone. I have an interesting story, if you'd like to hear it." I said.

"What's that." They asked.

"Well, my friend told me that he knew of someone who drew a picture of a woman he was told that he would meet. He never met the person before. So he drew it. Then a year later, that person appeared, the picture matched, and the two of them met. He said it was an event that changed his friend's life forever."

"That kind of stuff never happens." Said Jamie in a disdainful, unbelieving voice, as she stood up to go to the bathroom. When she left, I looked at Marie, smiled, and said, "it did happen. It happened to me."

"Who was the person?"

"Remember Kendra, from the Kung Fu Club?"

"Ah ha! I knew there was an odd chemistry going on between the two of you. I saw what was going on. Did you tell her?"

"Right before I left, I sent her the picture, and told her the story in a letter. I was hoping she would throw them away."

"So you just ditched her."

"I was freaked out! Think about it, what kind of stuff like that happens to a person? Have you ever heard of something like that ever happening?"

"No, I've never heard of something like that ever happening. Usually someone tells them that they're going to meet someone, and then they meet. But you're the first one I know who has physical evidence." Marie said, and then added, "although, you better be careful Dave, what you did might backfire on you. She might not throw it away, and she might keep it even closer to her heart."

"We'll see. As far as I'm concerned, I'm here, and she's there in the USA. That's a huge distance. What can she do? Nothing. What can I do? Nothing. That works well for me. Jamie's pretty jaded huh?"

"The irony, Dave, is that it's people like her who watch romantic movies, saying, 'oh god, how could they not meet? They deserve each other!' It's like they can believe it so fully in a movie, but they can't accept it in real life."

"Well, it happened in real life, to me. But, I want my adventure, and I have to satisfy my wander lust."

"And you're a totally uncommitted bastard." Marie added.

Later, Marie and Jamie went to tour Macchu Picchu. I continued touring Cuzco, exploring the alley ways, and parts of the city. I went to the central market, which was full of stalls, and reddish brown skinned Quechua women, who wore traditional skirts, and rainbow colored shawls. All the women had bowler hats, which was a left over custom from the colonial days when the Spanish imperial government forced the women to adopt some European customs and dress. I talked to the children who played in the streets, especially when they came up to me and asked me, *"are you Japanese?"*

"No, I'm north American. My family is from Vietnam."

"Vietnam? Where's that?"

"Asia."

"You look Japanese. Can I practice my Japanese with you?"

It exasperated me that they didn't seem to understand me, and I was adamant that they got my ethnicity correct. I knew it was wrong to expect people to be less ignorant about where people came from, but I still wanted it to be that way. I was still reacting as I always did, from what I used to deal with in the US. It would take me a while to eventually calm down, and for me to realize that racial perceptions were vastly different in Latin America.

I walked into art galleries, and fell into an addiction for churros, a Peruvian pastry deep fried in oil, and filled with sweet cream. I walked far from the tourist center to where only the locals went to get my churros, and soon, the cooks affectionately started calling me, "Chinito." Café Haylilly became my place to go to for breakfast, and sometimes lunch, and the owner, Sally, and the staff, greeted me warmly. They even began cooking custom dishes adapted to my diet. I was slowly adjusting to my new surroundings, and making friends with the locals. Yet, each day, at breakfast, I opened my notebook, and looked at a question I'd written inside.

"Something inside of me told me to come here. Something told me that I'm going to meet someone important. Who is it, and what for?"

****

In the South American Explorer's Club, I read an explorer report about their bicycle trip from Lima to Cuzco. Marie was right, it took at least two weeks at a daily pace to get to Cuzco. I read the report about what the explorer encountered along the way. I pulled out another binder of trip reports into Macchu Picchu, and flipped through the write-ups from travelers before me.

"Are you looking to go to Macchu Picchu?" A warm, Latino accented voice said behind me. I turned around and saw a reddish brown man, with an eagle like nose, and slight smile. His face was wide, and he looked strong. He was my height, and took a look at the binder I opened. He told me about how special Macchu Picchu was, and how he used to be a guide there. And then the conversation took a curious turn.

"There are many ancient Incan temples and ruins on the Inca trail, yes. But there are also strange lights." He said.

"Strange lights?"

"Yes. Who knows you might see them."

"Tell me about these lights."

"They come only at certain times."

"Are there any cities, or towns there?"

"No."

"Lighting storms, or thunder storms?"

"No. They appear during clear nights."

"Where do they appear again?"

"From behind the mountains, to the east. There are no cities there. Nothing."

I stopped and thought for a moment. "I've forgotten my manners. My name is David." I said as I extended my hand.

"I am Ernesto." He said as he shook it and asked, "so how long are you going to be here? Two weeks?"

"Two weeks? No, more like a month. I'm extending my trip."

"That is good. Too many Americans like you come here for just two weeks. You cannot learn anything in two weeks, especially in a city as rich in history as Cuzco." He grabbed his back pack, and started towards the door.

"Ernesto, do you come around here often?" I asked.

"Yes. You will see me again. Come talk to me if you have any questions." He said as he left.

"Strange lights?" I thought to myself as I walked up to my hostel. The air was clear, cold, and crisp, and despite the light pollution from the city, I saw stars. Several attractive women approached me as I walked to a restaurant I frequented in the plaza. The girls came up to me, and handed out flyer's for the local clubs and discos. I got to know one of the girls, Tammy, a pretty girl who was about nineteen, with shiny dark eyes and long black hair, who originated from Lima. She always wore a sweater, and a jacket, but her tight jeans accentuated her well proportioned curves beautifully. My Spanish was improving just from listening and talking, and every time I saw her, we went through our conversation again.

"Daveed, how are you tonight?" She would say sweetly to me. I of course, would smile, and say, *"I'm fine. Your eyes are precious tonight as usual."*

"Why thank you! You're very sweet. So, are you going to Club Lobo with me tonight?"

"Well, I will. Just not right now."

"Why not tonight?"

"I've got some things to do."

"Aye, Daveed, I know you're a busy guy, eh?" She'd wink, and then say, *"but please don't forget me. Before you come to my club, come see me."*

It was the same shtick. The women were paid to bring in patrons to the club, not to go on dates, and I knew this. Once the guys were in the club, the women would have them buy them drinks, since this was how the clubs made most of their money. I didn't feel like falling into that kind of trap with them. I wanted to date a girl who didn't think of me as the beer tap. I continued on to the restaurant to meet up with Kate, an American girl I met in the clubhouse. She was from Vermont, and was traveling through South America for three months. Kate had short cropped brown hair, and was a recent graduate from Dartmouth University. Kate traveled a lot during her years at Dartmouth. She spent nine months in Kenya, three months in

Mexico, and was working on her Spanish skills in Peru for the last four months. So, we spent time talking about her travels, infectious mosquito borne diseases, bad anti malarial medicine which made her shake like an epileptic, adventure, and our cultural obsession with work.

After dinner, I walked into the local craft shops to buy a sweater. Ernesto's words rang in my ears about the "strange lights". Macchu Picchu was just a ruin, but the lights, to me, indicated that there was something living. As I browsed woolen textiles of colorful, hand woven ponchos, alpaca sweaters, and pullovers, an elderly Quechua woman came up to me. She spoke heavily accented English, and I bought a rough, wool sweater from her. I realized that she was an old Quechua, and maybe she'd know about the strange lights. She probably saw many things before Cuzco modernized during the last twenty years. We introduced ourselves. Her name was Kristine.

"Hello Kristine. A pleasure to meet you. Say, I heard about a strange thing around here, nearby Macchu Picchu. Maybe you know about it?"

"What is it?"

"A strange light was seen by my friend as he went to Macchu Picchu. Do you know what it is?"

"A strange light?"

"Yes, he sees it at night, when there is clear sky. There are no cities or towns nearby, and it comes from behind the mountains."

"Ahh. That is Spiritual la Tierra. Only the *acclhaska* can see those."

"The acclhaska? What's that?"

"I don't know the word in English for it. But the acclhaska is very special, only he can search these things. The lights show the way to lots of gold."

"Gold?"

"Yes. But only the acclhaska is permitted to see the lights, and the gold."

"Acclhaska, is that a Quechua word?"

"Yes."

Acclhaska is a Quechua word, and I repeated its pronunciation. "Ackla-haska." Tired, I went back to my hostel. It was cold out, and the shower was out of propane for heating the water. The showers were outdoors, in a little wooden stall in the open. I chose to wash my face, changed into my long johns, and went to sleep thinking about Ernesto and the old Quechua woman's information.

I spent more time at the clubhouse, and while browsing a book on the Incans, a pretty woman in her early thirty's came into the clubhouse. She had red hair, and sharp eyes, and we saw each other instantly the moment she walked in. I became a mainstay at the clubhouse, and even helped out the staff while I was there, so I gave the lady a tour. Her name was Michelle, she was an American, originally from a Midwestern town, and she was looking for an apartment to rent in Cuzco. After showing her around, we sat down and started talking about her travels. She lived in Nepal for two years, learned the language of the Sherpas, and she was an entrepreneurial woman who traveled around the world, filmed places in video, and then sold the video. Her lifestyle seduced me, and I started dreaming about being an adventurer, making money where ever I went.

We talked about how she saved for three years before taking off on a trip, and did things like scrounge dormitory halls for used toothpaste tubes, cook at home, and keep the goal of the journey in mind constantly. She was an investigative documentary maker, and after working around the world for a few years, she came to Cuzco to investigate the properties of the San Pedro plant.

"Dave, put your feelers out there regarding that plant, and let me know what you find out."

"What exactly is San Pedro?"

"It's a plant that has psychic enhancing properties. It's a mind altering drug, to be blunt, but when used properly, it gives the mind access to other areas that you typically wouldn't be able to access. Here's the cool part. When I was in Tibet, they did a study where they gave some of the monks a small dosage of a mind altering drug, but it didn't do anything to them! The monks naturally produced the chemicals in their minds as the meditated, and they were already accustomed to the chemicals. So, we're all equipped with the same capabilities, but we've forgotten how to access those areas of our mind."

"Wow. So, by meditation…"

"You're already accessing the 95% of the mind that you normally don't access through day to day, or even intensive thought. Everyone only uses 5% of the brain, no matter how hard they try consciously. But in a state between conscious and unconscious, you're accessing enormous areas of the mind. The question is how to get to that. In the East, in Asia, they typically do it naturally, except in isolated cases. In the Americas, they use the aid of plants and mushrooms to access it. The only problem with meditation is practice, and knowing the right method; if you know the right method, and practice it, your mind gets stronger. Plants are like a crutch; they'll get you there, but they're still a crutch, so you don't get stronger."

"So why do you want to know about San Pedro?"

"I'm building up documentation that the proper use of the plants, by the shamans, who regard them as sacred, gives the mind access to knowledge that westerner's took 2000 years to figure out, where as the shaman's had their Gods explain it to them. You have to feed your mind with more than just knowledge. There are certain nutrients that, in small quantities, and used with respect, expand the mind."

"Hello David!" Interrupted Ernesto as he walked into the club.

"Ernesto! I've been looking for you!" I said back, smiling.

"You were? Well, it's a good thing I decided to come in today. I usually don't come in, but something inside me said to come. So I am here. What can I do for you?"

"Those lights that you were talking about, I need some more information on them."

"So you are now curious about the lights? That is very interesting. Most people don't care about the lights, but you are." He looked at me curiously, then added, "OK then, let me tell you about them."

"Oh! I keep forgetting my manners again. Michelle, this is Ernesto, and Ernesto, this is Michelle." I said as I introduced them.

"Why don't we go to a café, and discuss this?" Asked Ernesto

"Good idea." Said Michelle.

In a small bistro around the corner, over some hot tea and fresh bread, we sat down and started talking about the many strange mysteries in the Cuzco area, and how it related to us and our world. Somehow, we wandered into mathematics, and then into science, but more particularly, western science.

"The beauty of math is it's such a universal language." Said Michelle.

"That is true. You cannot mistake the interpretation of numbers of geo-metrical forms." Said Ernesto

"Well, I'd like to use science to figure out the ruins around here." I said.

"Really?" Asked Ernesto

"Science, huh? Kind of like the stuff that came up with the atomic bomb?" Asked Michelle.

I soon found myself in a corner defending Western, reductionist science from the two. Both were adamant that Western science itself was the source of all the problems of the world. Now, Ernesto and Michelle weren't Luddites or ignorant. Both were well educated, and more importantly, well read. They were also quite good at mathematics. Both were also spiritual as well as contemplative. Still, something about science really bugged them.

I tried to get them to understand that to me, science, like spirituality, was truth. It just is, and it's just how things work. However, man's application of science, known as technology, and man's application of spirituality, known as religion, is actually the reason the world has seen so many problems as well as solutions. I didn't succeed in my goal, so we moved on to the characteristics of the strange lights.

"So, what exactly does the light look like, Ernesto?" I asked.

"It looks like there are two moons."

"Two moons?"

"Yes."

"And where did you see it?"

"On the third pass on the way to Macchu Picchu. I saw the lights five times, and I concluded that they are not Aurora, because we are too far from the poles and the light's origins are too low in the sky. They come from the bottom up. They are not lighting flashes, because there are no thunder clouds, and in four of the cases, there were no clouds in the sky. It only occurs at night, and they fit into a strange pattern. At first I thought they were random, until I noticed that they had a pattern. It starts off small, in the beginning, and then the energy form expands until the entire mountain range is lit up. So, that would not be a city, or town, because it happens at once, and it covers the entire mountain range."

"Do the locals know about it?"

"Not all of them. Only a few know."

"What about travelers and tourists?"

"Most of the tourists stop to sleep in the hostel after the third pass. Almost nobody stays in the third pass, and even then, the lights are selective."

"How so?"

"I've gone with other people, sometimes in a group as large as ten. Five people saw it, and five others did not."

"Did you ever try to locate the source of the light?"

"Yes, one time, a looter witnessed the lights. He followed a trail to the source, and found a large stone slab covering a hole in the ground. He had a metal detector with him, and scanned the area, and the detector registered large quantities of metal. So, he marked the spot, and returned with a group of men. They moved to slab, and found the area empty, as if the metal had "moved." This frightened him and the men, so they ran."

"What do you think it is Ernesto?"

"Some people think it's El Dorado. Other's think it's Paititi. What do you think of it David?"

"I'm not sure. I won't know until I witness it. Let me make a few expeditions, and find out."

"OK. Well, why don't I take you to a few places around here to introduce you to some of the problems that we have here? Who knows, maybe you might be able to find a solution, or put us on the right path to understanding the things around here."

"What things?"

"There are many ancient ruins, and sites. I used to be an assistant to many white researchers, archaeologists, and anthropologists. Their theories that they come up with, write about, and eventually teach in their schools trouble me, because they never listened to me when I told them what we, the locals know about these things. They have always been very arrogant to us. Are you religious, David?"

"No, why?"

"What religion are you?"

"I don't really hold onto a religion, but I am Buddhist in name. I don't think you can call Buddhism a religion."

"That is fine. You are an engineer, but you have another perspective. That is what we need here. I will call you next week, and then I will take you to some of these places."

As we departed, Michelle said to me, "You'll be around, right Dave?"

"Oh yeah. I'm not going any time soon. I think I just found what I was looking for."

"Well, let me know. I'd like to see you again."

****

I was on the verge of a major bowel dysfunction. I was four kilometers away from the nearest toilet. On top of that, the Peruvian toilets typically didn't have toilet paper. I found myself in this compromising position when Ernesto took me out to some little explored areas to start my investigation. We were looking for tunnels in the mountains surrounding the Cuzco region.

One of the major local legends of the Cuzco area is about a major network of tunnels running underneath the four corners of the Incan Empire. The Incan Empire was as large, if not bigger, than the Roman Empire. Many true and not so true stories abound about the tunnel network. The true ones involved people going into the tunnels, and never coming back, or they came back stark raving mad and died immediately afterwards. The legends stated that the Incas hid a massive amount of gold in the network after the death of Altahualpa, the last Incan Emperor, to get it away from the murderous Spanish. Since then, numerous intrepid, yet poorly equipped treasure hunters have disappeared into that system. Due to the increase of missing adult reports, the government tried to seal up the entrances. They also must've mistaken the sewers for tunnels as well, which I found evident in the malfunctioning toilet systems.

The Peruvian government wasn't particularly thorough, because Ernesto and I found a major entrance to the tunnels on our first try. We went out on a crisp, cold, and clear night to explore the local ruins, sans tourists. I dislike tourists, despite the fact that most Peruvians considered me one. My grist with tourists is that most of them don't engage or try to make contact with the people and cultures that made a place special in the first place. The Quechua were the direct descendants of the Inca, and they're the ones who built these ruins. It made sense to get to know them. The tourists, especially the ones from Europe and Israel, always kept making references to "all these savages", which I found to be insulting. Surprisingly, the few American travelers I met didn't make such references, nor did the Canadians, or the Japanese.

When we got to the monuments, it was twilight. There is nothing more awe inspiring than seeing enormous, megalithic stone monuments in the glow of the Milky Way and a crescent moon. The Inca, or more likely, their ancestors who built the magnificent monuments must've had this idea in mind. I stood there with Ernesto, and I tried to get into the heads of whoever it was that built these structures. What were they thinking? What great and awesome purpose could have possibly motivated such a magnificent civilization to build such monstrosities?

We first went to visit the Qenko monument in the pale moonlight. Qenko looked like someone took a 600 ton rock, plopped it in the middle of plateau, and carved a tunnel straight through the solid rock. On top, numerous altars and channels were carved into it. Upon exploring the cave, my mind began its first series of stomach twisting, mind bending, mentally headache causing thought processes. How this was done without even basic modern technology, let alone steel tools was mind boggling. Inside of the rock were smooth bore walls and altars, as well as an area that looked like a kitchen and a bathroom. Right angles insider of the windows and cubby holes were carved out of the dense rock.

The rock itself is Andesite, which is a type of dense, hard, volcanic stone. The Andes are full of Andesite, since the Ring of Fire runs alongside the vast mountain range. The Incans had no iron tools, just copper alloy, or bronze tools. Strong, carbonized steel is necessary to do some basic stone work. If it was done with rocks, which was the prevalent theory on much of the older constructions, then how did they manage to cut straight angles into the stone? Cutting and forming sharp angles outside the stone is one thing, but cutting into it? On the outside was a ridiculously huge 200 ton pointed stone, also planted with an Incan wall surrounding it. Ernesto told me that Qenko wasn't well known to most tourists, because no one ever figured out how the thing was built, or what it really was for. What he did notice was that on the solstices of the year, there was a slit through the rock that was precisely 30 degrees off the moon, which would be compensated if the earth was rotated 30 degrees to put the rock in its place to match the solstices. It was a real mystery.

Ernesto then asked me, the present scientist and engineer, how it was possible. I simply said, "I don't know." Funny those three words, "I don't know." It wasn't until I uttered those three humbling words, "I don't know," that I really understood what it was that irked Ernesto and Michelle about science, and for that matter, the western approach to science.

The problem is humility. To be humble is to be able to suck it up, and say, "You know, I haven't a single clue." For me personally, I don't like being lied to. Science won't lie to you, because that is just the quest for truth in nature. The problem is the human aspect of science. When you ask a scientist something, you expect an answer. The problem is that option D, "I don't know," is missing from the vocabulary. We had this option as children, when we were all natural born scientists.

Kids are great. They're totally open minded, unbiased, honest, they ask tons of questions to drive you nuts, and are willing to test things. Even I had fun with the fork and the electric socket when I was an impressionable four year old. Still, those are the hallmarks of good science. Yet somewhere in college and graduate school, everyone became pundits. Everyone's got to have some kind of answer. Whatever happened to the magic three words which often got most people out of trouble? Whatever happened to saying, "I don't know?" The beauty of those words is that they're honest.

Another problem with western scientists is that it consists of dissecting and separating everything so much that people in general can't connect to it. They're missing the whole. In fact, there currently is a battle brewing between the scientists of China, and Asia, for that matter, and the scientists of the West regarding the evolution of life. The Asian scientists are look-ing at things from a holistic view, and are putting the connections together. The western scientists in general, are continuing to dissect. This was really evident at a recent conference on evolution, where Chinese scientists were proposing another theory to evolution based on their studies of the fossils in the Mongolian region. What the Chinese scientists were seeing is a science of "harmony", or how things aren't so much competing in terms of natural selection, but somehow the competing traits were actually cooperating, and that another force other than genetic selection was at play. It'll be interest-ing to see how this current shouting match goes. The funny thing is a lot of people were relating to the Chinese scientist's viewpoints.

Those three magic words also connect to the 99% of the world who pro-fess to some sort of spirituality or religion. Many people attach themselves to these beliefs out of a sense of the "I don't know" factor. For some, it gives them a sense of security, for others, a sense of awe. For me, it gave me a clear sense of my ignorance.

Our next site was the eerily named the "Ex-On" site. Ernesto told me how the locals had spotted tons of UFO's in the vicinity of the site. It looked like a 100,000 ton rock that was sliced and diced with a ginsu knife in some areas, like a mad chef carving a cake. I thought the name was cute, until I saw the multiple caves and tunnels lacing the outcropping. As soon as I saw the cave, I dove right in. The tunnels and crevices seemed endless. They went right through the Andesite rock, and what was even more amazing was the number of tunnels that were carved through the rock. What really perplexed me was that several of the entrances, had carved stone stairs that descended all the way down, to the dirt. When I scraped out some of the dirt, I found some more stair case. The stairs led down somewhere, but someone decided to fill the hallway with soil. So, I decided to follow one really deep tunnel as far as I could go, until I realized that for all the squeezing and squirming, I was stuck.

Suddenly, my body told me something strange. It started with a rumble in my stomach, and then a twitch in an unnamed area. "Crap", I said, and I didn't mean that in the expletive. Beyond me was a hole in the ground, marked by multiple altars indicating an important entrance to a vast underground network. At the time, I didn't see it as an entrance. I saw something quite different. I saw the john, and I was seriously thinking about doing something sacrilegious, only because nature was calling.

"Are you alright in there, David?" Called Ernesto

"I'm stuck."

"Oh my. Can you reach for the stairway?"

"Yes, hold on."

I sucked in my stomach, and slowly crawled out of the tunnel.

"Please be careful, some of these places are still dangerous." Said Ernesto.

"I will."

After figuring out that my body wasn't ready for the outhouse we headed to the Incan fortress temple ruins of Sacsayhuaman. It's pronounced "sexy woman", and from an ogling point of view, it was definitely worth a look. The enormous curved stones, the gorgeous geometry of the placements, and quite frankly, the hills and the valleys of the "sexy woman", were indeed a sight to behold. At night in the crescent moonlight, she knocked my boots off.

Sacsayhuaman is best described as a gigantic terrace of stones. The bottom, leading terrace had the monster rocks; the centerpiece was a 300 ton, Andesite monolith. It wasn't the only one, as next to it were stones that were on the order of 250 tons. If we multiplied the average, of say, 200 tons per stone, conservatively speaking, with about 100 stones for the first terrace, which is probably an underestimate; that brought the total tonnage of the first level of Sacsayhuaman to about 20,000 tons worth of stones. To present a relationship, the US aircraft carrier Nimitz weighs about 97,000 tons, the battleship New Jersey is 15,000 tons, a typical destroyer class ship is 5-7000 tons, and a 4 story nuclear reactor can be 670 tons.

But 20,000 tons was too much to even consider first. So, we examined the monster, the beast of the rock in the wall. At 300 tons, it was a stone that most modern day equipment would have lots of problems moving. In fact, there was only one piece of equipment that could move it, and that was the cargo cranes in massive shipyards. On top of that, it was carved precisely into a polygonal shape and then set into the wall. I stood there gazing at her with my mouth wide open. Ernesto then asked me what I thought of the archaeologist's opinions about how the monstrosity was built.

"David, you're an engineer. You're the first engineer that I've worked with. Most of the people I've worked with were white, western, archaeologists and anthropologists. They never listened to me, or to the locals when we tried to tell them what our ancient stories were about this sight. You aren't white, you're an engineer, and you seem to have an understanding in two different systems of thought, so I would like to know what you think about this."

"Ernesto, let me be frank. Those guys are on crack. That's probably what they came here for, because I can tell you right now, any construction engineer is going to have problems with their theories."

The current theory is that the Incans built the wall using stones to pound them flat, placed the stone, lifted it up again to see the impression, and repeated the process to make it fit. I had a major problem with that theory. This was a 300 ton, Andesite monolithic stone, and it was just one of many. Andesite is a remarkably hard substance, which would make it a great building material, if it weren't so dense, hard, and heavy. The only way to confirm that theory was to lift up the 300 ton stone, and see if there were any dismembered hands or bodies in that tight fit. Accidents were bound to happen with that technique, and I couldn't even get my diving knife into the cracks.

To top it off, no sources of Andesite were located in or around Cuzco. The Andesite was quarried in several sources, one at a source that was 35 kilometers away, in Rumiqolqa, and another that was 100 kilometers away, in the north. So, to present the problem, somehow, this 300 ton, Andesite monster was carved out of a quarry, transported up the mountain side, on

Incan roads that were staircases, to the top of the mountain, carved, and set into the wall. The angle of the staircase heading up to Sacsayhuaman was, on average, 45 to 60 degrees, and there were several hundred meters of staircase, from the center of Cuzco, and it wound around the mountain. Sacsayhuaman was at the top of the mountain, overlooking Cuzco. And finally, repeat that a hundred times, hope there weren't any accidents that would kill off the man power, and that was just for the first terrace. There are three terrace levels.

When I thought about it, I immediately threw out the obvious. I decided to use the pyramids as a baseline, since so many people tried to theorize how the pyramids were built. One theory said that they used boats to float the stones up. How can a boat work on the side of a mountain that's 3400 meters in altitude? Another was that giant earthen ramps were built around the pyramids. So, someone's going to tell me that someone moved the equivalent amount of earth of a 3400 meter high mountain, that's several square miles wide, just to drag up the stone?

Another theory was that they dragged it up across the stair case, and Incan roads, which are on a 45 to 60 degree incline to the top of the mountain, up 3400 meters in altitude? Of course, they somehow, transported the rock across rope bridges, across canyons, through valleys, and then up the mountain! OK, let's give them credit, they would have to build a road, around the mountain, all several square miles of the mountain. That's like building a road around the sides of a volcano. Doable, but it was a hell of a lot of effort to boot. However, if the Incan roads were any indication, the spiral around the mountain would've been a staircase, not a smoothed road.

It was easy to see why I had problems with the archaeologist's theories. They didn't do their math. The best way to explain the construction would be to do the math. Archaeologists aren't particularly good at math, because after we worked it out, we looked at each other, and again in awe, professed our ignorance.

So, how come the math doesn't work out with the western archaeologist's theories? How could they have built the monument in the first place? Well, before you can ask the "how did they build it", you have to ask the, "how much?" as in "how much energy does it take to build this thing?" It's a very simple question, and one that anyone with a basic understanding of physics and engineering can do. The best part is that it doesn't matter what kind of structure you're looking at; the energy requirements are going to be the same regardless, simply because you cannot change the laws of nature.

First, you have calculate the amount of energy it would take just to cut out a stone of that size. Then you have to calculate the energy it takes to lift and move it there. This also has to take into account, the distance of the quarry, either ten, thirty five, or a hundred kilometers away, across dips, and valleys, canyons, rivers, up the staircase, up the mountain, up 3400 meters, to the level just above Cuzco. Then you have to calculate the amount of energy it takes just to cut the stone precisely. Then you have to calculate the amount of energy it takes to set it in place. And here's the part that most people seem to miss out, especially archaeologists, when it comes to engineering logistics. You have to calculate the amount of energy it took to develop, harness, and construct the technology it took to actually do the work in the first place. You also need to understand that it takes experience, a fundamental understanding of strengths of materials, weights, and measurements, and you at least need some kind of established technology. Finally, you need to see what the established time frame is. Whether it's with sticks, stones, ropes, and men, to trucks, cranes, and lasers, the fact is you cannot ignore the laws of physics, energy, and nature. Those requirements are the same.

Unfortunately, that's what a lot of archaeologists do when they go around proposing that they know how the things were built. I would not trust an archaeologist to build my house. I'd trust a construction engineer. When it came to that 300 ton stone, which wasn't single or unique in the structure, I knew that a lot of people had some serious problems with the western archaeologists, and among them was Ernesto. He had many opportunities to work with them, and he considered them to be extremely arrogant.

The real question then, is not how it was built, or even why. It's how much. That is the basic, fundamental question that must be answered first before any kind of theory could even be set regarding the logistics, organization, and mechanics of moving the stone, and then do it a hundred times for the first level.

We decided that other than asking that basic question and doing some basic calculations, to also add an, "I don't know." The energy requirements were immense, and the area of Sacsayhuaman, at the top of the mountain, in that little plateau, was too small to have enough men, ropes, and sticks or logs, to support the building of that structure. We didn't even bother to calculate what kind of rope and structural support was needed, because even with multiple ropes, and really thick logs, it wouldn't have supported the weight, and the bulk of that material added even more mass, which required even more energy to move the thing and the machines themselves. My father was a mechanical engineer who always said, "engineers can do anything, as long as they have the right technology."

That night, both Ernesto and I professed our ignorance, and were awestruck as we watched the crescent moon, and the milky way, turn it's cosmic turbines over the monument of Sacsayhuaman.

Chapter 7

The Strange Light

I was knocked out with a bout of the flu, as I sat in Café Haylilly in the evening, trying to nurse my body back to strength. My Spanish was still poor, but I had a vocabulary of about eighty words, and I struggled to explain to Sally that I needed ginger tea, and garlic. Finally, I gave up trying to ask her for ginger, and settled for chamomile tea instead. She did understand that I needed raw garlic, and gave me a clove. Sally was almost motherly, because when I tried to eat another clove, she said no, that I shouldn't take too much, and to let my body rest. While I had the flu, I tried to write in my notebook, and spent a lot of time pondering the mystery of the lights, and the enormous stone structures.

After a week, I had a bout with food poisoning for a day from some bad milk products. Never in my life had I seen so much stuff come out the other end, especially when I barely ate a thing. The flu was over in a few days though, and I coughed up green phlegm, as my system cleared itself of gunk. Soon, I felt better, and I was ready to see just how well acclimatized my body was. It was one thing to feel fine in thin air, but it's another thing to work the body at more than two miles high in altitude. I took my bike out for a ride through Sacsayhuaman, and the entire ruin. I saw them at night, and now I wanted to see them in them in the daytime.

Nature had a funny way of blowing the steam out of me. By the time I reached the top of Sacsayhuaman, I discovered just how far I had to go to acclimatize myself. As I ascended the staircase, I felt my body burn, knees creak, head spin, and my lungs were on fire. I knew I was out of shape from being sick, but I still wanted to push myself, and see if I could at least make it to Sacsayhuaman.

I made it to the top, sat down, took a breather, and then I toured the ruin. I wanted to take some pictures of the 300 ton monster which made up part of the wall. As I wandered the cyclopean stones, it dawned on me that everything I learned back in school, the states, and on TV, was wrong. What I learned came from a perspective that wasn't my own.

"Hey! Hey you! You can't do that! You can't bring the bicycle up there!" I heard a man yell out to me. I saw a Peruvian running to me with a badge. He pointed his fingers at me, and made quick motions for me to get off the terrace. I walked down the terrace, and then he yelled at me in Spanish.

"Don't you know the rules? Don't you know you're not allowed to bring a bicycle in here?" He said. I couldn't understand what he said, but I heard the word bicycle several times. While he berated me, two men, who were about five feet in height, stepped up to the man. They were dressed in spandex cyclist pants and shirts, and wore helmets and goggles.

"He's with us." Said one of the men. I looked at the guy.

"Well tell him to obey the rules next time. And the two of you get your bicycles out of here!" Said the man.

"Ok, we will. Hey, we're Peruvians, so take it easy OK? The guy is obviously a foreigner. How would he know? He can't even understand you."

The guard looked at me, and than said, *"oh. I thought you were Peruvian. OK, fine, fine, just go."* He thought I was Peruvian? We left the ruin, and walked down a road to where it split. The two started talking to each other, pulled out a map, looked at it, and then pointed down the road. The man who spoke for me waved a hand. They introduced themselves as Jaime and Jesus.

I joined them. The two looked unassuming, but they exhibited a fitness that made me feel out of shape. They effortlessly took off to ascend another five hundred meters up from Sacsayhuaman as if it was flatland.

We went from one ruin to another. We stopped at an Incan hydrological work of canals and fountains, where the Incans blended water worship and water production into one structure. The structure was built into the side of a small hill, and had several steps of fitted, polygonal stones, and aqueducts that ran from a reservoir located up the hill. Again, I got into trouble for jumping down the ruin, and Jaime had to come in and save my behind.

Then we stopped at the ruins of an Incan farm commune, with trapezoidal doors, stone walls, and walkways. It was roofless, but it epitomized one of the standard constructions of the Empire. It was a four walled structure, with a high, triangular stone form on two sides of a long rectangle that formed the structural support for the roof.

Then we stopped at an Incan messenger outpost. The messenger outpost was a round, circular, stone hut, where the ancient couriers slept. In the four corners of the Incan Empire, which spanned from the north of Ecuador to the South of Chile, into the Amazon, and present day Argentina, legends said that a message took just three days to get from one end to the other, thanks to the network of runners. As we headed back into Cuzco that night, I learned quite a bit from them with my rudimentary Spanish.

Jesus was a pharmacist who enjoyed new age music, and Jaime was a watch repairman, and an inventor. He designed and built most of his outdoor equipment with pure practicality and functionality in mind. He built a convertible backpack, which turned into panniers for the bike, and could be assembled into a standard mountain backpack for mountaineering. I asked him if he could build me one.

When we arrived at their residence in Cuzco, the differences in how we grew up became apparent. I came from a country where anything can be had for a price. Even though Americans considered ourselves to be the most inventive people in the world, we forgot the fact that we're taking credit for the work that comes from a particular type of people who make the inventions. Those people were from developing countries who immigrated to the US, like Jaime. Most of our high tech industry was built on the backs of immigrants. It's been estimated that half of the entrepreneurs and inventions from Silicon Valley came from Indian and Chinese engineers, scientists, and researchers.

The immigrants come from a background full of problems that needed to be solved. I never had to worry about clean water and food, or working equipment. I just assumed it worked. Yet, the immigrants didn't, and they had to work inside boundaries to come up with new ways to do things. My father has that hallmark coming from Vietnam. If he even patented half of his nutty ideas, I wouldn't be surprised if he started several brand new businesses himself. As for me, I was a Philadelphia suburban kid. What did I have to worry about? School. Work. Mundane stuff. The only thing I have spent a lot of time tinkering with was my bike, and even there, Jaime was bubbling with ideas that the bike industry hadn't tried yet.

Jaime borrowed his cousin's apartment for the night. The apartment was down the mountain slope of the city, in a barrio of Cuzco, and with my crude Spanish and sign language, we communicated as we ate. Their food was basic, and consisted of bread, water, cheese, and some fruit which I shared with them

After returning home that night, I was still hungry. I walked into a local restaurant, and made a major linguistic faux pas. I was dressed in my bicycle shorts, which were spandex, and they were skin tight to my body. I walked up the owner, and tired, I smiled and said,

"Yo tengo hombre, quiero comer."

"Que?"

"Yo tengo hombre, quiero comer!"

"Mira, somos un restaurante decente. No quiero homosexuales aquí!"

"No no! No soy homosexual! Yo tengo, ah, mi estomago. Quiero comer.

"Quieres comer tu estomago ahora? Estas loco?"

"No! Quiero comer!"

Here's the translation.

"I have man, I want to eat."

"What?"

"I have man, I want to eat!"

"Look, we're a decent restaurant. We don't want homosexuals here!"

"No no! I am not homosexual! I have, ah, my stomach, I want to eat."

"You want to eat your stomach? Are you crazy?"

"No! I want to eat!"

I was supposed to say, "Yo tengo hambre, que quiero comer."

"I have hunger, I want to eat."

I went to another cafe. The waiter came up to me, and he thought I looked like Bruce Lee's son, Brandon Lee, and must have been a half brother somehow. This was probably the fourth time someone referred to me as being Bruce Lee, related to Bruce Lee, or being associated with Bruce Lee, which I didn't mind at all. Bruce Lee was a man I greatly admired, who destroyed racial stereotypes, created a whole new industry in the movies, inspired millions of people, and revolutionized the martial arts. I hoped that one day I could do something revolutionary for humanity like he did.

As I ate, I felt the aches and pains in my body. I thought I was swallowing something, but I wasn't sure if it was a loose organ or the meal. Of course, I'm a masochist at heart, so I told Jaime that I would join them for a hundred kilometer, monster downhill ride the next day. I went to sleep and dreamed of growing some new body parts.

The next day I met them at the Plaza D'Armas. In every town and every city in Peru, was a central plaza, which functioned as central square. Couples flirted and kissed, families casually strolled, and it was a great area to relax. I met up with the two Peruvian supermen, as well as two Japanese cyclists who cycled around the world for the last three years. They were Yoshi and Kenji, and they came over to look at my bicycle. Kenji had a mustache, and he was slightly taller than me. Thin and muscular, he had a powerful handshake from thousands of miles of gripping the handlebars. He smiled warmly as we shook hands, and asked if he could take a look at my frame, and components. He gave me two thumbs up. Kenji circumnavigated the globe twice via bicycle, in a span of three years. Yoshi joined him a few months ago. They did the northern hemisphere first, and then the southern. Now they were doing the Equator, but Kenji was anxious to return to Colombia. I asked him why.

"He has a woman!" Joked Yoshi.

"My girlfriend is there. She's Colombian, and it breaks my heart sometimes being so far." Said Kenji.

"When did you meet her?"

"Four months ago," laughed Yoshi, "look at him. He's like a puppy dog when he talks about her."

I smiled and laughed with them. It was interesting to meet them, because I figured that I wouldn't meet many Asians, or Asian Americans traveling, or for that matter, traveling solo for extended periods of time. Yet, there were two other guys were Asian Americans, and the rest were white, Caucasian women. There were few, if any, white men, and if they were traveling, they were traveling with their girlfriends or they were there with a group for a short tour. I didn't meet a single, solo, white male traveler. In my twenty nine days there, I met several cyclists. Almost all were either from Asia, or were Americans of Asian descent. The Americans I met of Asian descent were John, a Korean American investment banker who had enough with corporate life, quit, and backpacked alone through South America, and Jack, a Filipino guy who bicycled from Oregon all the way to Peru, sold his bicycle and trailer, and went into the Amazon to do some volunteer work for the next year. The other two were white: a Spanish guy, and an Australian woman.

In the States, the general media perception of Asian men was of the passive, boring, geeky, persona who didn't do anything except stay on the sidelines. It was either that or the asexual, martial arts champ who was deadly serious, or a goof. And of course, in the films, he usually didn't get the girl.

Yet I met these Asian American men who were having the time of their lives, with outrageous adventures, and just doing things that were totally opposite of the media portrayal. The stories they shared would make any adventure movie in the US weak. I was glad that I was outside of the influence of the american media. The media is infectious, fake, and acutely pervasive. There's no way to escape it, other than to get out of the country, and find out who the person really is inside. The media's perceptions were so insidious, and molded a person's perceptions of self before that person even had a chance to form his own identity.

For me, the racial perceptions changed significantly the moment I crossed the Rio Grande. At first, on my first day, I was defensive, but as the days went on, numerous incidents began to tell me that the Peruvians, when I didn't open up my mouth, thought I was a Peruvian. In some cases, they would talk to me in Spanish, and then suddenly, stop, then say, "Oh wait, are you Japanese?" Which annoyed me.

In Peru, there's no such thing as "Chinese Peruvian", or "Japanese Peruvian." They're called Peruvians of Asian descent, chino, or chinito, which was an affectionate term for anyone from Asia. Peruvians rarely distinguished race, since it was always nationality that came up first. If a person spoke Spanish with the Peruvian accent and colloquialisms, regardless of their skin color and ethnic appearances, they were Peruvian first. In contrast, in the US, there was this obsessive need to segregate, divide, distinguish, hyphenate, keep, and maintain the races and ethnicities in different groups.

It was strange for me, but the camaraderie that I received from the locals, Jaime, and Jesus, endeared me to them. Of course, I could only hide my nationality for so long. As soon as I opened my big mouth, the locals would hear a strong accent, and then they'd yell, "Hey, American!" That became my name, besides all the Bruce Lee and Brandon Lee references. I'd never been called outright an American, even in the States. until I got to Peru. It was a strange experience, and it would take me a while to accustom myself to it.

Jaime, Jesus, and I headed up to the top of the mountain. We bicycled through fifty kilometers of countryside, where I watched peasants working on their fields, tending their goats, or sheep, and herds of llamas. Winter time was passing through, which made the fields look barren. Mostly women and children tended the flocks, and the llamas went by us with red tassels in their ears. The children waved at me, and we waved at them in turn. The sun was setting, and we could see the deep red and yellow pigments bath the sky, as snow capped mountain peaks in the distance glowed at dusk.

"We're almost there Daveed!" Said Jesus with a smile. *"Are you good?"*

"Yes. I'm good." I wheezed.

"Good, because here, we're going to go zoom!" Cackled Jaime.

We were at the top of the mountain. I took stock of the situation. I was on a mountain bike, at two and a half miles up in thin air. I looked down from the summit, and before me, was an incredibly vast, steep, and winding highway going all the way down for forty five to fifty kilometers into the Sacred Valley of the Incas. Along the way were sheer cliffs, with drops of a thousand feet or more, no barriers and fences, sand piles, unpaved roads, paved roads, huge cargo trucks rumbling up towards us, road debris, and mountain upon mountain as far as the eye could see. We watched the headlight glow in the descending darkness. The sun was setting, and we had to move quickly. We had at most fifteen minutes of day light left.

With nothing more than my potential energy, I raced down the road at forty five to fifty five kilometers an hour, without pedaling. The wind raged in my ears; all I had to follow was the pale glow of the road stripe, if there was one. My nose was stuck to the handlebars for aerodynamics, and I felt the vibration of the road make my bicycle become resonant. The cycle shook, and I reminded myself of how Aleks and I worked to make sure everything was tight. As we went down, I felt the incline of the road get steeper, and steeper. Soon, it felt like my butt was higher than my head, which it probably was. The wind screamed in my ears, as we raced through a downhill of a roller coaster ride; night fell, and we were in the glow of a half moon and the milky way.

Sharp turns with drops to uncertain death met us at almost every corner.

71

There were no barriers, no shoulders, and no margins of safety. As we sped down, we hit a patch of sand, and I struggled to control the bicycle as it fishtailed. The challenge was control as well as turning at the corners. I had to be careful of the pressure I applied on the brakes, because if I squeezed too hard, then I would fishtail out of control, or worse, fly over the handlebars.

We sped down the road, and I heard the rumble of a loaded eighteen wheeler coming towards us. I looked up from the shade of my helmet, but I looked up too high – suddenly, my eyes were blind – I struggled to control and quickly slowed the bike down, as I tried to blink the flashing blobs, the artifacts of a light in a dark adjusted eye, out of my eyes. Abruptly, I felt the front wheel hit something, and instinctively, I gripped the brakes and swerved the bike to the side, as I crashed and skidded. My body fell underneath the bike frame, and I felt the road slam into my thighs and calves. I came to a stop, and my foot touched a log on the side of the road. I crashed into a pile of wood. Luckily, I wore a pair of double lined nylon exercise pants, and the two layers slipped over each other, and helped protect my leg from the worst of the fall. A dull ache throbbed my leg, as I got up, and Jesus stopped to take a look at the wound,

"You're fine Daveed!" Said Jesus.

"Yeah, it looks good. Not much blood." Said Jaime. He pulled out a water bottle, and we doused the wounded area with it.

Then we took off again. Despite the sting on my leg, the trip was mesmerizing. My skills were good enough that on some of the less curvy sections, and I looked at the mountains on the side as we flew down the escarpment. They were huge black silhouettes, with dark gray clouds, glowing with moonlight.

From the escarpment of the mountain side, came a bright flash of light. For a few moments, as if time was suspended, the wind, the speed, everything became a blur, and then silent. All that existed was the light and I. In slow motion, I saw the light grow from behind the mountain side. Suddenly, I heard the rushing of the wind in my ears, felt the vibration of my bike, and I blinked into the darkness of the road.

At the bottom, near Pisac, I was surprised when Jaime said there was more road, on the way to Ollantaytambo, which was the farming village near the end of the valley. It's also the site of some spectacular ruins, which are even larger than Sacsayhuaman. So again we took off. This time, the way down wasn't as frenetic, but we had a new obstacle. Along the way, Peruvian dogs ran out at us, barking, and snapping at our feet, as they chased us either for fun, or to defend their territory. Peruvian dogs were territorial, but I grew tired of them trying to snap at us, so I developed a technique to scare them off. I biked straight at them screaming my head off which shocked them into a tail between the legs retreat. It worked. Jaime and Jesus adopted the technique, and late in the evening, through the valley, I was sure the Quechua villagers heard us.

****

After biking several kilometers from Pisac, and being hounded by large groups of dogs, we looked at our watches, and realized that we still had a long way to go to Ollantaytambo. So, we did what many travelers did outside of the USA. We hitchhiked. Hitchhiking was still accepted as a valid form of transit, and in general, people didn't harass hitchhikers.

We stood on the side of the road, and stuck our thumbs out as several headlights passed by us. No one slowed down. So, Jaime and Jesus got serious, and exposed their bare legs into the headlights of an oncoming car. It stopped, and I heard the radio of a police officer as a dark silhouette stepped out of the vehicle.

"That's the ugliest bunch of ladies I have ever seen." The officer muttered as he looked at us.

"We're not women! We're Peruvian!" Yelled Jaime.

"What? You stuck you're legs out there like a woman. Ah hell. What do you want?"

The officer looked at us, as Jaime approached the officer. After a few terse words, the officer told us to get in the station wagon. Unfortunately, there was no back door to the vehicle, so for twenty minutes, Jaime held onto the bicycles in the back, while Jesus and I held onto Jaime for dear life, as the car bumped, rumbled, and drove towards Ollantaytambo. My wrists were straining with the effort, and I could feel the burn of my muscles in the isometric position.

The officer dropped us off three towns away from Ollantaytambo, near the town of Calca, so we still had a small distance left to go. As we biked in, I looked up into the mountains, and from the corner of my eye, from behind

73

the escarpment, came the flash of light again. It was bright enough to look like two moons.

"*What is that?*" I said.

"*Jaime!*" I called out.

"*What's going on?*" He replied.

"*Light! There!*" I pointed.

"*Where?*" He asked as we slowed down. I pointed again to the glow behind the mountain. The moon was directly overhead, so it couldn't have been the moon. It did look like two moons were there. They both looked in the direction that I pointed my hand. It was away from Cuzco, and Ollantaytambo, pointing towards the direction of the Amazon basin.

"*What light? Oh!*" Jaime and Jesus looked with me, at the strange light that glowed from behind the mountains. I looked overhead at the moon, and then back towards the light.

"*Is a city there?*"

"*No. It's mountain range, and then jungle. There are no people.*"

As quickly as it came, the light disappeared. I looked at Jaime. He shrugged his arms, with a face of, "what was that?" Jesus looked at me as well.

"*See that before?*" I asked Jaime.

"*No. This is the first time I've ever seen it.*" He said, as we resumed biking. What was that light? Was that the light Ernesto told me about?

We headed into Ollantaytambo, the ancient fortress, agricultural outpost of the Incas. It was also the end of the road in the valley. On the Inca trail, Ollantaytambo was the last sight of civilization. For the next six days, the trail consisted of a hike through the ancient Incan highway to Macchu Picchu, or due east for six months into impenetrable rain forest. The escarpment is one of the great frontiers; it was full of enormous unexplored territories. In fact, the entire Amazon Basin is the size of the continental United States. It was incredible to believe, that in this day and age of satellites, modern technology and population density, large expanses of territory remained unexplored, and it was still full of human tribes that never had any contact with the outside world. I mulled about it as we biked into the Plaza D'Armas of Ollantaytambo.

Jaime's aunt lived inside of the fortress commune, which was seven to eight hundred years old. As we walked up the cobblestone steps, I saw the fortress loom in the darkness in front of me. It was enormous, looked like a castle, but it was built with the Incan style of stonework. Along the sides of the fortress were water channels, and I heard the flow of water. I inhaled, and smelled the scents of hay, flowers, and llama manure. I looked up, and saw the halo of the moon, and in it, the fortress cast a deep shadow to one side. I followed Jaime and Jesus up a dark alley to a great gate on the side of the commune. We walked across a small stone bridge.

Jaime knocked the great knocker on the door. Jaime's Aunt greeted us as she opened the door, and then took a look at me. She stopped, smiled at me, and then motioned for me to come inside. I smiled back.

"Thank you." I said as I kissed her on the cheek in the Peruvian custom.

"For what? You are our guest."

We walked into her part of the commune. It was like a small apartment, except the apartment was up a set of wooden steps that stuck out of the wall. Around me were small dirt bays where they grew flowers. His aunt led me to a hand pumped fountain.

"Wash here."

"OK."

After rinsing off, we ate some bread, fruit, and water. We tried to talk, and I noticed that I wasn't getting anywhere, until Jesus asked me, *"do you know martial arts?"*

"Yes. I teach."

"Show me some."

We walked into the tiny courtyard, where I showed them some basic Tai Chi movements, Kung Fu, and a few yoga movements. We laughed and joked as I got them to try the moves on me.

"How did you do that?" Asked Jesus when he found himself on the ground with his arm behind him. I did it in slow motion, and made sure to catch his back. I showed him it again.

"What I really need Dave, is something to relax." Said Jaime. I heard the word for relax, so I said, *"do yoga."* I showed him the mountain position, and then the tree. We laughed as Jaime tried the tree, and discovered that his sense of balance wasn't as keen as his road sense. Finally, it was time to sleep. We all had smiles on our faces, and I felt better, since I imparted something of value to my hosts. I had wondered how I would pay Jaime and Jesus back for their hospitality. Jaime figured the yoga instruction was

a good trade. Part of being a vagabond was knowing how to barter. So far, I was able to barter English lessons, Kung Fu lessons, Tai Chi lessons, basic yoga lessons, and even the occasional computer fix in the internet café, for kitchen privileges, food, free internet time, and in this case, room and board.

It was time to sleep, so Jaime's aunt led us to our beds in the apartment. The whole place was open to the outside, and the wooden floor creaked as I walked in. I felt the breeze come through. We were at a lower elevation then Cuzco, so it was warmer in the evening, but the breeze felt cool on my skin. I laid down in my bed, and watched the moonlight stream through the glassless windows. The room was open to the outside, and I saw the mountains in the moonlight; yet, the llama blankets were warm enough to keep out the night chills.

I woke up the next morning to the crows of the rooster. Jaime went out with his two cousins, Lizbeth and Ola to help them with their business. The girls ran a tourist stand outside the train station, and they catered to the tourists who stopped on their way to Macchu Picchu. The stand was a small shack made of corrugated aluminum, and they sold sandwiches, snacks, pastries, and juice drinks. I washed my face, and listened to the town stir in the morning. All around me, I could hear the muffled sound of flowing water. Quietly, I opened the door, and stepped out of the commune, to see the beginnings of day to day life.

In the soft light of the early morning, about 7 AM, a line of school girls, probably between the ages of ten and twelve, walked to class. They were dressed in green and white uniforms, which contrasted with their dark brown, reddish skin, black hair, and they had backpacks on as they giggled and skipped on the way to class. Then in the opposite direction, a group of boys, also about the same age, dressed in the dark blue uniforms, with back packs walked to class. The children hurried past men and women in traditional rainbow colored Quechua attire. The men had slacks, and fedora hats, but they had ponchos that were rainbow colored. Next to them walked women, many of whom were thick and strong, and they were dressed in long skirts, and loose blouses. They wore bowler hats, and carried goods to the market, or went to work in the fields with the men. Two cows, led by a gentleman in a sweater and a fedora hat walked down the street, and then several donkeys walked in the opposite direction. Soon, a herd of llamas with bright red tassels in their ears walked down the street as the small village was slowly waking up.

All over the streets were open aqueduct systems with rapidly flowing streams of water. The water rippled and flowed in the light, and I saw the sparkle of the liquid as it flowed, crystal clear. The Incans were obsessed with water, and their ancient plumbing still worked beautifully for the people, even after 800 or more years. As the sun rose up, the fortress ruins of Ollantaytambo on the steep mountain sides lit up. Ollantaytambo still used the ancient Incan constructions for its residences. Each city block was called a "concha", which housed several families. The structures outlasted earthquakes and the ravages of the Spanish destruction. As I walked down the street, roosters crowed in people's courtyards as children fed their chickens. Jesus woke up, and saw me walking down the street, so he joined me, and started to teach me some words. I would point at an object, and he said the Spanish word for it.

"The cow"

"The chicken"

"The rooster."

"The carburetor tuned motor engine block fed by diesel that pollutes the air."

"What?" I asked, confused.

"Sorry. The car."

I repeated the words after him, and he corrected what I said. The air was crisp, and it smelled fresh, like the smell just after a rainfall. It was peaceful, and idyllic.

It was the site of one of the bloodiest, ferocious, and greatest battles of the Incan-Spanish war. The Incans, in a brilliant tactical move, rendered the Spaniard's main weapon, the horse, useless. Using their plumbing, they maneuvered the canal gates to flood the valley around the Spanish, miring the horses. Without horses, the Spanish were helpless, and the Incans streamed out of the fortress to rout the Spanish back to Cuzco. I celebrated the victory that morning with some waterworks of my own as I got routed to the outhouse.

Later that day, after spending some time for lunch with Ola and Lizbeth, we headed back into town to take the bus back to Cuzco. Back in Cuzco, we hiked up the mountain back to the center of the City, and as we walked, I noticed the behavior of Jaime and Jesus that I soon adopted for myself.

Whenever we were behind women, they would whistle. Curious, I looked at the direction their eyes were in, where I noticed that they never looked at the head, the back, the shoulders, or the arms. No, these two looked at the most favored body part in all of Latin American culture, the ass.

As we walked up the street, and practiced our wolf whistles, Ernesto and a taller Peruvian, walked up to us. Ernesto introduced us, and the man's name was Marco. I introduced Jaime and Jesus. Ernesto spoke with Jaime for a bit. Then I turned to Ernesto, and said, "Ernesto, can you tell Jaime and Jesus that I said thank you very much for your hospitality, let me know if there's anything I can do for you?"

"Sure." Ernesto translated what I said to Jaime and Jesus. They both smiled brightly and shook hands before leaving. I turned back to Ernesto.

"By the way, I think I saw it." I said.

"You did?"

"Yes. Let's meet up later in the week. I have some ideas I need to put down on paper first. My intuition is telling me something that makes sense to me. I don't know how you'll take to it, but I need to clarify some of my thoughts first."

"OK. This Friday we will meet."

"Ernesto has told me about you. I would like to hear more about what you are investigating." Marco said.

"I'll be happy to enlighten you." I replied.

****

A Letter to Ernesto: Hypothesis of the Megalithic Constructions

Dear Ernesto,

OK, based on some of the research I've done, and the places you've shown me, and after witnessing the strange energy form, I'd like to lay the problem out.

1.) Macchu Picchu, Tiwanaku, Paititi, and Nazca are all pre Incan, and megalithic in nature. They are big, solid, and made to last the effects of time from the start of the original construction.

2.) Each point seems to have unusual properties; the most telling is the Nazca lines ability to withstand being buried from sandstorms, according to the local and Marco's information, as well as Paititi's legendary disappearing and reappearing act. I don't have enough information on Tiwanaku or Macchu Picchu.

3.) Sacsayhuaman does not look like the head and teeth of the Puma, but it is definitely the head or a critical point of something.

4.) Cuzco is the navel or the center point of some kind of something.

5.) Cuzco and Sacsayhuaman are also pre-Incan in origin, and composed of two hundred ton plus stones. From what we can tell after exploring Cuzco, most of the megalithic structures are still there.

6.) Sacsayhuaman seems to be some sort of control point, and does not seem to have a ritualistic fuction or practical function, like as a map representation. It does not denote constellations, symbols, or anything that exhibits a pattern.

7.) It seems more likely that Nazca is some sort of user manual, not a map, as several theories have posited. After inspecting the maps of Nazca, we are unable to trace patterns of repetition. However, there seems to be a mathematical representation. We can see repetition of math, like the spirals, the strange hand glyph, and a few other glyphs.

8.) There are legends of tunnels linking all four sites and Cuzco

9.) The sites seem to be within geometric distances from each other. There seems to be symmetry.

10.) There is a release of energy in the area in the form of light, which appears in areas where there are no cities, in skies which have no clouds, and from below the mountains. Aurora would not work because we are too close to the equator, and the light comes from the ground up. Something is accumulating and then releasing energy, and that release is enough to create a glow like a full moon. That is the biggest mystery to me.

Synopsis: My feeling is that the entire area of the four suyo's is some kind of "machine". It feels like a sort of planetary energy device. I'm not sure why, but my intuition is really strong in terms of viewing the structures in that perspective. The time and effort to build the megalithic sites is so immense, that to simply build them for ritualistic or representative reasons using two hundred ton or more stones is impractical. We calculated that the lower level of Sacsayhuaman is composed of at least twenty to thirty thousand tons of giant stones, set close to the peak of the mountain. A tyrannical ruler would want to see a finished product. It took time to build the pyramids, and that was with ten to twenty ton stones, and that was at sea level.

Many of these stones are at least two hundred tons or more, and they were hauled up to 3280 meters above sea level, from those two quarries, which are thirty five or a hundred kilometers away.

Whoever built these were damn good engineers, highly advanced, and had a functional purpose. To add to that, it once worked, and I believe it can be made to work again. In addition, unlike the pyramids, it is an active system. The pyramids were built as a passive computational system, in a seismically inactive area, where there are little to no earthquakes. The pyramids were built with the predisposition of regular, natural planetary and cosmic cycles that are easily observable, and it calculates periods of time, and functions as a marker of the center of the world land mass. This we've read in several of the books at the clubhouse.

Cuzco, Sacsayhuaman, Ollantaytambo, and Macchu Picchu were built in highly active earthquake zones, using stones that are at least 10 times the size and weight of the stones that make up the pyramids. A lot of potential and kinetic energy courses through this area. Therefore to build such giant structures in a seismically active area would have to require the following:

1.) A good scientific understanding of the geological processes and cycles.

2.) Immense engineering knowledge of structural building to withstand earthquakes and other forces.

3.) A bona fide reason for wasting the time and effort to do it with two hundred ton stones when it could be done more efficiently with five to ten ton stones. Five to ten ton stones make sense to build temples, maps, and calendar systems. This we can see in the Coricancha temple, which is earthquake proof and built with much smaller stones. Three hundred or more tons is not logical for the use of a simple structure, or even a fortress. Any engineer is going to eventually realize this in the building process, because the logistical requirements in terms of man power, cargo load, and energy is too much for the altitude, angle of the mountain's slope, and distance of the quarry to the work site.

4.) If there is a bona fide reason to do this in such an earthquake prone area, than the reason appears to be more functional than passive.

If I was the engineer who planned this, I would need a reason for such large tonnage. My hypothesis is that whoever planned these structures foresaw the need to build these things to last for periods of thousands of years, and to endure earthquakes that are as much as ten on the Richter scale. If I had that as the criteria to fulfill, then I would need to fulfill the following requirements before I even build this thing.

1.) Build it with durable materials in such a way that it would always be present, could not be buried or toppled, and would endure all the natural destructive cycles. The material would have to be crystalline and flexible, so concrete or quartz is out. That includes anything with calcium oxides, since they erode easily in carbonic acid. Silicon oxide based rock is best. I would use something that's been melted and cooled, volcanic, vitreous, or granite type stones. I guess Andesite fills this requirement?

2.) Build it on an available, dependable, and accessible energy source, which can also endure the test of time for thousands of years. This rules out nuclear, electric, solar, wind, gas, coal, oil, biomass, and human power. Water and hydro geological, earth made steam, are also ruled out due to the need to build machinery which will break down. Since the whole site seems solid state, there are no moving parts to break down, that would also rule out volcanic or earth kinetic, like earthquakes. Both are highly chaotic and hard to control. What's left? The earth's magnetic field, and then there are the esoteric, yet detectable, unproven, and untapped energies. Yet they are documented, and have been known to be accessed by ancient cultures, and today are still accessed, especially in China and India. I know I'm stretching my mind to include these, so let us stretch, shall we? These include earth energies, ley lines/dragon lines, and the earth's life force energies. However strange and unproven to our modern day world, the energies just mentioned above would have all the characteristics which fit the requirements.

3.) Have a manual which is easily accessible, dependable, and readable. Do not use a written language since that can easily change in meaning. There is only one common language in the universe which exists; that is mathematics. Therefore, the user should have good mathematic skills, say up to basic trigonometry, geometry, and the ability to do matrix transforms, since we can transpose the coordinates of the structures into a basic matrix. Euler functions, nonlinear math, and anything which includes the mathematics of harmonics would be ideal, since we are dealing with energy, which consists of waveforms. Somehow, the math would have to be transcribed into either: symbols, geometries, codex's, or patterns which are identifiable, translatable, and when proven with probability, are proven to be 95% or better to not be a coincidence. That means there's a 95% or greater probability that it was done on purpose.

4.) And finally, to make sure that the device is not accidentally turned on by accident, a key is required. The key is not some esoteric jewel, object, or thing which can easily be lost or destroyed in the ravages of time. The key, like the energy form, has to be something that is an inherent characteristic, sequence, code, or form that anyone can possess, or figure out using insight and understanding based upon the mathematics of the manual.

Now, those are the criteria I'd need to fulfill to build these things. However, to get to the level where I can even begin to think about filling that criteria, let alone creating that criteria, I must have the following background.

I would need a good understanding of the geological processes, materials of construction, and possess the adequate technology to do so rapidly and efficiently. I would also need experience in prior construction on seismically active areas, a complete understanding of all the energy forms and how to harness those forms, the ability to make the system simple enough so that someone with a basic solid background in math and science as well as some insight can figure it out, and most importantly be able to operate it when the time is right.

That's actually the last key, which is to operate it when necessary. This is a huge device, which must harness and control immense amounts of energy. That sort of power is not something you want to be playing with. So that brings us to the last question. What is the right time, and under what circumstances?

So, we need to read the user manual, plug in the power source or sources, and then turn it on. Then we have to know how to operate it, and when. Whoever built these things were humans, and their descendants are the red skinned Quechua and Aymara. That much is obvious.

The biggest clue that the ancient builders of these structures are the indigenous is in the Aymaran language itself. The fact that the Aymaran language was used to create a computer program called Atamiri, by the computer scientist Ivan Guzman de Rojas is also a huge clue. Aymara is the only spoken language in the world which was proven to program a computer. On top of that, it is the only language, compared to C, C++, Pascal, et al. which can efficiently translate one human based language into another. No other language, artificial or human based can do that as well.

In addition, the characteristics of the Aymaran language consists of a yes, no, and an in-between modality. No other language is like this. Current computers are binary, using 1 and 0, or yes and no. There is no in between. However, quantum computers are molecular, and based on the spin state of a molecule, which is yes, no, and in between. Therefore, Aymara would be the ideal language for a quantum computer; this obviously raises several enormous questions.

What are the Aymara doing with a highly logical computer language as their form of communication? Why, is the Aymaran language so highly logical and efficient, in other words, it doesn't resemble the rest of the human based organic languages.

That is enough evidence for me to postulate that the ancient builders were advanced. Very advanced. Come to think of it, after learning Spanish, I'd better go and learn Aymara, and Quechua. Comisariqui!

Also, and I'm not sure why my senses are buzzing on this, but there is a significant metaphysical component to the device. Unfortunately, I haven't added these because I haven't completely made a connection: the sites relationships with the elements, Earth, Wind, Water, and Fire. The idea of Cuzco as a chakra point and Sacsayhuaman as the head of the chakra point, and as centers for energy collection and harnessing is a possibility. That would explain the strange lights that we've seen, since light is just a release of stored energy, or the conversion of one energy form into another. Now that I think about it more, and after writing it out, the above arguments make a lot more sense to me.

This is one hell of an engineering problem. It's a good thing I didn't have to do something like this in the University. The rocket project is peanuts compared to this. Can't wait to meet with you later this week to see what your thoughts are.

Later,

Dave

P.S. Why do I feel like I'm missing one more clue, and/or criterion?

****

I sat down in Café Haylilly in the evening, after I sent the letter to Ernesto. The TV was on, and the Spanish version of CNN was talking about the election of Alejandro Toledo to the presidency of Peru. I asked Sally to turn the volume down, as I ran the criteria through my mind again. I wasn't feeling well, as my body was still recovering from the flu. However, my mind wasn't well either. My rational mind wanted to puke. How could I come up with such a nutty idea? Yet a strange, unsettling calm reassured me, and said it was the right track.

Was I insane? The hypothesis made sense to my intuition, but my rational mind was having a fit. Of course, it had an upset stomach when the picture incident happened, and it practically vomited when the bird went through the window. Yet through it all, my intuition kept saying, "You're on the right track Dave. This is normal Dave." How the hell was this normal? Then again, how could it be normal for me to just leave my family, friends, established routines, safety, and comfort of the States, to a complete unknown, and somehow, as if on cue, people appeared to give me clues, and slowly, in front of my eyes, a mystery opened up like a flower, petal by petal. Each petal held a clue.

I was still missing something important. I sat in the café, as I re-read my criteria, over and over again. What was I missing? I needed the energy form, the key, and the book. As I read over my notes, Sally watched over me like a concerned mother. She knew I was ill, and earlier in the day, I hunted for ginger to make a tea for my throat. As soon as she saw it in my hand, she said, "Jinjibre!" I looked at her, smiled, and said, *"Tea please?"* She smiled broadly, and gave it to the staff to boil.

I was about to start my classes in the next week at the Latin American Academy in Spanish. With such an enormous mystery, and such a shortage of information in English, it made sense to get as fluent as quickly as possible to read the myriad papers in the libraries that were written by the local explorers. I was also tired of talking like a three year old.

Sally placed a large, steaming cup on the table, and I thanked her. I breathed in the vapors, and drank. The ginger tea worked its magic as my air passages opened up, and forced me to hack up more of the green goop clogging my airways. I spat into a napkin as I drank. As I drank, Sally started to close the wooden shutter doors on her establishment. It was 10:30 PM. I looked at her, and she said, *"no, you rest here. You can leave when you want to. You seem preoccupied."*

"Thank you."

I looked to the back of the room, and watched as she sat down with an elderly, white, bearded and bespectacled gentleman. Next to her sat down two ladies who looked Chinese, and the rest of the staff who looked Quechua. Sally herself looked like a blend of Chinese and Spanish. They started conversing with each other in Spanish, and I noted the fluidity of the conversation. As they spoke, several words caught my attention: Atlantida, geométrica sagrada, energia sagrada.

I coughed, and decided that it was time for me to go. I walked over to the table, and thanked Sally for the tea. She asked me what I was working on, and I mentioned the strange light and energy I saw in the sky. She and the people around the table wanted to know more, but I needed to rest, and would tell them about it tomorrow.

I waved to everyone and said good night. The elderly man watched me as I waved, and I smiled at him. He smiled back, and said, *"tell us more when you feel better."* I nodded my head with a smile, as I withheld a cough. I walked out, and felt the cold dry air in my throat. I chomped down on a bit of ginger, and felt it mix with my saliva, and relieve my throat. My hostel was a few blocks up the mountain. Before going to sleep, I looked at the criteria again, and thought to myself, "was this the reason I was called down here?"

The next day, I sat in the Explorer's Club, where I made an enormous batch of ginger tea. I went through the books and explorer reports in the library to see if there were any references of the strange lights. There was nothing. I sat down on the couch, and looked into my notebook. I was lost. What kind of an energy form would fit the first criteria?

"David!" I heard a voice call out. In walked Michelle, and she had her sunglasses up in her red hair. We hugged and caught up. She saw me walking by the Coricancha Temple with Jaime and Jesus. Michelle was busy preparing for her expedition, and scouted out a Yamaha dirt bike as a potential purchase. She also asked me if I heard anything about the San Pedro plant, and informed me that she was headed to the States for a week. She rented a cheap apartment in Cuzco, and needed to move her things from the States to Cuzco.

"When are you leaving?"

"Tomorrow."

I sighed. "Well, let me know what happens. I'd like to know what your experience was like in Nepal."

"Yeah man, I'll bet you've got some stories to tell too. But looks like you're going to have to get rid of that cold first."

"Flu. I'm done. I'm just hacking up the green shit."

Michelle laughed, and said, "it's always like that when you get to a new place. The first thing you have to deal with are the new viruses. After that though, when you feel better, you feel a lot better. It's not like the States where you just get well. Here, you get really well. So I heard from Ernesto that you saw that weird light."

"Oh man, I've never seen anything like it. Over our head was the moon, so it wasn't the moon. There were few clouds in the sky, but over the mountain, there were a few clouds. Get this, underneath the clouds was the light. But it came from an area where there are no cities, just mountain, or jungle. Then the light went away. Weird, huh?"

"That is strange."

Michelle left the club after dropping off a few of her things for storage, we hugged and agreed to meet up again. I went back to reading another report, when I was interrupted.

"Excuse me mate, but did I just hear you talking about a strange energy form?" I looked up, and on the gray couch was an older man, about mid fifties, with a long gray beard and mustache, with a small fedora that looked almost conical. He wore a thin pair of glasses, and smiled at me, as he said,

"I'd say that was an interesting bit of conversation I heard there."

"Yes. I just saw it a few days ago. It's weird, because the moon was over hour heads, but the light came up from behind the mountain range, where there's no cities, towns, or anything. It's either mountains, or you're headed into the cloud rain forest."

"Go on."

"Well, it seemed to spread out a baseline and then radiate up. So, it's not a pinpoint light source, like a high beam. It looks like a large part of the mountain range was glowing."

"Now that's interesting mate. It looks like you've discovered something."

"Me? Other people have seen it. I wasn't the first to discover it."

"No, mate, but you've seen if for the first time. It's a discovery by you. And not everyone has had a chance to see it."

"What do you know about the light?"

"I don't know much about it, other than it's selective. What's your name by the way?"

"David."

"Last name?"

"Nghiem."

"Ah, you're Vietnamese, aren't ya?"

"That was impressive. Most people wouldn't have figured that out."

"That's because I had many Vietnamese neighbors in Sydney. Good folks, nicer than sunlight. Always got a smile on their faces. Hard working too. So, tell me Dave, what brings an, American or Canadian?"

"American."

"An American like you here? Crikey, you're American? Born there or escaped to there?"

"Born."

"Well, what brings you here?" It was the first time someone asked me that question.

"I was just here on a joy ride. I'm planning on bicycling to Buenos Aires, eventually. How about you?"

"I got sick of day to day life in Australia, saved up, and I've been traveling the world for the last year. It's been interesting for an old man like me."

"Hey man, it's never too late. You have to eventually make your dreams happen, otherwise, what's the point of living?"

"That's good someone young like you would realize that. I think I'm an example of too old smart."

"So what brings you to Cuzco?"

"Well right now, I'm pumped up on antibiotics, so I'm just here for the medical treatment and to recover."

"What happened?"

"My appendix burst while I was volunteering out in the rain forest. I was teaching a tribe some English. They flew me into Cuzco, and fixed me up, although I had a battle to see if my travel health insurance would pay. That was bloody hell, but the doctors were kind enough to stitch me back up. So now, I 'm just relaxing here, and listening to some interesting things going on around here, like your energy conversation."

He took a sip of tea, and then said, "about that light, have you met Marco?"

"I think so, why?"

"I swear, I think he's a reincarnated Incan. Marco has a knack for finding ancient ruins that no one else knows about. He's shown me a few. This place is full of them. The entire Andes and some of the cloud forests are full of them. If there's anyone who'd know what to look for, that would be Marco. And speak of the devil. Ah well, there never was such a thing as a coincidence." Said Geoff as Marco walked in.

Marco was taller than me by a couple of inches. He was brown and sturdy looking. He walked up to us, and we shook hands.

"Hello Marco."

"David! Ernesto has told me much about you. I have many things I want to talk to you about."

"What did he say?"

"He showed me your theory that these things are part of some kind of machine."

"It's a hypothesis, and it's based on what I've observed. It's not a theory yet."

"Still, it is a good idea. A very good one. I have also worked with the western archaeologists and anthropologists, and I did not like what their theories were. They never listened to us."

I looked at Geoff. He nodded in agreement.

"David, I also think that the westerners are missing something vitally important. Who knows, your Vietnamese background and perspectives, along with your training in the west, could make you a bridge. You could figure this out, where many others failed. I myself don't agree with the westerners. They're like me, from a white background. We're missing too many important things, because of, who knows, ethnocentrism, Eurocentrism, whitecentrism, racism, and God knows what else. We have too much baggage on us from history, from our own arrogance, and from what we did to the native peoples. You might get insights that others don't."

"Ok," I looked back to Marco, and asked, "did you go over the email I sent to Ernesto?"

"Yes! It is very good, and I agree, many things are not practical if done from the other perspectives. But what you said, that it is more functional in design, and that there is an energy form - I too, have seen that energy form."

"How did you see it?"

"Do you know the story about the looter who went to the source of the lights?"

"Yes."

"I was part of the party that came with him."

"So, why did you guys run?"

"Because, it was so strange. We knew there was a lot of metal in there. We had detectors. But then the metal moved. We have legends of people who wander the mountains, and disappear. We did not want to disappear, so we ran."

"There was nothing under that slab of stone?"

"No. It was very strange, because we had four detectors, and two were new. How could all four detectors be wrong? We detected a lot of metal."

"That is strange."

"Yes, and that is why when Ernesto told me about your theory, he said that you were on to something."

"Did they still detect the metal when you lifted up the slab?"

"No, there was no more metal."

"And the slab wasn't metal."

"It wasn't. It didn't even register."

"And no one changed the settings on the detectors."

"Nobody."

"I'll say that's a mystery. Marco, I'm missing some information for the theory, mainly I want to double check if the source of the rocks at Sacsay-huaman is correct. Are there any local sources of Andesite?"

"No. I will show you what the archaeologists say is the source, and you will laugh."

"OK. When do we go?"

"Let us go these weekend. I have much too show you. I showed the archaeologists, and tried to tell them what the locals know. They did not listen, so I've stopped showing anyone these places. Many are secret, ones that no one knows about. I did not show the westerners those, because I no longer trust them."

"Alright, let's meet up this weekend then. What time?"

"6 AM. We have far to go. Very far. It is a long walk. You will be amazed at some of the things that I will show you. You will be very amazed."

Chapter 8

Guidance

"David?"

"David, are you awake?" A loud knocking woke me up.

"Huh? What the..." I turned in my bed. I was stuck in my sleeping bag, as my long johns caught the nylon sides.

"David! It's Marco! It's 6 AM."

"Ah shit! Sorry Marco! I forgot! Hold on, let me get changed."

I got up and changed into my day clothes. I saw my breath in the air, and quickly washed my face. The water was freezing cold, and it rudely snapped me to attention. The rising sun was poking through the window as I rinsed my teeth. I opened the door, to see

Marco with a back pack and a walking stick.

"Hello Dave! Are you ready?"

"Yes! Give me a moment." I grabbed my courier bag, and put in a roll of toilet paper. I had my basic survival kit, and some food I bought the day before. We left the hostel, and started hiking up the mountain, opposite of the city.

"We're going in this direction?"

"Yes, because few people ever bother to go this way. There are many things around here. Most of what the tours show, is only the things that are known. But where we are going, there are places no one has ever bothered to explore, until now."

"Why is that?"

"They did not think of them to be significant. Or the archaeologists ignored me."

"Man, every time I hear the two of you talk about them, it sounds like you both have an axe to grind."

"Because they are telling the world about us, but they don't listen to us. They are not us. Why should the gringo represent us, when he's not us?"

"Good point."

"It is bad enough what they did in the colonization. It was bad enough what they continued to do to us up until 1980's. Now they have to talk about us?"

We continued up the mountain, far from Cuzco, and soon we entered farmlands, and a few forested areas of eucalyptus trees, which were brought in from Australia a hundred years ago. Few, large, hardwood trees could exist at the high altitude, and the eucalyptus proved to adapt well. Unfortunately, it's an invasive species, introduced a hundred or so years ago from Australia, and although it provided wood, it changed the ecology in dramatic ways. One eucalyptus sucked up inordinate amounts of water, and many of the streams and springs that once fed the city were going dry.

We continued along an ancient Incan road, hidden in the canyon, and descended into a stream bed. In the middle of the stream bed was a large red boulder, which weighed about six hundred tons or more. Large rectangular incisions were carved into it, and the incisions were about 4 feet wide, by 1.5 feet deep, by 3 feet down. We climbed on top, where an ancient altar once stood. On the sides of the boulder, the ancient builders built an Incan wall into the boulder, and carefully meshed the polygonal stones seamlessly into the rock. On the top, several channels flowed to the river.

"This was the first strange place I showed to an archaeologist. He didn't think much of it. What do you think?"

"Was this an altar?"

"Yes. The Incans had many altars. Whenever they conquered a nation or a tribe, they brought their gods here, and honored them equally. This gave respect, but also forced the nation to come here, to Cuzco to pay tribute. When the Spanish came, they tried to destroy every single one of the altars. Some of the altars survived, but even today, if they are found, Catholics will come out to deface or destroy them."

"It's still that bad, huh?"

"Yes. That is why those of us who know of the altars, we keep it secret."

"I don't blame you." We continued down the stream. Soon, we came up to an enormous rock overhang. The face of the rock wall was about 40 feet, by 30 feet, and a large cross like incision was made into the rock wall. The incision was in the form of a plus sign, but layered within each other. The cuts were 1.5 feet in depth.

"This is called the southern cross. It is an ancient religious symbol to the Inca, and the Quechua."

I looked at the cuts, and noted how they were precisely in right angles.

"The Incans didn't have any iron or steel tools, right?"

"That is correct. They had bronze. For stone work, supposedly they used stone."

"For round stones, those are very precise angles cut into the wall.. although I'm sure with some practice they could get some pretty decent angles in. Although, I'd like to know how they made the incisions into the rock in the first place." I said as I pointed at the incisions.

We continued down the river, and then up an ancient Incan staircase up the canyon. Soon, we were far above the city of Cuzco, on the side of a mountain, and we came up to another wall of rock. Again, there was the rectangular incision, and enormous one, that was about 15 feet long by 10 feet wide, and 2 feet deep.

"The archaeologists say that these is where the Incan got the stone for Sacsayhuaman from."

"The giant stone?"

"Yes."

I looked at the depth of the cut. It was only about 1.5 feet deep. The giant hundred ton stones at Sacsayhuaman was at least 4 to 5 feet in thickness, and there were others that were even thicker.

"Did they even bother to measure this before they came to that conclusion?" I asked.

"No, but he put it in his PhD dissertation. What do you think? Are you ready to laugh?"

"You have got to be kidding me."

"Even worse, this is not Andesite. These are another type of stone. There is no source of Andesite within twenty kilometers of Cuzco."

"You want to know what pisses me off, Marco?"

"What."

"Those guys are the ones who put their bullshit up in the text books for kids to read, and into TV documentaries on PBS declaring that everything is solved. I mean, what the hell?! He could at least use a tape measure to confirm the thickness of this thing. That's so goddamn basic."

"Now you know why Ernesto and I do not like them at all. I had many arguments with the gringos."

"I don't blame you. It pisses me off when they make presumptions about my family's culture, most of which aren't true, and then propagate that into society. That's where the bullshit stereotypes come from."

I looked at the incision, and said, "if they just used this as the source for their stones, why did they bother to smooth out and cut perfect angles into it?"

"That is a good question. There are no altars here."

"Oh yes. David, I want to show you something very strange, later today."

"OK."

We continued hiking into another canyon and valley system. As we hiked, Marco explained to me about the foundations of the Incan Empire. The Incan Empire was just the latest in a long line of empires, and it only lasted for a few hundred years. Before that, the empire was known in another name. The empire was unique in the world in many ways. First of all, it was a confederation of nation states, who displayed loyalty to the ruling elite in Cuzco. It was monarchical, with an emperor, a leading family, and it had a house of lords, who were the noblemen, but they ruled via a federalist system. The economic system of the empire however, was socialist, where the people provided labor, and in exchange for the labor, everyone was fully fed, clothed, housed, and taken care of. The credo of the empire was, "No lying, no stealing, no laziness." The architectural constructions, the water works, the sanitation works, the distribution system, the tracking system of goods, and the communication system were all a testament to this credo.

Their agricultural efforts were incredibly efficient, and they used microclimates and genetic selection to produce thousands of varieties of potatoes, corn, quinoa, and other crops. Potatoes, one of the principal crops of the world, originate from the Andes. On the mountain sides, the Incans were able to produce enough food, in the smallest amount of land, for a population that was in the order of millions. Water was central to Incan society, and it was holy. Many of the major Incan water works are incredible feats of sustainable, reusable hydrological engineering, where water was collected, cleansed, and transported to the far corners of the empire in this mountainous region. In today's world of consumption, recovering even a piece of that technology would solve many of the world's food and water problems.

The Incan empire was unique in the world. When the Spanish came, the Incans had several forces working against them. So many people loved to glorify that all it took was a hundred and eighty men to conquer the empire in the 1500's. This is completely incorrect and inaccurate. The Spanish were allied with several tens of thousands of warriors from nations that the Incans had recently conquered, and they were hungry for vengeance. On top of that, the Incan Empire had recently suffered a civil war, and civil society was fracturing in all the Incan States. These factions allied themselves with the Spanish, bringing in thousands of battle tested warriors who spoke the language and knew the terrain.

Although many scholars would like to point out that small pox was a major factor in decimating the empire, the Incan army still had a well trained force of 80,000 men, who were experienced, combat ready, tough, and well supplied due to the highly efficient agricultural, production, distribution, and tracking system of the Incan bureaucracy, which despite the illness, still functioned well. In fact, the Incan war against the Spanish didn't end for almost forty years, thanks in part to the efforts and tactical abilities of several Incan army generals, Ruminahui, Zope-Zapahua, and Quisquis. It was not the rout that many people in the West portrayed it as. It was a long, bloody, and nasty war that went from large armies in the field into guerrilla style warfare. Afterwards, the indigenous allies of the Spanish found themselves betrayed, enslaved, murdered, or worse by the Spaniards. Their lack of foresight got them their vengeance against the Inca, but in the end, their revenge boomeranged back on them, and they themselves were betrayed.

In Cuzco, what was once a glorious architecture, unique in the world, with clean streets, clean flowing water, and systems that quickly and efficiently removed waste, people who were fed and trained, was destroyed. The Spanish sought to annihilate everything they could. Soon afterwards, it was documented that what was once clean and efficient was now full of trash, human waste, and it was a stinking hole, due to the Spanish.

Yet, despite the colonization, genocide, ravaging, wholesale enslavement, subjugation, and rape of the Incan Empire, the confederation of nations that made up the Incan Empire managed to preserve much of their traditions to the present day. Using the guise of Catholicism, they were able to make the PachaMama incarnated as the Virgin Mary, among other things. Many of the old rituals were still practiced in secret, and during the 80's and 90's, a revivalist spark was running amongst them, due in part to white people traveling to Peru to seek out the ancient traditions.

It surprised the people who'd been humiliated and exploited for over five centuries. Suddenly white people valued their traditions, and many ancient stereotypes and perceptions were being turned on their heads. White people came to seek out shamans and ancient wisdom. Quechua men would talk about their latest conquest of a white woman, which surprised many people because for ages, the lowest rungs of society in terms of attraction were the indigenous peoples. For the first time in history, during the festival of Inti Raymi, an ethnic Quechua was finally in place as the symbolic head of the festival, as opposed to a white man. The Quechua were rediscovering their history and their pride. Interestingly, the indigenous peoples of the Americas, like the Asians, the Arabs, the Indians, the Africans, the pacific islands peoples, maintained the memories of the injustices, which were continuous from the 1500's to the present day. I wasn't at all surprised when I heard the loathing in the voices of Marco and Ernesto.

We continued down a small trail into another canyon that was hidden away. Inside the canyon, was a strange circular ruin, and it had an arch inside it.

"This, David, is an Incan ruin. Take a look. What do you see is unusual?"

"Well, it doesn't have the typical, earthquake proof, trapezoidal Incan door."

"Exactly. Yet, the archaeologists all say that Incans had no arch. Here, right here, where you and I are standing, we see with our own eyes an old ruin, with an arch."

"I can see why you get pissed off with them. Did you try to show them this?"

"Yes. They didn't want to go. It would interfere with their pet theory."

"And yet another piece of bullshit gets published, and my tax dollars pay for it." I mumbled.

"Did you see the tunnels with Ernesto?" Asked Marco.

"Yes."

"You only saw the small ones. I will show you a gigantic one, that shows how powerful the technology these people here possessed."

We hiked around the rim of the mountain, to an area that had the airport in view. As we rounded a corner, I came to a giant cave opening; it was 30 feet wide, by 15 feet high. It was completely walled up.

"El presidente Fujimori sealed these systems, because too many people were wandering in, and dying, or going missing. What do you think?"

"This wasn't a mine?"

"No, the cave entrance is too large. And there are no rail road tracks for mineral cars."

I looked at the parts that weren't covered with cinder block and concrete. The cave wall sides were smooth.

"Two years ago, in the newspapers, one man followed a tunnel all the way through to the center of Cuzco. He was almost five kilometers away when he started. He came up through the grate in the Coricancha temple. He said that the tunnels were not natural. They are large, and smooth, so they are artificial." Said Marco.

"That's amazing! I guess that's where the legends come from of Atahualpa hiding lots of gold in them."

"I have something special I would like to show you now." Replied Marco as he led me down a trail.

It was approaching the evening, and we'd been hiking for hours. The sun was setting, as Marco took me to an outcropping of rock. On the rock were several holes.

"Can you take a look at this, and tell me what you think?"

I put my hand in the hole, and started to feel around. At first I thought someone pounded a stone in to make the hole, until I noticed that the edges of the hole, as my hand went along its sides, went away from the opening. If someone pounded it, they apparently pounded it on the sides, creating something like a vase lip. As my hands traced the surface, I noted how smooth the surface was. They also made the effort to smooth the roughened surface as well. But, it was odd, because the surface was smooth, and perforated with many bubble like blister holes, that were too tiny for any kind of hand tool. The best way to imagine the hole, would be to imagine a Styrofoam board, and then to imagine pouring acid on the board. The acid would eat a hole away, and as it evaporated, it would leave smaller holes with sharp edges.

That's what the hole felt like.

"Dude, this doesn't feel like someone pounded away at it with a rock."

"Uh huh, and?"

"All these blister holes make me think of, the hell? Acid?"

"And?"

"Like acid? The heck? Did someone pour acid on this rock?" I looked at Marco, bewildered.

"What kind of an acid eats away at stone like this?" I asked.

He smiled at me, "no one believed me when I told them about this."

"Holy shit, did the Incas use something else? Just how advanced were they?"

Marco kept smiling at me. I think he felt vindicated that someone else came to the same conclusion he did. I felt the inside of the hole again, and the texture of the blister holes in my finger tips. My mind was buzzing.

"There are legends that the shamans know of mixtures of juices from the rain forest, and when mixed together, the juices could dissolve rock."

"Well, if these are calcium oxide rocks, like limestone, then that would make sense. But these rocks, aren't these silicon oxide rocks? In the lab, to etch silicon wafers for computer chips, we use fluorine acid, and that stuff is nasty! It doesn't dissolve your skin, but the vapor eats through your bone. What ever it was that did this, I wouldn't want to mess with it."

At nightfall, we headed back to Cuzco. The next day, we met up again in the Clubhouse.

"So what do you think of what I showed you?"

"Damn man, a lot of the stuff I read and saw on TV about the Inca is bullshit."

"Now you know."

"Yeah, tell me about it. At least we know now that there are definitely no sources for the rocks of Sacsayhuaman around here. And those cut out rocks don't fit into Sacsayhuaman because they're too thin. That means that the sources are still those two quarries that are thirty five kilometers and a hundred kilometers away. In Rumiqolqa, right? And we still have that weird energy form. Marco, we need someone who understands other energies."

"Yes, we do. But who?"

"I don't know. Let me go over my notes again, and see what I come up with. Anyway, we're still at square one. We need the manual, the energy, and the key."

"What would the manual be?"

"I don't know, something symbolic I guess?"

"I know of a site, with many strange symbols. Again, they say the Inca had no writing, but that is not true. We must go to this site then, if that is what you need. There are many symbols there."

"When can we go?"

"We must wait for the weather. It is a very dangerous place, almost 5500 meters high. It is also a secret site, and forbidden to outsiders. But you are my amigo, and so far, you have proven yourself to me. I will show you it. We are already acclimatized. It is difficult to get there, because of the weather. I will check with the airport to see what the predictions are."

Marco left for work at the airport, where he worked in a control tower. I sat down at the table, and started outlining some of what we'd seen. So far, all we'd seen only proved that the source for the stones of Sacsayhuaman was distant, and there was nothing else that indicated anything close to fulfilling my criteria. I was still there with a mystery on my hands, and no real clues to even start with. On top of that, I was dealing with an energy form that I had no idea about. I needed an expert in energy.

"Hello, is this the South American Explorer's Club?"

I looked up to see a blond haired lady, whose hair was pulled back, looking at me. She was slim, and looked like she was in her late 30's. We introduced ourselves, and I gave her a tour of the club. Her name was Sara, and she was a Canadian. We sat down, and started talking about our travels.

"So what brings you to Cuzco?" I asked.

"A strange force, something I can't describe told me to come here."

"You too?"

"What do you mean you too?"

For some odd reason, I trusted her enough to tell her about the strange events that led up to my journey to Peru. I told her about the bird incident, and my parent's reaction.

"David, I'm not surprised that your mother acted that way, given her background. You said that her grandmother was a Buddhist shaman/healer, right? I think in general, your culture is supposed to look at miracles as simply manifestations of the mind, and to not put such an enormous influence on them. Otherwise, it will distract your from your purpose. So, did you find what you were looking for?" She asked.

"What I was looking for?"

"The reason you came down here."

"Well, I did get sucked in with this weird mystery. I came up with a hypothesis into the megalithic structures around here. There's also a strange energy form that I witnessed, and right now I'm trying to find someone who knows about energy."

"Maybe I can help you. Let's meet up for dinner later in the week and go over it."

****

Later in the week, I met up with Ernesto, and Marco. I told Ernesto about the phenomenon I saw, and described it as if there were "two moons."

"Ah yes. That is exactly what I told you. It looks like two moons. You described it exactly right. It is very significant that you got to see it."

"Well, now that I saw it, I'd like to make two or three more expeditions to these passes here and here to see if I can get a better idea of where it is."

I pointed to two high mountain passes on the map. Both were in excess of 4000 meters.

"I figure, if I can get two more coordinate points, than it's possible I can track down the source of the phenomenon. It might intersect here."

I pointed at a point on the map that said "unknown area." Peru's most current topographical maps had lots of "unknown areas."

"David, you know, the area you are planning to go to is unexplored jungle. You will encounter several tribes of Indians there, known as the Machenga. You will need their help to get through it."

"OK, I'm sure I can muddle my way through to do that."

"There's a catch though. There is a custom. You must have sex with one of the chief's wives. It is their way of saying hello. If not, they will kick you out, or they will kill you."

Marco stood straight up and grinned at the prospect.

Ernesto smiled and said, "Be careful. If there are no women, then you must fuck one of the men. That is the custom." Marco sat down really quick.

Ernesto continued, "Hm, yes. And the jungle has it's own set of difficulties too, much like the high mountains. There is the heat, humidity, and it is difficult to find food and water without a guide. There are insects that lay eggs in your skin, which gestate in your circulation to reappear out of your pores as flies. There are all the jungle diseases. Mosquitoes are horrible too. Supply lines and help are nonexistent. You must plan for at least a month in the jungle."

"I'm not that interested in entering the jungle. I just want to find out what this phenomenon is." I replied. Marco left the room. Ernesto subtlety changed. It was like he was orating for someone.

"David. You do know that what you are looking for, is the lost city of Paititi."

"Paititi? You mean the city that those rich Belgian gringos couldn't find, despite all the satellite evidence, GPS, and massive amounts of equipment and money? I'm not interested in that. I just want to find out what the 2nd moon is. To me, that's alive. Macchu Picchu, Nazca, Tiwanaku are all dead monuments. Paititi is probably one as well."

Many expeditions set out each year from Cuzco to search for the lost city of Paititi. It's often mistaken for "El Dorado", The City of Gold. No one succeeded. The search for Paititi claimed lives, money, equipment, and time. Satellite reconnaissance had photos of man-made structures in the jungle, and yet when the expeditions went to those exact points, they found nothing. It was a strange mystery, and because there were so many failures, many people decided that Paititi was just a myth. That didn't stop the expeditions from trying each year though. Another one recently left, armed with GPS, satellite recon, guides, canoes, and condoms. They didn't succeed. Some even died. "David, why are you so interested in the second moon? No one else ever has any interest in it. Yet you, you're the only one."

"Because, that is a phenomena that deserves investigation." I replied.

"Do you think it is Spiritual La Tierra?"

"I don't know. That's what that Quechua woman called it. We have a term called 'Gaia,' but that's a mechanistic term for the Earth's life process. You're talking about the 'The Spirit of the Earth'. Well, now that I've seen the lights of the second moon, I really want to know what it is. To me, that is far more interesting than any of the old, dead ruins around here. Then again, maybe Gaia does exist. She might actually be alive."

The "Gaia Theory" is a theory proposed by a NASA scientist, James Lovelock, about how the earth is a living organism. He was assigned to research methods into detecting life on other planets. He denied that he suggested that the earth was actually a living entity; he was simply saying that the processes essential for life are all part of a gigantic mechanism, and the mechanism is life itself. The carbon cycle, water cycle, organic compound production and waste digestion, and the retaining of heat are essential components for the Gaia Theory. It's the reason life can exist on our planet. They tested the theory on Mars, and Mars is so dead it can't even push up daisies.

On the other hand much of Asia, Africa, and the native Americans consider Earth to be a real living entity. They believe in a "life force", and according to the Chinese, they actually use this life force in acupuncture, traditional Chinese medicine, and health. So, it actually is a working force, and western science is still baffled at how it functions, despite India and China's use of it for several millennia. They also consider the "Gaia" to be capable of evolution. The ancient Europeans, Africans, and most of the world before "modern" times also believed this. Intuitively, I figured this tied into "Spiritual La Tierra" and the strange second moon that I saw.

Then Ernesto hit me with his main question.

"Why did you come here David?"

I looked at him. Ernesto now had a strange, searching, expression that I hadn't seen before on his face.

"You know, that's the same question my father asked me before I went. I told him - I told him that I didn't know. I just had to go."

Ernesto smiled. "It always starts that way. The legend of Paititi is that only those who are selected may see the city. Otherwise, it appears and disappears at will, confusing those who are not worthy. It is for those who come here beyond there own will."

Beyond their own will? What the hell... I started getting a strange buzz up my back. It's the kind of feeling that I would get whenever I knew that something major was up.

"David, do you think that you are the 'Escogido'?"

"Escogido?"

"The name that the old Quechua woman called you was Acclhaska. Do you know it what it means?"

"It means searcher, right?"

"No... It means 'Chosen One'"

I was silent. "Very funny Ernesto I'm going to have strange dreams if you keep this up." I smiled and tried to lighten the suddenly heavy atmosphere of the conversation. Ernesto looked very mysterious.

"I'm very serious. Do you think you have been chosen? Only those who have been chosen can see the second moon. No one else sees it. Yet, you have. That is incredibly important. So tell me, do you think you have been chosen?"

"Whether I have been chosen or not doesn't matter to me. I just want to know what the cause of this phenomena is. When I'm done, I've solved the mystery for me, and then I'm off for Bolivia and Tiwanaku. It's just a scientific interest."

Ernesto had this odd smile. It was a smile that said, "I can tell this is far more than a simple curiosity for you. There is no escape this time David. You are bound to it. You cannot stop now. You cannot leave. You must solve the puzzle, at all costs. For my sake, for your sake, for all sakes. We have lived in an eon of darkness. Now, the mystery must be solved."

A very distinctive and creepy feeling went up my back.

"Uh, well, at least that's the plan. I also just want to see if my theory on the purpose of the four Suyos, Sacsayhuaman, and Cuzco are possibly workable. If everything is a gigantic energy device for the planet, than, we'll see. But it's just a theory. A crazy, crazy, muy loco theory." I finally said.

"But a very good theory. Better than the one that many of the archaeologists have proposed. Yet, once you have the knowledge, what will you do with it?"

"I beg your pardon?"

"Say Paititi exists, and you are chosen to enter. The inhabitants teach you all that you are to know. Your past, your future, our past, our future. New ways, and new technologies. Then what will you do with it? What will you do with that knowledge?"

I thought about that for a moment. I had no intention of looking for Paititi.

"To be honest, I don't know. I usually share my knowledge, unless instructed otherwise. It... It depends." I said.

"Hmm... you see, perhaps you are not the Escogido. I am different. I think knowledge should be kept secret for those who are worthy. Knowledge, true knowledge transcends language, and passes without word to those who are chosen. That is why the Inca and those before them had no writing. Yet look at their achievements. Now, look at today. There is so much abuse. Do you think powerful knowledge should be shared?"

"I really don't know. I won't know until I know the situation I'm in."

"Hmm... Let us say you had the money, and access to the resources you need for an expedition to find Paititi. Would you do it?"

"Of course. It's only natural."

"Hmm, then you are different. I think most people would spend that money for material things."

"Whatever the case, I don't think I'm ready for an expedition of the sort that you're thinking of."

"Really. I think you're ready. I think you've been ready for a long time."

That night, I went back to my hostel after dinner. I was uncomfortable with all this "Escogido" business. This was my vacation, time out, kick back, have fun, and have a good time. But then there were the things that drew me to Cusco, and there were too many questions that I needed to answer.

****

I looked at my watch, and saw the date was September 10th, 2001. Sara and I dined in a vegetarian restaurant. She wanted to see my theory. Sara used to be a teacher in the northern parts of Canada, until she quit and started a natural healing store. She then left that because like me, something beyond her will drew her here.

She was also knowledgeable in the "esoteric energy" spectrum. Speaking as a scientist, esoterica is frowned upon, because it's difficult to quantify. That's the main reason western science has a problem with esoterica. The other problem is academic prejudice.

Sara quietly tied her blond hair back, and put her glasses on. She had an elegant demeanor about her as she concentrated on my conclusions. I had trouble containing my energy. After exploring the area with Marco, I told him we needed an expert on energies to understand the device. Now here I was talking to one, and I needed answers. I told her about the second moon that I saw, and how I felt it was connected to all of this. I ordered some ginger tea for the lingering bronchitis.

"So, what do you think? I mean, the logistics and the methods needed for those stones is enormous. No one would put that much effort just for ritualistic, social, or political purposes. It's just too much. Even a megalomaniac wants to see his structure done. No matter how you look at it, you still can't change the laws of physics. This has to be functional." I said.

"Your theory is logical actually. It is more of an energy device than a simple building. This whole place is just coursing with all kinds of energy."

"You mean Life Force, right?"

"It's the same thing." She flipped the page.

"What you're reading right now is what a design engineer would setup as requirements, if he or she were tasked to design an energy device to last several thousand years. It's got to be the craziest theory I've ever had." I said as she read the pages.

"It's not a crazy theory, and in fact, when you think about it, it's quite logical. Are all the megalithic monuments on a grid?"

"Yes. Two librarians did an enormous amount of research on that. Their names are Flem-Ath, and they have a website and a book, called the 'Atlantis Blueprint'. He shows that when you use the Giza plateau as the Prime Meridian, every single megalithic monument lines up precisely at equal distances from each other. It forms an entire planetary system."

"Good, then we can go from there. You have an interesting section here regarding all the energy forms, eh?"

"Yeah, and that's actually where I need your help. Part of the design criteria requires a constant energy supply. Nothing we have today can last thousands of years. Nuclear, hydrodynamic, electric, none of these is constant. The Earth's magnetic field is too weak, and then there's the "Dragon Lines", or earth energy lines. Those would be the only constant sources I can think of. But that's an area I have no knowledge about, and pretty much everyone in the West ignores it. There's no research on it here, and I can't read Chinese."

"The magnetic lines aren't weak. And they can shift, you do know that, eh? Not as in the poles will shift, but as in the entire crust of the earth shifts in the field, changing the polarity of the crusts."

The Earth's magnetic field according to NASA is about a hundred times stronger than the sun's field when measured from the earth. That field is the reason we're not glowing green from solar radiation. The interaction of the charged solar particles and the field generates huge amounts of electricity in an amount equal to several hundred nuclear power plants. Much of it gets funneled into the earth's core, and it does things to the core that we haven't figured out yet. A lot also gets funneled through conducting points on the earth's surface. That's why power stations and grids go out whenever there's a solar flare impact.

As for the pole shift, according to paleontologists, the rocks in the earth have different polarities corresponding to different periods. What was once the north was the south and vice versa. This happened several times in the past. A lot of people argued whether the Earth's core simply flipped, or the crust itself flipped. Either one could be catastrophic to some degree. Floods, earthquakes, storms, and televangelist marathons of biblical proportions are usually the result. The televangelist marathons would be a nightmare. The rest would also be a nightmare according to the cataclysmic geologists. The opposing faction are the uniformitarians, who say that the Earth goes through ultra slow geological changes.

Both groups despise each other, but the fact is both are right. The asteroid that killed the dinosaurs? That was a cataclysmic event, and it wasn't the only asteroid in history either. The live volcanoes erupting in Hawaii? That's a uniformitarian process.

"Yes, that is a pity that they don't look into earth energies, eh?" Sara grew up in the farm country, and nature was her teacher. Like Jane Goodall with the chimpanzees, she would meditate to connect to her surroundings before making her studies. She understood the very processes that were going on around her at a deep level. She was like a geomancer, someone who could connect to the earth on a level most of us can't comprehend. Or at least, that's what they say. At this point in time, I wasn't sure what to make of things. My adventures were pulling me further and further into something far more bizarre than I had imagined.

"Dave, do you know how the energies of the Earth work?"

"No, I don't."

"I didn't I tell you why I came here, eh?" She asked.

"No. Do tell."

"I had several dreams. The first one showed the planet, and there were stacked grids of energy lines. The other one was literally a command, to go straight to Peru. I never had a dream like that before, so I immediately obeyed it."

Once upon a time, I didn't put much stock in dreams. Most of my dreams were too bizarre and strange to really make sense to me. I did have a couple that came true a few years later, in that strange sense of deja vu. Yet it wasn't until two years ago that I had that peculiar sequence of paranormal events that concurred with my dreams and intuition. Then I finally decided to take them seriously. I learned that when it came to the esoterica, like dreams or intuition, to not belittle them. They could be far more important to life's meaning than any scientific analysis.

"The grids are several energy layers, stacked on each other. You do know that all matter is energy."

"Yes. Einstein's law states that. All you have to do is get it to the speed of light squared, and presto, enough gamma radiation to turn you green."

"OK. Well, it's not just what the scientists are saying though. You have matter, which has it's own set of vibrations. Than you have mental vibrations, the intellectual layer. Your thoughts have an energy to themselves. Than you have a Life Force layer, the energy which keeps you alive. And then you have a higher potential layer or the spiritual layer."

"I didn't think of it that way. I thought the Life Force and Spirit might be connected."

"*Everything* is connected." She replied.

"That's what some of those people mean by four dimensions?"

"Yes. It's not just three lines and time. That's just one way of looking at it. But in a metaphysical way, four dimensions means you're looking at the four aspects of being."

"And these four layers, do they extend from a person?"

"Absolutely. Think of yourself as a being composed purely of auras, energy fields, or force fields if you'd like. Those fields extend far beyond you, and they effect your surroundings, others, and your very reality."

"Does Gaia also have her own set of layers?" She thought about that one for a moment. A smile crept onto her face.

"You know Dave, it's no surprise to me that you're here. This place draws a lot of people here who are in tune within themselves, and who are very aware of their levels of being. But, you're an anomaly. You're a scientist, and yet you understand the other systems of thought. It's no surprise that you're of Vietnamese descent. I don't think a third generation white American would be saying the things that you're saying. Have you told anyone else about this?"

"Just Ernesto, Elio, Marco, and Sally. I don't think most of the others would understand."

"Because I will tell you that what you're getting into is enormous. This encompasses the entire planet, and it's important that you know who to talk to. Do you think you're the only one on this?"

"I feel like it. I feel like I'm alone in figuring this out. It's actually getting really scary. The sheer potential of this thing is enormous. This is the entire planet after all. Is there anyone who could understand what I am studying, without the academic bias?"

"Yes, there is a core group of scientists, Nobel laureates among them, who know that there is a lot more going on here than what science decides to dictate. They're not on the fringes either. Some of them are deep in the academic world, but they don't voice their views because of the prejudice and politics. I can put you in contact with them."

"Great, because quite frankly, I need help. I really need allies."

"Have you heard about the hundred monkey theory?"

"Like the eight hundred pound gorilla? I thought that was for smokers."

Sara smiled.

"No, like the concept of critical mass."

"Oh yeah. Once you hit critical an enormous change takes place."

"You do know what a collective conscious is, right? The human mind is incredibly powerful. It will mold and shape your realities. When they say that we can move mountains, really, they mean we can move mountains. I'll give you an example. I recently saw a video from China using a branch of their medical system. What happened was a woman got on the operating table. There were two live video feeds, one using ultrasound, and another to measure time. In the ultrasound monitor was a tumor in her ovaries. No instruments were attached to her. What happened next was extraordinary. The Chinese doctors, there were three of them, simply closed their eyes. In three minutes, the tumor began to quiver. In two more minutes, the tumor began vibrating at a high rate and then it disintegrated. The woman got up, thanked the doctors, and left. Apparently, they treat thousands of patients this way."

I didn't know how to respond - yet I trusted that Sara believed what she saw. I left the story open. I didn't know whether to believe it or not. There are many cases where patients were put on a placebo system and were able to use their minds to get well. They just believed that they were getting well and they got well. It didn't matter what disease they had. If this was true, than the Chinese doctors were able to advance their abilities to the next level, or they already had this skill for eons.

Sara continued. "When you have a critical mass of similar thoughts, or wills operating on a certain level, you'll be able to make changes on an enormous scale."

"Oh yes. Which is why Hitler wasn't guilty. The entire German nation was guilty for collectively being behind him. We just scapegoated him."

"Absolutely. If you think about it, instead of thinking of God as a sentient being, which isn't really correct, it's more correct to think of Her as a Sentient Reality."

This was getting heavy now. "Sentient... Reality." I chewed on a piece of ginger as I let that sink in. The heat of the herb gave a bite to my words.

"Yes. It's a lot more accurate to describe her that way. The Reality shapes and molds at will. When you see her that way, suddenly, all the things that occur on this planet make a lot more sense. Realities bend and shape according to the will of the occupants in that reality. That's why I said, the human mind is incredibly powerful. Once you understand that it's more like a reality, than you can see how the layers of energy fall in place. Collect an enormous pool of consciousness, and the reality bends to the wills of the pool. Everything from the Big Bang, to the formation of life, to war, to peace, everything is done according to the will of those in that reality. The reality also reacts according to that will. Good, Bad, all of that makes the Sentient Reality. It's the Yin and Yang. Lao Tzu got it right."

"I think I get what you're saying. I've had my own name for it. I always called it the 'Field of Pure Potentiality.'"

"Correct. So if you think about it, you have non-animate matter, and then life force induced beings, starting with plants, sentient beings, like animals and us, then you have Gaia, the solar system, the local systems, then galaxies, and the cosmos. Each thing functions in the Sentient Reality. Everything is connected. Gaia isn't the only one manifesting herself."

"So then, the manifestation, and this planetary device..."

"is important because now, Gaia is expressing herself in the Sentient Reality." She finished.

I was silent.

"Have you considered making a website to pool similar minds into your concept?" She asked.

"No. I keep getting the feeling that someone is trying to keep me hidden. I can't shake the feeling that I have a protector. It's like there's an opposing force that they don't want knowing about me. I only send out my travelogues to a select group of friends who I intuitively feel I can trust with this. It's strange actually. I can't shake the feeling that I'm some kind of 'genetic bomb'. It's like someone's using me as a wild card, but when the time is right. All I can do right now is continue my investigation, and figure out how to operate the device."

"Listen to your feelings. That's good. You're a scientist, but you've learned to operate using your body's feelings and perceptions as well. There are two kinds of scientists. The ones who are so rigid and narrow that they just push pencils. They can't feel at all. They just add bits and pieces to the overall body of knowledge, and it doesn't really do all that much for humanity. Then there are the ones who've been able to tap into the deeper, spiritual part of themselves. They're the ones who can form quantum leaps in understanding."

Sara sipped her mint tea. "When do you go to that marked ruin again?"

"This week, on Thursday."

Marco and I planned an expedition was to go see a possible entrance into a mountain tunnel system. It was marked with a petroglyph. Marco discovered it last year and kept it hidden. It's never charted or documented. The strange thing is that none of the cultures, Inca, or pre-Inca, had any evidence of writing. Yet there was a petroglyph. None of the other ruins, cave entrances, nothing had any markings of that sort. For that matter, nothing in Peru had anything like it, except for maybe the Nazca Lines. That meant that this ruin was unique to the area, and possibly the world. It's been unexplored and unknown to outsiders. I'd be the first to see it. My survey was to see what the entrance was, and if anything was in the way, how to remove the obstacles. To make things even harder, it was 5500 meters in thin air, through incredibly harsh, and steep terrain, and it was subject to the elements. At that height, mountain weather was chaotic and extremely dangerous. That reason alone explained why it was undiscovered by others. I would have to take things a step at a time.

Figure 8.1: The massive, cyclopean, polygonal stone walls of Sacsayhuaman.

Figure 8.2: An altar carved into the boulder.

Figure 8.3: Part of another altar carved into a large boulder.

Figure 8.4: The usually purported "source" for the stones for many of Cuzco's monolithic monuments.

Figure 8.5: Marco pauses in front of an arch on an old Tambo, which was a resting place for Incan messengers on the vast network of Incan roadways.

Figure 8.6: A large tunnel entrance in a remote location near Cusco.

Chapter 9

September 11th, 2001

It was the day everything changed. Monday morning in Cuzco. I got out of my hostel, and the sky was clear, and blue, and I walked briskly to the academy. As I walked, the city was alive with Quechua going to work, and the first diesel fumes were beginning to color the air.

I walked into the academy, and we started class. The class was about the use of the subjunctive. We had a break at 9:30, when Luis, a Peruvian who arranged tours for Macchu Picchu, came in to the conference room in a fit. I was chewing a piece of fresh bread when he burst into the room, and next to me were three Belgian women. We were talking about the trip to Macchu Picchu.

"We will fight back! This effects everyone! Peruvians, Chileans, Argentinians, everyone!" He said as he counted his fingers.

"What's going on?" I asked.

"The USA has been attacked!"

"What?! What the hell? Where?!"

"It is on the television!"

We ran upstairs, and there was a white couple were watching the TV. It was CNN. The couple was white and blond, and the woman, who was American, was crying. I looked at the TV, and live, on TV, I watched as the second plane flew into the far corner of the building of the World Trade Center. I watched, numb, as much of the fuel erupted, and blew out the corner in a large, orange, black explosion. The TV then replayed the first impact, where the jet slammed smack into the middle of the towers.

I knew, from that moment on, that there was no turning back. I knew, from the moment of the impact, that I had no choice. I watched, in disbelief, as the white woman screamed, *"whoever did this, had been well integrated into our society!"*

I've heard that statement before. That statement put honest Americans into prison camps during world war II, the Japanese Americans. They sacrificed their lives, were the most decorated military unit of all time, and they still weren't allowed to be US citizens until after Martin Luther King marched. That very same statement almost got the Chinese Americans, Americans, born and raised in the US, sent to China after the Chinese Communists won their civil war in the 1950's. That very same statement was hurled at any one who looked Indian or middle eastern during the Persian gulf war. It was uttered after Oklahoma. Ironically, it was a white American who perpetrated the attack. During this attack, many Muslims were in the Trade Towers. They died, and their families grieved for them, but did the rest of the country even stop to think about that?

I looked at her, and I wanted to yell out in anger at her, "It's racist motherfuckers like you that destroy everything!"

But I didn't. I couldn't. I had many Arabic and Muslim friends, and I feared for their lives. I knew how nasty and racist the States were. When she said that, my blood boiled, and my stomach began to churn. I knew she was in shock and anger, but the venom that came out was the same venom that was hurled at us after we bombed and incited our own set of terrorist activities in the Middle East. How much longer could this cycle be continued? I wanted it to end. I've endured plenty of racism and violence. I didn't want any of my friends to go through what I had to go through.

Instead, I looked at her, and said, and I wanted to cry as I said it,

"There's a lot of innocent Americans who are Muslim. They didn't do this."

She looked at me, and with a tone of nastiness in her voice that I never forgot, said, "They're your friends?"

"Yes." I said back in anger as I glared at her.

She didn't look at me. The blond man, who was British, gave me a dirty look, and went back to comforting his wife. I stared at the TV, in disbelief. An hour later, on the TV, something happened which threw me off completely.

I watched in disbelief, as tower 1 imploded in itself, and then tower two, where earlier, I saw much of the fuel erupt out the corner edge. I watched as the video provided close-ups, as puffs of smoke blew out on the corners, as if in sequence, and then the tower collapsed. The announcer, who was sitting on a building watching all of this, then said, "we have news that the Pentagon has been hit." I watched in disbelief as my intuition screamed out to me, "this is utter bullshit."

I knew for sure, inside of myself, that the attacks were not Islamic. I knew that. This was far more insidious than any religious or political cause would engender. I watched as somehow, the events that occurred even defied the laws of nature, of physics itself. I watched, as a hydrocarbon fire melt or soften rigid, fire proofed steel, when to even soften it, required not just pure oxygen, but acetylene, and temperatures which exceeded 2000 degrees Fahrenheit and it had to be maintained at that ideal condition for several minutes. Hydrocarbon fires, even under ideal conditions where pure oxygen is being fed in, can only reach 500 degrees Fahrenheit. Yet, here, in a smoky, oxygen starved office complex, it was able to reach 2000 degrees? This information is easily found in any welder's reference manual.

I watched a trillion dollar defense system, which in the past *always* sent up fighter escorts the moment any plane deviated off course, regardless of what happened inside of the plane, suddenly and inexplicably, not follow it's own rules and regulations, and even de-throttle their own jets. An F-16 at full throttle can cover the entire East Coast of the US in fifteen minutes. Yet, there were three *uninterrupted* impacts, one fifteen minutes from the first, and the other an hour and a half after the second!

I watched, and the more I watched, the angrier I became, when later in the day, the announcer on CNN said, "We have reports that World Trade Center 7, which was not hit by a plane, has been demolished by a bomb." I watched Dan Rather comment in awe and bewilderment as he watched World Trade Center 7 collapse in on itself. When I saw Building 7 collapse because some idiot owner called to "pull it", which was the word for demolition, and when I saw it collapse in a demolition, my rage was pure. I knew from that moment on that I was watching the biggest, staged massacre in history. That night, I sent off an email to some of my friends, where I said, "I don't believe the Muslims have anything to do with this. I think our own government did this."

Joe responded, "That's damn bloody if our own government attacks our own people!" Mistrani responded, "Dave, I think that this will unite our country against a common enemy. As tragic as it is, perhaps some good can come of it." Tasnim responded, "Dave, you don't know how horrifically this has affected me!" Michelle sent me an email back from the states that said, "Dave, I'm stuck, this has been a fucking mess!"

I sent emails to see if any family was lost in the attack. My brothers reported back that so far, everyone was intact, but some friends were missing. I felt sick in my stomach, as the images went through my head. We weren't attacked by some crazy hijackers, that I knew. I also knew that if I said anymore about what I felt, especially with the nation in hysteria, that I was destined to become a target. I'd just witnessed the American version of the burning of the Reichstags. It was the official start of the coming authoritarian rule of the USA. And that meant that what I was investigating, what I was learning, could put me in danger.

When I went to sleep, I prayed for my friends, the victim's families, and especially my Arabic and Muslim friends. I prayed for their lives, and for their families. I went to sleep, and prayed. Those who died, were dead. There was nothing I could do for them. They were in God's hands. Those who were alive, I prayed for them.

Chapter 10

Strange Symbols, Strange Ruins

We were in the pursuit of the unknown. On that day, Marco and I decided to make a survey mission of the strange, marked ruin. The ruin lay 5000 meters above sea level, or, about three to four miles above flatland. Are you out of breath? Low on energy? The mountain and it's wild nature will eat you alive. I kept that in mind the morning during my preparations for the expedition. At that altitude, anything can happen. Blizzards, powerful winds, rain, hail, hypothermia, land slides, falling boulders, and extreme altitude sickness will claim you as a trophy.

As we scaled the obstacles, hacked through thorns, and trekked further up, I noticed the sheer cliffs which were blocking our way to the ruins. The verticals were hundreds of feet high. We didn't have any rock climbing equipment, and most of our effort was through sheer muscle and finesse. To add to the difficulty, we carried hand axes, knives, compasses, food and water, extra clothes, emergency equipment, cameras, and walking staffs to double as weapons. One of Marco's concerns were treasure hunters roaming the mountains. A lot of looters were still looking for Inca gold. Many were armed with machetes or guns.

As we hiked up, we found a small mountain stream. Many birds flew around us. Tadpoles swam in the small pools that collected. Multiple varieties of flowers were around, despite the dry season. The landscape changed from dry dusty farms, llama dung, and dirt roads to an Eden of green glens, trees, strange plants, exotic flowers, and flocks of birds.

"PachaMama has blessed this place. There is much life here because of her." Said Marco. PachaMama is the local Quechua term for "Mother Earth." The reverence that the locals have for their environment runs deep in their culture. There are many rituals to celebrate PachaMama. As a tribute to Earth, the locals spilled maize beer, or chicha. Chicha beer is produced by Quechua women chewing, spitting out, and fermenting grains of corn. Offerings of flowers or grain in the altars that dotted the mountainous horizon was another ritual. Respect for the Earth runs deep among the farmers. It doesn't with the city folk, and that's where we ran into some major problems. We were city folks, and we completely forgot an essential element that most locals do before climbing a mountain. We forgot to give tribute to the Earth.

When we started in the tiny farming village at the valley, the sky was perfectly blue with a few clouds in the distance. Going up the road was uneventful. On our way up, we began to approach 4000 meters when the weather began to take a nasty turn. The entire sky turned gray, and the winds began to whip us about. A little bit of rain started to fall. Still, we kept moving up. We really couldn't go down, since the way was already blocked with obstacles, and going down was actually a lot more hazardous than going up. The slope became significantly steeper, and we noticed there were no more trails.

As we started our ascent at the base, an army Antonov troop carrier flew around the mountain we were flying. Those planes were used to carry paratroopers. Marco and saw it. As soon as he saw it, he asked, "What the hell is that doing here?"

According to Marco, who was an airport tower controller, the military never did operations in the area. In addition, the mountain we were climbing was forbidden to all air traffic due to it's height and the violent convection currents which rose on its sides. Those currents can rip through a plane like a soda can. Yet, there it was, making risky maneuvers as it flew over us in circles. It was looking for something, or it was looking for us.

"Marco, you're sure no one's been here?"

"Yes. The locals are superstitious of this place. That is why there were so many thorns in our way. It is forbidden to come up here. It is also very difficult to get here, and most of the time, violent clouds cover the top. Visibility is at most five feet. We are lucky today. We can see all the way to the top."

I looked around the slope, and tried to find a way up. There were no trails. The slope was getting close to vertical, and one slip meant a long way down through cactus, thorns, and boulders. The drop before hitting any kind of plateau was at least two hundred meters. I dug foot holes with the heel of my shoes, as we attempted to navigate a way to another plateau. The weather began to change.

In mid-ascent through turbulent weather, a white, unmarked military reconnaissance plane circled us as well. Marco thought they were insane to fly in such conditions. "What is a recon plane doing here?! Is he mad?!"

We took cover under some trees as it went by. I couldn't shake the eerie feeling that they knew we were coming up the mountain, and that someone wanted to stop us. The pilot of that plane was either intent on finding something, or suicidal to fly in those conditions.

After the plane passed, we continued our ascent. As I grabbed some dry grass for a handhold, I saw a periwinkle snail shell on the ground. Periwinkles come from the ocean, but we were several hundred kilometers away from the ocean. We were also 4500 meters above sea level.

"What the hell is a seashell doing up here?" I asked. I picked it up. It looked fresh, with the meaty remains inside of the snail. It definitely wasn't a fossil. It was also out on the dirt, clear of any dust or wear.

"I think it might be an offering. But that doesn't make any sense. There are no trails here. The last trail is way back there." He pointed into the valley. The trail ended about 500 meters down the slope.

"Usually they make offerings with shells, but that is on the altars. That is the custom."

I put the shell back, and continued up. We got closer to the top, and we saw a massive pre-Incan, Huari culture wall surrounding the top. It was at least 20 feet high. It was well formed with stones, and vertical.

"There's a huge wall up there Marco!" I yelled. He was below trying to find an easier way around, but there was no easier way around. The slope steepened, and high speed winds came down the mountainside, pushing us off the slope. In the distance, I could hear the rumbles of the convection currents. At this altitude, hot air rose quickly, and it rubbed on the cold air. The friction from the two created rumbles that sound like thunder. It's disconcerting, especially when approaching 5000 meters, and those convection currents can whip a person off the mountain.

"What do you think of the wall David?" Marco yelled out.

"Well, it's definitely not defensive. Only an idiot would try to attack from this side of the mountain. I think it was made to hide something." I yelled over the rumbling. I felt like a mosquito trying to buzz a snoring giant.

"That is exactly what I thought."

"Can we climb it?"

"No. Those rocks are loose. If you pull the wrong one, then you will have a landslide of several tons of rocks on you."

"Huh. And I promised Fiona I'd bring you back alive." Marco smiled. Marco was great. He was the sort of person who would go barreling into anything, regardless of the situation, which was exactly what worried his wife. I looked at another mountain top about ten miles away, and gazed in fascination at the snowstorm on top.

"Marco, that other mountain top, will those clouds come this way?" I yelled. It started hailing.

"Possibly. But I don't think so. Look over there David." I looked east. A huge black cloud was taking shape. It looked like a giant wall coming straight for us.

"That cloud, and the one right above us, they are going to become very good friends. When that happens, it will get really rough."

"What do you think? Will it effect our mission?"

"We have some time. PachaMama is holding them there for us. I think we have enough time to get there, but I think she is angry at us."

"No, I don't think she's angry. I think she's testing us!" Marco smiled when I said that. He liked my optimism. Due to his job in the control tower in the airport, Marco's knowledge of cloud formations, weather conditions, airplanes, and terrain was impeccable. Still, despite his confidence, he seemed reassured when I went with him. He knew the area and the terrain, and I had the techniques and skills to get through them.

We spotted a rock outcropping that formed a cliff. We just needed to get around to the top of it, where we could find a place to rest and secure ourselves in the wind.

"David! Here is another one. This is strange. This place has no other tracks except mountain deer. No llama, nada."

He tossed a white sea shell to me. I looked at it. It looked like someone just picked it up from the beach and gently placed it on the mountain side. "Weird", I thought as I put it in my pocket – and then I accidentally broke it. Suddenly, a huge rumble erupted from around us. I looked at a peak nearby. A bright flash of lightning struck the top and knocked a boulder down. Shock waves reverberated through our heads.

"Shit! How long before that gets here?" I yelled.

"PachaMama is angry with us! But I think she is holding it for us!" I looked at the top. The mountain seemed to be holding the clouds there.

"We're almost there. Is there a way around that wall?" I yelled.

"Yes. I remember a rock fall. We must find it!"

Marco hiked off to find the rockfall. I attempted to see if it was possible to climb over the top. The Huari went through a lot of effort to build a wall of this size and height at 5000 meters above sea level. Something about the site made it incredibly sacred for the locals to keep it away from the everyone, including other Peruvians. Marco found it with his intuition, and he hiked there from another route.

We attempted the ascent on this side of the mountain, because we didn't want anyone to be suspicious of our intentions. We also didn't want to pay an entrance fee at an archaeological site at the base of the mountain. The wall itself was a kind of camouflage. From the bottom, it looked like a part of the mountain, and there was no indication from a distance of being man made. There were no trails to the top, and the clouds kept the peak covered. I wondered how many other sites were undiscovered in the vast cordillera. There were thousands of peaks.

Marco yelled my name. I ran down to find Marco. He found the rock-fall, and we pulled our way over it. Behind the wall was a plateau, which appeared to be man made. Dirt filled in behind the wall up to the top of it. On the plateau, the only thing we saw was the edge of the horizon. The well blended in well with the mountain, especially with all the plants growing on it.

In the horizon of the mountain top were massive piles of Andesite boulders. They looked like the fallen remains of a fortress wall.

BOOM! A giant white arc flashed in front. We looked south. There was more lightning and thunder. The weather got violent, and we were surrounded with stormy weather. The wind picked up its pace and tried to sweep us away. In all directions was lightning and thunder, striking the mountain

123

tops. Hail and rain was in the valleys. A gray curtain of rain, wind, and hail surrounded us.

"I think we really pissed off PachaMama." Said Marco. I nodded my head in agreement.

"Any sign of the troop carrier or that recon plane?" I yelled.

"No. Thank God. Do you think they were after us?"

"I don't know."

"Whatever they're doing, it is suicidal to fly around here."

We hiked towards several outcrops of boulders. As we walked, I felt a powerful surge of energy. My head felt like it was swelling.

"Marco, does you head feel normal?"

"No. It is swelling."

A swelling sensation is normal for getting used to acclimatization, but we were already acclimatized. Maybe it was an after effect. We didn't bring any coca leaves with us for the altitude. Still, it was mild, so we both ignored it, but I couldn't ignore the feeling of the place. I looked around the horizon, and saw the gray cloud closing in on us. We didn't have much time. The weather was violent, but at the moment, it was mostly wind. I looked down the horizon, sweeping my eyes back and forth as we hiked. Then we both saw it loom out of the horizon. On the mountain, in the distance, was a giant rock portal on a pedestal of stone.

****

At the edge of the plateau, stood a giant portal made from rough cut rocks. It had an arch, which was a surprise, given the age of the structure. Arches aren't earthquake proof. Yet here on top of a 5000 meter mountain, was a large, looming, ancient looking portal. I began to salivate because it made me think of a giant bagel. The Incans weren't known to build portals. None of the cultures in Peru made portals. What was this doing here? Marco walked up to it. Marco stood about six feet high, and the portal easily dwarfed him. I looked at the key stone. It had to be at least a ton. I knew something was up with this site, after all, why would the Huari build a wall to hide it? There was no way an army would take the effort to climb what we had to climb to get up here. There were no trails, no roads, and the locals refused to come up here. This place was ancient, and there was something sacred about it. My intuition started to buzz - something was alive here. I looked at a stone on the right supporting the structure. It had to be twenty to thirty tons, at least. I watched as the rain dripped down its water eroded sides. Green lichen grew in some places, and contrasted with it's black hue.

I took a photo of Marco next to the portal as a reference. I walked through the center, feeling the hair on my back stand up. It was enormous, and it even had a base that the rocks stood on. The base went into the ground, and behind the portal was an enormous pit.

"It was once a cave, but it is filled in now." Said Marco

"How did this stand up to the earthquakes?" I wondered.

"I don't know. That is a very good question."

We walked to a cluster of boulder groups. As we got closer, we stumbled on another oddity in the ground. It was a perfectly rectangular, carved, stone made of a whitish rock. What made it unusual was all the other rocks around the area were dark colored Andesite. The rock measured five feet by six feet, with perfectly straight sides, and it went into the ground. There were no other carved rocks around it. It could have been ten, or even a hundred tons.

"What is this doing in the middle of nowhere?" I asked.

We stared at it. First there was that portal. Then appeared this perfectly cut white stone, surrounded by piles of dark Andesite stones. We spent some time photographing it and making measurements. I checked the angles. They were perfect right angles.

KRACK! We immediately turned our heads to the sound, which was in the direction of the snow covered peaks. The ominous clouds held there, while the wind kept blowing in our direction.

"Where did that come from?" I yelled. The convection currents were rumbling on both sides. The Mountain Giant was waking up.

"About thirty kilometers south of us! But it shouldn't get us for some time!" yelled Marco. We hiked around the boulder outcrops.

"Ah! David!"

"Fuck!" I yelled as I ran for where I heard Marco.

As I cornered around the pile of boulders, he stood there bent over something. He was bent over a hole in the ground. I stopped and muttered in surprise. The hole was deep. Inside was a quartz stone roof. And below that, was an entry way to a hallway, but to what?

He jumped into the pit, and I followed him in. A large, rectangular, monolithic carved quartz rock formed one side of the entry way. Quartz formed the top, and on the right side was a section of quartz, carved and fitted into the arch of the entryway. What was a hallway doing at the top of a mountain? And why was it made of quartz? Everything, in every single other culture around the area carved their constructions out of Andesite, granite, or some other hard rock. Quartz was uncommon.

"This pit wasn't here the last time I came here. Someone recently dug it up." Marco said. I looked around us. Behind us was an ancient Huari stone wall inside of the pit to our backs. The entryway was in front of us. Whoever built the wall, meant to seal this thing in forever. I pulled up two of the rocks that were on the ground. They were clear of any dirt, mud, or clay.

"The rocks are clean." I said. Marco looked at me with concern.

"That means that they were dropped in here." I said as I put the rocks back down, and touched my knife. We looked at the entrance way of the hall. Two thirds of the entry way was buried, but with loose dirt. Scratches marked the wall of the entry, showing the tell tale signs of frantic digging.

"Shit. The looters got here before us. I will kill them." Muttered Marco.

"That's not all. The dirt is loose. Did you notice that on top there was a small pile of dirt that matches the color of the dirt in here? It's wet on top. And then in here, this must've been at least 100 cubic feet of dirt, but it's all dry. It's been raining here, hasn't it? I think that's why the hallway is half filled. Whoever it was that came here, they dug out the hallway, and then reburied it again, not too long ago. Maybe even today. Do you suppose they're hiding something?" I asked.

"I think so. But, you are right, the soil in here is dry. They just left." With a concerned look, Marco drew his knife, and got out of the hole to take a look around.

KRAK BOOM! A lightning bolt flashed directly above the pit, as Marco dropped back down into the hole again. The air above us exploded, sending shock waves through our body. For a minute, we had trouble hearing. The storm was right on top of us now. There was no escape. We would have to stay in the pit and wait out the storm. That was if the PachaMama would let us escape.

"I don't think anyone is around. If they are, they will be dead soon. PachaMama is making conditions out there very dangerous."

"In that case, do you want some lunch?" I asked Marco, as four more bolts of lightning struck around the perimeter of the pit.

"Sure." He said, as another bolt of lightning flashed above us, giving the pit an eerie light.

BOOM! As I munched on the fresh baked bread, I let the aroma of garlic go through my nostrils. I tried to stick my head into the space of the hallway, and searched for any possibility of a clear excavation. I didn't see farther than five feet. The roof was built out of stone. This lead somewhere, but it would take some work to clear it. Whoever it was that dug the site before we got here, they were bound to be back and armed. Looters are protective of their finds. We spent the next twenty minutes photographing the half buried tunnel, and thinking about how to get out.

"David, it is good that we found this, but we have to survive to figure out what to do next."

"What we have to do now is find those petroglyph's. That's the key. If we have that, we can start figuring out how the device works."

The lightning stopped, but it continued hailing as we got out of the pit. Things seemed to calm down, but in the distance was the peak with the snowstorm. The winds were blowing in from that direction. I looked at my watch; it was 4:00 PM.

"Marco, do we have time?" The sun set at 5:45, and it would take at least two hours to get down the mountain. I didn't want to get stuck when the blizzard hit.

"Not much. Maybe fifteen minutes. But you want to see the petro-glyph's, yes?"

"OK, ten minutes max to find the glyphs. If we don't find it, we get the hell out of here."

Marco nodded in agreement. That wasn't much time, and the top of the mountain was big. We hiked around another pile of boulders. As we walked around, I got the impression that there were massive stone buildings, and that some kind of quake, cataclysm, something disastrous demolished them where they stood.

"It is here! David! Get over here!"

On top of a now buried cave, was a large flat stone, about six feet long by five feet wide. On it were numerous petroglyph's. There were spirals, some in sequence, and others connected by a line, and circle pits in formations. One spiral was extra complicated, and stood apart from the others. I watched in awe as the rain and hail made the stone seem to come alive. Lichens and moss covered the top. They were eroded away, and there were smooth ridges where sharp cuts once existed.

"We have to get pictures! This is the key." I took pictures until I ran out of film. As Marco took pictures, I walked to a small gathering of stones nearby. Something drew me there, and as I walked into the center, I noticed that there were more petroglyph's.

"Marco, get the fuck over here." I yelled. It was a circle of stones, and one of them, the one with the most spectacular petroglyph's, was cracked right down the middle. According to Sara, rings of stones indicated areas of enormous energies. I walked to another stone with glyphs. It's surface was almost glass smooth. It's glyphs were barely intelligible as the rain made its surface glisten. The wind began to pick up pace as I used up my last roll of film on the stone circle.

"David, promise me you will not tell anyone the location!"

"Trust me, that promise is already kept!"

KRAK-BOOM! A huge flash lit above us. We ran to the edge of the mountain. Below us, was a vast range and valley that we had to cross. We jumped down, and started rock hopping as quickly as possible down the slope. As we went down, something in the back of my head nagged me.

"Marco, you said that the locals used the periwinkle shell in rituals to pay tribute to the PachaMama, right?"

"Uh huh."

"What happens if you break it?"

"Bad things happen."

I pulled out the fragments of the periwinkle shell, and showed it to Marco. He was dismayed.

"Why did you break it?"

"What do you mean? It was crushed when I put it in my pocket."

"Because that was an offering to the PachaMama! That's why we had so many problems up there!"

"What? I don't understand."

"David, whenever you go up the mountain, you must respect the mountain. When you broke the shell, that was disrespect."

"I'm sorry man, I didn't know."

"It is OK. Even though you disrespected PachaMama, she still only did enough to teach us a lesson. It could've been much worse."

About a hundred meters away from the peak, the sky behind us turned blue and clear. We heard bird songs, as I watched the sunset on our descent. We both looked back. There was no sign of the clouds at all, or of the violent wind, hail, or rain. The lightning vanished, as if it never was there. No rumbles came up the sides. The sky was clear, golden red hues colored the horizon. It was like the mountain giant went back to sleep, satisfied that two annoying mosquitoes went away. The stars of Orion's belt began to show themselves in the darkening sky above. I looked at Marco in astonishment. He smiled.

"It is always like that. Whenever you go to a place that isn't meant to be seen, it is violent, turbulent. We were lucky, because today, PachaMama decided not to blanket us with clouds. It could have been much worse. We were very very lucky. You *are* the Escogido." He said as he looked at me. I put both my hands up in defense.

"I think we both are. We have to go back, you do know that. There's something in that hallway, and it might lead to the clues we need to operate the device. We need to get a better idea of how everything connects, that stone circle, the giant portal, and the petroglyph's. Still, I feel that she wanted us to see those things. It was like she held back just enough to get us through. Don't you think so?"

Marco smiled. We made our way down to an ancient Incan aqueduct that appeared out of the side of the mountain. It was a long aqueduct that ran from the top of a mountain, down to a reservoir that opened up into fountains and hydrological works. As we walked through the still working Incan water works, the swelling of our heads intensified.

"Marco, hows your head?" I asked.

"It feels like it is swelling", he replied, "I think something about that site did something to us."

The ancient Incan waterworks served as a water center, to store, divert, and release water in controlled amounts into the valley. A lot of the architecture endured the ages, and still worked. Most of our "modern" techniques paled in comparison to the capabilities of much of the local Incan techniques. They had water through all the seasons, in filtered, clean quantities. I wondered how much of the old technology could be used in the States.

As we hiked down the road towards the tiny farming village, I looked into the sky. The night sky was clear, and the milky way painted a huge grayish band. We walked down, letting the twilight light our away. Crickets sang their songs, and the sound of running water allowed us to hike in peace. The air had a scent of eucalyptus.

Both of us wanted to do something about the looters. Marco wanted to purchase a rifle. I contemplated making a pair of nunchakus. Suddenly, a bright white flash hit our eyes. We stopped in our tracks.

"What was that?" I asked.

"I don't know. Lightning?" I looked up at the horizon. There weren't any clouds.

We continued to walk for a few seconds, and slowed down as our minds processed what just happened relative to the environmental data that flowed through our senses. Something didn't compute.

"Where's the thunder?" Asked Marco.

"I don't know. That was weird."

We walked for two more minutes as I watched the ground for objects. Then I had a revelation.

The eye is composed of rods and cones. The rods interprets light as shades of gray. The cones interpret light as reds, blues, and greens. At night, the eyes manufacture a chemical called rhodopsin that allows the eyes to see in the dark. Rhodopsin is such a light sensitive chemical that under controlled circumstances, it can capture a single photon.

Whenever you shine a bright light in your eyes, you lose your night sight, because it activates all the rhodopsin that your eyes produced. Whenever that happens, you lose your night vision, and you're usually blind for about ten seconds, and then it takes about five minutes, or however long the rhodopsin production rate is, to regain your night vision. In addition, the light fires off signals in the optic nerve, which is why after a light is flashed in your eyes in the dark, you have blobs of light in your eyes, even though your eyes are closed or in the dark. Of course, you will only have that reaction if the light strikes your eyes.

We didn't lose our night vision. We didn't have any blobs of light after the flash. I stopped, and explained that to Marco. He was stunned.

"Did you lose your night vision Marco?"

"No. Did you?"

"No, I checked the horizon and the sky right afterward. That's impossible. Your eyes will always react that way." I said.

I stopped and looked at him. I could still discern his features. I looked at my watch. I could still see the dim green glow of the hands.

"But that's impossible! How can we get a bright flash in our eyes and not loose our night vision?" I asked.

"Unless it wasn't in our eyes." Replied Marco.

"That means it was internal! In the optic nerve, or in the part of our brain that processes images! But that's not possible." I said as we looked back at the mountain behind us. The hairs on my back stood up once I understood what just happened. We walked faster. As we turned a bend, we started walking in the direction of the mountain again. Then we then saw it.

From the back of the mountain, where there wasn't a single cloud in the sky, came three flashes.

"Did you see that?" I asked Marco.

"Yes."

"Do you hear any thunder?" I asked Marco.

"No."

"Do you see any clouds?"

"No. And there are no cities behind it. It is just mountain range."

We kept walking. We saw it flash twice. I turned my head away to avoid looking at it, and then stopped. We looked at the direction of the mountain. Nothing. Maybe it was just lightning. That didn't explain the light in our eyes though. We were facing away from the mountain before hitting the bend. Marco pulled out his flashlight, and turned it on. It was bright.

"When did you change the batteries?" I asked him. The last expedition we went on, his batteries were so low that I was lighting the rest of the way with my flashlight.

"I didn't. Here are the new batteries I just bought." He showed me the package of fresh alkaline cells. We looked at each other. I took his flashlight, and pointed it into the sky. It formed a visible beam, and I pointed it at the the three stars in Orion's belt. We could follow the beam all the way into the black night sky. We looked at each other again.

"They're not rechargeable. They're alkaline." He said.

"Marco, let me try an experiment."

I shone the light in his eyes, and then my eyes. Suddenly, we were blind as bats, and as we waited to recover our night vision, we stumbled over piles of road debris.

"What the hell is going on?" I muttered.

"OK, now please confirm to me that you also lost your night sight and saw colored blobs after shining the light in your eyes?" I asked. I saw the usual reaction of light blobs.

"Yes, I did."

"OK, so I'm not crazy, or we're both going loco."

"I don't think we're both going loco." He said. It took us four minutes to regain our vision. We both looked back at the mountain. As if in reply, we saw it again. This time in another pattern. Flash Flash.... Flash Flash Flash.... Flash Flash... Flash Flash Flash...Flash Flash...Flash Flash Flash. 2, 3, 2, 3, 2, 3.

It was repeating two prime numbers. We looked at each other. The time in between was perfect, as I counted "one Mississippi, two Mississippi" in my mind. This wasn't just a concentrated beam of light. The entire mountain range was lighting up evenly across the entire range on top.

"I think it scanned us" Said Marco.

"No *shit*! It fucking scanned us in our heads!" I replied.

"What do we do if whatever it is comes after us?"

"Nothing. If it can scan us in our head, it can already kill us." I replied.

We walked further down, until we hit the outskirts of the village. A family was hiking up the mountain. Marco stopped to ask them if they had seen the lights. They didn't. We kept walking.

"My head is still swelling, and we're already 2000 meters down. The altitude effect should be over by now." Said Marco.

"I know. Mine too. You do know that we have to go back." I said.

"I know. But what do we do about it?"

"I think those are the lights Ernesto was talking about. I don't think it's Paititi anymore. This is different."

"Do you suppose it is a UFO?"

"No. If it were, then the locals would've seen it. I think this is a property of the planet. There's something about this place that's special." I replied.

We got to the bus stop and a bus drove up. We boarded, exhausted, scratched, bruised, hungry, thirsty, and still disconcerted from the flash in our eyes and the swelling in our heads. Something about the site effected us physically. Had I gone alone, I would have dismissed it all as my imagination. But Marco was there to confirm it.

When I got back, I was paranoid. A troop carrier came by us when there was supposed to be no military activity in the area. Then a pilot risked flying up the mountain into turbulent winds in a tiny Cessna to buzz us. Then we got scanned by God knows what. I walked to the door of my room, and grabbed the handle in the dark. Something soft brushed it. I jumped back, and saw a note. I got into my room, and read it. Ernesto wanted his mountaineering guide book back.

"Geezus Christ Ernesto, you scared the living shit out of me." I mumbled. The next morning, I jolted out of bed, breathless, and said, "Oh my God, She's Intelligent!"

Figure 10.1: We approach a strange wall at the top of the mountain that blends in perfectly with the surroundings.

Figure 10.2: We get close to the wall on the steep mountainside.

Figure 10.3: Right up against the wall. Up close, it's definitely a wall. From a distance, it just looks like mountainside.

Figure 10.4: The Portal.

Figure 10.5: Up close to the portal. Note the crude arch where the two boulders meet.

Figure 10.6: Marco stands in front of the portal.

Figure 10.7: The strange rectangular stone at the sacred site.

Figure 10.8: I stand on the edge of the pit.

Figure 10.9: A partially excavated tunnel entrance lays at our feet at the bottom of the pit. I try to take a look into the entry way of the tunnel inside of the pit.

Figure 10.10: I stand next to the rock table full of ancient, eroded glyphs.

Figure 10.11: Close up of one of the glyphs on the rock table.

Chapter 11

Analysis

I stared at the photos Marco and I took of the stone circles, and the flat table rock. In front of me, were ancient, and eroded Andesite rocks with symbols of spirals, and pits. Spirals popped up everywhere, and finally, I understood why it struck such a chord inside of me when I first saw it on the monkey's tail in the Nazca desert. What was the spiral? What did it mean? I sat down in café Haylilly, when an older white man, with a gray beard and spectacles sat down in front of me.

"Hello!" I said when I recognized him from the other night with Sally. I smiled to him, and said, *"I met you the other night with Sally."*

"Yes yes! I remember you. My name is Elio." We shook hands.

"My name is David."

"Ah, David. Are you Japanese?"

"No. Vietnamese, but I'm American."

"You will want to be careful before identifying yourself as American."

"Why is that?"

"Americans are easy targets these days, with all the things going on."

"Oh."

"So tell me, what are you doing here in Cuzco?"

"Well, I originally came to travel for fun. But now, I'm investigating a strange mystery."

"Ah yes, so I've been told. Sally tells me that she sees you often in here writing. So, what is this mystery?"

"A strange energy form, which comes out as light. It seems to come

from the ground, and illuminates the mountains in places where there are no cities, no clouds for lightning, or volcanoes. In one place where we saw the light, we found strange symbols on the rocks."

"May I see them?"

"Sure."

I handed him the photos, as he looked at them. He smiled as he perused, and then he handed the photos back to me, took out a pen, and pointed at my notebook. I took out a page, and gave it to him.

"David, I used to be a chemical engineer in Argentina, but working with the toxic chemicals gave me horrible reactions. So, I quit, and became an artist. I tell you this so that you may understand the background that I come from."

"OK."

He started to draw out a spiral, and an equation for it.

"Let us start with the spiral. There is a concept of geometry, known as the Flower of Life. It is based on a specialized geometry, known as Sacred Geometry. This is a knowledge that has been passed down through the ages. The Chinese have it in there I Ching. The Russians figured it out in the 1950's. Most Americans, unfortunately, are unaware of the concept."

He continued, *"the geometry is based on the Fibonacci sequence, a theory in calculus which says you can get close to the pi ratio of 3.14, but you will never end it. If you go to infinity, you will hit 1.618, which is the exact number you'd be off of perfection."*

"OK, but what does this have to do with the site?"

"Ah, ever seen a nautilus shell? Or DNA? Or Leonardo Da Vinci's drawing of a man in a circle with curiously arranged triangles?"

"Yes."

"All things in nature, move according to the Fibonacci. It is the rule of the Universe itself. If you ever wished to find a fundamental mathematics of biology, then the Fibonacci is where you must start. Let me show you those petroglyph's."

He pulled out one of the photos with the spiral.

"The ancients knew of the spiral, and it's properties. Look here." He said as he pointed to a photo where two spirals were opposed to each other, and connected with a line.

"Seek symmetry. This is your key. Have you been to Tiwanaku, in Bo-

livia?"

"*No.*"

"*I was there. I found these petroglyph's.*" He said as he drew a spiral, a square wave, a square with lines radiating lines from the corners in 45 degree angles, a volcano like glyph, and three pits in a triangular formation. He then drew a sperm cell and an egg.

"*These are part of the mystery. But, the spiral is the key.*"

****

I sat in Cafe' Haylilly, in Cuzco, and watched CNN Español go on about the terrorist attack in New York. Two weeks into the aftermath, and I was sick of it. To my dismay, the cafe managers switched it to the CNN American version to accommodate their customers. There were two messages coming out of the tube. One was "War and Retaliation", and the other was "How's the stock market doing?" Great, war and greed was what my country now stood for. When the managers switched it to the CNN Español, the message was, "*was this attack allowed to help the Star Wars Defense bill get passed through the government and to boost the flailing US economy?*"

Something as significant and horrific as September 11th, would have some kind of reverberating effect on all of humanity. But was there a way to detect this? As it turned out, there was.

Sara and I had a conversation about the ways and methods to detect energy forms before the expedition to the forbidden site. She had a unique way of detecting the energy forms that no instrument in existence could do.

"David, I carry this with me." She said, as she pulled out a neck pouch from her shirt. From the pouch, she pulled out a crystal point attached to a string.

"What is that?" I asked.

"It's my dowsing pendulum."

"Dowsing? Like those guys who claim to find water with sticks?"

"You'd be surprised at how effective it is." She said.

I was never a believer in dowsing. For me, it was unquantifiable, and it smacked of something even more off beat then the other crazy theories and practices that I'd heard. Yet, as I did some research, I found that I was wrong.

Before I went on the trip, I read a website known as the "Global Consciousness" site, or www.noosphere.org. The background of the site is based on twenty five years of research in a Princeton University Laboratory known as the "Princeton Engineering Anomalies Research" Center, or PEAR. The center was dedicated to the scientific study of consciousness related physical phenomena. It was founded by a plasma rocket systems engineer and professor at Princeton University.

The basis of the research used a highly rigorous and thorough methodology to see and question the following: does thought effect machinery and electronics, is it quantifiable, and are there patterns?

The basis of the research was through the use of random number generators, which, when plotted over time, looked like white noise. In a controlled experiment, involving thousands of tests, test subjects, male and female, tried to mentally manipulate the numbers to hit a numerical goal. They tried to decrease randomness. When the directors of the labs began the experiments, they didn't expect anything. As it turned out, they were baffled with the data they received.

They found that the human mind was able, through the use of thought, to decrease the randomness of the number generators to such a degree that it could not be explained away with mere statistics. In other words, Sara was right. Our minds can, indeed, influence things. It got more interesting.

In an extension of the project, random number generators called "eggs", were placed around the world, without operators, to see if there was a possibility that humanity, unaware of their existence, could influence the generators. The Noosphere project was coined for this experiment, and it monitored things like the World Cup and Princess Diana's death. However, three weeks after September 11th, when I took a look at the site, I saw the biggest shock of my life.

In the report, in the days before 911, the generators began to decrease in randomness. Suddenly, the randomness dropped significantly, a day before the attacks. On the fateful day, it looked like it was flat lining, and it didn't resume noticeable randomness until several days afterwards. The report cautioned not to draw any conclusions, but to me, the data was clear. There was a global consciousness, there was a sentient reality, and the reality knew of the events before they took place, and it was affected, as the events took place.

To take it further, Sara's dowsing was the crude equivalent of a random number generator, and her subconscious mind interacted with the field of the sentient reality, giving and receiving feedback. There was a global consciousness, and there was now data to prove it. Even Einstein said this about dowsing. *"I know very well that many scientists consider dowsing as they do astrology, as a type of ancient superstition. According to my conviction this is, however, unjustified. The dowsing rod is a simple instrument which shows the reaction of the human nervous system to certain factors which are unknown to us at this time."*

Since the mind produces energy forms which are measurable, in the electromagnetic spectrum, then the thoughts we produce, are things. Our thoughts are measured as energy. If we look at thoughts from a quantum point of view, than we would see thought forms as packets of energy, like a photon, continuously streaming from our minds.

If we take the light photon, and the mental energy packet we'd see that both have similar characteristics. Both are measurable. Both have frequencies and wavelengths. For a light particle, it's expressed in the electromagnetic spectrum. For a thought to register on equipment, it shows up as alpha, or beta waves.

Then, it wouldn't be a stretch to say that a thought form has the equivalent in properties of a light particle.

Now, let's go to hyper-dimensional theory, which seeks to unite the four forces of the universe by expanding the characteristics of energy and force into five to ten dimensions. The goal of hyper-dimensional physics, according to Michio Kaku's "Hyperspace", is that *"the laws of nature simplify when self consistently expressed in higher dimensions."*

Part of the theory involves the use of strings as the basic construct of particles, like quarks, leptons, and the entire pantheon of particles. String theory's basis is that any particle, when closely examined, is simply a harmonic of a vibrating string. Therefore, our thoughts, as energy particles, are composed of vibrating strings.

Now, here's where it gets crazy. String theory only works when mathematically explained in 10 or 26 dimensions. In other words, nature, our physical natures, which are really just compact bundles of energy is best explained, mathematically speaking, in 10 dimensions. Therefore, our thoughts exist in 10 dimensions, and as quantifiable energy, like particles, they interact with a multitude of particles that form solid objects, like machines, or are expressed in the electromagnetic spectrum, like a number generator, or in Sara's case, a dowser.

So what happens when you take a single human emitter of thought forms, and mix them with 6 billion other humans? What a mess! Yet, if we were to apply fractal theory to this vibrating soup of energy forms, we'd see a strange order out of the disorder. This order, and its changes, I think, is what the global consciousness project is measuring. It's either that, or Gaia herself. Or quite possibly, we are part of the neural network of the enormous body of Gaia. We on a collective scale, are her conscious and subconscious.

****

Geoff and I sat in a small shop outside the abandoned train tracks. We watched the children play in the red, sandy soil. The smell of urine and human waste reeked, as clouds of dust swept through. The sun was bright and clear overhead, and it gave everything a strange western movie feel. I watched as a little girl played with a balloon. Peruvians were poor, and their poverty can sometimes wreak havoc on your sense of reality and morality. Still, they were also a proud people, and for the most part, people had enough to eat. This wasn't like Africa, where a bad season would leave people in famine. Food was plentiful, and almost everyone had a roof and access to basic services. The materialism that Americans are so used to is the only thing that wasn't present. Peruvians were able to live their lives in relative comfort with all their basic necessities. Besides, who was I to judge if they were poor or not. After all, it really is relative.

Sometimes you have to ask yourself these questions. What is being poor? What is being rich? What makes you happy? A house full of stuff? That stereo and a new car? A new love interest? That paper degree you got from an expensive institution? Fame and seeing your name in a newspaper or on TV? I already experienced all of that, and nothing made me feel as free or as rich as exploring on a bicycle with little more than a few clothes, some basic equipment, and my wits. I guess I was poor compared to a lot of my fellow countrymen, but here, I was rich beyond belief. Really, what was being rich or poor? I remembered a quote from a traveler, you can be broke a few times in your life, but you can never be poor.

Geoff poured a beer out of a dusty bottle into his glass, as I patted the little girl's head. All around us was trash, waste, and peasants selling their vegetables and wares on the tracks. Their rainbow colored clothing stood out in the reddish orange dirt. Children played in the waste, and picked through the trash for anything of remote value.

"Krakey. Nothing like a cold dusty one, right mate? Ah."

I watched as he tilted it back. He looked like he didn't have a drink in years. Geoff was a fifty something Australian who decided to travel the world. He recently spent three months doing volunteer work in the heart of the Amazon, teaching the native tribes English. His long, graying beard, glasses, Peruvian leather hat, and mystical twinkle in his eyes reminded me of Merlin the Magician.

"So, it seems you've stumbled onto something really remarkable."

"You're telling me. Gaia really is manifesting herself, isn't she?"

"Well, from what you've discovered, it would seem that way. Krakey though, it seems you're in a bit of a bloody mess though ain't it?"

"I beg your pardon?"

"Well, let's see. You're definitely on to something. The structures around here certainly are functional. But you seem to be forgetting something."

"The key?"

"Yeah, you've done a lot of exploration in the outer world. Yet, have you bothered to explore inside? You have to go in, inside of yourself."

"Inside of myself?"

"You know. Internally. In your spirit. Have you ever bothered to just let go of everything, and then sink deep inside of yourself, to that quiet part of you. I'll give you an example. You have a brain. And yet, you're only accessing 10%. What happens with that other 90%? And in that 10%, most of it is, I am Geoff, Geoff does this, Geoff does that. It's mostly filled with the crap of everyday. Ya gotta let go of that ego that is you, because it'll only get in the way of your discoveries."

"Oh no. My mom's been bugging you to remind me to meditate, hasn't she?"

Geoff smiled and winked.

"Do you really think that whoever built this system did it solely for mechanical or energetic purposes? No. They were multi-functional. Like those energy spirals. They spiral out, but don't forget mate, they also spiral in."

"So that's what Anita meant, when she kept telling me that 'Silence is Golden'. I finally figured she just wanted me to keep my mouth shut."

"Wow Dave. You sure are perceptive. Cute girl tells you to shut your arse and you keep blathering on."

"Eh... yeah. Thanks for reminding me." I grinned. Geoff poured another beer into his cup.

"Until you can get rid of all that mental crap and tap into that part of you that's breathing and living, you'll never understand the purpose of the device."

"Gee thanks Geoff. You sure are encouraging."

"Think about it Dave. *'You can't solve a problem on the same level that created it,'* Einstein said that. You need to get to another level."

"I would think that by today most of us would be on that other level."

Geoff suddenly laughed, startling me and the little girl.

"Do you really think that all this progress that our civilization has done has really improved our lot? Come on! We still scream bloody hell at each other, and are ready to stick a knife in the other person's chest. We've destroyed most of the life systems that support on us on this planet. And now look at this whole terrorist attack. Do you really think it was unprovoked? Be real. Your country has been murdering people for a long time. It was only a matter of time before it came back. And now, my country, Australia, the bloody bunch of fucks, won't even let the afghan refugees in. Those refugees really need the help, but when they've got no one else to turn to, that desperation..."

"Turns into anger, and then hate, and then destruction."

"Exactly."

"Great. Just great. My entire country..."

"Is being lead by a bloody bunch of fools who are ready to capitalize on their own people's will to take the lives of the downtrodden so that they've got something to show to those who elected them, and to maintain their power."

Geoff was such an optimist.

"Until your countrymen start thinking, 'you know what mate, it's not them that's really wrong. There's something that we're doing that's wrong', then your country will continue on its path to annihilation. It's a shame really. I wanted to live to see the end of this decade too. Oh well. I've still got a few more years to see the rest of the world. No worries."

I sighed, and looked over to the tracks. Two boys played with some pieces of plastic and toy cars. A few dogs pecked at the debris, scratching around for food. Geoff took another swig out of his glass.

"There's always a way out you know. The future was never set in stone. There's gotta be a way to derail a Train to Nowhere." I said.

"Ah, I can hear that Vietnamese part of you talking. You've got to change the mind of the conductor and the passengers... But it's hard to battle the collective wills of a blood thirsty nation."

"Then what's the point of me pursuing this planetary device? I might as well just keep traveling until everything is finished. It makes no sense for me to change, only to see everyone I love and care about collapse into destruction."

"Oh... No longer the jolly, happy go lucky, optimistic Dave all of the sudden?"

Geoff grinned. Then he looked very serious.

"Dave. Keep doing what you're doing. It's important. Gaia needs you. Let the right people know too. Maybe their hearts aren't so frozen by the attack that they too can see and even join you in your quest. Just remember though, it'll all be for nothing if you don't take the time out to be at peace with yourself. Remember, your greatest enemy is yourself. Your ego is the thing that blocks you from what you want to do."

"I'll bet my brother Jeff's been talking to you to, huh?"

"Of course mate! That telepathic little bloke is a sharp one alright. You should listen to him. The fact that he pointed out that this area is Gaia's central nervous system was pretty good. I'll tip a cold one to him too."

Jeff analyzed some of my emails describing the things I'd seen, and he astutely pointed out that the areas which were full of active energy forms, whether volcanic, kinetic, solar, or esoteric, were also areas that had the most biological diversity. He said it was possible that the area we were in was a nervous system point, like an acupuncture point on a human body. In fact, a good analogy to the planet would be with a human body. Across the body, are numerous points that Chinese acupuncturists stimulate. Interestingly, many of those points when analyzed with Western medicine, didn't have any intersection with nerve endings, or even vessels. Western medicine is still baffled at how acupuncture worked, but for the Chinese, it made perfect sense. The human body is mapped with energy lines. By working the energy lines, certain responses were created. Take that analogy to the earth, and the earth's energy lines, work those points, and there'd be different effects.

I watched as two elderly women in top hats struggled to carry their infants across the tracks. The rural areas were tough areas to make a living, and you could see it on their faces. I waved hello to them, and watched the toddlers wave back.

"Just remember my friend, as the prophecy states, the Star of David appears in a few days. It's the last thing we really need in these interesting times. It hasn't shown it's bloody arse in over 4000 years. When that comes, it will be a time of tumult and chaos. The old Chinese curse rings true as always."

"Chaos works for me. I live off of it."

"Then all the more power to you my friend. You will need everything you can get."

****

Pictures of the artifact and site lay sprawled across the table. Spiral forms, pits, circles of stones, buried hallways, strange energy emissions, and giant portals flashed through my brain as I tried to make sense of everything. In the aftermath of contact, I understood that Gaia was a real, living, breathing, and *intelligent* entity. I woke up to an incredible epiphany. That she made contact with us was even more startling. Something was happening to the entire planet. Sure, the Cassandras spoke about the doom and gloom of the environment and how global warming was wrecking everything, but something inside of me stirred after we made contact. If Gaia truly was an intelligent super-organism, then surely, we were just moments in time to Her. She knew how to take care of herself. The question was what She wanted to do with us, and why did She make contact with us.

What do you do with a cancer that's metastasizing in your body? You remove it. Were we, the homo sapien species, the current harbingers of change, a cancer? From the condition I saw of the planet, it sure looked a lot like that.

Before I even contemplated taking a trip anywhere, I read James Lovelock's theories of Gaia, ecology, deep ecology, energy systems, and feedback. One of the things I noticed was that we already had a theory for Chaos.

154

Entropy factors in as well. Entropy is where everything just breaks down. Yet, there weren't any real theories regarding order, other then fractal theory. But fractal theory doesn't deal with consciousness. There wasn't a science of consciousness that I knew of.

It came to my mind that as you get more complex in your series of order, you were going to hit a critical point of complexity. When you hit that critical point, consciousness, at least, in my eyes, was born.

Is Gaia approaching a critical point of complexity? If so, then She was already past the point of attaining consciousness. Now the question was, what was She going to do with Herself and that new found consciousness? I sipped my tea in the cafe as Sara looked through my photos. Classical music floated through the air.

"You know Sara, I think what we're looking at is a global system. I think it works like this. When you have the accumulation of mass into a planet, it forms a simplistic grid of energy. That's inherent in every planet. Then, depending on the conditions, with that basic energy grid supplying the order and control, it forms the basic ordered series of molecules. When you get to your first critical point, you have molecules which are capable of replication, like RNA. Then I think the grid at that point also hits another stage of evolution. It goes to the next level of complexity, and in symbiosis, the replicating molecules evolve again. Then you have your first cell formations, etc, until both the grid and the cells evolve again. I think we're looking at the force of evolution here."

Sara stared at me. Her Celtic blue eyes didn't blink or waver.

"Keep going."

"OK. Now imagine that at a certain point in the planet's stage, after several quantum leaps of order, you form the first organic consciousness. They're intuitive enough to sense the intersections of these grid points, and assemble simple structures at these points which can harness those earth energies. Then you approach the next set of quantum leaps in consciousness."

"Yes, that would be dolphins, cetaceans, elephants, and I guess we should include humans."

"Just not the one's in Capitol Hill. I'm sorry, bad joke."

Sara chuckled, "go on."

"Each quantum leap in complexity advances itself, and the energy structure at the same time. Now imagine that in our 100,000 year history of existence in our current genetic form, we had a magnificent, opulent civilization. They understood this system, and were able to harness it on all levels, energetically, materially, transport, communication, genetic engineering, and spiritually. Now imagine that they were able to build enormous structures specifically to connect and harmonize those points, like acupuncture. Then imagine that something went terribly wrong, and they had to deactivate, or put the system on standby mode. I think what we're looking at is the system in standby mode."

I sipped my tea for a moment.

"Oh My God. You know what this reminds me of? 2001, A Space Odyssey, by Arthur C. Clarke! He got it right!" I said.

"Except more appropriate for this would be 2001, An Earth Odyssey, and instead of David Bowman, it's David Nghiem." Said Sara.

"Very funny Sara." I smirked. The similarity was amazing though. It was like I walked into the Monolith, which gave early man intelligence. Except it smashed me in the nose to wake me up.

"Wow. This whole thing just gives me the shivers thinking about it. Whooo! This is amazing! So now that you know this, what do you propose to do next?" She asked.

"I think it's important to reactivate the system. I think that's the most important thing to do."

"It's not."

"What do you mean? Gaia is manifesting herself, and somehow this device ties in with Her."

"David, you said that as ordered complexity increases, you will hit a critical point to attain consciousness. So we know that She's intelligent, and that She's hit that order of complexity."

"But is She awake? She could just be dreaming. I think this might be like a way to just wake Her up."

"David, do you realize what has happened in the past few weeks?"

"Besides Contact?"

"No, I mean in the human world. The terrorist attack, everything. Remember how I said that everything was accelerating now?"

"Yeah, you did. You mentioned that."

"What I am going to tell you next will help you to understand. The planet, as in Gaia, is currently undergoing what's called a 'dimensional shift'."

"OK."

"Let me give you an example. There are two trends that are happening right now around the world. The first, is the birth and appearance of many children that most people would consider mutants."

"Mutants?"

"Yes. They're called 'Indigo Children'. They have a lot of interesting traits, but the most telling is that many of them have ADD."

"I have the dreamy type of ADD, the one that effects girls usually."

"No you don't. I worked with children who have 'ADD', but what I am seeing is something that's completely different. Let me explain. In China, there's a large group of children being born with extraordinary psychic powers. Discover magazine went in to test them, and they found that they had extremely powerful telepathic, intuitive, and remote sensing powers. The second group they found was in the United States. These kids have had certain sections of their DNA activated. When their cells are tested with HIV and AIDs, the cells repel the attacks, even when they're overloaded with them. They're impervious to diseases. David, you don't have ADD. Your family and friends don't have ADD. ADD is a figment of society. You're here to aid the planet. That's why you have those extra intuitive traits. You and those who were born before 1985 were among the 2nd wave. The Indigo Kids are the third and final wave. You and those who you consider close to you are functioning on a different frequency. That's why nothing seems right in this world to you. We're here to aid Gaia, that's what those extra skills are for."

I took a long sip of tea before responding. This was getting way too strange.

"The second trend is in Gaia and the solar system Herself. I'm sure that as scientist, you've noticed from your astronomers and scientists that many new structures and events are happening which currently defy their theories. A lot of the events will indicate a sequential order, like something conscious was producing it."

That part, I knew about. Lately, the speed of light became inconsistent after a group of scientists were able to slow a photon down, and even make a photon move at a measurable speed. A Boston University scientist looked all the way to the beginnings of the universe, and found that the laws of physics for electromagnetic phenomena had evolved with time. That was the only way they could explain the strange absorption rates of light since the time of the Big Bang. What was going on here? Physics, of all the sciences was supposed to be solid, not evolving. Evolution of a physical property meant that something fundamental was changing. Why?

"In other words David we have a big job to do here. You're making all the right steps. But I'm telling you that activating the system is not the most important task. It is important, and you have until 2012 to make sure it's fully functional. No, your important task is letting in more Love and Light in."

"That's really touchy feely Sara." I smirked.

She chuckled.

"Now I know that sounds really kooky, but I cannot stress to you how important it is at this time period. Imagine the world's on a balance. It can fall one way or the other. One goes to destruction, the other to creation. Take your pick."

"Oh. The hundred monkey theory."

"Exactly."

"It was painful for me to see some of my friends choose vengeance after the terrorist attacks." I said.

"They're not ready for it yet, and they're not functioning at that level of awareness yet. You'll just have to be patient."

I took another sip. Gaia was going through a "dimensional shift"? That might explain the existence of the strange portal. It might be a Stargate for all I knew. The top of the mountain was under clouds almost all of the time, so it didn't make sense to build a giant multi-ton portal pointing to the horizon for constellations. It was on top of a 5000 meter mountain, next to a circle of stones with petroglyph's that looked like galaxies and pits that looked like planets. Interestingly, the pits were in patterns of four and five. Was it possible that they represented the 4th dimension or 5th dimension?

"Dimensional shift." I said.

"Correct. Part of the shifting is a period before it which you might equate with pregnancy. It's painful, traumatic, and absolutely an ordeal, but afterwards, something wonderful is born. And it's wonderful."

"You're starting to freak me out. What about the troop carrier and the recon plane that buzzed us?"

"There will always be an opposing force. Don't worry about them. My feeling is that your family has already taken the necessary steps to safeguard you. Just meditate more and do what you have to do. Speaking of your family, I'd love to meet your mother. She sounds like a very remarkable woman."

"So then the device - it's still a necessity to activate it?"

"Of course! But it's a huge job David. This is the whole world. Not to mention it's a big adventure. You do have time though to work and develop your theories into something that's practical."

"Well, now that we know that anything is possible, I'm going to go back to the site and see if I can access a planetary memory core. If what my brother Jeff said was correct, than I might be able to tap into Gaia's memories, and maybe even find a manual on how to operate the device."

"How do you propose to do this?"

"Meditation."

"You have to be careful David. There are stories about people who weren't at the right frequency in their consciousness, and the effects on them varied from disappearing to absolute shock."

I sipped the last drop of tea from my cup.

Chapter 12

Macchu Picchu

I arranged for a trip to Macchu Picchu, and I knew it was time to do the tourist thing. During my stay in Cuzco, I did things most tourists didn't do. I befriended the locals, went to see things far off the beaten track, dated a local girl, and I was invited to Peruvian parties. It was at one such party that I befriended Paulo, who was a local Spanish teacher, and Bill, a Philadelphia native.

Bill was an interesting white guy, and a libertarian. He grew up three blocks from where I lived, but he spent many years on a ranch in Texas as a cowboy and ranch hand. His fellow cowboys used to call him the crazy man, because he'd get up after a fist fight, adjust his jaw, and then say, "Let's try that again." He later became a white hat hacker, and analyzed computer security systems from his abode in Mount Shasta, California. Now, he was exploring Cuzco, and considered setting up shop in the city, hacking and improving networks for pay, while exploring South America.

Bill was the first white, male, solo traveler I met, and as a libertarian myself, we got along easily. We talked about his home in Shasta, about the interesting people the volcano and surrounding lands attracted, and about how independent minded the people were. Bill used to work with Vietnamese people in one of his odd jobs in Texas, and he even knew a few words of Vietnamese. He became good friends with a Vietnamese family, and admired their fierce independence. When September 11th happened, Bill didn't fall for the official theory, and he became even more suspicious of the government when he analyzed the reports.

"If them feds ever come out to Shasta, we got our own private militia, and mountain men. We can handle em. I'm tellin ya Dave, we can sure use a fella like you out there. We think alike, especially regardin the gov'ment."

It was a fun party, and I enjoyed getting to know Bill and Paulo better. Paulo, who was gay, introduced me to some of his female friends, saying, "David, you should meet some pretty girls, nice girls. Not the ones in the clubs. Good girls. You're the type who should have a nice, pretty girl friend."

"I'm flattered Paulo."

Paulo introduced me to Marita. Well curved, cute face, slender, with long dark hair and eyes, and a smile that was flirtatious, she gave me the eye for the rest of the night. We danced the salsa several times, while Bill cheered us on with his cowboy hat.

That night, after getting Marita's phone number, I walked to a small shop in the center. I was hungry, so I bought a packet of roasted macadamia nuts. I chomped down on one, and then another, and on the third, as I crunched it in my teeth, I smelled something that reminded me of an old sewer pipe. Before I knew it, I automatically swallowed it. Since I had to leave early the next morning for the Inca trail, I went straight to my hostel, and fell asleep.

The road to Macchu Picchu started with a train ride from the city to Ollantaytambo. We got out, and started our hike at the two day point from Macchu Picchu. Along with me in the group was a newly wed American/British couple, an Argentinean woman who was a biochemist in town for a conference, and two guys who were ex spooks of the Israeli army. We descended into the green, misty, mountain valley. There was moisture everywhere, and we were well below the altitude of Cuzco. As we hiked by the ancient, misty farm communes, the trail became steeper and narrower. The communes were built along the sheer sides of the mountains, and they were surrounded with many terraces. The plants and trees glowed with a thick, green lushness in the moisture. Rain began to fall, as we followed the trail.

In the afternoon, after lunch, I felt my stomach cramp. I dismissed it, and drank some water, before we continued our hike into the valley. Later, while resting in the ruins of an Incan relay post, I felt the cramp turn into an ache. Still, I held fast, and tightened my muscles.

We followed the trail from one ruin to another. All the ruins were made of a light colored stone, and the stones of each ruin were no bigger than 600 pounds. In each construction, they were set polygonally, which ensured their earthquake proof characteristics. The trapezoidal Incan doors withstood the tests of time. I contemplated the millions of people the empire once supported. With a record system based on knots in colored strings, called Quipus, the Incas tracked the movement of thousands of goods and food stuffs. The quipus system provided both a database and a system of communication for the Incas. Unfortunately, because of the Spanish Inquisition, the knowledge of how to read the ancient libraries and records was lost.

Finally, in the evening, we reached the first base camp, and that night, we had a spaghetti dinner. My body felt better, and the cramps subsided, until night fell. I set up my tent at the bottom of the stairs of a small dormitory. I slept. Within an hour I felt my stomach grumble, and growl, and then a pressure on my backside began to erupt. Immediately, I leaped up, got out of my tent, and ran for the outhouse, only to find it occupied. After waiting an eternity, which was three minutes, I stumbled in.

A Peruvian outhouse is unlike any other. In the States, an outhouse is usually made of plastic, and a funny smelling truck frequently comes up to empty it out. When I went to Taiwan, I lived in a Buddhist temple. The outhouses were holes in the ground with foot places above, where a person would mount on the foot placements, squat, and listen to the sounds of shit falling. How were the outhouses in Peru? Well, they had places for my feet, but there were no holes in the ground. In fact, the Peruvians covered the holes with concrete. I couldn't figure out why they did that, since it didn't seem to make the outhouse more effective. Walking into one was like doing ballet in a mine field, but when my body wanted to empty the tank in a series of hurried squirts, the last thing I could think about was swan lake. I think I stepped on the Italian's lunch when I stumbled in that night. I refused to touch my shoes after that.

When I squatted, it came out like a water hose, and I listened to the splattering behind me.

"You've got to be kidding me." I muttered as I looked at the concrete sealed hole. All through the night, for another nine times, or one or two for every hour, I dashed to the outhouse, and squirted. I knew my condition worsened, since I lost a lot body fluid. In my tent, I used up my pack of handy wipes, since I ran out of toilet paper. I lay in on my pad, groaning, and cursed the bad macadamian nut that gave me a case of food poisoning. Finally, early in the morning, two Peruvians saw me collapse on the hand rail of the stair case. They picked me up, and took me to the infirmary. After a long night with my two best friends, Ciproflaxin and Metrodizole, and God knows what else the nurse fed me in the infirmary, I felt a little bit better. In the early morning, I felt strong enough to complete the trail and see Macchu Picchu.

As we hiked, I watched the black mountains rise up like islands in the gray ocean of mists. We walked by water falls, and the mist draped like curtains aside us, and politely swirled out of our way as we walked past. As we approached the ruins, on the side of the trail was an enormous 500 ton or more monster of a crystal like rock, planted on the side, and surrounded with an Incan wall. It looked like an ancient temple guardian, who stood there to decide who went in, and who didn't. When I arrived at Macchu Picchu, it was blanketed in mists, and a single tree appeared amongst the giant, looming boulders of the Incan walls. After a moment's rest, the first thing I did when we got there was to head straight for Huayna Picchu, which was on the mountain behind the ruins. As I jogged there, I felt energized by either the site, or my own adrenaline. A German woman in a tour group loudly asked the guide, "Vhere is dat man going?" as I jogged by. I was in a hurry. I had no desire to go with a group guide. I walked through the gate, signed my name in at the guard hut, and scaled the spiral staircase that wound around the mountain to the top of Huayna Picchu. At the top, finally, in a fit of exhaustion, alone, I collapsed, rested, and then meditated until the mists cleared.

As I descended, I walked around the peak and found something that was never described in any of the guidebooks, or references. Pointing off into the Amazon basin, was a stone stellae, carved, it seemed, to resemble a man's face and head. It stuck out from the base, and the only way to see it was to go through some bushes that hid it. No one else knew it was there. I stared at the stellae, and looked off into the distance. However, before I could think about it anymore, I had to go to the bathroom.

I got to the modern toilets of a luxury hotel that was built next to the ruins. Of course, as with all things in Peru, when I got to them, an avalanche crushed the main water pipe. As a result, the men's room was locked and marked, "out of order." So, I walked into the ladies room. After a few screams and strange looks, I explained my situation, and the ladies were much more understanding.

"Now you know how we feel when there are no toilets for us." Said an American woman.

Afterward, I went back again to Huayna Picchu, and this time, I went down the mountain, to the temple of the moon. For an hour, I slept amongst the ruins. When I awoke, I walked further to the back of the temple, and saw a giant, Incan stair case that descended into the cloud forest. It was covered with detritus, and I walked down it. No one, it seemed, had ever bothered to excavate, clear, or restore the staircase, and the stair went on for several kilometers. Finally, after about a kilometer down hill, I saw that the stair case seemed endless, and I didn't have enough time to continue. The Incan road went far out, into the mountains, and into the Amazon Basin. Was this the road to Paititi? I didn't know. I didn't have time. So, I went back to the main ruins of Macchu Picchu.

I had no desire to listen to the guide's explanation of where the rocks came from. I already had my own conclusions after seeing Sacsayhuaman. So, instead of the guided tour, I simply walked the ruins, and imagined myself as a Quechua, who was born, and raised in the ancient city, and tasked to taking care of the rituals and observances there. I walked amongst the giant stones, some which were as big as the 300 ton monster in Sacsayhuaman. Macchu Picchu probably had some of the finest stone masonry of all the Incan empire, as I walked to ruins where the organic shapes were formed with such precisely fitted stone work.

After the tour, I took the train ride back home. Back in Cuzco, after recovering for a few days, I met another traveler, Diane. Diane was a solo, 30ish, single American woman traveling through South America. We agreed to meet up in three weeks to go to Bolivia together. After all, we only had three weeks left before the winter was over, and the seasonal, daily down pouring would begin. The rains would leave the roads a muddy mess, and getting through it, either by bicycle, or by bus, would be hell.

Figure 12.1: Macchu Picchu's cyclopean stones, weighing many tons, fitted together in customized, polygonal forms, attest to what was once the world's greatest masons. Functionally, the stones organic fit is also earthquake resistant.

Figure 12.2: Macchu Picchu.

Figure 12.3: The anthropomorphic head near Huayna Picchu.

Chapter 13

Apologies to the Pachamama

Ernesto wanted to meet up with me at the clubhouse to go over the discoveries that Marco and I made. I was armed with fresh experience and information. First, everything started with the energy form that Marco and I experienced. It's characteristics were as follows:

1. It's an energy form expressed in the electromagnetic spectrum as light

2. It's intelligent or the forces behind it are intelligent

3. It's capable of psycho synaptic response, ie. it can appear in the neurons in our heads

4. It's also physically present in response, ie. it can appear physically outside the neurons in our heads

5. It expressed intelligence to us in prime numbers two and three which indicated that it was not a natural occurrence

6. It appeared in a seismically active area, where potential energy can be released as earthquakes or in volcanoes

7. It definitely is not, as far as we can tell, the result of human activity, lightning, or static.

8. It's expansive since it seems to glow the entire mountain range. This indicates that it's not a point source of light, and would toss out any possibility of beams or radiating beacons. It's more like a giant glow stick laid out along the mountain range

9. It comes from below, so that rules out any possibility of aurora. In addition, aurora is not possible to be seen from that latitude since we're too close to the Equator.

10. It's capable of conversion into chemical potential as shown by Marco's flashlight suddenly becoming "charged."

Ernesto looked at the notes, and said, "David, you forget, it can respond to you."

"What?"

"I was in the pass, and I was sleeping in my tent. Then, through the tent, the light came. I got out of the tent, and all around me, everyone in my party was sleeping. But all around me was the light. It is like being surrounded by the light. So, by now, I was accustomed to it. So, I tried to go back to sleep, but the light began to make patterns, like it was blinking at me. It acted like, 'Come Ernesto, come and play with me.' I said, 'No, I need to sleep, I am tired.' So, the light changed patterns, and it would try to get me up again. Finally, I said, 'OK, OK, I see you. But I am tired.' So, then, the light went away."

I put another note down.

11. The light responds intelligently, it is curious, and playful. We looked at the characteristics of the light.

"Well, we have our energy form, or at least, one expression of it." I said.

"Yes, it is very good, your analysis. But tell me David, do you understand the purpose of the device?"

"Not really. I think it could do something mechanical, or more likely it's solid state. It might convert energy into some kind of kinetic expression."

"No. You are forgetting something very important. You are forgetting the reason we as humans, exist."

I looked at Ernesto, as he made a one handed prayer salute like a Shaolin Monk.

"You must realize that the Inca, and their predecessors were deeply spiritual. We are here as expressions of spirit."

"What? You think the device..."

"No, I know."

"So, why would they use giant stones at the node points?"

"The stones are simply, like your theory on a possible energy of order, are there to advance consciousness. What is consciousness but the spirit? Like you said, David, in Western science, we have, as an analogy to the West, the ability to break things down in entropy. But that is all Western science can do. There is no theory of ordered complexity which becomes consciousness.

What is higher ordered complexity? Making something more complicated does not mean it becomes aware."

"That intelligent energy form, do you suppose it's...".

"You said it yourself, everything synchronizes with each other. As the quantum leaps occur, Earth, PachaMama herself leaps with us."

"So, we start with intelligence, or an evolving intelligence." I replied.

"Correct. David, when are you and Marco going back to the forbidden site? He told me about your 'accident' with the sea shell."

"Yeah," I said, embarrassingly, "ever since my mistake, this giant black storm cloud has enveloped the site. Marco keeps a daily look out on the weather from the airport, but it hasn't left."

Ernesto smiled, and said, "this is your first lesson in the way things are here. I would recommend you either find a shaman to bless the two of you, or that you make an offering to the PachaMama. Let me tell you a story. I was a guide for four European trekkers in Huaraz. We were going for several days, when we ran out of water in the high mountains. Finally, after much thirst, and time, we found a stream. The Europeans ran to the stream, drank, and gave no thought to how we had water. They even pissed nearby the stream. The place where we found the water, was a sacred place, and I made an offering to the PachaMama before drinking to say thanks. Later, they got sick, but I did not. You must remember, always give thanks to those who give to you, even if you cannot see them."

"Lesson learned." I said.

"So, what do you plan now at the site?"

"Well, I've got a possible direction in terms of the symbols. But I want to document them better, and I want to meditate in the site."

"Do you think PachaMama will talk to you?"

"I don't know. She was the one who made contact with us. This time, I'm going to try and contact her. Maybe she'll have some information we could use."

Ernesto smiled, as he said, "The PachaMama's secrets are never given. They must be earned."

****

It was our last chance. The Humboldt current, which flowed from Antarctica all the way to the Arctic, was driving the seasonal rains. Once the rains came, any access to the mountain would be delayed until the next winter. It was time for me to leave, since the rains would reduce many of the roads to mud. We had one more week left. Marco and I met up in the clubhouse, to go over our plans.

"This is it, man." I said, as I looked out the window of the overcast sky. The days and skies in Cuzco were no longer blue and cold.

"I know. The black cloud is still there."

"Then we have to take drastic measures. This Friday is our last chance, right?"

"Yes. After this week, any kind of mountain activity is very dangerous."

"What do I have to do?"

"We must make an offering to the PachaMama."

"How?"

"We must offer coca leaves, a sea shell, and holy water. These were valued as symbols of the PachaMama by the Inca, and the Quechua."

We went to the market, and amongst open sacks of rice, corn, and stalls of vegetables and fruit, we found a coca leaf vendor. The coca leaf is an ancient, religious and spiritual symbol to the peoples of the Quechua, Aymara, and many other indigenous nations. It's non addictive, and the best analogy for it would be spinach with caffeine. It provides more biologically active calcium than milk, more protein than most other plant groups, as well as high concentrations of all the vitamin groups. The stimulant, which is an alkaloid, is one of fifty to sixty other alkaloids in the leaf, which the human body selectively uses. It's a medicine for soroche, stomach aches, and pains.

Cocaine is an invention of an Austrian scientist in the 1890's. It's the isolate of just one of the alkaloid compounds in the leaf. Because the active alkaloid in cocaine is present in such minute quantities in the leaves, it literally takes a kiloton of coca leaves and a toxic brew of kerosene, methyl ether, and other toxic chemicals to produce just one kilogram of cocaine. Interestingly, the primary market for cocaine is for the rich kids of the USA and Europe.

Because Americans wouldn't take responsibility for their own drug problem, the American government poured billions of dollars into Peru, Bolivia, and mostly Colombia to eradicate the coca crop, train Para military groups, and support dictatorships. This created billions of dollars in revenue for herbicide companies, arms companies, and chemical industries. The chemicals destroyed landscapes, jungles, tropical rain forest, cloud forests, as well as contaminated water and soil. The toxic effects of the herbicides caused mutations, illnesses, and death in wildlife and humans.

As a result, the indigenous, in their own homelands, found their ancient cultures criminalized and stigmatized. It was easy to understand why many of the indigenous peoples weren't fond of Americans.

I purchased a bag of coca leaves, and thanks the Quechua woman, who had bright red cheeks.

"What are you going to do with it?" She asked me in halting Spanish. For much of the Quechua, Spanish was a second language.

"I have to apologize and make an offering to the PachaMama." I said. She nodded her head, and said, *"you must always respect the local traditions."*

I nodded back. We purchased some periwinkle shells, some water, and chalk dust to gently fill in the carvings, large tracing paper to sketch on, and some charcoal. The day before, I fasted and meditated to purify myself.

As we ascended the mountain, at first, the sky was over cast, with a few patches of clouds. But as we got closed, we saw the black cloud around the peak. Closer, we inched to the top, only to feel the ferocity of the convection currents as they tried to swat us off the mountain.

"We must do it now, David!" Yelled Marco over the roar of the rumbling currents, "put the leaves under a rock!"

"A rock, a rock." I muttered. I couldn't find a rock! We were headed to a peak full of giant rocks, and I couldn't find a single rock within twenty feet of me? The sides were almost vertical - we clung to the mountain and held fast in the powerful wind.

"Ya gotta be kidding me, where's a freaking rock?" I said to myself.

Finally, I found a rock, a big one, lodged into the side of the mountain.

"Found it!" I yelled. Marco was further up ahead, monitoring the black cloud.

"Put the leaves under the rock, and then pour water on it!" he yelled back.

I did as he said. Before I poured the water on, I put the water bottle to my forehead, recited a mantra, and asked to bless the PachaMama. I poured the water onto the stone.

"Done! Now what?!"

"Put the seashell in the ground, pour water on it, and apologize!" He yelled out. The roar of the currents was deafening as the air rushed past my ears.

I put the shell on the ground, put the water bottle to my forehead, closed my eyes, and repeated the mantra, and then said, "PachaMama, if you can hear me, I am truly sorry. I did not know." I then poured the water on the shell.

"OK! Done!" I yelled to Marco.

"Good! Let's go!" The convection currents got stronger, and as we clawed our way up the mountain, and the wind became fiercer. When we got to the rock wall, suddenly, the wind turned into a breeze. We looked around in astonishment. The sky was still overcast, but the black cloud lifted and turned gray. Marco looked at me, and smiled, "PachaMama smiles upon you. But, are you ready?"

"Yeah." I said, as I turned and looked around us, incredulous at how suddenly the peace came to what was, just minutes ago, a roaring, windy nightmare.

We walked to the circle of stones, and I sat down on my sleeping pad. Marco wandered off to see if there were any other ruins we might have missed. I closed my eyes, and relaxed. Slowly, I began to sink into myself, and into my heart. I felt something warm on my face, and opened my eyes. A single ray of sunshine, cut through a hole in the overcast sky, and lit my body up.

"You have got to be kidding me. I will never disregard local traditions again." I said, as I smiled, and closed my eyes again. It made absolutely no sense to me scientifically, but as my father told me, "there are some things that you just don't mess with." As I meditated, I felt a surge of images, colors, and thoughts, pour into me. It was like drinking out of a gushing fire hydrant. It was overwhelming, and I couldn't make sense of anything. Thirty minutes later, I emerged from my state, and Marco came by.

"Finished?"

"Yes."

"PachaMama is very happy. Let's go trace the symbols."

We gently poured chalk dust onto the carvings, taking care not to make any permanent, or embedded marks, and took photos. With the tracing paper, we charcoaled the glyphs onto the paper, and documented every symbol we

174

could find. Thankfully, there were no bandits. When we got to the pit in the ground, and the tunnel, I got in and a two hundred pound stone fell near me. We decided not to clear out the hallway, due to the risk of more rock falls.

We also discovered some new petroglyph forms, including one that resembled a sperm and egg. We finished exploring, I repeated the mantra, and thanked PachaMama. We found an ancient abandoned Incan stairway on a side of the mountain that we hadn't explored, and descended in that direction. As we left, the sun shone on us. We smiled and joked about what the possibilities were for the giant portal, and where it might lead to if it was ever opened. As we approached the bottom, we looked back up the mountain. We descended almost 1500 meters in altitude. At the top, the furious black cloud was back, and it covered the top. I saw a ferocious rainstorm, like a thick gray blanket that covered the peak. Marco looked at it, and said.

"PachaMama is cleaning away the chalk. She let us in. Remember that what you were given, is a gift, not a right. Even if we are chosen, we are still guests."

Figure 13.1: Glyph 01 from the strange circle of stones at the peak of the mountain.

Figure 13.2: Glyph 02.

Figure 13.3: Glyph 03.

Figure 13.4: Part of the circle of stones.

Figure 13.5: The strange stone table with glyphs now clearly visible using chalk dust.

South America - Bolivia

Chapter 14

Lake Titicaca

"Comisariqui!" I said to the little Aymaran girl in her native tongue.

"Waliqui!" She replied back.

I knew just a few words of Aymara, as Diana and I toured the reed island, in the middle of Lake Titicaca, nearby Puno, Peru. Her face was red brown, and she wore a wide brim hat. The sky was clear, and I sat down in front of her on a mat, made from the totora reeds. She was dressed in a white smock, with rainbow colored sweaters and a white skirt, as she showed me her hand-made jewelry. We were on an island, made of mats of totora reeds, which gently floated on the still waters of the lake. There were many man made reed islands like this one. The Aymara of the lake, escaped the Spanish onslaught via these islands. Even the Inca couldn't get the Aymara to submit to their empire, since so many of them lived on the waters of Titicaca. I watched as the little girl smiled at me, and said, "Konichiwa!" I grimaced, held my temper in check, smiled back at her, and said, *"thank you."*

As I walked on the island, I felt the sponge-like feel of the ground, as it bounced and gave way to my weight, and I went from hut to hut, and eventually bought a medallion of the Sun Gate of Tiwanaku. The homes were made of woven reeds, supported with poles, and roofed with corrugated aluminum or plastic. Village life on the island consisted of making handicrafts for the tourists, harvesting trout or pejerrey, a native fish, from their aquaculture farms, and trading in Puno for foodstuffs, and other goods. Most of their economy was based on tourism.

In ancient times, they made reed boats to paddle around the lake. Today, they used aluminum boats. A stubborn people, they maintained their ancient culture, language, customs, and techniques, but they did adopt a few modern day amenities. Almost every home had a solar panel. I walked back to the boat, after finishing the tour, and looked at the fresh green reeds being prepared for another island.

"All done?" Asked Diana. I looked at her, and smiled. Diana struck an interesting figure, as an attractive, 30ish, Jewish American, New Yorker, with a leather cowboy hat, a north face jacket, and leather cowboy boots.

"Yeah." I replied.

"Neat, huh?"

"Amazing. I'm surprised they've maintained their culture."

"Yes, it is amazing, isn't it? Let's hope it stays that way. I'd hate to see them lose themselves in all this globalization."

Diana and I traveled together for the last two days. We both left Cuzco just before the rains came in, and shared rooms and meals together. She had the ideal personality to travel with: laid back, easy going, take it as it goes, roll with the punches. I thought that was interesting, considering she was a New Yorker. Later that evening, we dined in a restaurant in Puno, and made plans.

The next morning, we parted company.

"I'll keep an eye out for you, Dave," she said, and then added, "just in case you get to me before I get moving."

"Maybe on the isles of the Sun and Moon, we'll meet."

"Let's meet in Copacabana, at the Hostal Americano."

"Deal."

I pushed my bike down Puno's central road into the town market for supplies. I bought bread, cheese, and fruit, as well as some powdered fruit drink mix. The stalls were on push carts, with large umbrellas for shade, and the people smiled as I bought my supplies. Bread, cheese, and fruits were my rations, as well as an assortment of nuts. Looking at my map, I noted the distance between towns. It'd been a long time, and I'd have to take it slow on the bike.

There's a certain majesty about the Andean landscape that fills the soul with wonder. As I biked down the road, alongside me were giant, snow capped peaks on black mountains, where clouds climbed the sides, and turned from white puffs into angry dark storm clouds. Because of the high altitude, the air's thin quality made everything clear. Vast plains of brown, dry grass in the winter, rippled in the wind. There were no trees, as it was too far above the tree line for anything other than grass, potatoes, and the native high altitude plants to grow. Campesino women, Aymara or Quechua, dressed in gray or black skirts, and colored sweaters, with top hats or broad brimmed hats, crossed the road with their flocks of sheep or llamas, and children honked horns on their old style, single speed, Chinese made bicycles as they passed by me on the way to school or home. Sometimes they asked me for money, other times, they waved a simple hello. Once, men ran alongside me, saying, "gringos have dollars!"

On one lonely stretch of road, a headwind pushed me off the bike, and I pushed the bike between two mountains to a sparkling, beckoning azure of Lake Titicaca. I stopped to eat and drink, and then to stretch my muscles.

I arrived in the town of Juli at 7:30 PM, where a family put me up in a lakeside room, above their family room. On a meal of rice, potatoes, tomatoes, ketchup, and salad, with cheese, I looked out of my second story window as a distant thunder storm lit up the lake, while above us was the clear, star studded sky.

The next day, I met a Peruvian bicycle traveler, and we exchanged tokens. I reminded myself to keep a collection of trinkets for exchange and memories for other bicycle travelers. Later, while crossing on a ferry through a narrow passage between Desaguadero and the border of Bolivia, I watched a sunset on the lake, and breathed in the cold air. I was out of shape, and spent the night in a hostel in a tiny township alongside the lake and the ferries. I sat down in the boat and felt my knees.

I arrived at the Peruvian Bolivian border, and I passed through to a road with a long line of vehicles. I looked at the cars waiting in line next to me. There were expensive Land Rovers, and sixties era European sports cars, little roadsters, and all sorts of old and new vehicles. It was a continental road rally, and to the chagrin of some of the drivers, I rode by them while waving my hand. I couldn't help myself. I was the non-petroleum powered vehicle, and I beat all of the drivers through the customs process to enter Bolivia. Nothing brought a more visceral response than riding on a fully loaded bicycle, pedaling through a dirt poor country, and passing by Land Rovers that cost more than the collected village's material possessions.

They perspired in the heat at the customs office along the border of Peru and Bolivia. After some hand shaking, picture taking, and some dinner invitations, I decided it was best to head off into Copacabana.

The road was made of cobblestones, so I got off my bike and pushed up the hill. After 3 miles of pushing into the evening, I came to a cobblestone downhill. I wasn't in the mood to decrease my sperm count, so I stood on the bike as it bounced and jostled down the road into Copacabana.

Many people think of Copacabana as a warm, sunny place in Brazil. Copacabana, Brazil, was actually named after Copacabana, Bolivia. The name, Copacabana, is a transformation from the Aymaran word Kota Kahuana, which means "View of the Lake."

I found Dawn's hostel in the center of town. I checked in, and found she already reserved a bed for me. She also left a note for me to meet her in a restaurant nearby. I walked into the cobblestone courtyard of the restaurant, and smelled the heady scent of fresh pizza.

"Dawn!" I said, as she got up from the table full of European travelers.

"Dave! You made it!" She said as we hugged.

"Hell yeah. Told you I would."

I was introduced to the table, and ordered a pizza. She introduced me to Cornelia, a Norwegian, 25, and traveling mostly solo through Bolivia, Peru, and Chile. She was just at the start of her travels. We talked about travel as a form of therapy, and about the reasons we were traveling. I listened to each woman talk about their relationships and the problems with them that they were getting away from. Eventually, the relationship steered towards my reasons for my adventures.

"And what are you running away from, Dave? I mean, I know you're on the track of something really interesting, with that planetary energy stuff, but how did it start?"

I told her about the picture, and Kendra. They were shocked, and intrigued at the events.

"And you what? You sent it to her, and then you just *ditched* her?" Said Diana.

"Hey, I was in this, 'I can't take Fate phase'. I'm still, sort of in that phase. I was hoping that she'd wig out with the story, and that she'd toss it away. Besides, I figured maybe she'd get freaked out that maybe I was stalking her. I hope she threw it away."

"You don't seem like the stalking type. I don't know Dave, if I was her that would have me hooked for a long time, especially when you just *left*, and on top of that, *left the country*. If I was her, that would be the most beautiful, and intriguing thing to happen to me. I wouldn't toss it away. If anything, I'd become obsessed. I'd start stalking *you*." Said Diana.

"Yeah, just because you ditched her, doesn't mean she's going to toss it." Added Cornelia.

"Will you two quit it with the ditching?! Great, just freaking great. Hey, you know? I'm here, she's there, and I'm going to have an awesome time. That's all that matters."

As we finished a desert of apple pie and ice cream, Diana brought up the subject of the importance of dreams and how they related to life. Diana and Cornelia were good at analyzing dreams, so I became curious. I had so many strange dreams that never made sense to me. I decided to have them analyze a few of mine, and the strange events that occurred during my journeys. It captivated them to realize that the strange events in my life and my dreams were so inextricably intertwined, that Diana said,

"OK everyone, remember your dreams tonight. Then we'll talk about them, especially you Dave. I want to see what happens next that connects them. You have a very interesting life."

"What exactly is a dream, anyway?" I asked.

"Dreams, are the 95% of the mind that you don't use, that's in operation. Think of it as the most powerful part of your mind. Dreams are a way that the 95% of your mind expresses solutions, events, and foresight of things to come."

"Oh. So, it's the subconscious?"

"More than that, it might even be the super-conscious."

"The super-conscious? What's that?"

"Think of the super-conscious as the collective unconscious of, I don't know, everything and anything. Think of it like this. Your conscious mind, your day to day mind, is the driver in a car. That's the minuscule 5% we use everyday. It's still important, because it steers you, presses the gas, brakes, and directs you. Now, the 95% of your mind that is the subconscious, that's the car, the engine, and the power. That takes you down the road. Now, the cool thing is, the road, the environment, and how everything interacts with you, that's the super-conscious mind."

"Cool. I never thought of it like that before." I said.

"Not many people do. Very few people realize that in most of their lives, their reality is what they make of it."

"So I can get rid of Fate, right?" I said, hopeful.

"Nope, you can't."

"Why not?"

"If you can get 6 billion people to work with you, then maybe you can get rid of Fate. But, it's so hard to just get one person to work with you. Everybody's mind has a part and a role in the super conscious mind."

"Well, other than the Fate thing, this is too cool." I said.

Later we watched the sunset on the horizon of the lake. The entire sky was blanketed in a dark red, and the blue waters became black, and reflective, and we saw the mirror image of the sunset.

****

I couldn't move. I was absolutely helpless. Nothing about my body worked. My arms floated in front of me, mocking my former strength as I looked at them. I tensed my muscles, only to see that I was completely paralyzed. As I floated there in midair, I stared at the thing that I presumed was paralyzing me. It was a giant ball of light, spinning against a misty background of clouds. I tried to see with my peripheral vision, and I noticed that I was utterly naked, but I felt warm.

"What the hell is going on here?!" I yelled. There was no answer from the ball of light. "Why can't I move?! Who are you?!" I demanded. I tried again to twist around, to see what was going on around me to no avail. "Let go of me!!" I protested. Then a voice punctured the air. I felt like a giant ear as I listened to what it said.

"The quest is quite simple," said the strange, ethereal voice, "The quest is to find Gaia. That is the purpose of your journey. It is your mission. You must journey the world and find her. She is a planetary entity. She does not exist in one place. She is everywhere, yet now where. You must know her. But you must do it in such a way that you yourself do not harm her. By doing this, she will understand your true intentions. You have a long journey ahead of you, David.

Remember. You must see your own world before you can see another. Do not forget what she told you.

Find Gaia, David. You must find her. She's a very young entity. It's time for her to wake up. She should not awake to this current nightmare. No. You need to be there when she wakes up. Find her."

It started to draw me in closer, and my vision began to blur as the light blinded my eyes.

BOOM! My body jerked out of bed. A flash blinded my eyes. My head snapped to the window. I heard rain pouring outside. A lightning bolt flashed, as I felt another thunder burst explode through the sky. I put my head in my heads. My heart was racing.

"What the hell." I muttered. I glanced at my watch. Its iridescent hands glowed, and it reassured me that I hadn't lost any sense of myself. It was 5:30 AM. I moved the curtains aside and saw another lightning bolt illuminate a wall of water falling in the courtyard. "Where am I." I thought. I looked around the room. The dim outlines of my bike, bags, and a sleeping traveler made the darkness real. I was still in Copacabana. I lay back down in the bed, staring up into the ceiling. Another lightning bolt lit the room.

It was the first intense and memorable dream I had in a long time. My mind was blank. My head was still shaking from the dream. My body quivered as I realized that I could move again. I shook my legs and hands as I checked to make sure that I wasn't in another dream. The hot warmth of my body's skin against my hands was reassuring. My shorts were still on, and I wasn't as vulnerable as I was during that dream.

"Ugh," I thought, "this is just going to screw with my mind even more. I'm done with Cuzco and its sites. I did my job." I went back to sleep as the rain came down in torrents.

The next morning, I walked out to the landing dock with Diana and Cornelia. We had plans to take a ferry to the Island of the Sun, the legendary birthplace of the Incas. It was clear outside, and a brilliant, cloudless blue sky welcomed us at eight in the morning. As we got into the ferry, I sat down next to Cornelia.

"So, did you have any interesting dreams last night?" She asked me.

"Oh God. Next time I have a conversation with you two, I am not going to discuss dreams anymore."

"Why, did you have one?" Cornelia asked with sudden interest.

"Yes, and it's been a while since I've had a really intense dream. I had one last night. I think it's significant to this crazy adventure I'm in."

"Do tell." She said.

I described the dream to her, as I watched her green eyes widen.

"That's major," she said, "Fate or destiny is calling to you."

"Yeah, as if all the crazy adventures I've been having haven't been enough."

"Consider yourself lucky. You're in something that at least gives you some sense of purpose. Do you know how many people are out there wandering around without a clue as to what they want to do?"

"Well, yes. But it's not exactly something I wanted to do with my life."

I watched the azure waters of Lake Titicaca. The Islands themselves were sandy in color, with scrub brushes, some eucalyptus trees, and terraced sides for farming. Even though the population of the Island was at most 400 people, it required the resources of the entire island to sustain them, and that didn't include the tourists. Using the ancient farming techniques of the Incans, the islanders produced enough food for themselves, have a surplus for hard times and for us. Aquaculture farms produced trout and pejerrey, adding proteins to their diet. I watched the islanders go about in customs that were thousands of years old, but with modern technology, like their boats and solar panels. Sometimes I wondered about how modernization affected ancient cultures. In this case the cultural effects were benign, and for a small amount of change, they derived an enormous benefit.

I went for a hike with James and Brian, two British travelers. We hiked over enormous boulders that made up the bulk of the trail. They seemed set in place to make a giant, stone path to the northern point of the island. At the northern tip were ancient ruins of a temple, where the Inca went to worship the origins of their people. The ancient legends talked about the islands of the Sun and Moon as a place of great holiness, and from there, the first man and woman emerged, Manco Capac and Mama Occla, birthed by the sun god, and were given a golden rod. From the islands, the couple walked, until in Cuzco, the rod sank into the ground, thus forming the foundations of the Incan Empire. Manco Capac taught irrigation, cultivation of crops, and crafts to the men. Mama Occla taught spinning, weaving, and sewing, to the women.

We swam in the crystal cold waters, and at the highest point on the northern end, I watched a spectacular setting sun, and the crescent moon rose above the blue, red, black waters. Where ever the Inca originated, this desolate, beautiful place, was appropriate for its holiness.

Later that night I spent some time with Fernanda, a Brazilian woman I met on the island. We had a candlelit dinner next to the waves of the lake. The stars glittered over the waters. A light breeze danced on our lips as we sipped the coca tea. We conversed for a while about traveling the world, and what I thought about the USA's actions in Afghanistan. She had tears in her eyes when I told her my thoughts. I read about the Afghani's horrible turmoil four years before September 11th.

"Most Brazilians do not like the US. We think that they are the worst country in the world." She said.

"So I've heard. A lot of people think that way."

She paused before speaking.

"I hate your country. It is because of your country that my people are suffering. When that terrorist attack happened, at first I thought "good, they deserved it", but then I stopped the thought and prayed to God to forgive me for thinking that way. A lot of innocent people were killed that day."

"How can your country be suffering? I thought Brazil was supposed to be like China in its industrialization."

"Ha ha ha! Brazil is more like Bangladesh. Only a few people are benefiting, and they are the ones who have influence or American support. Our real (Brazilian currency) is tied to your dollar. Whenever your financiers decide to play, is when our real drops. Your country also tries to extract so much of our resources without any thought to our country's people. They are like locusts. Our country is left with nothing when your country is done with us, and we're not the only one. Your country is destroying everyone."

I thought about the massive protests I saw in Peru regarding an Amazon highway to Peru's coastline. The protest wanted the highway, since it would provide more jobs, but it was backed mainly by American companies, who wanted the virgin rain forest lumber. A large percent of the Amazon was already clear cut, devastating the ecosystems, native tribes, and biodiversity. Large numbers of species were lost, due to our thirst for lumber. There were more productive and profitable ways to harvest the rain forest without destroying it, but those methods were ignored by the American corporations.

"I came here to Bolivia for a vacation, and I see how the American drug war is destroying these people. You Americans are so ignorant to how other people live and their way of life. You think that you can just come in and destroy someone to stop what is your own problem. It is your people that created the drug market, not them. These people require the coca to cope with the altitude and their working conditions. It is part of their sacred culture." She said.

The ignorance of the coca leaf was rampant in the States. As an example, the US senate authorized the drug war, but they were ignorant of the culture and the geography. One senator said, "we should have a carrier on the Bolivian coastline, and fly jet planes to bomb the coca plantations." Bolivia doesn't have a coastline; it's landlocked. The bombing part of his statement showed what the mentality was. It's simple and thoughtless to rely on high technology to achieve their goals. The USA thought of the world as an enormous video game. On CNN, I listened to the report of a US pilot describe the Afghan war effort as his place in the "Super Bowl". When I heard that, I listened to several British travelers, say, "God, those fucked up Americans."

The current drug war in Bolivia and Columbia was a dirty, nasty business. When the spraying was done and the crops were destroyed, the farmers were left with nothing. They tried rotation programs to grow food crops like yucca or corn, but the profits from those crops barely sustained a family. Tax subsidized factory farms from the US dumped their goods at below the costs of even the poorest farmer. There was no way he could compete. Growing coca for the US cocaine market became the only option, yet no one in the States knew about this. Several billions in tax payers dollars were going out of the States to solve a problem that we created ourselves, and it had no effect accept to raise prices and increase cash flow to the parties involved in the drug war, which included the corporations who manufactured arms, chemicals, and food, and the US and the Colombian government. And as a taxpayer, I was indirectly responsible.

Fernanda opened her jacket, and revealed a t-shirt with the coca leaf on it. It said "Coca is not Cocaine."

"As a judge, I have to see so many cases of people who are suffering, and are arrested simply because they are poor. There is so much suffering. But they are poor because most of the time someone else is trying to make sure they stay poor."

"That's a lot like the US. Homeless people in Boston are put into jail simply because they're poor. Our president also got rid of the real estate tax. He effectively recreated an aristocracy. Even the richest people in the country, like Warren Buffet, opposed it. He said that what Bush was doing was taking away the meritocracy that rewarded effort in the country."

She watched me eat my fried potatoes in silence.

"You... you are strange. I have never met an American like you. You... are critical of your country."

"Look at my face. Do I look like a typical American? I've always been an outside observer, which was difficult socially, but at the same time, it gives me perspective. I also try to see through things and people. I don't like being lied to, and I do believe in what my country originally stood for. I hate the fact that it's being a murdering hypocrite to the rest of the world. I don't like subterfuge and I try to find my own truths."

Fernanda stared at me curiously for a few minutes, before talking again.

"I will go to Vietnam soon. Even though you were born in the US, you still retain much of your family's cultural characteristics, their intelligence and rebelliousness." She said.

"You will love the country and the people. Everyone I know says that out of all the countries of Asia they've been too, Vietnam and Nepal are their favorites. The Vietnamese people are very passionate about all kinds of things: politics, fighting, family, food, art, poetry, and love; especially poetry and love. Some of the greatest poets in Asia were from Vietnam. Ho Chi Minh himself was famous for his poetry. That's his other claim to fame, other than defeating the French and the Americans."

She sipped her tea as she contemplated the dark waters of the night time lake.

"I really admire your family's people and heritage. They've been fighting for freedom against oppressors for so long. First the Chinese, the Mongolians, the Japanese, the French, and finally the US. The US is a superpower country, yet the Vietnamese won. So many of us in South America admire that." She paused before continuing, "come see me in Sao Paulo when you come to Brazil." I looked at her when she said that. I could almost see the Milky Way's reflection in her eyes.

Chapter 15

On the Road to La Paz

I stumbled into Huajtajata, a little town that wasn't on my map, on the out-skirts of Lake Titicaca. It was night time, and I was worn out and aching from the long ride. I walked through the tiny farm village. There were no lights, and all I could see was the shadows of rooftops through the starlight. My legs were soaked after falling into a ditch. I could smell the faint twinges of llama dung. All I wanted was to find some place to sleep, and maybe some cold water to give myself a sponge bath. My right knee quivered. I could feel the ligaments swelling. This was typical, since at about 10:00 PM, most villages were already asleep.

I knocked on the door of a farm house at the waterfront. I had enough with the wandering and pushing of my heavily laden bike. All I wanted was a small corner to prop up my tent and sleep. A woman's voice cut through the air.

"Who is there?"

"Good evening Miss. My name is David. I'm looking for a hostel or a place for a tent."

A small boy's face peeked out from behind the door.

"Sir, there's a hostel over there. In front over there." He said as he pointed.

"Over there? But there are no lights over there."

"Yes, but you have to knock. Knock hard."

"Thank you."

I walked a few blocks until I came to what could've been a parking lot, except it was concrete. There was a two story building, and its dark outline rose up like a tower in the little village of single story homes. I dumped my bike on a telephone pole and walked into the courtyard.

"Hello! Good evening! Is there anybody here?" I yelled. All the dogs in the neighborhood started barking. A light turned on, and it cut like beacon in the pitch black of the lake and the village. As an elderly man walked down the stairs, I felt my knee give out. It held up for 80 kilometers, and now it was time to let it rest. I biked for almost five years, through longer routes than this, but the heavy load on my bike put added stress on my knees. I made a mental note not to get stuck in one place for too long. Two months in Cuzco deteriorated my body muscularly. In the high beam of a flood light, I saw a bright red face come out the door, wrinkled from the sun and age.

"Hi! Please sir, I'm trying to find a room. Do you have one available?"

"Yes, yes."

The old man let me in, and showed me my room in the two story, half finished hostel. There were no working showers. After getting the room and a bucket of water, I gave myself a sponge bath in the cold, and then slept. My body rested on the soft bed, and I felt the weariness of my muscles.

The next morning, I ate breakfast in the restaurant attached to the hostel. There wasn't a single traveler, tourist, or even any locals in the hostel. On the lake, the Aymara worked their nets catching trout. I sat watching the peaceful movement of clouds in the horizon.

I munched on a buttered piece of bread. The dog that barked at me the night before trotted up to me, and pawed me to pet him. Bolivian dogs were much friendlier than Peruvian dogs.

Bolivia is the 2nd poorest country in the entire western hemisphere. Yet, it was largely unspoiled, spectacular in its landscapes and people, and as a whole, it was peaceful. With a landscape that towered above 4000 meters, to lush, tropical rain forests, mountain cloud forests, and everything in between, I was in the Tibet of the Americas. The locals weren't pushy, and the dogs liked to be petted. I liked Bolivia. Its vibe was much more tranquil than Peru. It was also an adventurer's paradise, since it was still untamed, and occasionally, politically unstable.

As I ate, I felt my knee throb. I'd have to spend a day there just to heal enough to bike the next eighty eight kilometers to La Paz the next morning. I made a mental note to sell off the load of tools and spare parts that I carried, in La Paz. It was a lot of weight, and I figured I could travel for another week and a half on those funds. So far, every long term biker I met didn't need spare parts. I met a Canadian couple who were mountain bike touring through Bolivia, and they recommended keeping the parts clean and in good repair.

I walked around the restaurant, and browsed through the newspaper clippings on the walls. There was Thor Heyerdahl, the Norwegian scientist, rogue archaeologist, bane of academic archeology, and captain of the Kon Tiki, the famous balsa raft expedition to the Polynesian islands. Another clipping had Kitin Muñoz, a Spaniard who sailed a reed boat from Arica, Chile midway to Rapa Nui, also known as Easter Island. He sank in the torrid waters. There was an article on Phil Buck, an American explorer and navigator from Ashfield, Massachusetts, who successfully completed a reed boat voyage to Rapa Nui, and was planning another one to Japan, Australia, and the Polynesian Islands.

I looked around me, when I began to realize in astonishment, just where I was. I was in the home of Maximus Catari, chief engineer of the ancient techniques and arts of reed boat building, and he was, with all probability, the only expert in the world in those techniques. The possibility that ancient man was sophisticated enough to explore the world's oceans in these reed boats was captivating. That meant that the entire world was being navigated long before the current time of "academic theory", and by cultures that are traditionally put down as "primitive." My personal dream was to explore the other planets as an astronaut. That's been my focus for as long as I could remember. In truth though, I'm an explorer and a wanderer at heart. So there I was, a former engineer of a NASA rocket project, staying in the hostel of the engineer of some of the most daring expeditions that the world had ever known.

Mr. Catari spent part of the morning and the afternoon taking me through a tour of his little museum, as well as some videos of his crafts exploits. Although what I worked on was exciting, what he worked on was far more daring.

Mr. Catari made reed boats in a way that demonstrated a deep, and sophisticated knowledge. The boats weren't just clumps of reeds held together. They were wrapped in a special way, where the inside cross section of the reed became a sort of pontoon, with a shell of reeds around it. They would make several of these pontoons, each about a foot to two feet wide, depending on the scale of the vessel, making a boat that looked like a reed version of Noah's ark. We walked through his museum, and he let me watch a video of Kitin Munoz's voyage. As he showed me around, I noticed that Mr Catari had a contentedness about him, and it intrigued me.

He appeared to simply be the owner of a tiny hostel and restaurant, and yet he designed and built some of the most intrepid exploration devices known to man. He had fame, recognition, TV appearances, documentaries, everything. Yet, he was perfectly content living in this remote village, making tiny models of boats to sell to the tourists, and making five bucks off of me, the only tourist he's seen in months.

Mr. Catari didn't say much, when I tried to ask him how he felt about his exploits. He just nodded, and smiled, and left the room when I was done with the video. I spent the rest of the day resting, writing, and watching the sunset.

****

La Paz is one of the most beautiful cities in the world. The city is situated inside of a canyon. When I rode on the Altiplano, I saw high, deserted plains, small villages on the sides, and enormous, bare mountains. It was a landscape high, harsh, forbidding, and at times, alien. As I approached La Paz, I still couldn't see it because it's inside the bottom of the canyon, and along the sides. First, I rode through the campesino slum of El Alto, the satellite city that bordered the high plains. Then suddenly, the clouds broke away and an enormous bowl of a city inside the canyon, with great mountain ranges and peaks shimmering in the distance, greeted me. La Paz, even though it's in a canyon, is still 3900 meters above sea level. Clouds and all sorts of micro climates form on the sides.

Sky scrapers stood along side the colonial buildings, while local campesino women populated the streets and markets in their traditional rainbow colored garb and bowler hats. Men with cows walked up the canyon to the markets in El Alto, while a brand new Toyota would drive down the road. It's a city where the ancient, colonial, and the modern have mixed together on all levels. There's a magical charm about La Paz, and it came out when I wandered through the streets and the markets. Maybe it was all the Aymara and Quechua folks dressed in their traditional outfits going to the market

198

and daily life in El Alto, or it was the vibrant student population nearby Sopocachi, where the University of San Andres held classes, or it was the night life of the clubs and expensive restaurants in the warmer, higher air pressure Southern Zone. There was the ancient colonial section higher up the canyon from the city center. I didn't know, I couldn't put my finger on it. The air seemed cleaner, and the people were friendly and vibrant. I smiled, they smiled, everyone smiled! So, I stayed in town for a few days to take care of errands.

At an internet cafe, I found that my brother emailed me that the package of prints and film from the forbidden site had arrived. I initially sent several rolls of film, 2 packages of prints of the strange site, and 2 drawn pictures. When it arrived, he told me that there were no prints, and that the package had been tampered with.

Figure 15.1: Some models of Mr. Catari's boats.

Chapter 16

The World's Most Dangerous Road

"The World's Most Dangerous Road... what a name", I thought as I ascended the heights from La Paz to La Cumbre in the packed micro. I recently met up with two other travelers, Mitch, a British cyclist, and Joe, another American cyclist from Washington. We got together in a La Paz cafe, and then we decided to go and see for ourselves just how dangerous "World's Most Dangerous Road," was. We wanted to take the road for the next sixty kilometers to Coroico, the cloud forest's emerald village which lay in the mountains at the edge of the Amazon.

The road from La Cumbre to Coroico claims about twenty six vehicles a year. That figures to about one vehicle every two weeks falling off the sides of the road to a definite death one kilometer below.

The road was the only route to Coroico and Rurenabaque in the Amazon Basin, and there was no luck in trying to find an alternative route. As a result, most drivers took some time out to pray before heading off down the road.

Presumably, it was a lot safer to traverse the road on mountain bicycles, since bikes were tiny compared to the buses and trucks that drove through. The width of the road in some places was just wide enough for a single vehicle to pass through. Of course, if you're stuck at on one of those sections, than you either got run off into the abyss below, or you flattened yourself on the side of the canyon, and hoped that your head didn't get taken off with a side mirror. The attraction was the sheer downhill. Seventy kilometers of downhill meant several hours of high speed, white knuckle, and moderately technical riding.

We got to the top of the road, where a few Bolivians were having trouble with a flat tire. Joe and I pulled out our patch kits and pumps, and did some dirty work to help repair their bikes. Then we went to the edge, had a lunch of bananas, tossed the peels over the sides, and looked down. We didn't see much, since there were clouds blanketing the entire way. Visibility was about six feet at most.

"Nice bit of pea soup we've got here." I said.

"Alright you girls, let's get going. Vamos." Replied Mitch in his London accent.

"Last one at the bottom is... alive!" I yelled back as I hopped on my bike. Joe laughed at that as he hopped on his bike.

We took off. As soon as I got on the bike, I noticed that we were speeding at about thirty five kilometers an hour, and soon we were flying at fifty five kilometers an hour. Soon, hail pounded our helmets and faces. Visibility was still just six feet, and at the speed we were going, sheer cliffs appeared in front of us instantly. It took some deft maneuvering to handle the curves. I felt like I was flying in a cloud, and my fingers started to freeze up. The first twenty five kilometers was tarmac and relatively safe, but the last thirty five was dirt and rock. Since it was cut into the side of a canyon, with widths in some areas that were just wide enough for a car, and tight tunnels, where any kind of vehicular encounter meant death, I made sure to yell out what was coming up.

We passed by many head stones with plaques, memorializing the numerous victims of the road. Three weeks before us, three cyclists fell to their deaths over a curve, since they couldn't see and react in the mists. Given the risks, we were dancing on the razor's edge.

We dropped about 500 meters in elevation, and I could feel the pressure change in my ears. Crickets made a cacophony around us as we entered the upper parts of the cloud forest. The hail turned into rain, and then a light mist. Mud caked us and our bikes.

As we descended, we looked around to see if the mist would clear. As we rounded a corner, we were able to see the mists clear just enough to see a vehicle on the canyon opposite of us attempting to go through the road. The vehicle moved slowly. Its wheels were right on the edge of the road, off a sheer cliff. I got close to the edge to see if I could see the bottom. I gave up after my eyes scanned down to about a kilometer.

I looked to the vehicle. Dirt and rocks were falling down from where the vehicle's tires were gripping the edge. I watched, and hoped that nothing would happen. Yet at the same time, it felt like watching those tasteless videos on television, where you wanted to see a disaster unfold in front of you. We stood there, mesmerized and watched the vehicle make its way through.

Mitch decided to take off first towards the cliff, and I pedaled after him. There were sections where whole parts of the road were falling off into the abyss. Mitch tossed a rock down, and we strained to hear any impact sounds. Nothing.

"I'd say that's bottomless." I said.

"Shit. That's a bloody long way down." Replied Mitch.

We stared at the tire marks and tracks of vehicles that weren't so lucky. The skeleton of a tire loomed through the mist, and we got the shivers looking at it. We took off again, and this time I took the lead, and headed down the canyon gorge. We stopped at sections where a wall towered above us for hundreds of feet, and a waterfall at the top poured on us. All around us was verdant, tropical cloud forest, and flocks of parakeets. There were other birds, but we didn't see them. We heard them. Their sounds were unlike anything I had ever heard in my life. One sounded like a wooden drum and flute, while another made a "ra ta ta ta twaaaaan" sound. The sound reminded me of an electronic synthesizer. I got off my bike and walked a small portion of the road just to listen to the sounds. Later we saw the giant wing span of a condor, it had to be six feet wide, as it soared the thermals of the canyon. It looked like a Pterodactyl in flight, in our journey into a lost and prehistoric world.

After about four more hours of twists, cliffs, canyons, waterfalls, high speed descents, rocky road, and lots of mud, we came to a turn and saw below the cloud line. The town of Coroico poked through the mists and clouds.

Both Joe and Mitch cycled for the last seven kilometers. It was an uphill of 1000 meters in elevation to Coroico. I tried to keep up with them, but then I encountered engine trouble. My chain kept getting stuck when I shifted, and it forced me to stick with the highest gear. I did a slow motion, and painful cadence up the hill, as I cursed my bike. Along the way I lobbed stones at dogs fiercely guarding their territory.

Cursing your bike for its mechanical problems is unproductive, and yelling attracts inquisitive locals.

"What's this crazy gringo doing, yelling at his bike?" Asked one local. I gave him a dirty look and began walking my bike up the path. I had no vocabulary in my mind to describe the problem. All I wanted was to get to Coroico, take a hot shower, eat some food, and get some sleep.

I looked back at the winding cliff road that came up from the canyon. I did come up a long way, and on a malfunctioning gear too. I relaxed and smiled when I looked westward to the sunset. The red glows highlighted the clouds floating up the forest as howler monkeys made mating calls in the evening. When I arrived into the town, I was exhausted. I sat in a café, muddied and bloodied, and I was a curiosity for the locals passing by.

Figure 16.1: A ten wheeler slowly makes its way down the narrow road, while it's wheels teeter on the very edge.

Figure 16.2: The cloud forest along the walls of the canyon.

Chapter 17

Salar De Uyuni

After a fourteen hour bus ride in a crowded bus without shocks, on unpaved roads, while sitting in the back with a six year old boy clinging to my leg on my left, who lost control of his bladder, a seven year old girl clinging to my leg on the right, and an old man to my right who must've been dreaming about a boxing match since he kept elbowing me through out the night, I finally joined Joe, Mitch and two British school teachers, Brian and Angela for a four day tour of the Southwest deserts. Initially, I wanted to see if I could cross it on my own on the bike. I was glad that I didn't do that. After learning about the conditions, I wasn't in the mood to become a freeze dried platter.

Bolivia is a country of contrasts. In the lowland north and east are humid, tropical rainforest's with some of the highest densities of exotic flora and fauna on the planet. In the southwest is a high altitude, desolate, UV scorched wasteland. The Southwest is coined as the definitive place to see the "Real Bolivia". Most of the Aymara and Quechua peoples inhabit this region of the country, and they've retained most of their ancient cultural traditions. The allure of the southwest was the taste of exploring another planet.

The area, at over 4000 meters above sea level, is a geologist and biologist's dream world. Strange geysers spout, sulfur springs boil, azure blue, bloody red, emerald green, and golden yellow lakes teamed with flamingos. High winds churned the lakes color full waters into a foam that would criss-cross on the shores of the lakes. Geothermal pools provided relief for weary travelers, and huge black volcanoes erupted in the distances. The sulfur springs were warm, but the stench and the yellow mud bubbling wasn't particularly inviting. Giant expanses of desert, smoking steaming volcanoes in the distance, coupled with strange, eroded rock forms were colored with strange green, bright red, fluorescent like orange, browns, and blues from all the seeping mineral formations would leak onto the rocks. The southwest was a cubist painter's nightmare, or dream, and even Salvador Dali couldn't hold a candle to what Nature came up with. The southwest also held secrets that were not found in any book, and I soon discovered one of them on the very first day of the tour.

It's also an area of extremes. Its temperature can go as high as 110 in the day, to minus 30 at night, depending on the season. Without proper protection, a person could get the amount of radiation as a suited astronaut on Mars. Strange life forms and landscapes inhabit the Southwest. Its plant and animal life forms come right out of a bad science fiction movie. I found one evergreen, mossy like plant that felt like a rock. It oozed turpentine like fluids that the locals used as cooking fuel. Odd squirrel looking rabbits hopped among the rocks, feeding off scraps of vegetation.

The prime attraction of the Southwest is the Salar de Uyuni, or the Salt Flats. Affectionately known as the "Salar", it's the remains of an ancient inland sea, which evaporated about 15000 years ago. The sea once stretched from Lake Titicaca all the way down to what is now the San Pedro Desert of northern Chile.

It's also the biggest stretch of salt in the world. When the sea evaporated, it left behind enough sodium to support various economies, and Bolivian exported the salt internationally. The locals gathered salt for their potato chips and salteñas. With all that salt and desert, water is a prized commodity. They also used the salt to build a hotel in the middle of the salt lake, which we visited on the first day.

The hotel was closed, since its sewage was contaminating the salt flat. The people of Uyuni were protesting the pollution, and about two weeks before we arrived, they managed to blockade the entire town from transportation. They also kept a number of foreign tourists from being able to leave the town. It was like a hostage situation. Some of the tourists tried escape at four in the morning in the desert. The problem was they had no idea where they were going, and where they were. It was one of the dumbest decisions I'd ever heard about. For me, I had my bike, so if anything happened, I knew

I could at least get to a small village where some buses ran through.

It was prohibited to enter the hotel, which I didn't know; I managed to find an open window which was out of view, and I went inside. The hotel was completely made of salt. It's furniture, beds, chairs, a pool table, the entire thing was one giant cake of salt. I walked around the empty rooms as I eyed the strangeness of it all. It was like a giant ice house, but one that existed at 95 degrees. I wondered what would have happened had the house been made out of sugar, and it was tempting to just take a lick of one of the chairs.

Once the rest of the tourists saw me inside, they all wanted to go in. As a result, the grounds keeper got into a heated argument with the tour guides about who did it, whose fault it was, and who would be responsible. After fifteen minutes, I decided to end what was becoming a long argument. So, I confessed. As a result, I found myself apologizing to the director, the tour guide, and the grounds keeper for breaking and entering. Personally, I just wanted to get on with the tour.

Later, that day, we went to the Isla del Pescado, where I discovered something out of place. We went to the island to end the day watching a sunset over the vast salt sea. When I got there, I didn't follow the rest of the group, and instead, I hiked a kilometer or more over the harsh, rocky, cactus filled terrain to the very end of the island. I found a cave that had two openings, so there was air flow through there.

There was tropical coral, encrusted on the sides. Coral reef occurs in tropical to subtropical waters, below the sea. The current theory of the Salar was that it rose from the ocean over a period of millions of years. I would've been fine with that theory, if it weren't for one thing. In the high, 3650 meter altitude, with winds that could kick up to forty miles per hour, and with so much corrosive salt and sand, wouldn't that have eroded away, completely, the soft calcium corals? Yet, as I picked up a piece of coral, and noted the lack of erosion, I felt that something else was going on.

We ended up at a small clustered hostel in a tiny agricultural village for the night, where I met two Americans, a man and a woman, Brian, and Jennifer. They were Peace Corps Volunteers, who were working on a sustainability project to get tourism to help the locals. We spent the whole night talking about the salt hotel, and their project. I listened to their stories of trying to find ways to help the locals sustain themselves. The problem was that the locals were trying to sell their hand made textile products to tourists, but not many of the items were actually selling. So, Jenn, one of the volunteers, decided to try and see if she could use the internet to find other designs that could perhaps be more attractive. I thought it was a good idea. If something doesn't work, and you're trying to produce a result, then try another method.

I love the Peace Corps, or more accurately, I love the concept. I had no idea about the politics of the Corps though. They're probably one of the few groups who were presenting what I felt was the true face of American people. Most Americans are represented by our media, our military actions, and our corporations. Going further, what those three groups are doing is opposite of what Americans stand for, or at least, my version of Americans. Yet, the groups who were representing Americans were tiny, underfunded, undermanned, or poorly managed. But to me, the Peace Corps and those NGO's were the real Americans, the ones who actually went out and gave a helping hand. To me, that was America.

I had that view because my parents were Vietnamese refugees, who came over penniless, destitute, and escaping the inhuman horrors from the War. Yet, it was the local "Peace Corps" of American churches, adopted grand-parents, uncles, and aunts who would always give advice to help my parents sustain themselves. What my parents did was almost superhuman in my eyes, but it was Grandma Sue and Uncle John, two protestant senior Americans in the outskirts of Philadelphia who helped my Dad find a way into engineering companies in a time that was still hostile to Asian Americans, or minorities. It was Elizabeth, an elderly woman and widower, who my family affectionately called "Bama" for decades, who gave moral support, Christmas gifts, birthday parties, and thanksgiving dinners. Numerous adopted "uncles and aunts" would also visit and see how we were doing. They were white people, they took us into their lives like we were their family, and they all transmitted that one all encompassing understanding to us. "No free rides, but we will assist you in adapting your traits of strength and independence to America." They were my family's Peace Corps. That was also the motto of the Peace Corps. It was all about empowerment of the self. That was what I grew up with, and that was what I believed in. Yet there were so few out there representing the true USA.

The next day, we got into a discussion about the two Peace Corps volunteers and their efforts. It quickly turned into a heated debate, which was me, versus all of them. The point of it was the salt hotel on the flat. Brian and Angela wanted to stay in it, and they had trouble seeing what the point of the protest was for. They thought it was just as bad when the people went out to harvest the salt, and would take a dump right on the flat. They didn't see the difference. Mitch didn't see the point of closing the hotel, or the whole point of eco-tourism. The whole point of the protest was to close the hotel from polluting the flat, since the flat was where the local communities would gather salt, halides, and other minerals that were consumable for export. It was their livelihood, and obviously, sewage on the salt didn't make the locals too happy. The locals were also contesting the right of the hotel to be on the flat, since it was built by an ex tourism minister, who had connections and money. Ownership rights over the flat are still being contested to this day. Obviously, the Peace Corps were in support of the local people.

Still, closing the hotel didn't make some tourists happy either. I made a point of defending the Peace Corps volunteers and their opinions, since for me, I found it admirable what the people were able to do despite their obstacles.

On the 2nd day, we headed out to see the multi colored lakes, and the brilliant Lago Colorado. The Lago Colorado is a gigantic and brilliantly red lake that was about 5600 meters above sea level. It was extremely cold. During the trip, we spent most of the time watching Mitch get pissed at the driver for not being able to hook up a radio for some tunes. I decided to take a walk around the multi colored lakes in the area.

The Lago Colorado's brilliant red hues are created by a nasty mix of dissolved minerals and floating microorganisms. The shores of the lake are pure white. I walked around on the high hills surrounding the outpost, gazing at the desolate, cold, and its remarkably beautiful landscape. I watched the sun set behind me, as its golden orange hues turned a strange volcanic looking mound into an enormous mouth. I felt like I was being swallowed by a Bolivian giant.

Later that night, I dined with the Canadians, Jen and Anne. Dan later joined us. Dan's a Canadian who worked full time with an NGO in Cochabamba. Anne was Sara's daughter, the Canadian energy lady who helped me in Cuzco. I hadn't seen Anne since I ran into her and Jenn in La Paz at a club. Still, we were on the "gringo" trail, where most backpackers tended to run into each other over large distances. I reminded myself to leave that trail. We caught up on what happened since then. Anne wanted to know more about what I had discovered.

"Do you have any idea why they would take your prints?" Anne asked.

"No. I mean, what can they tell from it? The only thing I can think of that would be significant would be the arch. The spiral forms are common at most of the world's sacred sites. But a giant megaton arch? That's uncommon, especially here."

"Any idea who would take the photos?" Asked Anne.

"No. That's what bugs me the most. There were eight film cannisters in there. Why didn't they take those cannisters? Whoever it was left everything behind except for the two packages of prints."

"Well Dave, I can tell you this. The mountain is a major Apu for the locals. That mountain is incredibly sacred, and it's forbidden for outsiders to go there." Said Dan.

"The other thing to remember Dave, is that what you've found might have been deemed so sacred that those people might know the right ones to track you down and, well, relieve you of your photos."

"That doesn't explain the military presence though."

"The military activities are recent. It's more to do with the rebel groups nearby."

"Oh, the Montevideos. That still doesn't explain why a tiny Cessna recon plane would risk its life buzzing us."

"Yeah, that is pretty weird. I don't know man. All I can recommend to you for now is to lay low and have a good time, eh?" He replied.

"It's not normal for things like that to disappear out of the package though, is it?" I asked.

"Definitely not. They do sometimes open packages to inspect them. But they don't take things out. Whoever did this had to know who you are, and what they were looking for."

The thought of being monitored by some unknown entity disturbed me. Still, if someone was following me, then with my luck I was going to run into them one way or the other.

We got up at four in the morning to head out to the sulfur springs and the hot water baths. After three days of not bathing, it was paradise. Even though the air was just twenty degrees above zero, it was that need to just let all the dirt, grime, tension, and ache out of my bones. Laying down next to three Swedish women in bikinis also helped to heighten the experience.

Later, we entered an area with some of the strangest rock formations I had ever seen in my life. The powerful winds combined with the sand formed a high powered sand blaster, and it gave Nature a wonderful tool to carve with. It was also enticing when I saw the innumerable handhold's that I can grab onto. Obviously, I couldn't resist.

My folly was at the peak when I was at that height without a harness and a rope. I wasn't that experienced yet to try free hand climbing, so I figured that at most four meters would be safe. The problem is that it's difficult to judge heights when you're on the wall and looking down. I also didn't consider that in order for the wind to carve the rocks into such strange formations, the rocks had to be soft. When I was sprawled on the wall, I decided to hold on to one hand hold and rest my other hand. Some people watched me, and I also got a little cocky. That was my downfall. I swung my body around to take a look, and then I turned back. When I turned back, my handhold broke.

I checked my two ribs to see if I re cracked them. After falling seventeen feet the first thing I said was, "Ow."

I took a look at my chest and stomach. I could feel the sting, and I watched the blood drip out of the scratches on my stomach and two very bruised ribs. I was lucky that Mitch pressed me right up against the wall as soon as he could reach me in my descent. The friction broke my fall considerably. Still, it left an indelible mark on my body. I silently scolded myself, as Jen gave me some antiseptic cream.

"Sheesh, Dave."

"I know, I know, I have a habit of getting myself into a pickle. Well, it was a fun climb, despite the fall."

"Yeah, but it wouldn't have been fun if you broke something."

Later that night, in a small dusty town, I cleaned up the wounds, and sat down to a game of cards with my group. Then later on, it was just me, Jen and Anne in the dining hall. I attempted to teach them poker, since they never learned how to play.

The last day of the trip was the long drive back to Uyuni. Everyone was in a good mood. It was the end of the trip, we'd seen a lot, and we knew we'd soon be back to some sort of civilization and personal space. We watched herds of llamas and the rarer vicunas graze in the rare river valleys and streams.

We went back into town, and hung out at the restaurant, where I met another American woman, Janine, a blond, 30ish teacher from Boston. She was getting ready to take the tour, and we traded tips and travel advice. Suddenly, I heard a thunderous roar rumble into town, and then suddenly stop. Curious, I walked to the hostel, to see what was going on, when suddenly, I heard a familiar, feminine voice say,

"Well, now there's a familiar face!"

In the courtyard, five motorcyclists took off their helmets, one by one. Each one was pale, and bearded, except when the shortest one took off the helmet, and I saw a shock of red hair fall out over a lovely face.

"So, how's Mr. Mystery Man doing today? Did ya find the lost golden toilet paper roll holder for the dysfunctional Peruvian lavatory ruins?" The woman joked as she looked me in the eye with a grin.

Michelle! We hugged each other.

"Hey! Well, I did find a working toilet. Now that's a treasure. You made it back! I thought you were never going to make it back with all the crap going on."

"Me? You're talking to the lady that managed to sneak marijuana past the borders of Nepal, Tibet, and India, and all three have customs where you're in prison and dead for drug smuggling. You think something like that could keep me from coming back? I'm not going to let you hog all the adventure. So, what's happened to you since I left?" She asked.

"A whole lot of shit went down. More than you can imagine. I'm still barely digesting it right now."

"More of that weird energy stuff, huh?"

"Yeah, but right now, it's over for the moment, and I'm having fun. Where did you ride in from?"

"Remember how I had my eye on a motorcycle in Cuzco?"

"Yeah. This is it?" I said as I pointed to her Yamaha.

"Yup."

"So, where'd you meet El Loco Max and the gang?" I said as I made a thumb point to the her companions. One of them looked at me, I smiled to him, and he grinned back at me.

"Oh these guys? They're Colombian. They know what goes on down here, so they've been showing me how to get through some pretty dangerous areas. It's easier when you have someone who knows the lingo and knows how to get through things."

"Awesome." I shook hands and said hello to the Colombians. They were headed in to a bar for some beer.

"Let's get some food and catch up, Dave. It's been a while, and I want to know what's going on with you."

We ordered a pizza in the local cafe near the plaza.

"Did you find anything out about the San Pedro plant?" She asked.

"Only that it's an Andean cactus, and it's so holy that only Shaman's can properly use it. They use it for their spirit visions."

"Nothing I don't already know. Anything else?"

"Just that there's another plant that's far more sacred, I think it's called Ayahuasca. Michelle, I'm curious about you're doing. What exactly are you trying to do here, I mean, I know you're documenting the effects to prove the Shaman's access to some kind of knowledge."

"It's part of my studies in ethno-botany."

"Ethno-botany?"

"It's the study of the cultural uses of plants and cultures, and how it gives them access to other realms of consciousness, awareness, and maybe even to God."

"Does that mean they used drugs? I mean plants?"

"No. What they did was put their bodies through such extremes that the brain chemistry was stimulating the production of the very same chemicals that are already in the plants that these shaman's consume, and that was when they had their visions. I saw that happen in Tibet, where these monks would fast for days, and when they gave them the chemical, it didn't do anything to them. They were already producing it."

"What do you think Michelle? Do you think these visionary states are the results of a delirium?"

"What's the definition of a delirium, and according to whose standards. Your reality isn't my reality, or vice versa."

"Good point."

"The interesting thing is between the shaman's and the monk's, there's a lot of consistency with what they're seeing. We're talking about two sides of the world, who aren't in communication with each other."

"What's the consistency?"

215

"They see patterns that are the same. Same forms of creatures, like elves, or alien like beings. The monk or the shaman is in a fully conscious state, but they're in a different reality. What's odd is that the two of them see the same thing, or they describe the same thing. So, with that consistency, we have a possibility that just maybe, they're seeing another world in parallel with ours."

We finished dinner, and played a Bolivian game of dice called cachi with Mitch, and then called it a night. The next day, we parted ways, and Mitch, Joe, and I went to Potosi, in the Southeast, where we separated.

Figure 17.1: The Salar de Uyuni.

Figure 17.2: The hotel made of salt.

Figure 17.3: Isla del Pescado (Island of Fish) on the great salt desert, the remains of what was once an enormous sea.

Figure 17.4: The remains of a coral reef, without major marks of wind erosion in a cave passage way, in the Isla del Pescado. Photo by Anthony Khan.

Figure 17.5: Powerful wind erosion carves some strange forms out of the rocks in the desert.

Chapter 18

Potosi

When I decided to check out the Collective Silver Mines in Potosi, I carried around enough explosives in my courier bag to take out one or two military tanks. The collective mines are a legacy of Spanish enslavement. The city and the mines of Potosi were the source of capital for the entire Spanish empire. When they discovered the mines, they took every single Aymara and Quechua they could find, and enslaved them into the most inhuman conditions in the world to finance their empire. When many of the indigenous people were dead, they brought millions of Africans slaves to mine the mountain. Because the Africans weren't adapted to the extremely high altitude, they died even faster than the indigenous. The few Africans who survived, escaped to the Yungas region, where they became an Aymaran speaking tribe.

The legend stated that enough silver was mined from Potosi to build a bridge from Spain to South America, and they'd still have plenty left over to carry to Spain. After looking at how Spain today still has a financial legacy from those mines, I'd say they could have built even more. Just two years earlier, one of the collectives found an untapped silver vein, and in the lode, they bought homes, cars, and some property. Stories and events like that continue to motivate the miners, and today, even though most of the mines have been tapped out, the miners still continue the tradition of mining out of choice, and for the prospect that they might one day strike it middle class. Still, it was the job from hell.

When we got to the mines, we carried items with us to give to the miners. The miners are among the poorest people on Bolivia, and they couldn't afford many of the things that kept them productive. Even basics, like simple dust masks were out of reach for many. Most miners died by the age of 30, from either the high concentrations of asbestos, silicosis, black lung, cancers from the witches brew of chemicals that floated through the mine, or from getting lost. The locals found mummies of miners who lost there way in the labyrinths.

Even more died from dynamite accidents, gas explosions, and cave falls. Yet, they continued to work. They would work 36 hours straight, before going home to sleep, and then continue the next day. Cocoa leaves were vital for them to do this. The coca leaves removed any sense of hunger or a need to sleep. They became organic robots, stopping maybe to eat a little, or go to the bathroom where they were. They didn't wear protective masks, and many didn't even have flashlights. They used acetylene torches as a source of illumination in the depths.

When we got to the entrance of the mine, the first thing the guide did was inspect the dynamite. I had a fuse, a cap, a couple sticks of dynamite and batch of nitroglycerin. The guide, Eduardo, put the parts together to form the final explosive: He stuck the blasting cap at the end of the fuse, inserted it into the dynamite stick, and then put the stick in the bag of nitro-glycerin. Then he took it out of the bag. Then he lit the fuse while holding the dynamite with his teeth. I noticed he was missing a couple of teeth, and I wondered if a blasting cap blew up near his mouth. He then handed the thing to me, lit and smoking, to inspect the detonator cap. He gave me a warning as he handed the live explosives to me.

"You must be careful! Because, when the cap is activated, you will be blown to bits." He said.

I peered into the stick, noting that the cap was deep inside. I had about four minutes left of fuse before it released it's energy. I gave the stick back to him. He took the stick, and put it back into the small bag of nitroglycerin.

"How powerful is the explosive?" I asked Eduardo.

"You can take out an armored vehicle if you put this in the right place."

He gave it to a nine year old girl who was selling minerals from the mines. She took the smoking explosive, sniffed it, then inspected it for a minute, looked at the guide, smiled, and then casually sauntered off into the distance with the explosive. After putting the explosive down next to a pile of rubble, she bolted back to us, and hid behind a rock. Everyone ducked down, while I stood up. I saw Eduardo was standing, so I trusted him to know what the blast radius was. I put my fingers to my ears.

KABOOM! A huge cloud erupted into the air, and the pressure wave washing over me was immense, as the ground shook. Bits of debris, blown by the blast fell on us. That was just one stick of the dynamite and a small bag of nitroglycerin in my bag. We would give the rest to the miners, and they would explode the things with us in the mines.

We followed Eduardo in for about ten minutes into the tunnels. The ceilings were low, since they were designed for the campesino's height. As we plunged into the depths, I noticed that the Korean girl behind me held her torch a little too close to my bag.

"Myung! Will you watch where you point that thing?" I said to her with an urgent voice.

"Huh? Oh, I'm sorry David. I forgot you have several bags of explosives with you." She said as she moved the torch further back.

Myung was a traveler from South Korea, and she spent a couple of months in Peru, before heading into Bolivia. She loved to travel, and we decided to take the tour together. The further we went in, the more cramped, stuffy, and damp it got. The further in I went, the more the walls of the cavern would close in on me. The miners carried the minerals out on their backs, so there was no room for a rail and cart. The floors were damp and wet, and I felt the coldness go through a hole in my boot. When we got to a wider area in the mine, I watched as a fourteen year old boy and his mentor pounded spikes into the walls. They made deep holes to put the dynamite in.

Three blasts rocked the cave, as muffled sounds rattled the earth all around us. I watched as the debris fell down on both our sides. The blasts didn't deter the two workers. They just kept pounding away at their stakes. TANG! TANG! TANG! The ringing of the stakes made my ears buzz. According to Eduardo, the average miner started work at the age of thirteen. Many worked as ordinary workers, but this boy in particular was an apprentice to an explosives mentor. In twelve years, the boy would become an explosives mining expert.

"How much do they get paid to do this?" I asked.

"Twenty bolivianos a day."

Twenty bolivianos a day was about $2.94. In one week, that amounted to

$20.58. It was no where near what the average Bolivian needed to survive. We descended further into the deeper shafts of the mine. I looked around the walls. We were about a hundred meters underground, and the air weighed on us. I shone my lamp onto the wall. There were millions of crystalline like hairs hanging off the walls. It made the wall almost furry and alive, and I was tempted to pet it. I was glad I didn't. The guide said the fur was naturally occurring asbestos, which resulted when the minerals mixed with water and seeped through the porous rocks out into the open.

I wondered how many years of my life were shortened by the exposure to the asbestos in the room. I reassured myself as I realized that the fibers usually settle into the ground, and that to get any kind of effect, a person had to be bathed in it, and be a smoker as well. Since the ground was wet, it kept the fibers from rising into the air. We ascended up a ladder from the room, into another tunnel, and then into another room. Inside the room was a red plaster statue of the devil with an enormous penis.

"This is Uncle George. He rules the depths down here. Above the earth, is God in heaven. Under is the Devil in Hell."

Eduardo poured some rubbing alcohol on the dick.

"When you do this, it is for good luck, for when you mine, or when you go home to your woman. Because so many of the miners are macho, they try to show how macho they are. So they have six or seven kids at a time. For good luck, they pour alcohol on George's penis."

He poured some more alcohol on the dick, stopped, took a sip, and then poured the rest on. I figured he was in the mood for some fun with his wife that night. Still, the more I thought about it, the more I realized just what people meant when they said that Bolivia was the poorest country of South America. A miner had to support six kids on a salary that didn't even support one human being. In addition the women had no control over their reproductive rights. As a result, many of them had children they couldn't support, and many of them were abandoned by the men.

I watched as a ten year old boy walked in to meet us along with the other older miners. They all had a puffy left cheek. The cheek was stuffed with coca leaves, which they chewed and activated with ash or lime. He had a confident swagger, like he was one of the big boys of the caverns. I shook his hands and gave him the bag of coca leaves that I brought with me. Ten years old, and he was working in what really was the job from hell. He didn't act like any ten year old I knew in the States. He acted like a small version of an adult, and held himself with a confidence and knowledge that no American child ever could. I had trouble believing it. The conditions were appalling, and here was a little boy working to support his family! I shook my head as I watched him. The conditions put him into this, and made him grow older than he seemed. I felt spoiled and petty after seeing that.

"Sometimes, we miners become lost in the mines. When that happens, in about 48 hours, if no one comes to find you, you will die. I have brought out many mummies of dead miners who became lost in the mines for many days. I once became lost for three days. I had to drink my own piss to survive. I was very lucky, because then my brothers and sisters came to find me. After that, I decided to quit." Said Eduardo.

"So now you just guide people here." I said.

"Yes. It is better for me and my family. Better pay too. But not everyone can do what I do, because I can speak English."

Eduardo continued his story about Uncle George.

"There is a story with Diablo and the miners. He walks among us in the mines. No, he doesn't look like this nor does he have a big penis. He looks like us. You will only meet him when you are alone. He will ask you if you want to find a rich vein of silver. If you do, he will ask you to give him your soul. When you agree to do that, then you will find the vein. But there is a price. The price is you must give him your soul, and then you will be his. And so will your children."

I gave the rest of the explosives to the miners, and watched them smile. They shook my hands, and said thank you, before they ran off into a hidden corner of the mines. After ten minutes, they came back.

"We must immediately leave now!" said Eduardo. The miners planted the charges, and we had about fifteen minutes to get the hell out before the caves shook with a tremor akin to an earthquake. We hurried out of the cave, into the welcoming glare of the midday sun. At 4500 meters above sea level, Potosi was one of the highest cities in the world, and the clear light striking us was painful to our unadjusted eyes.

I felt three tremors shake the earth underneath me, and then silence. Dust floated out of the cave opening as we got into our return vehicle.

I looked back as we went down from "Cerro Rico", or *"Rich Hill."* Witnessing those conditions troubled me. I wondered how many of my friends

225

would suddenly wake up to a shocking grasp of just how bad a shape most of the world's people were in. I didn't want to think of the number of times I had to endure listening to friends talk about how lousy their job was. I didn't want to listen to myself about how lousy my job was.

Figure 18.1: Eduardo holds a lit fuse, dynamite stick, nitroglycerin bag, and blasting cap in his mouth.

Figure 18.2: I try my hand at making a blast hole in the mine shaft.

Chapter 19

Sucre

After a haircut in a traditional barber shop that looked like something out of the early 19th century, where a pleasant barber cut my hair with hand held clippers, and then shaved me with an open razor blade, which, incidentally, was the closest shave I ever had in my life, I spent some time in Manazana Magica, a vegetarian café that was nearby my hostel. I took a look at my budget so far for the rest of the year. At most, I was spending about ten dollars a day, and this already factored in hostels, good, sufficient amounts of food three times a day, Spanish language classes, and side tours. At this rate on my current travel funds, I could travel for about eight or nine more months. Travel is not expensive. One of the problems that most Americans have is they think travel is expensive. Then again, most of them go to Europe, where it was comfortable to travel. My only real cost was my plane ticket, which was $800 for the round trip.

I thought about that as I worked out my budget, and had a spicy, filling gluten and lentil soup that Frank, the Bolivian restaurant owner, cooked up for me. I sat back to savor the richness of the soup. It'd been a while since I had a decent meal, but I didn't have long to take it in.

BOOM! The restaurant shook. I looked around in shock. Cerro Rico was kilometers from here. Any explosion would be muffled by the mountain. That blast sounded close. "Plop", something fell into my soup. I looked up at the ceiling as more small rocks fell on my face. I turned and looked at Frank.

"What's going on?"

"It's a protest of the miners. They're marching, but, I think they are also using dynamite."

I ran out the door to take a look. The sounds of chanting rumbled in the distance. As I left the door, Frank called out,

"Where are you going?"

"I want to see what's going on?"

"You crazy enough to want to die?"

"No, I just want to see what's going on."

I walked down the hill to the main street, and there, before me, was a large group of miners marching in protest. One of them was holding some kind of stick. It sparkled. It was dynamite, and it was lit.

Next thing I saw, he threw it in my general direction. A group of school girls in uniform in front of me ran towards me, with a look of hysterical panic in their eyes.

"Run you idiot!"

A little one screamed at me, as I stood there, watching in dumb fascination as the dynamite arced up through the air. It felt like slow motion. Everything seemed to move like molasses. It then occurred to me that I fully understood what the little girl was screaming at me. So, I turned, and started to run back to the restaurant.

I took one step, then two steps, and then three steps. Time moves very slowly when you're anticipating something huge. Suddenly, I couldn't hear a thing.

BOOM!! The shock wave of the explosive was unbelievably close, as I felt the pressure roll right through me. I shook myself after the blast was over, wondering if anything embedded itself into my back. As my hearing began to come back, I dusted myself off, and looked around to see if any of the school kids were hurt. None of them were. I ran back to the safety of the restaurant.

"Yes, you are right. They certainly are using dynamite"

Frank looked me over, smiled, then said, *"you're shocked? I told you so. Next time, if you're not careful, you won't be walking"*

Because of my re-found distaste for hanging out with tourists, I stayed with the locals. So, I wandered into a university gymnasium to watch a local university groups and clubs from the practice for the folk festival to occur that night. After that, I spent the night watching folk music, chaco dance, which looks like a blend of morrison dancing with cowboy outfits, saya, an African derived dance that was now part of the Yungas, and Tinkuy, a dance straight from the Incan Empire.

Tinkuy is one of those cultural traditions that failed export or presentation in other countries, and for good reason. The basis of tinkuy is it's a festival where everyone, men and women, get together as equals. On the first day, there's synchronized dancing to tinkuy music, which is the ancient and traditional music of the Andean regions. It's a combination of songs, Andean flutes, the charango, a kind of tiny strumming instrument, and drums. They were dressed in rainbow like costumes with helmets that looked similar to a Spanish conquistador's helmet, but with feathers, and in a coordinated dance, moved to the beat with flair and beauty. It looked like a cross between hip hop and martial arts. Then that night, they all go out to binge drink.

They drink rubbing alcohol because it's easy to get plastered quickly. The next day, in a drunken stupor, they brawl. Challenges are issued, insults are thrown, people are accused of stealing, robbing, having affairs, cheating, you name it. Rocks are thrown, and then they start pounding each other. The whole point of the second day is to beat someone to take care of vendettas. People often die, and the deaths are considered a sacrifice to the PachaMama. I imagine the Incans sanctioned this as a way for the people to let out their aggressions on each other, as opposed to the empire.

The version I saw that night in the University hall was the ritual sobriety before the drunken stupor. That was the opposite of Boston's student parties, where there's an orgy and dance of idiocy first, and then a day after of hangovers and sobriety afterwards. I had a rude reminder of that as I hiked up the mountain back to the hostel. Even though I was well acclimatized and I didn't drink, I abruptly had a fainting spell.

First, I walked up the mountain, and then suddenly the sky fell on top of me, or did I fall on top of the concrete? I laid there for a few minutes to get my bearings and head back. Luckily, I didn't hit the ground hard with my head, as my sides cushioned the fall. What happened to me? Was I too high in altitude? Potosi was 4090 meters above sea level, which made it the highest city in the world.

Or was it because earlier in the day, while wandering the central square area, which was a mix of an outdoor and indoor market, I walked by a place where a woman saw me, who bore a striking resemblance to Kendra? When

I walked by the shop, a shoe store, I glanced in and saw the woman, as she suddenly looked at me. I continued past, and suddenly stopped. "Did I just see... no." I turned around, and walked back to the shop. She wasn't there. I walked into the shop, where the women behind the counter came out to help me.

"Hi! Excuse me, but, was there a woman here, just a moment ago with dark eyes, and long dark hair?" I asked.

"Sir, all the women here have dark eyes and long dark hair."

One of the girls giggled.

"Oh. Thanks."

The next day I went to Sucre, the spiritual and judicial capital of Bolivia. Currently, the legislative and seat of government capital of Bolivia is in La Paz, but Sucre is still considered the constitutional capital, and it was one of the most beautiful cities in all of South America.

It's also the educational capital, and the University of San Francisco Xavier is older than Harvard University. The University was famous for producing the "Doctors of Charcas", leaders who were famed in their exploits for liberty, revolution, and for freedom from the Spanish empire. And Sucre, like any other educational capital, with a young and healthy intelligent population, was also prone to protests.

Lots of protests. It seemed to be a favorite past time of the people in Bolivia. Everywhere I went, I saw newspapers, TV reports, and in front of me, people being angry at their conditions. It was like that old joke about an American president's wife who went to Mexico. She went to a bullfight, and the Mexican president said "this is our favorite past time." The first lady, who was an avowed animal lover, replied, "That's revolting!!", to which the Mexican president replied, "No, that's our 2nd favorite past time!!"

I experienced enough of Bolivia to get a handle on what the favorite past time was. It was easy to see why they revolted. Bolivia is the most corrupt nation in the western hemisphere, but unlike Mexico, few people got a part of that corruption. In Mexico, everyone knew the government was corrupt, and that everyone would get a piece of the action. That's why Mexico still managed to function. In Bolivia, people knew there was corruption, but they didn't know who was corrupt, or how to get a piece of the pie.

Economic liberalization programs, where many national utilities were sold off and privatized under International Monetary Fund and World Bank conditions for loans, decimated their society. The companies were bought by international corporations, who ran roughshod over human and environmental rights. The most infamous was an American multinational, Bechtel Corp., who bought a Cochabamba water utility. As soon as the company gained control, Bechtel stopped all repairs, turned off services, and then jacked up the price. Water is life, and understandably, the people protested. Several people were killed, and Bechtel left the country, but not before attempting to penalize the Bolivian government for financial compensation for "lost future revenue".

One night, I saw a giant procession of students, professors, teaching assistants, and administrators walking down the street carrying torches, and shooting fireworks into the air. They were all chanting, and in the early hours of the evening, it was like a long blanket of fire lazily creeping over the ground. Naturally, I got curious. I started walking with them, and became friends with Roberto, an administrator at the university. We talked about what the march was for.

"Why are you walking with the students?"

"Because we are protesting the Director's administration. He had 10 million dollars for the university, but now there is no money. Nothing. No one knows where it went. Corruption here is horrible, and afterwards, the students suffer a lot from it."

I continued with the crowd and Roberto until we got to a large intersection in a residential neighborhood.

"Where are we going?"

"Ah ha ha! To the Director himself! And we're gonna show the Boss what we can do!"

I didn't like the sound of that. I stopped in the middle of the intersection, and watched the students surround a section of the residential area. Then I heard explosions, as a group of students started running towards me. What started as a group, became a horde. They were in a rush to get away. In the distance, I saw policemen in bulletproof vests and riot shields. One of them aimed a thick pipe like thing in my direction.

POP! I watched smoke come out of his pipe device. Then, immediately, about two meters from me, something exploded, and a white mist started to flow out. It was teargas

I started walking, calmly, to the side of the road, looking for a way out.

The police blocked off certain sections, and more canisters of gas exploded nearby me. I found an open door, and a pretty Bolivian girl stared at me. We looked at each other for a few seconds, before she looked out the door, grabbed, and pulled me in. She shut the door behind us. She smiled at me after closing the door, as we listened to more exploding canisters of gas go off nearby. Below the steps was an evangelical Christian congregation, but since some of the women veiled their heads, I thought I walked into some kind of mosque. As the the gas canisters exploded, she gave me a handkerchief to cover my nose and mouth. As she did so, she looked at me, and smiled.

"What's your name?" I asked her.

"Janeth. And you?"

"David. Nice to meet you"

I kissed her on the cheek. Her brown skin glowed when I did that. I watched her Quechua features glisten in the air, and as we stood next to each other, I felt the heat from her body.

The custom in South America is when you meet a woman, you kiss her on the cheek. That came naturally to me. I like to kiss, but I was also instantly attracted to her. It was the same for her likewise. After that, we couldn't keep a distance of more than half a foot from each other.

Bolivian women are beautiful. Come to think of it, South American women, in the Andes regions, are beautiful. Most of Bolivia's population is majority Aymara, Quechua, with the rest being mestizo, with small minorities of black, white, east Asian, and Arabic. Their mixed features remind me of Italian, Arabic, Latin, or south Indian women who I formerly dated. It drove me nuts walking through the main plaza of Sucre. There were beautiful women everywhere. Everyone walked and the ladies immediately engaged my eyes and held my gaze.

Janeth and I conversed for a while, as we waited for the teargas to disperse a bit. I asked her if she wanted to go out to a café. She demurred, and we sat down to two fruit-shakes and wrote love poems in Spanish to each other. Then we walked through the city plaza, sat down on a bench, in the park on a warm Sucre night amongst the palm trees, and talked for a while.

The next thing I knew, we were in each other's arms, and making out like an eager high school couple. I checked my watch and noticed that three hours passed. After a while, we conversed some more.

"So, do you have a girlfriend in your country?" She asked.

"No, I don't have one." I replied.

She gave me a funny look.

"You're sure you don't have a lover?"

"Absolutely! There are girls I'm very attracted to in the USA, but no definite girlfriends."

We made out for a long time after that. Then she asked me the million dollar question.

"Tu estas mentiroso?" When I heard her say the word mentiroso with such a seductive, beautiful voice, I thought it was a lovely word. But I didn't know what it meant. I flipped open my pocket Spanish dictionary, and hunted for the word. She stared at me as I searched frantically, but I didn't want to lose the moment so I closed the book, looked her in the eyes with a smile, and seductively said,

"Si, si. Yo soy mentiroso. Yo soy mentiroso grande!"

Mentiroso means liar. Here's the translation.

"Are you a liar?"

"Yes, yes! I am a liar! I am a grand liar!"

Her facial changes were abrupt. I'd never seen someone's facial expression instantaneously turn into something completely different so quickly. One moment, her face was one of pure, lovely, radiating ecstasy, and suddenly, in the next, her face was regarding me with suspicion, confusion, and caution. I looked back at her, smiled, and asked, "what's up?"

"Oh, nothing. I have to go now."

"Oh, well, I'll walk you home."

"OK."

I saw her one more time after that, and she took me to an evangelical church for our date. We had a very romantic evening sitting on the hard cold pews, with her making sure I was paying attention to the preacher, and me trying not to fall asleep. I guess she wanted me to repent for being a liar. I never saw her again after that.

****

For two weeks, I stayed in Hostal Sucre on Calle Arenales (Arenales Street). Each morning, I got up and went for a walk around the city, to a park, a museum, or a café. I often went to the markets, just to drift away into

235

a backdrop of hurriedness and white noise of the campesinos vending their products. Sometimes I sampled some of the local fruits, a pear, a peach, a succulent, and sweet chirimoya, and if I felt really adventurous with my digestive system, a fruit shake at one of the many health stands. It surprised me to see the signs above the stands, which said, healthy shake, protein enriched, vitamin full, or sweet without the carbohydrates. At the stands were brown Quechua women, their strong features smiling at me, as I sat down and drank the rich, sweet, and creamy glass, while reading a newspaper.

Mornings were bright blue, cool, and there was a dry San Diego like climate desert air that was cool, but fresh. The diesel fumes from the public transit added some flavor to the air, but not in a smoggy blanket, like Lima, but in a slight touch, where the taste of a bus as it went by simply meant there were many people inside. Quechua, Aymara, Mestizo, and creole walked to work, classes, or to eat. By the afternoon, I'd go to Restaurant Kaypicchu, a popular international flavored vegetarian restaurant, where two gentlemen, Marco and Roberto, served lunch. Kaypicchu means "Here it is" in Quechua.

Roberto was a Peruvian who escaped the terrorism of the shining path guerrillas in Peru to the peace of La Paz. He was about an inch shorter than me, with short cropped, graying hair that was slightly balding, and he always had some stubble of a two days old beard. One of his eyes was slightly off center, and it had some discoloration of gray. Roberto had seen a lot; he was mature, and calm in the way he dealt with people. However, behind his seriousness was a laughing heart; he always took the time to enjoy a good laugh. When he spoke with me, his speech was relaxed, and well paced, and it afforded me the time to understand and absorb what he had to say.

Marco, was the opposite. Younger than Roberto by about 10 years, he sported a full head of black hair that was always combed back, and he was full of hyperactive energy, that came out in bursts when he laughed. He was the main waiter for the restaurant. He was also about an inch shorter than me, with a big Basque nose, and a grin. Marco was native to La Paz, and he had teasing quality about the way he spoke.

The outside of the restaurant was on a corner intersection inside of a large, two story colonial building from the 1800's. Kaypicchu was on the second floor, above a pharmacist and a doctor's office. A large wooden plaque said "Kaypicchu" outside, and I walked through the large, heavy, wooden double doors into a small courtyard, turned up the wooden stairs with a heavy banister, and walked to the second floor. The restaurant had high ceilings, waxed, wooden floors that creaked, and a cavernous dining hall that echoed. It was furnished with finished wooden tables and stools, and on the walls, the restaurant felt more like an art gallery than a place to eat. There were paintings, cubist paintings, and I developed a fondness for one painting, which was a canvas of a naked woman in a techno colored dream scape.

On this day, I came in at noon. Marco greeted me with surprise as I sat down and opened up the menu for lunch.

"You're here early." He said as he looked at his watch, *"it's noon. Don't you usually arrive at 2PM?"*

"Yes, I am early. I slept earlier last night."

"Ah. Less partying with the ladies?" He smiled.

"Me? What's your definition of partying with the ladies? Like getting dropped with Janeth? I don't want to do that again."

Marco laughed.

"Señor, you need to work on your vocabulary"

"Yes, on that subject, do you know of any good tutors around here?"

"Just one. Did you try the Spanish American academy?"

"Yes. I visited, but I don't want to do any more classes like that. I want one on one instruction."

"Maybe one of the Peace Corps can help you."

"There's Peace Corps here?"

"Yes, many. Let me ask one of them for you to find you a tutor."

"Well, while I look for one, I need to work on my conversations. Do you know if there are local students who will do that in exchange for English conversations?"

"Hmm, let me ask one for you. Oh it is lunch time Señor. Would you like something? Your usual?"

"Yes, avocado sandwich with three cheeses."

"Lettuce, tomato and onions? Remember, we do treat the lettuce for you."

"Yes. Thank you."

He smiled and walked to the kitchen. I'd just finished touring a local history museum to learn more about Bolivia's history. Bolivia, is named for the famous Simon Bolivar, the Great Libertador, who liberated much of

South America from Spain. Bolivar recruited many able lieutenants from the University San Francisco Xavier, as well as a few highly regarded women warriors from the province, one of whom was Juana Azurduy de Padilla, a Bolivian guerrilla leader who waged war against the Spanish. She was a mestiza who, after the Spanish withdrew in ignominy, lead her forces and carved out her own republic in Bolivia. The domestic airport in Sucre is named after her. In the museum Simon Bolivar, I admired her painting, which depicted her brandishing a cutlass with a beautiful, fierce and fiery face. She was dressed in her red military outfit with long black hair flowing down her side. Now here was a woman I could fall for; she was definitely my kind of lady. Marco came out with my sandwich, and interrupted my thoughts.

Women were on my mind for the rest of the afternoon. After Janeth, I had a strong desire for a local romance. I didn't know why. I also felt something inside of me which said to just stay put for a while in Sucre. I wasn't inclined to argue. There was something about the atmosphere of Sucre that swept my heart, and for the first time in a long time, I could think unfettered and uninterrupted. Maybe it was the population. This was a college town, and Sucre was demographically a young city. It was young, intelligent, and there was a strange energy which I gravitated to. I couldn't put my finger on it. It didn't matter. As I ate, I read a Bolivian travel magazine with a lot of assistance from my dictionary. The new words rang in my mind, and soon I was overwhelmed. I really needed a tutor.

Roberto came over to collect my plates as I worked my way through the article. He refilled my glass with refresco, a drink made from boiled dry fruits or pits.

"Señor Nghiem, how was your meal?"

"Excellent. I should learn to cook some dishes from the two of you. Oh, Marco mentioned that there were Peace Corps here."

"Yes, there are many."

"There's a holiday in the USA, called Thanksgiving. Can you ask them if they're celebrating?"

"Certainly I can."

"Thank you."

Every year for Thanksgiving, I made my annual visit to see my family. Thanksgiving with my family was always an exploration of the melding of cultures. As always, there was plenty of food, albeit with a Vietnamese vegetarian flair. Sure, there were the usual staples, mashed potatoes, cranberry sauce, salad, stuffing, apple and pumpkin pie, but we also had mashed sweet potatoes, sweet potato pie, textured soy steak and chops, noodle soup with spices, curries, and peanut sauce, and a vegetarian mock "duck" lathered in rich oyster mushroom gravy with onions sautéed and sweetened. We also had pineapples and papayas for desert. I missed that, especially the mock duck with the sauces. What could I do, or eat in Sucre, for Thanksgiving?

Later that evening, I returned to Kaypicchu for dinner. In the soft candle light, as quiet Brazilian music played an ethereal, almost alien like melody that calmed and soothed, in walked a couple who sat down next to me. I started talking to them, and learned they were newly wed Americans from Massachusetts. They were honey mooning by traveling and volunteering through South America for six months. It was the best idea I'd heard of for a honey moon.

"So what are the two of you doing in Sucre?" I asked.

"Ed's looking for volunteer work, as well as me, and then later we're going to Chile." Said Megan.

"Megan's going to finish some course work in a university in Chile for her masters." Said Ed.

"Are you two going to stay in Sucre for Thanksgiving?"

"Yes."

I tried not to invite myself, but the loneliness was biting into me. I'd made friends with a German girl, Hilda, and a French girl, Delphine, who I hung out with for lunch and tea almost everyday, but neither of them knew what Thanksgiving was. I was happy to have met Edward and Megan. I finally couldn't hold myself in any longer.

"So, what do you plan to do for Thanksgiving?" I finally asked.

"Well, Megan wants to try and do a vegetarian Thanksgiving." Edward said, as he shrugged. My brain leaped for the open opportunity. I looked at Megan, grinned, and said, "I can make an apple pie." I thought I made a good sales pitch with that. I looked at Edward. They knew what I was hinting at.

"Why don't we make Thanksgiving dinner together?" Asked Megan.

"Sure, Dave can make the pie, you can make the stuffing, and I can wash dishes." Smiled Edward.

"That settles it then. Let's meet up on the weekend?" Asked Megan.

"Sure! I'll help get ingredients!" I excitedly replied. I was ecstatic. The prospect of Thanksgiving with some company and a chance to cook one of my favorite dishes had my mind racing as I mentally listed the ingredients I needed.

That evening, after they left, I finished my meal and continued translating the article. It was an article in the local paper about the recent protests. It was almost 10PM, and a tall, white haired, Brazilian accented man sat down in the corner, dining on a lasagna. With him sat a short, dark, brown man, with strong Quechua features, and he was dressed in a collared, buttom up shirt and pressed slacks. Marco and Roberto came out with several trays, and sat down with the two, as well their two mestiza employees, the kitchen staff. All of them sat down on the long wooden table to their evening meal, after Marco locked up the doors. Roberto looked at me, and beckoned to me with his hand. I walked over and sat down with them.

"Señor Nghiem, you said you wanted to practice your Spanish, so, we'd like to invite you to converse with us." Said Roberto.

"Yes, we'd like to learn more about you." Said Marco.

I introduced myself, as did the other two. The tall man with graying hair was Fernando, a Brazilian civil engineer from Säo Paolo state, Brazil. I'd seen Fernando several times previously in the restaurant, and he always had a smile on his face, and a gentleman like courtesy with his warm, jovial manners. On my first day at the restaurant, he smiled at me and said hello. It always took me by surprise how in South America, quite often the locals were the ones who initiated the contact of saying hello to me, and compared to the Northeast of the USA, it was culture shock. I was always the one who initiated random hellos on the streets in Boston. Most of the time I would get a smile back, but no one ever initiated a smile with me.

The other man was Willy. Willy was from Sucre, and he was a systems engineer and programmer who worked for a small accounting firm in the city. Willy had a strange sense of humor, and he laughed at almost anything, even at the things that weren't humorous. In fact, he seemed to laugh at anything which ticked his fancy. Still, the others knew him well, and tolerated this as a normal trait of his.

"So where are you from, David?" Asked Fernando.

"I'm from the USA."

"Ahh, the USA." He said, as he looked at Marco and Roberto. I was getting the feeling that the USA wasn't popular.

"Don't worry, we won't hold that against you. What about your racial background? Are you Japanese?"

"No, no. My family is from Vietnam."

"Ah! A Vietnamese! How wonderful! I've never met a Vietnamese before." Said Fernando brightly, with a smiling face, as he added, *"well then, welcome to Sucre my friend. For a moment, there, I thought you were Japanese, or at least Brazilian."*

"Brazilian?"

"Yes! Many Japanese are Brazilians. They're called Nisei. Wonderful folks, I have a friend who married a Japanese man. Well, he's Brazilian, but you know what I mean. His family came over a long time ago. In fact, the largest population of Japanese outside Japan is in Brazil."

"Really?"

"Yes. Now, I have a coworker who is actually from Japan, but he's a naturalized citizen."

"Really?"

All through my journey, I was getting an education in immigration patterns, racial integration, and racial/sexual politics. It was completely 180 degrees compared to the USA.

"Yes. He tells me that in Japan, everyone is strict and straight," said Fernando as he suddenly sat straight up on his stool, with a straight and dour face, *"but in Brazil, my friend said, 'here? We can dance!'"* And suddenly, Fernando broke into a sunny smile with both hands in the air as he danced on his seat.

I laughed, as I said, *"That's how I am. I dance in my seat a lot."*

"Well then you should come to Brazil."

"Yes, David, you should come with us." Said Marco.

"You both are going to Brazil?"

"No, not us both. We four." He said, as he pointed to Willy.

"Really? When?"

"For Christmas vacation, and then New Years. We are going for one month."

"Where are you going in Brazil?"

"Säo Paolo, to my house. You should come David. My wife will cook for you." Said Fernando.

241

"What about Carnaval? I've heard a lot about that."

"Ah, that's in February. It's much later, but that is also a fun time to visit. Unfortunately, I will be back in Sucre to finish my project."

"Are you going at the same time as Marco, Roberto, and Willy?"

"No. I will leave one week before Christmas."

"Well, we are going, David. Let us know if you want to come with us." Said Roberto. I thought about it for a moment, and decided against the temptation to take off. I'd just arrived in Sucre, and I wanted to work on my Spanish.

"I just got here, and I'm still working on my Spanish. Maybe later, but thank you very much for the invitation."

"Why." Said Marco, Roberto, Willy, and Fernando.

"Is is the custom to say 'why' after saying 'Thank you' ?" I asked.

"Yes, it is a regionalism of Chuquisaca, but it's a way of saying your welcome with out the your welcome. If you think about the words for 'your welcome', or 'de nada', they are actually saying, for nothing."

For the rest of the night, we talked, and my ears and mind were overwhelmed with the new words, the tempo, and the context. There were so many words, so many regional phrases, and colloquialisms, but the four made sure to slow the pace of the conversation down. Finally, I asked them,

"Do you like jokes?"

"Yes. Do you have some to tell?" Asked Roberto.

"Many. I have a ton, but they're ah, how do I say it? Inappropriate?"

"You mean dirty." Said Marco.

"Yes! I have many dirty jokes to tell."

"Well, we're all men here. Tell us one." Said Fernando.

"I have to go home and translate them first."

"OK, then bring them in later this week. We'd like to hear them." Said Roberto.

Later that night, as I walked back in the cool, dry, night air, I looked up at the milky way in the sky. Even though Sucre was a city, it's light pollution wasn't significant enough to block out the stars, and I admired the dreamy landscape of colonial buildings amongst the many lit lights in the sky. I smiled to myself as I entered my hostel. I had some new friends, and a wonderful place to eat. Now, I just had to try my brand of humor out with them.

****

I listened to my footsteps echo into the empty hall in Kaypicchu, and entered. It was empty except for three people sitting down at the opposite end of a long wooden table. One of them was Willy, and two women. One of the women, a Japanese Bolivian, got up and thanked them, and then walked out of the hall. The other one to his right was a remarkably beautiful woman. She wore a yellow blouse, as well as close fitting, long white pants, and sneakers. He long dark hair flowed down her back, and her large, bright, dark eyes sparkled.

I smiled at her as I walked right over to the table; our gaze never wavered from each other, and I sat down in front of Willy. Her skin was light brown, and her smile was as bright as the sunlight coming in through the windows. I broke our gaze, and looked at Willy.

"Hello Willy! How are you today?" I greeted him as we shook hands.

"Hello David. I'm fine today."

"Hello, how are you?" I said to the woman. We both got up and kissed each other on the cheek.

"I'm David."

"I'm Claudia. Pleased to meet you."

"So Willy! Are you a shy guy? Is this your girlfriend? You didn't tell me that." Immediately, Claudia made a grimaced face, and Willy's face was in shock.

"No! I'm not his girlfriend!" She vehemently exclaimed.

"No, no, we're just friends." He said.

"Oh really?" I looked at Claudia, grinning, and I said, as I touched my heart, *"I'm sorry, I didn't know. I thought I walked in to see the two of you, with her being so pretty and striking, and you looking so happy, well, I thought, you know."*

"No no. we're just friends," said Claudia, *"so, where are you from?"*

"I'm from the USA, and no, I'm not Japanese. I'm Vietnamese. I'm from a completely different culture, land, and language. Besides, I was born and raised in the USA."

"Really? So you're not Japanese. You don't know Yuki, the Cruzeña?" Asked Claudia.

"No, I don't know her."

"God, I love that accent!" Claudia suddenly said in English.

"You can speak English?" I asked in surprise.

"Just a little bit. *I was in an exchange program in the USA when I was in high school for a year.*"

"*Well, let's stick with Spanish, because I want to practice more. Would you like to hear a dirty joke? I just translated it. It's really good.*"

"*A joke? OK. A dirty one? Why not.*" Said Willy.

"*Yes, a joke? Give it, David.*" Said Claudia.

"*Adam and Eve were in the Garden of Eden, when one day, a hyperactive and excited God came in running like a madman. 'Adam, Eve, You won't believe it! I've got the two best gifts for the two of you! They're the best inventions!'*

Adam said, 'God, what's up?'

'I've got these two incredible gifts for the two of you!' He excitedly said as he held out two wrapped gifts.

'What are they?' Asked Eve.

'It's a surprise. There are two, but each of you can only pick one.'

'Just one huh?' Said Eve, who then added, 'OK then, Adam, you go first.'

'OK. What's in that one?' Asked Adam as he pointed at one. God smiled brightly.

'That's the ability to pee while standing up!' He said with pride.

'That's a great gift! It sure beats having to squat all the time!' Said Adam, happy at his new found ability. Now, Eve, was pessimistic. Adam got a great invention. She pointed at the other gift and asked, 'what's in that one?'

God smiled.

'That one? That's my crowning achievement!'

'What is it?' Asked Eve.

'Multiple Orgasms.'"

Willy choked on his food, while Claudia stopped, with her spoon of soup in mid air, in shock. Willy laughed weakly, while Claudia, with an uncomfortable smile, slowly laughed.

"*Was it too dirty for the both of you?*" I asked. I spent two hours translating and reworking that joke the night before, to make sure the delivery was right. I also spent an hour practicing and saying it out loud.

"*No! No, it was, ah, it was good, but surprising.*" Said Claudia.

"*Oh, well, I've got more!*" I grinned.

Marco and Roberto came out with trays laden with lunch, and sat down with the three of us.

"So, David, we heard you tell Claudia and Willy your joke. How was it, Claudia?" Asked Roberto.

"David? He's rough, and he needs work." Said Claudia.

"Really? Is it that bad?" I asked.

"Bad? It was awful! Goodness, it's so indecent!" She said.

"Yeah, but admit it, I saw you laugh."

I winked at Claudia, as I chuckled. She started to giggle, and then stopped herself.

"I only laughed to be polite." She said.

"Well, Señor Nghiem has told us many times that he had some good, dirty jokes to tell, except that he needed to translate them. Do you have anymore?" Asked Marco.

"Yes!" I said

"Goodness, look at the time!" Said Claudia, as she started to get up. She looked at me, and said, *"I apologize, I'd love to stay longer, but I have final exams. But it was a pleasure to meet you, David."*

"It was a pleasure for me as well. The fact that you laughed shows me you're intelligent, and you have, how do I say it? A strong brand of humor?"

"I do not have that kind of humor! I have a clean mind," she said, *"well, Señor Nghiem, will you be here in Sucre for a while?"*

"If I find a reason to be, I will." I said.

"I will see you later then."

"Sooner would be better."

****

All through the night, I rode on the long distance bus with Edward and Megan. During one section of the trip, where I felt the driver twist and turn, I felt nauseous for the first time, so I opened up a window. The bus smelt of stale, humid air, and human odors, and I figured everyone was breathing everyone's already spent air. Someone immediately slammed the window shut. In a daze, I looked up, and opened it again.

"Please keep this window closed!" Griped a young woman. I stood up, looked her and smiled, as I tried to put her at ease.

"I'm feeling nauseous, and it's stuffy in here." I said reasoned.

"I don't want that window open!"

Across from me, Ed looked to the young woman, and said, *"excuse me ma'am, but he's feeling sick."*

"I don't want my child getting sick." I looked to the other seat, and in the dim light, I saw the little child.

"It's OK, Ed." I said.

"Are you sure?"

"Yeah, it's cool."

I put up with worse before. I chose to deal with it, and tried to go to sleep. I never slept well on moving vehicles. After a night of twists and turns, we finally arrived at the enormous Cochabamba bus station, where I immediately stumbled outside at 5:30AM.

"Ugh." I muttered.

"That, was a long bus ride." Said Megan.

"Yeah, let's find a hostel." Replied Edward.

We found a hostel near the station, got two rooms, and I fell asleep for a few hours. When I came to, Edward was knocking on my door, "are you up, Dave?"

"Yeah, give me a moment." I said as I put some clean clothes on. We went out to tour the mansion of an 18th century tin baron. Back in the 1800's, Bolivia was populated with some of the richest people on the planet, during the days of the tin, silver, and rubber robber billionaires. As we toured the lavish palace, I admired some of the intricate woodwork, and walked over to Ed and Megan.

"This is disgusting." Said Edward.

"Really?" I inquired.

"Yes. With this country's history, and extreme levels of poverty, this is just unbelievably disgusting."

"I see what you mean."

Extremes like this, with little to no system in place for advancement, a government which aimed to keep it that way, and an enormous population which, paradoxically, was marginalized, although how to marginalize 90% of a population is quite a feat, was a brewing fire bomb for revolutions. Not surprisingly, there were constant blockades and protests, which were the only way for the 90% to have a voice. The month before we took our trip to Cochabamba, all the roads leading into Cochabamba were blockaded for several weeks, and it effectively shut down much of the economy.

The blockade was in protest of the US drug war, which was rife with human, environmental, and indigenous rights violations and abuses. The locals were upset, and as a result, a US marine had disappeared into the hills, a few miles from us into the highlands region. Rescue efforts never found or recovered him.

For a long time, I heard many stories about the destructive and inhumane results of US foreign policy, but every time I heard about them, they were to me, purely anecdotal. Usually, an errant European would complain about the US, but I always considered them as jealous first worlders.

In Bolivia, however, it was the first time I witnessed and spoke with economic refugees, who were escaping the rampant destruction wrought by the USA's proxy institutions, the World Bank and the International Monetary Fund. While I was in Sucre, I initially made arrangements to enter Argentina, but at the same time, Argentina's economy and society imploded. Streams of Argentineans were making their way into Bolivia, Chile, Brazil, Uruguay, Paraguay, Europe, and the USA.

When it came to economics, I was more in favor of capitalism than socialism, but to a point. Argentina's downfall tempered much of what I thought was appropriate. We picked up a local newspaper, and read how Argentina went through six presidents in two weeks. This was a former second world country, that plunged into violent chaos from defaulting on their loans. Argentina became the only non-African member of a group of several nations to default on their loans.

All through the 90's, Argentina was the "successful" poster child for the IMF, and the World Bank. They listened, and implemented every single request of the IMF and the World Bank. Not surprisingly, as a result of those policies, all through the 90's, half of that decade was spent under economic hardship, despite the world press presenting Argentina as a posterchild of success and as a paragon of their policies. Push came to shove in 2001, when the gun barrel of the IMF, on December, 2001, withheld 1.2 billion dollars in loans. They imposed more conditions that Argentina had to fulfill. The country couldn't, and it defaulted.

Chaos followed the default. Long lines formed outside of banks, who, due to following the Washington consensus, were a fractional reserve banking system. They only carried just enough for day to day transactions, and there wasn't enough actual money for depositors to reclaim. Violence erupted, and I saw a photo of a Bank Boston building with a brick hole in it.

Food riots grew out of control, as markets were barren of inventory, since they couldn't buy inventory with their devalued peso. I saw a picture of starving children, who lay dying, and it looked like something from Africa, if it weren't for the blond hair and blue eyes. Riots broke out, and half the country was unemployed, and for the first time, there were mass migrations to Europe and the USA. Just a month before the collapse, the Argentineans weren't required to purchase a VISA for entry into the US. At the moment of the collapse, the US slammed the door shut after the crisis, and the Argentineans suddenly became like the rest of Latin America.

For many Latinos, they felt it was poetic justice. For too long, Argentineans looked down on the rest of Latin America, thinking that they were Europeans, not Latinos, and proclaimed themselves to be better than the rest of the mestizo, mulatto, creole, and indigenous continent. Now, they were worse off than the rest of the continent, and Bolivians noticed how they started to enter the borderlands of Bolivia, looking for a place to stay and work.

The IMF and the World Bank, both of whom have their headquarters in Washington D.C., are extensions of the Federal Reserve. Any country which takes a loan, usually at the behest and bribery from an "Economic Hitman" has to comply with several requirements. All major national industries, services, and utilities were to be privatized. Tariffs and taxes on trade were to be removed. Officials and wealthy members are bribed, and told to embark on massive infrastructure projects: highways, electrical generation, airports, ports, and industrial parks. The caveat is that the US or Europe must build the projects. As a result, the money never touches the hands of the local people. In fact, the money doesn't even leave Washington D.C. It just goes a few blocks from one financial institution to another. When the project is complete, the company that built it maintains ownership, so the local government has no say in how it is managed. Prices are raised, and recently privatized industries are absorbed by foreign corporations. Layoffs are almost always the next step, and then suddenly, not only do the local governments and people find themselves unable to pay their basic utilities, but with the loss of revenue in the form of taxes from laid off employees and once national utilities, the local governments are trapped between cutting off basic social services and administration, and raising taxes just to pay the interest off on a debt that their officials were bribed into accepting.

Argentina was caught in that bind, hence the budget shortfall of 1.264 billion, which the IMF withheld in the form of a loan, all while the IMF were the ones who made the conditions which created the problem in Argentina in the first place!

Bankruptcy and devaluation resulted, and even then, there was still a loan to pay in now devalued currencies, for a product which they never and could never own. With a nation on its knees, they are then forced to submit to in-equal treaties, a long forgotten relic that's still alive and well, and descended from the mercantile colonialist policies of Britain and the USA back in the 1800's. These in-equal treaties include submission to have a foreign military base planted in their soil, or to give up primary resource control over a national resource, such as oil, tin, gold, etc. The list goes on and on.

As for open, "free" trade, the first to go is usually agriculture. Agriculture is the biggest industry in the world, and Argentina has some of the richest farmland in the world. They produce eight times the amount of food than their population requires. Yet, while the Argentineans were starving, they were exporting their produce in order to bring in foreign capital!

To add insult to injury, at the behest of the IMF, Argentina pegged their peso to the dollar, and supported it with the issuance of government bonds. Much of the bond sales and handling was via foreign banks, located in New York. As a result, all Argentinean products were uncompetitive, since they were priced in dollars. No money was being made, nothing was being exported, and almost all the money going into Argentina was from foreign investors speculating on the bonds. Bond holders, naturally, expected a high interest rate of return. Interest in government debt is paid for by either tax revenue or via national industries.

So, what happened when most of the population wasn't able to produce and sell their goods overseas? Those revenues went down. The revenue that came from once public industries was also gone. The government still had services and administration to pay for, but their sources of revenue dried up, so they issued more and more bonds, which, I'm sure, were "backed with the full faith of the Argentine government". When the budget shortfall occurred, they petitioned the IMF. The IMF refused, and Argentina became the largest sovereign debt default in history.

Argentina, from the moment she signed those agreements with the World Bank and the IMF, had signed away her sovereignty, freedom, and future. And all it took to collapse the country was less than a decade. Not surprisingly, Argentineans had few kind words for the World Bank, IMF, or USA.

Bolivia was effected by this as well, but unlike the Argentineans, the Bolivians have a powerful bullshit detector in their indigenous populations. When ex-president Lozada privatized many of the national industries and utilities, among them was water. Water, is rare in the high Altiplano, and for thousands of years, the Quechua and Aymara worshiped water. Bechtel corporation, located in San Francisco, bought the utility, and immediately raised the price and cut services in Cochabamba. Protests ensued, people died, and the company left, but not before asking for twelve million in compensation loss from the government, which is akin to a bully requesting payment for emotional damage after getting his ass kicked in a fight he started.

As we toured Cochabamba, we noted how many of the buildings had large rain catches. It looked as if the protest was still on going, as people chose to be self reliant on water. All of these things made me temper my libertarian, pro-capitalist leanings. I understood that I also had a responsibility to both the people around me, and people I effect, as well as the environment. After all, we all live on one earth, and what goes around, comes around, and when it comes around, it often comes back in multiples in a boomerang.

We finished our tour, and met a family from La Paz: Christian, a 28 year old man, Elsa, his mother who was a scientist and director of eduction for the government, and Chyang and Claudia, a married couple from Santa Cruz. They invited us to see them in La Paz, and Christian, after I told him about some of the things I'd seen and learned about in Cuzco, as well as my theory on the device, was excited enough to ask that I spend a week with him exploring some of the more unknown parts of the Altiplano.

"If you want to see some unusual things, come to our home. You must." He said.

"Yes, David, you must come." Replied Elsa.

"And, Claudia will find you a pretty Bolivian girl." Joked Chyang.

"But I already have one." I protested.

"You'll change your mind when you meet her. But you must come see us." Said Elsa.

For lunch, we went out to eat in Govinda, one of the many vegetarian restaurants run by the Krishna's all over the world before parting ways with Elsa, Chyang, Claudia, and Christian.

Then we went to the market. Cochabamba's market was famed in Bolivia for the sheer variety and quantity of goods available. I loved to walk around the markets. The scents, and smells of peppers, dried spices, fresh fruits, and freshly baked bread wove a sense of dignity amongst the productive campesinos. I stopped in front of a cholita, a plump Quechua woman, with brown skin and a bowler cap, and asked questions about her produce. Her Spanish was halting, and I noted how Quechua was still the first language.

I strolled through the market. From food, pants, equipment, and parts, TV's, stoves, ranges, and bicycles, a market is an organic expression of human labors, desires, wants, and needs. Like a cornucopia, it all depends on individuals and teams of people seeing a place for themselves in society to provide for a need and a want. I found myself in the "taller de bicicletas", a bicycle shop, looking at their cheap Chinese and locally made frames. Despite the quality, it always fascinated me of what people did to fulfill the needs of the populace. I started playing around with one heavy duty clunker of a bicycle, a cheap, heavy, steel bike that didn't have wire cables for brake control. It used solid steel tubes.

I met up with Megan and Ed, and we went to a Mexican restaurant for dinner, where Ed noted a linguistic error I made as we walked by a girl vending sandwiches at a stand.

"You know, Dave, when that girl in the market asked if you wanted a taste, you basically said that you wanted to eat her because she's pretty."

"What? I did?"

"Mmhm." Nodded Megan, who was smiling at my naivety.

"I was trying to say I'm sure it tastes wonderful, because you're pretty. Whoops!"

"Yeah. So, how's your Spanish tutoring going?"

"It's going well, I've been using this." I pulled out a copy of a Schaum's Outline Manual pages of Spanish that my tutor gave me, and showed it to Ed. He and Megan looked at each other, frowned, and said to me, "you don't want English in your studies. That's like a crutch."

"That's how the Peace Corps does it."

"Have you noticed how we are with Spanish and how they are?"

251

"You two are much much better. The Peace Corps people still have trouble with it, even after two years. OK, I see your point. I'm getting a full Spanish text when we get back."

On the ride back, which was during the daytime, we got to see where and why the driver drove with so many twists and turns. The road twisted from one close call of a canyon to another, on dirt roads with no safety rails, and along the way, we saw a carcass of an overturned bus. At that moment, Ed, next to me, panicked, and yelled out, "We're gonna die!"

I looked at him, smiled, and said, "Ed, I've come close to death several times. Believe me, unless I go, you're not going. And I'm not going anytime soon."

Megan tapped his shoulder, and calmed him down, as I watched and enjoyed our razor edged bus ride on the edge of doom. We didn't die, and we got back to Sucre. As we walked into the Plaza, Claudia spotted me and jumped into my arms.

"Where were you?" She exclaimed as she kissed me on the lips. She looked at Edward and Megan.

"Hello Edward, hello Megan, where did David go?"

"He came with us. Don't worry, he didn't misbehave." Smiled Megan.

"Misbehave?" I asked, as Claudia kissed me again.

"Yes. I can be very jealous."

"Oh. Well, see you Ed, see you later Megan." I waved to them as they walked back to their apartment. Claudia and I walked to the Central Plaza, and I breathed in the fresh air in the mid summer night.

"Did you miss me?" Claudia asked.

"Of course."

"You didn't flirt with other women, did you?"

"Me? No, you know me, I'm very friendly."

"That didn't answer my question. Did you or no?"

"I didn't. Claudia, you know the only woman on my mind, other than my mother, is you."

She kissed me as we strolled through the plaza.

Chapter 20

Tiwanaku

When I appeared at the bus terminal in La Paz, I figured Christian didn't receive my phone message from the day before. So I walked over to a man in the phone tienda and started to dial his home number. I suddenly felt a tap on my back, and turned around.

"Dave! Hey! Sheesh, you... I was shocked when I got your message, and immediately, I ran here for you. I just got your message this morning!"

"Oops! Sorry, but I had problems when I was calling you. But, I am here."

"OK David. Well, it's good that you're here. My God! I had so much planned for us to do when I thought you were coming five days earlier!"

"I know, but I fell in love, then I fell in pain. I had a liver problem for about five days that took me out, and my girlfriend wanted me to stay and get better before I left."

"What did you do?"

"I had five avocados every morning for breakfast."

"You had what? Oh my god! Just once a week is bad enough! They are almost pure fat!"

"I know. But for me, avocados are like gold, because they're about one or two dollars a piece. Here, one or two bucks gets you thirty! I got a little greedy. Man, I'm never eating another avocado for several years, at least."

Christian smiled. We found a taxi and got in, loading my bicycle and gear in behind.

"I had so much... Aye. Dave, I could kill you."

"I know, I know. I will only be here for about three days before I take off for Panama."

"Well, I have to go to Santa Cruz for about four days to meet my professor regarding a paper for my thesis. So that means we will have..." He checked his watch, "ten hours together."

"Oh no! Well, in that case, I'd better fill you in on some of the things I had found. Did you make a copy of that book you were talking about?"

"No, but we can do that along the way. First lets drop your things off and get you washed up. We don't have much bloody time, but at least I can show you the strange bowl with the cuneiforms on it."

"Cuneiforms? What's that doing here? Aren't those supposed to be Sumerian, you know, from all the way around to the other side of the world in the south of Iraq? What are those doing here?"

"Well, they're from Tiwanaku, and the archaeologists assumed that it's Incan writing."

"Except the Incans used quipu knots in colored strings to record their history. Incans didn't use writing extensively,"

"Aye, I have much to show you Dave," Christian sighed, "if only you came earlier."

Along the way, I explained some more about what I had gathered with regards to the Planetary Device to Christian. He nodded his head and cursed me for not coming sooner, and not staying longer. Oh well. I knew I was coming back to Bolivia. It wasn't just for the device now. I had a woman now. We soon got to his home, a pleasant and small pink house on the side of the canyon that made up La Paz.

We dropped off my things in the lower house, and went up to the upper house. The house was composed of two houses, one on top of the other. His mother, Elsa, was in the kitchen.

"Hello David!" She said in her powerful Bolivian accent. I could always tell a Bolivian was talking with the way they tended to heavily accentuate the beginning of their words.

"How are you? We were waiting for you earlier!"

"Uh yeah, but I fell in love with my girlfriend"

"Oh ho?! You have a girlfriend? What is she?"

"She's studying in law at the University of San Francisco Xavier"

"So! David, then that is good, no? You are a scientist and engineer,

who deals with the exactitudes of life. She is a social and law worker, which
should balance the two of you properly. Very good choice, young one."

"*Uh. Yes. May I use your shower?"* I'd been sitting in the bus for five
hours, without a scrubbing or a brushing, and by now I was feeling dusty
and outright grungy.

"*No. You may not"* She smiled, *"David, we're Latinos. My house is
your house. This is our custom."*

I smiled back and went to get my things for the shower. After cleaning
up, Christian, Elsa, and Claudia had lunch with me. Chyang was working at
the time. We decided that Chyang and Claudia would take me out to see the
Valley of the Moon and Tiwanaku before I left. Christian and I would visit
the museum with the cuneiform bowl and make copies of the strange book
he had in his possession.

The book was the reason for me to take some time out in La Paz. Christian had in his possession a rare, strange book, published only in Bolivia,
and it was written only in Spanish. The book was one of a kind, and it was
about the hyper-dimensional mathematics of Tiwanaku, the oldest site in the
Americas, which has several pyramids and gates. The book, "La Teoria de
Unification en 10 Dimensiones", translated as "The Theory of Unification
in 10 Dimensions", was written by a Bolivian computer scientist, Xavier
Amaru Ruiz Garcia, who was an expert in Tetralectics, a postmodern logic
utilizing four dimensions. Mr. Ruiz, a computer and electrical engineer with
a specialty in digital communications and computational science, worked as
a test engineer for various high tech companies in Santa Clara, California.
His expertise was in number theory and its test applications in computation
via hardware and software. He took the formulas derived from the geometric
inscriptions on the Gate of the Sun, and programmed various test programs
with them; among them was a new, and highly efficient prime number generator, which utilized the algorithms derived from the Gate.

I set aside the nagging question of, "what the hell are advanced mathematics that derive advanced computer algorithms that run on modern day
computers doing on an ancient relic of the Aymaran peoples," when I noticed
that derivations of pi, phi, as well as some modular functions of Ramujan,
which are the core mathematics for hyper dimensional math, came from the
Sun Gate.

I puzzled over the book as Christian and I walked to the museum which housed the cuneiform bowl. We walked into the museum, as he guided and explained some of the local customs in exhibit. We then walked into the main museum which housed the artifacts from Tiwanaku, and then we found the bowl.

The bowl was carved out of a very large stone block, unlike all of the other bowls which were made of ceramic. Inscribed on the sides of the bowl were symbols of all shapes, and I noticed and ongoing pattern of the number three in many of the symbols. In the center of the bowl was a carving of a man in a fetal position, with his hands at his ears, and the thumbs pointing into his head. We had with us an old Bolivian newspaper article which had some basic descriptions of the symbols on the bowl, including a lot of mathematics.

I put the data of my journey together. First, there were the red skinned Aymaran people, who spoke an inorganic, highly logical language that formed the basis of a computer program, Atamiri. Atamiri is the creation of Iván Guzmán de Rojas, who used Ayamara as the the mother language for the Atamiri computer programming language, and Atamiri is used to translate human languages from one language to another, like Russian to Italian, for example. And, it's one of the fastest translation systems on the planet.

There is no other language like Aymara. No other human based language was proven to program a computer, with the exception of Aymara. There are some languages that experts claim can be used to program a computer, but so far, *only* Aymara was *actually used* to program a computer. I put together the flood of information: a spoken language that forms the woven threads of the Aymaran culture, and was used to create a programming language, and now I had a book which derived several fundamental mathematical constants, highly advanced modular mathematics which formed the basis of hyper-dimensional physics, and on top of that, was plugged into a computer as an algorithm to compute prime numbers in a way that was more efficient than modern day methods.

"What do you think?" Asked Christian as I ran my fingers along the symbols. I had too much information in my head, so I put it aside, and savored the roughness and smoothness of the stone, as I traced out the symbols on the bowl. It was a question that requested a lot, and I didn't have an answer for. So, I stuck to the bowl.

"Where did this come from?" I asked.

"Tiwanaku. But it has writing on it. I always think of the ancient Sumerian tablets with cuneiforms on them when I look at this"

I counted along the sides. The peaks amounted to three. The occurrence of three, for some odd reason, came up a lot in the patterns.

"Can you take pictures of this thing for me, and send it to me?" I asked him.

"Sure. I want to see if I can decipher the text as well. No one's done that before."

"This is the only thing they've found with writing on it? It seems pretty significant. Everything else here is in ceramic."

We went to find Christian's sister, Claudia. Claudia, Chyang's wife, was an architecture student studying in the University. Christian had to leave and catch his bus to Santa Cruz. I had two more days left, and now Claudia and Chyang would be my guides.

"*David! How are you!*" said Chyang in his rich Santa Cruz accent. Chyang Hwang was a first generation Bolivian. He moved to Bolivia when he was six years old from Taiwan. He grew up in Santa Cruz, and like the Cruzeños, he had a habit of not using the consonants s and z at the end of his words.

We ate dinner and discussed our plans. The plan for the next day would be to visit the valley of the moon in the afternoon, and on Sunday, if there was time, to make a trip to Tiwanaku. We talked about the differences in culture between South America and North America.

"*You know, Chyang, something here strikes me as very different from the States*"

"*What's that?*"

"*Well, when I was with my girlfriend, people thought it was normal. They even thought we were married. I never had any problems.*"

"*Problems?*"

"*Yes, racial problems. I always had hostility from other people whenever I was with another woman in the States. What was it like for you?*"

"*Here? No, we are not like the gringos. Their racism is very well known to us. Here, we are comrades, all of us. Here, the problem isn't always race, although that can be an issue between the whiter of the population and the more indigenous. That comes up from time to time because of the colonial brutality. Those days never really ended, especially with what the gringos*" *are trying to do to us, they are a constant reminder for all of us."*

"What about for Asians?"

"Asians? We are part of society. We always have been, and always will be."

"You never had problems when you were with your wife?"

"Never. Most Asian men here marry the local women. I've never heard of anyone having a problem. You have to understand, David, here, mixing is the least of our worries. Economics is foremost. Class-ism is the primary problem."

The next day we went to the Valley of the Moon. There were natural stalactite like mounds, sticking out of the ground and made from the surrounding mud. A canyon about 300 meters deep lay off in the distance, and as we hiked through, I couldn't help but wonder about how the water had to have flowed to carve out such an eerie landscape. It was a whole other world, all made out of mud.

Later that night, I cooked dinner for the family, making an Indian curry dish. Elsa recently acquired diabetes, and she really wanted to change her diet from the Bolivian diet, which was just meat and empty carbohydrates, to a vegetarian one to help alleviate her disease.

The next day was my last in Bolivia, so we headed out to Tiwanaku. The ancient site of Tiwanaku is, by all accounts, probably the oldest American culture. By some dates, it's probably even older than the Egyptian culture. Set out on the Altiplano at 3900 meters above sea level, all that remains of Tiwanaku are two pyramids surrounded with courtyards, and gates of unknown purpose. To the casual observer, it isn't very impressive, but not to someone who knows his math and science, and most importantly, engineering. The stones were far bigger than the 250 and 300 ton stones at Sacsayhuaman. The source of the stones was found miles away, there were no uncovered road systems, and they laid about the site at random.

I stood at the site of the pyramid of Puma Punku. The stones were the size of a bus, and even wider. One stone went further into the ground, and it was the size of a small house. This was the stone that was on top of the pyramid. Our machines of today can't lift a medium sized stone in Macchu Picchu or Sacsayhuaman. So, how in the world did these carved stones, which dwarfed those stones several times over in weight and size, get dragged, carved, setup, and then knocked and tossed about like this? At 3600 meters above sea level, the site was far above the tree line, so trees couldn't grow in the area due to the altitude. Course, since it was the altiplano, that meant there were no size-able, structurally useful trees for hundreds of miles around. There were trees in the lower altitude areas of La Paz, but they were Eucalyptus, which were recently imported in the 18th century from Australia. Several hundred miles to the south southeast, was an area of pristine Altiplano forest, with the native kinds of trees adapted to growing in those conditions. None of those trees were taller than five feet, and they resembled shrubs and bushes. To find trees of any usable quality, one had to go several hundred miles north east to the cloud forest, which also didn't have structurally useful trees, until one reached a significant distance into the Bolivian portion of the Amazon. Therefore, to even get structurally useful trees for any kind of construction required significant and extensive engineering and logistics. And that's just to get materials that might have a slim chance at moving, cutting, and transporting the gargantuan stone blocks.

The stone work of one of the blocks was exquisite. There was a large, perfectly cut, smooth, rectangular slab with no sign of erosion. It was about a foot and a half thick, and it measured eight feet by ten feet. It looked like it was cut with a laser, since the lines were perfectly square. Weren't the ancient Aymarans supposed to have just stone age or bronze tools? In today's day and age, to achieve such high level precision required diamond edged, tungsten alloy, or laser tools which, of course requires several hundred years of a body of engineering, science, and experience.

The courtyard with 188 faces of stone was also strange. Stone carvings of faces, stuck out of the wall. I counted 188 in total, each one different from the other, and every single one of them was defaced or damaged from what looked like striking blows. We walked over to the gate of the sun, and a strange stone with a hole that amplified sound. But none of those were as startling as the discovery that I made on the east of the site.

In the least impressive section, which also had a giant stone slab that was tossed about, under the mud and water, was a stone slab that reminded me of the stone Marco and I had found on top of the mountain. I got curious, and something inside of me said to stick my hand into the muddy water and feel around. I did, and I found something that I did not expect to find at all.

I found a spiral, much like the spiral Marco and I had found on the other site.

"Oh my god! I found a spiral!" I said, as Chyang and his wife ran to me in surprise.

"Why isn't this mentioned in any of the books about Tiwanaku?" I asked.

Chyang's wife got in the water with me and started to feel around for another spiral.

"Here! Here's another!" She said. Chyang looked on with surprise.

In total, we discovered several spirals, all buried in the mud. For some reason, the books glossed over it, and didn't mention the spirals carved on the stones. Spirals are considered a common thing around the world by many archaeologists, who consider them to be little more than fertility symbols. Yet, these symbols were around sites that were purported to have strange energies flowing through them. These sites were often considered sacred by their respective cultures. I had a hunch that the symbols meant more than a simplistic, materialistic explanation.

Finally, while exploring Puma Punku, I found Elio's discovery. I found the symbol that he said surprised him the most. It was on the biggest stone, which was on the top of the pyramid. The slab had an "official" weight of 150 tons, but the beast far surpassed the size of the stones in Peru which weighed officially at 300 tons.

On the rock, I found a very well weathered carving, and I pointed it out to Chyang's wife. We stood their staring at it before I finally asked her what she thought of it.

"What does that look like to you?" I asked her.

"Fertilization." She said.

"Exactly." I replied.

We stood there staring in disbelief at a sperm cell fertilizing an egg cell, imprinted on a gigantic ancient slab of stone, weathered away by thousands of years, made by a society that, according to western archeology, was at best bronze age, never had a microscope, or the means to see inside of a womb.

"I have to get to the Mayan Empire" I said, as we looked in the harsh sunlight. The windswept plain confronted me, as I felt the weight of the mystery grip my mind and heart.

Figure 20.1: The Gate of the Sun at Tiwanaku.

Figure 20.2: I stand next to the cap stones of the pyramid of Puma Punku. The rest of it is buried underground. According to the sign, the stone I'm leaning on weighs the 180 tons. The 300 ton stone in Sacsayhuaman is smaller than it!

Figure 20.3: I slide down the smooth, stone slab. The slab is perfectly smooth and flat, demonstrating amazing workmanship.

Figure 20.4: Sitting on the capstone, or top stones of the Puma Punku pyramid.

Figure 20.5: In front of the temple complex of Tiwanaku.

Figure 20.6: Inside the temple courtyard, with the 188 faces on the walls, all of which were defaced or damaged from what appeared to be striking blows from a tool or weapon.

Figure 20.7: I stand next to one of the monolithic stones of the temple walls.

Figure 20.8: A partially excavated arch of the Tiwanaku complex. Note the precise cuts into the stone, and the superb smoothing and workmanship that is consistent across the bottom of the arch. The cut has superb mathematical precision and it resembles an asymptote of a hyperbola. This precision was supposedly accomplished with stone age or bronze age tools?

Figure 20.9: I kneel next to a submerged stone full of etched glyphs at the Tiwanaku complex.

265

Figure 20.10: My hands frame one of the glyphs.

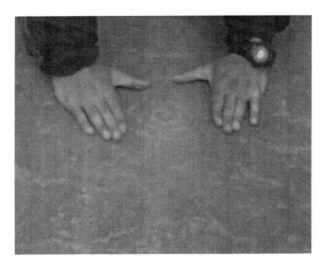

Figure 20.11: A closeup of the glyph.

Figure 20.12: The sperm and egg glyph on one of the stones. The egg is represented by a spiral.

Central America

Chapter 21

Costa Rica, Nicaragua

"Hey guys, let's go skinny dipping!" I eagerly said to my group of friends, Laura, Tracey, Don, and Meg, who were reclining on a towel on the sandy shores of a warm, tropical beach. The rhythmic beat of the waves crashing on the shore soothed our ears, and it was night time.

"No Dave, I think we're OK." Laura said calmly in her Chicago accent.

I watched as my friends covered their eyes, and took off my shorts. I was naked in the light of a half moon, as the waves of the warm, tropical Pacific splashed the beach of Monteczuma, Costa Rica. I spread my arms like an eagle, and turned to see my body cast a shadow on my friends. I looked back to see if anyone else was peeking at my completely naked body. I was free of my material trappings, free to run wild and naked in the waves, and I couldn't hide my glee. In fact, I tried to share it.

"You guys sure you don't want to go? It's gorgeous out!"

"Yes we're sure."

I spread my arms open, and let out a whoop, ran into the water, and dove in. The sensation was intoxicating, as I swam in just what the universe gave me through warm water.

I came out onto the beach, dripping with satisfaction. I shook off some of the water, and put my shorts on, and then I laid in the warm sand next to them. I grinned as I lay back and sipped on a freshly cut, green coconut. The night sparkled with the moon's beams on the frothing surf, and we listened to the slap of the waves, and the bursting of many bubbles. The air was seventy six degrees Fahrenheit, mild, and a calm breeze, gently touched and stroked

271

my skin. Two clouds floated near the moon, casting dark island shadows on the calm waters of the ocean, and we heard the palm fronds gently whisper and rub each other in the breeze. I smelled the odor of marijuana in the air, as my friends shared a joint. I put a piece of gum in my mouth, and chewed, as the quiet roar of the waves seduced our ears.

I arrived the day before at Punta Arenas, eager to keep my promise. Laura and Tracey were two friends I met my junior year at the University, and we often went out to eat, play volleyball, hike, and for coffee. They helped me keep my life balanced, so when I received word in Bolivia that they were going to Costa Rica, I knew it was time to go.

I took a flight from Santa Cruz, Bolivia, to Panama City, Panama. From there, I grabbed a bus to San Jose. It was a long 24 hour bus ride, and I arrived in San Jose at 3AM. The only hotels available were in the red light district, so I walked to the first one with a room, took a shower, and then collapsed. The next day, I rode out to Punta Arenas, where I took a ferry to the Peninsula, and then biked another six hours through dirt roads to the little resort town of Monteczuma. Along the way, the rough road conditions gave me a spill, and I fell on the road. An Israeli traveler on a motorcycle stopped to help me up.

I then took a long, rough, and curvy ride down the mountain to the beach, and arrived late at night at their hotel. They weren't there, so, dusty, exhausted, sweaty, and unshaved, I staggered into a restaurant hall in my rough cut off jeans, unbuttoned and dirty khaki shirt, and fedora hat. The entire crowd of mostly white, young, and dressed travelers stared at me in the dim light. I looked to the left, and saw a large screen, where they played a movie to the audience. I was in the way. I walked into the hall, well aware of how I stood out, when I suddenly heard someone say, "Dave?" in a familiar voice I hadn't heard in almost a year.

A large wave roared onto the beach, and we watched as the water flowed up near our feet.

"Yeah, you made it! Who'd a thought you'd come in like that?" Exclaimed Tracey. She took another puff of the joint, and passed it to Don. I listened to the waves crash, sighed, and fell half asleep on the sand, as it wrapped up and formed a perfect, comfortable mold underneath my body. I felt my knees throb. My knees didn't hurt as much as the day before when I arrived.

Laura was a gentle, Jewish girl from Chicago who went to Boston to study. I met her with Tracey, a Chinese American, from the Bronx of New York. Don was a taller, dark blond haired, white guy from Northern New Jersey, who decided to tag along for the trip, and Meg was a white girl from Vermont. Meg was Tracey's lab mate in a biological research center.

We spent the week in Monteczuma, but I wasn't fond of the place. I knew that the moment I stepped into a sandwich shop one night, to order dinner. A retired, sixty-ish white man, with a gray beard and mustache, walked up to the counter. He had horned rimmed glasses, and he didn't smile. I started to state my order.

"Hi! I'd like to get the 3 cheese sandwich." I asked.

"In English Please!" He growled.

"I thought this was a Spanish speaking country?"

"Well, they should speak English because we're Americans here."

I lost my appetite in that shop, and walked away from the counter. As I walked down the steps, I saw my friends walk up. We walked down the sandy path into a typical beach side restaurant. It had a thatched roof held up on thick palm wood poles, round lacquer straw woven tables. It was dimly lit with candles, as the sounds of the ocean waves filled the air, while the sounds of salsa from a far away nightclub faintly resonated in the air.

We ordered dinner, and talked about Boston, and my travels. I asked Laura about readjustment back in the States, since she spent a semester in the far reaches of the Amazon Basin in Ecuador, working on an environmental studies project. She didn't have any connection with civilization, or even the internet. When she came back to the States, I distinctly remembered her being disoriented.

"It's going to be rough for you Dave, especially after September 11th."

"I figured as much. After that happened, I knew for sure I couldn't go back home."

"So, what are you going to do?"

"Well, something inside me tells me to go to the Mayan Empire. I might find some clues along the way."

"You're going on your bike?"

"Yeah."

"That's awesome man."

"Does this have to do with that thing you found?" Asked Tracey.

273

"Yeah." I knew what she was getting to.

"Why did you cut me off your email list? You made us make a choice. I didn't think that was right." She said.

"I know, and I'm sorry. But after 911, I knew that everything was in a state of fear, and I wasn't sure about who I could trust. Suddenly the government decides if we're with or against the administration? My leanings would make me an enemy, since I'm against it. It was really confusing, and I hope you can forgive me. At the time, it was freaky. It's still freaky even now."

"I can Dave. You're still my friend." said Tracey.

"Thanks."

After a week of sun and surf, we returned to San Jose for Laura to return home, and to visit some museums. We sampled some of Costa Rica's well publicized tourist attractions: the famous tourist trap of the Monte Verde Cloud Forest; the nonexistent lava flows from the "lava erupting" volcano; the hot springs nearby said volcano, and finally to the ganja soaked east coast. Along the way, we were together twenty four seven, and conflict and frustrations hit a break point. Don and I traveled together to get away from the ladies down the east coast.

We headed to Cahuita, where we bicycled along the beaches, and hiked in tropical forests, where sloths and monkeys leaped and crawled along the branches. We camped out on the beach, ate breadfruit, plantains, and tamales made by local vendors, while we climbed coconut trees in secluded beaches to harvest water laden nuts. At night, we went to clubs, picked up women and danced.

After three weeks, Don, Tracey, Meg, and I returned to San Jose, where I bid them farewell, and I was grateful to once again travel alone. I wasn't used to traveling on a cramped itinerary, but I flowed with them. Still, I had to compromise, and I went along with decisions that I wasn't enthusiastic about.

I went back to the hostel, rested, and prepared for the rest of my journey through Central America. The next day, I went into the city to pick up equipment and supplies, and to get a haircut. I grabbed some pepper spray in a local weapons shop, and a new bicycle pump in a local bike shop. The next day, I headed out. I wanted to get to the Mayan Empire, and along the way, I knew inside that there were some people I had to meet. Who they were didn't matter. I knew that somehow, they would show up, and I would learn the answers that I needed.

****

I was back on track, and I cycled near the borders of Costa Rica and Nicaragua. It was evening, and as I rode, I watched the sunset in the sky. Swaths of red, orange, and yellow painted the sky around me. I looked to my right and to my left. I couldn't believe it; I'd bicycled for a hundred kilometers, and the entire stretch of road had barbed wire. The road was dusty, and a hot wind battered my body and face with sand and dust, as I looked at the desolate, desert landscape. Costa Rica had a good hype machine working in the US, which touted itself as a green, lush, and enlightened country, which preserved its forests and natural environments. Yet, the wind that knocked me over came from dry, parched, and destroyed cattle land. I was in the northwestern part of Costa Rica, in a lightly inhabited no-mans land that served as a buffer from Nicaragua. Still, Costa Rica did deserve credit for its efforts. The country did a lot better than most other 3rd world nations in slowing down the human destruction of the local ecology.

I cycled another twenty miles down the road, and the desert seemed endless. The sun was low, and I wanted to get off the road, due to the possibility of armed bandits. Ever since the Contra-Sandinista Wars in Nicaragua, armed bandits continued to travel between both countries. The Costa Rican police had many of checkpoints along the road, and they generally did a good job, but it was easy to avoid them. Still, my concern started to turn into anxiety as I looked for a place out of view to setup my tent. Then I spotted an opportunity.

It was a hole in the fence, and there were a lot of trees behind it. It was the perfect cover, and I made my choice immediately. As I looked up and down the road, I made sure no one was there, and then I dove through the fence. I walked behind the trees, and looked behind me to make sure no one followed. Suddenly, I stopped.

I looked down a precipice, and below my feet, before me, was an enormous valley of verdant, green trees, palms, mangoes, and tropical forest. In the distance were three active volcanoes and a glowing, bright, red, pool of lava. I'd stumbled onto an oasis in the desert, since everything else was barren for miles around. Fascinated, I watched as the strong winds from the valley ruffled my hair. The volcanoes were erupting, and I saw the mountain cough up bits of lava in fountains, while the lava pool shimmered in the horizon. I pitched my tent, and had some cold cereal for dinner as I admired the volcanoes. Then I laid down in my tent for some badly needed sleep.

I didn't sleep well at all. The winds got stronger as the night wore on, and they violently shook the tent. I lay sweating on my back in the tent, naked, my diving knife clutched in my right hand, and a can of pepper spray in the other. The strong wind rattled my tent, shaking the flaps, poles and ropes so violently the nylon fabric popped, sounding like sporadic gunfire. I stared at the dark, domed ceiling and shook with terror as a high beam from a vehicle slowly lit, and then left my tent. Could it be a bandito, a murderous ex-contra prowling the hills and valleys that lay in the shadow of a live volcano in the distance? Or was it a land squatter searching for a quiet place for a home and hearth? I didn't know. I didn't care. In the depth of my fear, I was ready to stab anyone who entered my tent.

I closed my eyes in the dark, only to confront an even deeper darkness. Why was I doing this? What sort of thing drove me to commit this mad, lonely act, to ride a bicycle across Latin America? It seemed so simple at first. It was supposed to be a leisurely three-month joyride across South America from Lima, Peru to Buenos Aires, Argentina. Instead, I was on the side of a road in an desolate stretch of north western Costa Rica, hiding from vagrants and highwaymen, perched on a cliff in front of a volcano, worn from my inability to sleep, and scared out of my mind.

I put the cold, steel blade on my bare chest, and wiped away a tear. I was thousands of miles from home, in an alien, hostile place, alone, exhausted, and overwhelmed from seven months of intense trials through three third-world countries.

I looked at my watch. It was 3 AM, and as I lay there, my fears came out. I repeated a mantra in my mind, to sooth myself, but the fears just grew stronger and stronger. Soon, the mantra disappeared, as I began to question myself, and my sanity out loud. All I could do was hug myself in the isolation. There was nothing around me except the roar of strong winds, a shaking tent, and the dread of being discovered by bandits.

****

I cycled into Nicaragua, and took a detour off the highway to the largest lake in Central America, Lake Nicaragua. After a long boat ride where I heaved my lunch and breakfast overboard, I spent some time in the peaceful solitude of the Isla del Ometepe, a volcanic island in Lake Nicaragua. Lake Nicaragua was the largest fresh water lake in Central America. It was quiet, and I had a nice little bungalow to myself. I spent several days wandering the volcanic sand beaches, tropical forests, and banana plantations, and flirted with the bar girl.

The lake was the only lake with a freshwater shark in it, although the pollution from cattle ranching and banana plantations decimated a lot of the life in the lake. As I rode by the shore, I observed huge spawns of green algae from fertilizer and pesticide run off. There's a long history of degradation in the Mexican and Central American countries to feed the appetite of the Northern Americans. Much of the cattle raised in former forest land, was exported to the US as grade D meat for many fast food franchises. When the land no longer produced, the companies and ranches left, and the poor came as land squatters. With no other options, they attempted to work a living off of it. I bought fruit from the children along the road; they held plastic bags of jacote, a hardy, dry forest fruit. It's also one of the few crops that grew in the wastelands. Most of the environmental devastation in these countries occurred in the last fifty years.

There was little variety in the people's diets, since most of the land was used for bananas or pineapples. Although Bolivia was poorer than most of the Central American countries, Bolivia was also blessed with having little influence from the US. As a result, the diet between the Bolivians and the Central Americans was starkly different. I had a varied diet in Bolivia of fresh fruit, bread, vegetables, and plenty of grains. In Central America, it was rice and beans, with some fried plantains. Much of the fruits and vegetables I saw in the Nicaraguan markets were poor in quality. As I traveled through Nicaragua, I saw malnutrition decimating the young and old. Many children had bowed legs from the lack of calcium. There was plenty of milk, but the body doesn't absorb calcium readily from milk. Vitamin D is necessary to absorb the calcium, which can only be found in green leafy vegetables or from skin exposure to the sun. Iron was another mineral that they lacked, but iron isn't absorbed without the vitamins A and C, which came from plants and fruits, to properly absorb iron. As a result, Kellogg's corn flakes were popular, since it supplemented the iron with those two vitamins. As I bicycled through the cities, I saw many obese people. In Peru and Bolivia, I rarely saw obese people; the moment I landed in Panama, I started seeing obesity everywhere. Interestingly, obesity was prevalent amongst people who were malnourished.

Yet, despite the hardships, the poverty, and the difficulties, I was readily welcomed by the warm hospitality of the people. Well, I was mostly welcomed warmly. I did leave one town where a Nicaraguan thought I was a CIA agent. I was eating dinner, and he sat down across me at the table. We started talking about each other, and he mentioned something about having to leave the USA quickly. He started saying, "I'm scared of you," and made a motion of what looked like a gun at me. I didn't take any chances. That's what I got when I talked about training people in martial arts in a country that was once their enemy. I also encountered a few obnoxious Nicaraguans who found it annoying to see an Asian man with a blond girl. I was hanging out with Gretchen, an east German girl and we were soaking up the waves on the beach. Actually, come to think of it, I was right at home, since that was the same reaction I got in the US whenever I dated non-Asian women.

Nicaragua was the most backwards country in Central America, due to the US embargo on the country after the Contra-Sandinista War. I cycled by horse drawn carts. The carriages were made of rusty, cannibalized cars, and the central markets in most of towns had meager offerings on the shelves, despite enduring ten years of an economic liberalization program recommended by the International Monetary Fund. Nicaragua had a civil war, which most Americans only knew by extension as the Iran Contra affair.

The Contras were the para-military that the US supplied and supported in Nicaragua against the socialist Sandinista political party. During the 1980's, the US sold weapons to the Islamic regime in Iran to generate funds for the Contras. Ironically, at the same time, the US also supplied Saddam Hussein in Iraq with enormous amounts of weapons, including chemical and biological weapons for their war against Iran. Even more money was generated by Colonel Oliver North's cocaine drug trafficking activities in the Los Angeles and California area. Oliver North and Noriega, of Panama, were business partners in the operation. In 1981, the Sandinista army defeated the right wing Samoza regime, which was a military dictatorship. They established a socialist government, and got to work on agrarian reforms, to establish medical, educational, and social services to the entire country.

Reagan decided to destabilize the country, and pushed efforts to supply money and arms to the contras. The CIA illegally mined the harbors in an attempt to enforce Reagan's embargo, and the international community vilified and condemned the unprovoked action. It was a war few in the US knew about, except through public trials where Col. Oliver North and Ronald Reagan were tried. Like Vietnam and other countries that fought for their sovereignty against US policies, they were placed under a heavy embargo, which was recently lifted. After the embargo, masses of Americans swooped in for land bargains, cheap labor, and private mansions. I cycled through Grenada and Leon, two colonial cities where Americans were buying up land and property at skyrocketing rates. A colonial home was worth almost 250,000 US dollars, yet the average Nicaraguan's monthly salary was at most $150. As I biked through, I saw children fill in large holes in the highway with sand, and then beg passing vehicles for money for the repairs. Nobody paid them.

The contras spread out into the northern Mosquito coast and the northern highlands. I was warned over and over not to ride along part of the Central American Highway that entered through those regions. The ex contras were still bitter, and they were still heavily armed with US weaponry. US weaponry was a heavy theme in my Central American journey. The M16 rifle, only manufactured in the US, the mainstay arms of the cold war, was everywhere. The left over rifles were confiscated from the contras, and saw use in the Nicaraguan police forces, in addition to the Russian AK-47, and the Israeli made Uzi.

In Leone, as I walked down the street, I saw a sign above a building that said "Museo." I looked in the door, and an ex Sandinista guerrilla, old and fat, with a bandanna around his head and a graying beard, ushered me into the Sandinista museum.

"Where are you from? Japan? Korea?"

"My family is from Vietnam." I refrained from stating my nationality.

"Ah! Come, come, look around my friend."

I stayed in the museum, going over photos, books, news clippings, and journals. Much of Central America was a war-zone, and sadly, all of it was the USA's experiment in perfecting its neo-colonial policy. The source of the enforcement of said experiment was the infamous School of the America's, founded, supported, and established by the US military, and funded by

279

the American taxpayer, it was regarded as vital to US foreign policy in Latin America. The world's pre-eminent techniques in torture, rape, terrorism, and execution was codified, documented, taught, and perfected in this school. It was established in Panama in the 1940's by the US Army. Its purpose was to train Latin American, right wing para-militaries in "counter insurgency techniques" and in the Orwellian double speak of "stabilization". By the 1960's, the school was so famous in Latin America for training most of Latin America's tyrants, dictators, terrorists, and henchmen, that it was known as the "School of Coups". Several Latin American newspapers called it the "School of Assassins." In the 1980's it was moved to Fort Banning, in Georgia, and then in 2001, the Pentagon renamed it the "Western Hemisphere Institute for Security Cooperation" to maintain funding from Congress. Thousands of Latin American military officers studied at the school each year.

From this school came much of the muscle for the US's Latin American policy. Every Latin American nation that had horrific periods of murder, genocide, gang rape, terrorism, civil war, and military dictatorship, was directly connected to this school. From Argentina's dirty war from the 70's to the 80's, Bolivia's numerous bloody coups, Chile's Caravan of Death under Pinochet, Colombia's right wing para-militaries, every single Latin American country that endured destabilization and organized death, the leader and his organization were trained there.

El Salvador was the scene of bands of "Death Squads," trained by US Special Forces, who indiscriminately murdered tens of thousands of innocents. Guatemala's civil war, the longest after Colombia, was the scene of a mass genocide against the Mayan people by right wing paramilitary groups, also supported directly by the US.

Panama was the scene of a horrific invasion, when George H.W. Bush decided to invade in order to cure an image of a "wimp" problem - when Panama did nothing to provoke them. They didn't violate international law, yet the moment the Panamanians requested that the US honor a treaty to return the Panama Canal, which was signed by Carter, and was due in 1990, the Administration, in 1989, invaded, bombed, and murdered 3000 civilians, the year before his administration invaded Iraq in 1990. It was done under the pretext that the president, Noriega, had violated US law - but in Panama. Ironically, Noriega was a graduate from the School, a business partner with Colonel Oliver North in the cocaine trade, and interestingly, on the CIA payroll since the 1970's. How US law applied to Panama, which was an independent and sovereign country astounded the international community, and defied all concepts of national sovereignty. Not surprisingly, the international community vociferously condemned the preemptive action.

The only country that escaped the conflicts was Costa Rica, and even then, the Costa Ricans were caught in a tight spot. They expelled the contras from using their country as a base, much to the antagonism of the US. Fortunately, Costa Rica was not considered a strategic point. The Costa Ricans made a concerted effort at a peace plan for Central America, which gave the Costa Rican president the Nobel peace prize. Unfortunately, Guatemala wouldn't conclude their civil war until 1996.

The museum was once the place where the Sandinista colonels planned their attacks. The old warrior showed me a wall, which was decorated with the weapons of the Cold War. In the middle center of it all was a big ceramic statue of a Chinese laughing Buddha. I looked at him, curious, and he pointed to his heart.

"I only want peace. I've fought for too long, and seen many comrades die."

I left the Museum, and went back to my hostel. Much of the history I studied in high school never referenced Latin America. Yet, much of what I saw, directly involved the States, and as I traveled, the pieces of a larger picture were beginning to fall in place. I was getting an education in US foreign policy in Central America.

In the hostel, I met John, another American traveler. He was bald, 30ish, white, and sported a five o'clock shadow. John was a Peace Corps worker in Guatemala, and he was traveling down the isthmus for a much needed vacation after one year of service. We went to the center of town for dinner, and ate in an outdoor cafeteria. We were the only ones there. A brown, slightly overweight lady pulled up a table, and cooked some fresh plantains. A little girl, dressed in ragged clothing came over to us. She was about nine years old, dark brown, with shoulder length dark hair, scrawny, dirty, and her eyes were tearing. I looked over her shoulder, and saw her mother, who was anxiously looking at us. Neither of the two looked well fed.

"Please señor, can you give me something?"

We both pulled out some cordobas, the local currency, and gave her a couple of bills.

"Thank you."

I looked at the mother, and nodded. She nodded back as the girl went back to her mother, and they both walked away. I watched them disappear into the city block.

"It's sad, but sometimes, when you see that so much, you get used to it." John said as he lit up a cigarette.

"It's rough. You can't help everyone." I replied.

"Yeah, sometimes the circumstances seem almost pre-destined, and no matter what you do, sometimes there's nothing you can really do. But, it doesn't matter. We try our best, and that's really all you can do."

"Was it difficult for you when you first started in the Corps, getting used to all the poverty?"

"Yeah, I don't think I ever really got used to it."

John was from Indiana, and he studied and lived in Boston for a while. He worked in the local government of a town in Guatemala as an advisor and consultant. As we ate our meal of rice, beans, plantains, and tamarind juice, we talked about traveling, some of the things I was investigating, what to look out for and where to go in Guatemala. I showed him the book that Christian gave me about Tiwanaku.

"The word Maya for the Aymara, and the Quechua, means one. I think the Mayans here might have a connection to them."

"Well, if you want to really get into the Mayans, I and a few other volunteers are going for an expedition in the Peten to find El Mirador."

"El Mirador?"

"Yep. The biggest Mayan city that we know of."

"What's the Peten?"

"You got a map?"

"Yes."

We spread out my Central America Map, and looked. The city was in the far upper reaches of the jungle border of Guatemala. There were marks that showed trails, but no roads. It was far from the main road, and it probably lay four or five days away on foot. John pointed to the archaeological mark on the map.

"We'll be going there." He said as he traced a trail from a logging settlement.

"Man, I'm with you. When are you going?"

282

"In about two months."

"I should make it to Guatemala in that amount of time."

"On the bicycle? Are you sure? That's a long way."

"Trust me. I'll be there."

"OK man, give me a call or an email when you get there. We'll be waiting for you."

Figure 21.1: A ceramic Buddha brings a sense of peace amidst the tools of war.

Chapter 22

Honduras

I rode hard through the west coast of northern Nicaragua. Heavily armed ex-contras roamed the eastern interior, so I chose to avoid them by taking the Pacific route. Also, there were numerous left over soldiers from the Salvadorian Honduran conflicts, so the locals constantly warned me,

"The interior is dangerous. We don't want you to die."

Despite following their advice, I encountered M-16 toting Honduran troops upon entry. They didn't bother me, since I didn't look like a typical tourist, but the experience alerted me to the fact that I was traveling through recovering war zones.

At the border station of Nicaragua and Honduras, I met two Norwegian cyclists, Jans and Sven. They started their journey at Tierra Del Fuego, in Chilé, and would finish at Prudhoe Bay, Alaska, covering the ends of the planet by bicycle. Driven to complete the journey as quickly as possible, they were a little cold when I asked if I could tag along. Fearful that I would slow them down, I reassured them that it was just for the day.

I had my reasons. After traveling alone for so long, I hungered just to have a decent conversation. Although I didn't mind going solo, the lonely nights were taking a toll. My only partner in this affair was my bicycle, and it wasn't an exemplary conversationalist.

Sven, a tall red head with a beard, and I biked the main road onto a dirt path, which lead into a town that didn't appear on our maps. Surprised it existed, yet also hungry, we loaded up on gourmet items - spaghetti, ketchup, salt, and Top Ramen. The other cyclist, Jans, went down the road to find fuel for our stoves, while Sven and I got back to the main road. Night settled upon us, but Jans failed to show up. Hours passed in silence. Where was Jans?

Suddenly, a light flashed in the distance, and a short man in a bicycling jersey walked over to us. I spoke to him, since I was fluent in Spanish.

"Hi, how are you?" I smiled.

"I'm fine. Are you friends with a cyclist?" He replied.

"Yes yes! He's got blond hair?"

"Yes! He's in my house. Please, come with me."

It was at this point that I learned about Central American hospitality. Despite their conditions, they were surrounded by hospitality, warmness, and friendliness. "Hey guys!" Yelled Jans, who stood behind a makeshift barbed wire fence. We followed the man into his mud and adobe home. It was roofed in corrugated metal and enclosed with plastic and canvas. The toilet was a hole in the ground, surrounded by 4 pieces of wood. Water was received about two or three times a week, and they often depended on rainfall. I later asked the Honduran if he was a cyclist. After he replied yes, he explained his reasons for the invitation.

"I'm also a cyclist, and we're all brothers in the world. Therefore, I want to extend my hands for brotherhood"

"Then my brother, we will receive your gifts. Many thanks, sir." I replied.

We walked into his home, and entered. In the dim light of a candle, we sat down on several aluminum chairs on the bare dirt floor. I looked around, and sitting on a broken TV were several cycling trophies. "Campeon de Honduras, 2000," said one trophy. On his jersey, in large letters, were the words, "El Campeon". Curious, I observed him. He was about 1.57 meters tall, dark, thin, twenty one years old, and with well defined quadriceps dressed in cycling shorts. Noting my sense of surprise, he led me to a corner of the room. On the wall were two bicycles, one of which was a Trek 5000, a two thousand dollar bicycle. He then showed me his prize - two Italian racing bicycles made of carbon fiber and specialized aluminum. Each bicycle was worth about three thousand dollars. He used one and his younger brother used the other.

"The champion?" I asked in surprise.

"Yes, of Honduras"

"My name is David. What is your name?"

"Melvin. Melvin Betancourt."

Later, his family came in, and because the Norwegians couldn't speak Spanish, I interpreted for most of the night. The mother, father, and his brother, all lived, literally, under one roof and in one room. His mother took the food we bought, and cooked for all of us. We had a wonderful time with the dinner conversation. I told jokes, while the family laughed as we ate spaghetti with ketchup, and fried plantains.

Still, being in Melvin's presence elicited a sense of admiration. How was it possible, in this poor home, that he could maintain his training and diet? I thought about the pampered people that I used to train with in the gym. I remembered how they complained about a lack of this or not having that. In the US, we had everything at our disposal: science, nutrition, equipment, and experts. He didn't.

"Do you find it difficult to train living here?"

"I was born in this, and with God, I do what I can." I noted the strength in his voice, as well as a sense of resignation.

"I admire you. You have done much, and you have much strength in your heart."

It was inspirational to meet Melvin. Despite his circumstances, he won through determination and hard work. Still, a question scratched my mind; how could he afford such expensive bicycles? The cost of just one of those bikes would help lift his family out of poverty.

"Are you a professional?"

"Ha ha! People here do not consider bicycling as a sport to pay for. We are not like football players (soccer) or baseball players. We are a minority here. Everything I do comes out of my pocket, and with the support of my family."

"Then, how can you buy your bicycle? They're very expensive." I carefully inquired. I didn't want to be too intrusive.

"They're donations from an association for poor athletes."

"Why not sell the Trek to help your family?"

Hesitantly, with his eyes looking at the floor, he replied, *"no one can buy it. It is expensive for the people here."*

I didn't want to pry any further when I felt his shame about his poverty. In the glow of the candlelight, we told stories, swapped training tips, and talked about ways to exercise. He would get up at five in the morning, eat a light breakfast, and then bicycle about three to four hundred kilometers. When he got back home, he would eat lunch, and help out his younger brother to sell food on the highway. They used a wagon attached to a bicycle. It was a rough life, and it trained him well. I lived and breathed training science and diet, and it baffled me when Melvin told me of his daily routines. Melvin subsisted on a diet of honey, whole grain cereal and milk for breakfast. He also ate whatever his mother threw at him. He had no access to vitamins, information, or experts. His training equipment was the Honduran roads, a keen sense of his body, tropical sun, rain, and hills. I asked him what his true motivation was.

"To go to the Olympics." If he made it to the Olympics, it would be a great victory for his homeland, the poor, and a testament to his determination.

"Have you competed outside the Honduras?"

"I want too, but it is difficult to find money to do that."

The next morning, Melvin decided to escort us for a portion of our journey. As he darted ahead of me, I silently cheered him on. I swore that when I got home, I would find a sponsor to help him. Still, sponsor or no sponsor, I knew he would find the determination to compete and win. I took that inspiration inside, and I resolved to complete my journey.

****

I met a man in the Honduras, a one armed Canadian cyclist, in the foothills the day after I left Melvin's home with Jans and Sven. Jans and Sven carried little equipment in their bags, so with their light weight, they took off. I meandered down the road, and slowly pedaled through the hot sunlight of the mid morning. Suddenly, I heard a man yelling at me in English.

"Hey! Hey you! Hey! Stop!"

I looked at him in surprise and stopped my bike as he ran and jumped over the barbed wire. He was half naked except for his bicycle shorts, lean, and burnt like a lobster. He had a big white patch of sunblock on his nose, and dark sunglasses, as well as short cropped, sun burnt, blond hair.

"Who are you?" I said in surprise.

"I'm a cyclist, like you. I left my gear up there." He said as he pointed to a tent and a colorful, rainbow colored, Mayan hammock next to his bike.

"Oh. What are you doing up there?"

"The same thing you probably do when you need to piss and camp at night, eh?"

"Oh, yeah, You're from Canada, aren't you?" I asked noticing his accent.

"Yup, Toronto, say, you look Canadian. Are you from the Oganagan Valley, or Vancouver?"

"Uh, no... what makes you think that?"

"Cause you look like one, and you're a lot nicer and friendlier than Americans. That and your accent is very Canadian."

We laughed and talked some more on the side of the road.

"What's your name?"

"Jim. And you?"

"David."

"Well, nice to meet you David. So you been traveling on a bicycle too, I can see. Where are you headed?"

"I'm planning on going through the Honduras to Guatemala. Say, what happened to your arm?" I asked, as I looked at his left arm. It was emaciated, and it stayed in a pocket that was sewn into his bicycle shorts.

"I lost the use of my left arm in an accident."

"And you're on a bicycle?"

"Yup. I make very good use of my other arm." He said as he flexed his right. It was twice the size of his left, the result of lifting and carrying his bike. I looked at his shoulder, and saw the long scar there.

"So where did you start, Jim?"

"I started in Mexico. I've been on the road for about 3 months now."

"And with one arm?"

"Oh yeah. I'm heading to Colombia. I want to work in Bogota, Columbia, when I get there." He said.

"What? Are you nuts? The place is a war zone! I ran into a bunch of refugees in Nicaragua, and they said the same thing. No one wants to go there." I replied. The war situation was getting out of hand in Columbia. This was the USA's Vietnam part three, after Afghanistan, which was Vietnam part two.

"That's exactly why I'm going there! Cause no one else wants to go, so it'll just be me and the Colombians!"

"That's actually not a bad idea. How are you going to get through the Darian Gap?"

The Darian Gap was a swampy, tropical separation between the South American Continent and the Central American Isthmus. It was several hundred miles of swamp, rain forest, and hostile native tribes and FARC guerrilla fighters. Every story I was told about it included something about going, and never coming back. How the tellers got their stories when no one ever came back usually made me suspicious. The native tribes themselves were among the most isolated in the planet. Some had never contacted an outsider before. Unlike the tribes in the Amazon, there weren't really any customs for greetings, except with a gun, bows and arrows, spears, darts, and anything else that guaranteed it to be the very last greeting.

"I figured I'll take the ferry from Colon to Cartagena, Columbia. I just want to get to Bogota."

"I heard that was a really nice place actually. Bogota is supposed to be one of the most educated, and progressive cities of all South America. It's a really enlightened, progressive, and nice place to live... except for the terrorists." I replied.

"Ah, I'll figure a way through. I mean, come on, what have they got with me? I'm lame in one arm. I've got nothing left to prove. I already rode through Mexico, and *that* was dangerous. Besides, I'm not American. They're not hunting for my nationality. The only problem is I look like one."

"Say, how was El Salvador."

"It was great! You know, everyone back home says to stay away from there, but as soon as I got there, they're all like, Hey, how are you? What are you doing? Can you come over for dinner?"

"Really?"

"Really! It's not as dangerous as they say! The people are really nice there. And because so few people go there due to it's reputation, you'll have a great time."

We parted ways, and I rode up the road for the next two days. I stayed in small town hostels near the ocean, and tried to sleep as next door, young couples looking for privacy from their homes had sex on creaking, loud, metal bed frames. It was a little depressing to hear them, especially when my girlfriend was so far away. I washed my clothes in the sink, and hung them on the balcony to dry in the warm westerly Pacific Ocean wind. On the third day, in the mid morning, I rode to a fork in the road. One went straight to El Salvador. The other, went to the western areas of the Honduras and on to Guatemala. I stood at the fork, straddled my bike, looked at my map, and then at the fork. It was close to noon, and I would have to make a decision.

I turned left, and rode down the road. Soon, I saw the border station as I cycled down the road. At the station, officers in their air conditioned chambers stamped my passport, and operated on their computers. I biked through the gates, and about a mile down the road, some little kids saw me and threw some rocks at me while they laughed. I ignored them and kept biking. The air was blazing hot, and the air above the road shimmered with waves of hot air, but I kept biking.

As I biked, I felt the sun's heat on me get stronger and stronger. I drank some water from my bottles, and continued to bike, but my head started to feel light. Then I felt an itch in my skull. It started small, but with each pedal, I felt the itch slowly turn into a screw. Suddenly, my head started to spin, and the road swam up above my head. I felt something land on my head with a loud "thud", and the next thing I knew, I saw blue sky. My bike came down with a crash. I'd collapsed onto the road, and I saw large bright spots in my eyes.

My head continued to spin, and as I laid on the tarmac, and my breathing was short. I grabbed my helmet, took it off, grabbed my head, and curled up in a fetal position. "The hell?!" I mumbled. I was disoriented, but I shook my body, and realized I'd fallen from sun stroke. I just lay there for five minutes, trying to get a grip on my skull. "Fuck." It felt like someone drilled through my brain, except I was the one spinning around, and not the drill bit. Finally, I managed to get up, pick up the bike, and walk over to the side of the road into some shade. I laid down, poured some water on myself, and rested for an hour.

Luckily there was no traffic on the road. I got up, ate some mangoes to replenish my blood sugar, and drank some more water. I pulled out my mat, and laid down to sleep for the next hour. I waited until 2:30PM before resuming cycling into the early evening. I searched for a place to pitch my tent. Some Salvadorians advised me to camp out in their grandfather's house on a hill for safety, but the route was blocked. Instead, I found a little knoll in the hillside. I squatted next to my tent, and contemplated the quiet calm of the countryside. It was lonesome and a light breeze touched my face. I sat down to watch the sunset in the Salvadorian hills, and lit dinner fire. My dinner was simple. With nothing more than some ramen noodles, ketchup, some spices, and a few vegetables from road side stands, I cooked yakisoba sautee. My meals were simple. In the mornings, I had cereal with cold soy milk, and whatever fruits or veggies that I picked up the night before. During the day, I had lunch at a cafe or a roadside stand. I would also pick up supplies for the evening, since I never knew if a roadside stand or café was available. Due to the physical demands, I constantly craved fresh vegetables and fruit, and I carried an iron ration of cereal, bread, water, noodles, rice, and cheese.

The sky glowed with hues of red and orange, and a thunderstorm erupted at a distance. The air was mildly warm, tranquil, with just a touch of moisture for the nostrils. Crickets sang, and I smelled cooking fires in the distance. I relaxed as I sat back, content, and hoped the thunderstorm would somehow avoid me, which it did. I sat down to eat and contemplate my decision to enter El Salvador. From what I heard along my route, other than Guatemala, El Salvador was considered the most dangerous country in Central America to travel in.

Figure 22.1: Melvin's trophies sit on top of the TV. His training diet, corn flakes, sits on the table.

Figure 22.2: Melvin and his family. I'm in the back.

Figure 22.3: Melvin starts his training for the day.

Chapter 23

El Salvador

The next day, I pedaled out to San Miguel, a large city at the southern border, and then down to the Pacific Coast. As I biked, I saw large numbers of US military personnel driving through the city and the highways. "How odd." I thought to myself, as I watched a line of military Humvees drive by. As I continued, I looked above, and every few miles was a sign across the highway that read, "Joint Construction Project of Japan and El Salvador, Donated by the government of Japan" or "Joint Agricultural Project of Taiwan and El Salvador, donated by the Government of Taiwan." There were many of these joint projects in Nicaragua, Honduras, and in El Salvador. I saw a few European Union projects, but most of the road construction, agricultural station, fishery, and some power station projects were called "Joint Projects" with either Japan, or interestingly, Taiwan, and many of them were donated by those governments. I didn't see any American projects, other than the military base.

As I biked, I watched huge volcanoes take up half of the horizon, while poor people walked alongside their straw, thatched bungalows, and little kids played soccer on the road side. During noontime, I took time out to avoid the sun. The bout of sunstroke I had the day before was painful. I passed through San Miguel, and then I rode down a hill looking for the intersection to turn right onto the Pacific highway. It was 2 in the afternoon, and I began to wonder if there were any food vendors. I had some basic rations, but I wanted to pick up some fresh produce, fruits, and basic staples. For the next hour and a half, there was nothing, and I started feeling concerned.

"Where am I, in a desert? There's nothing here." I said to myself. Then I saw a sign. I rode a little faster to see it. The sign said "Comedor LaFuente." I felt an unusual urge to go in.

I sat down on a plastic table shaded by a white tarp. It was quiet, and there weren't any other customers. I said hello to the waitress, and asked for a plate of rice, beans, salad and some juice. I was exhausted, and the sun was strong for the mid-afternoon. A strong looking, stout, barrel chested, and smiling Salvadorian sat down next to me, and we started to talk. He was brown, with combed back, black hair, and a hyperactive like energy that radiated from him. He smiled warmly, and we shook hands.

"Hey, whats up my friend! What are you doing out here? You out on a bike, I mean, friend! That's good, friend! I'm Liqu. What's your name?"

"David."

"Hey, so, why don't you take a load off, and sit back David? You know, take some time out, digest, and just enjoy yourself?"

"Well..."

As soon as I said "well...", blood started to well out of my nose. It surprised me as I held my face up and clamped my nose. Did the sun affect me that much?

"Agh! Excuse me, do you have a napkin?" I said as I clamped my fingers around my nose and squeezed it.

"Ah hah! That's a sign friend! You have to stay and rest! It's too hot for you. You can set up your tent in our yard over there."

The waitress brought a napkin and a large block of ice for me to put on top of my head. She smiled at me as I took the items, and I smiled back. Suddenly, I heard a commotion from behind the restaurant.

"Agh! You pervert! Get away from me!" Yelled a woman's voice.

"Ahahahahaha! Ah Manh!"

"Disgusting little... why I ought to..."

From around the corner, out ran a little boy with a fiendish grin on his face, and down syndrome like features. I took a closer look. He definitely had down syndrome. He ran straight to me, and then he tried to hug me. Bewildered, I just sat there and accepted his hug, while the waitress came over, scolded him, and then slapped him on the back of his head with her hand. He made a face, and then slapped her back on the butt, laughed his strange laugh, and then he proceeded to put on my helmet. The waitress reeled in disgust, and started yelling insults at him.

"You little twerp! How dare you slap my behind! Why I ought to… "

The boy made a grab for her breasts. The waitress quickly slapped his hand away, and covered her boobs with one arm, while she tried to slap him with the other one.

"Agh! You pervert! You disgusting little…"

I sat there and watched him put on the helmet. This was my first time in close contact with a child with down syndrome. In fact, I can't say I've spent a lot of time with retarded people either, and it was a fascinating experience for me. The waitress screamed and slapped him back, while she scolded him for putting on my helmet. I took the helmet back as I watched the little boy squirm and make faces at the waitress. I noticed that he couldn't form sentences, and none of his words were intelligible. He also started making strange hand signs at me. He opened his left palm, and had it face the sky. Then with his other hand, he pointed his index finger, and then he wiggled it at the palm. He kept looking at me and repeating the gesture. It looked like he was drawing spirals with his finger. The he hugged, kissed me on the cheek, and then he went back to accosting the waitress.

Giggle, spiral, accost, hug, kiss, slap a butt, accost, grab a breast, slap, get slapped, make faces, spiral, giggle, grab a butt, get slapped, scream, make a face, and then hug. I watched him in fascination. He kept making grabs for the waitresses, and they regarded him with anger and caution. Finally, Liqu, who amusedly watched the scene, spoke up.

"This is Tito, friend, he's my younger brother. He's got Down Syndrome." Said Liqu.

"I noticed! He also can't seem to keep his hands to himself."

Tito walked over, hugged, and mumbled to me again. I patted him on the head, and then hid my helmet, gloves, and gear. Liqu showed me a place to stow my stuff away from Tito, since he figured Tito would get mischievous and rummage through my things.

"You know my friend, given your condition, I don't think you can go any further. Why don't you stay here for the night? Back there in the bathroom we have a bath, so you can freshen up. I'd like you to meet my family tonight."

"OK." I said.

I pulled out my tent and spare clothes. I took a bath with a bucket of clean, cool water and a small pot inside the dark, moist, bathroom. I watched the water splash onto the bare, concrete floor, where the water sluiced down a drain in the middle. A sliver of sunlight broke the darkness from beneath the door and through a gap in the ceiling. It felt great to be fresh and clean again. Three days of heavy riding and no bathing wore down on me. I felt my muscles ache and renew themselves with each splash of cool water, and savored the cool moisture. Feeling refreshed, I dried myself and got dressed. It was warm, but I wore a khaki, cotton, long sleeved shirt for protection from the mosquitoes.

"Feels good to be fresh isn't it friend?" Asked Liqu, as I sat back down at the table.

"Oh man, I feel so light." I rolled my eyes in relief.

"Yeah, my friend! I told you! Don't you feel better? Hey, my father is coming home later this evening, and I want you to meet him. Say, what religion are you?"

"Oh, I'm Buddhist."

"Hey! My brother! Then you're in good company here! My Dad loves talking to people who have different belief systems. He and I are very different from most of the people here."

"How so?"

"Everyone here kisses the Pope's feet. If you're not one of them, then you're the demon."

"What? I guess there must be about 4 billion demons in the world then. Really though, is that true?"

"It's true brother, if you're not one of them, then you're one of THEM. There's no room for understanding or thought here. So, me and my Dad, we're isolated in the way we see things. He'll really be happy to meet you."

"What about Tito. How old is he?"

"Nineteen, friend."

I sat and watched Tito. Despite the first impressions, there was something about Tito that grabbed my curiosity. I couldn't quite put my finger on it, but I listened to my intuition, and stick around a bit. I wanted to know more about him.

****

It was the late evening, and I sat down to a meal of rice, beans, fried plantains, and vegetarian tamales. Tamales are mashed beans wrapped in rice and a banana leaf, and they're either fried or steamed. Usually they're served with beef, but I asked the waitress cook a couple meatless ones.

An imposing man walked in, and he had a square and stern expression on his scarred face. His face appeared to have seen and lived through enough to make most people cynical and pessimistic for the rest of their lives. Yet, it was also one which expressed an air of "I am the king here." He sat down at the table in front of me. I introduced myself, shook hands, and we began to talk. His name was Jose, father of Liqu and Tito, the owner of the restaurant and the surrounding lands. He explained that he was a consummate business man, but at the same time, I could feel that he was a haunted man. I felt like he had a million questions to ask me, and I hoped that I'd be able to answer them.

"My son tells me that you are a Buddhist."

"Yes, I am. But in truth, I'm really a person who believes that there is no real difference between the religions. The basic message is the same in all cases."

He reached over and shook my hand, and for the first time, he smiled brightly.

"Do you believe in a heaven and a hell?"

"No, I don't. It doesn't make sense to have either when there is an all powerful force. Existence would be pointless if you're not allowed to learn from your mistakes, and because we're not perfect in this world, we're bound to make them. To me, it makes more sense to have levels of understanding, where after practice and life's experiences, you can move towards higher levels."

Again, he reached over and shook my hand. His smile was even broader that time.

"Have you met Tito?"

"Yes."

"Then you saw that he has Down Syndrome."

"Yes. I know a lot about the disease genetically. I've never been in close contact with someone with the syndrome for a long time though."

"Good. Then you will answer my question."

He paused.

"Why did I have Tito? Why have I been punished? What have I done? Is it true that I'm being punished for terrible sins? Is it because I used to be

a terrible womanizer? I have had so many women, fifty, a hundred, I can't remember. I have three other children, healthy, beautiful children, and I have this successful business, and then I had Tito. Why? Why do I have him? Is it true that I am being punished?"

I listened to his questions, and felt a touch of agony in his voice. My response, was automatic, and I felt that I wasn't responding through my usual, conscious mind.

"There is no punishment. Tito is actually very special. My feeling is that he's a very advanced soul. He is here as a teacher, to teach us, to teach you. We all have a purpose here, and the most important purpose is to learn. I believe that you have something truly significant to learn from him. In reality, I believe that Tito is your greatest blessing."

Jose stared at me when I said that. His eyes glowed intensely. They pierced into me like laser beams with a ferocious focus, but then, slowly, in the silence after what I said, his eyes softened. Then, after a moment of silence, he spoke.

"What you said is true. Before I had Tito, I never knew how to love. I had many women, none of whom I loved. I did not care. My children, none of whom I expressed love to. I was a businessman, a powerful man, and then I had Tito. For sixteen years, I asked, 'why?! Why did I have Tito?!' For years I read everything I could on Down's Syndrome. My other children were perfect. Why, of all my children, did I have a child with this disease? For sixteen years, I asked that question. The priests said it was my curse. The evangelists, the catholics, they all said it was my punishment. The others said it was because of my affairs. I hated them and what they said. For sixteen years, I wanted to know why."

The anger in his voice made me stir, and I could feel a hate come out as he said it. Then he paused before continuing. He cooled down, and his voice softened, into a contemplative tone.

"Thank you David. What you just said is absolutely true. It was because of Tito, that I finally learned to love... and not just love, I learned uncondi-tional love. If it was not for Tito, I would not know this. It is because of Tito, that now, I know how to love without condition. Because of Tito, I learned faith, commitment, and loyalty. Now, I have one woman, who I've stayed with for 17 years. I want no other, and I've had no other. Because of Tito, I learned about what has true value. My children, and Tito are the greatest

blessings I have ever had. This great land, this property, this business, they are nothing compared to Tito. Because of Tito, I learned trust. Tito, I love him so much. Every time I look at him now, I can only love him. Before, I would get angry, and punish him. I thought he was a symbol of something wrong, a curse. But then I learned. I've told no one this. Not one person, because they never understood. But you, you knew the moment you came here. You told me this the very moment you came here. Thank you."

He smiled, and he radiated both relief, and happiness. He grabbed my hand, and shook it with a fierceness that I felt was a release of an age old burden.

"For many years, I thought I was mad to think this way. But now, I see that I am not the only one. You may stay here as long as you please. You are my honored guest, and my home is your home. Don't bother with the tent. We have a room, with air conditioning prepared for you. Please, stay there."

He called for Marcello, his other son, and told him to show me my quarters. After that, he bid me goodnight, and left in the darkness.

****

The next morning, Tito knocked on my door, and woke me up. He held a newspaper clip with a picture of a group of Salvadorian bicyclists. He showed me the clipping, and then pointed at me. I got dressed and ate breakfast at the table, and then sat down on a picnic table in the middle of a grassy yard next to some coconut and palm trees. A cool breeze brushed my face. Liqu walked over, dressed sharply in a collared, white, short sleeve shirt and khaki shorts. He wanted to take me on a tour of the property. Liqu, and his younger brother Marcello, took me for a hike.

The property contained two to three hectares of land, including hills, mountains, farmlands, cattle pasture, and of course, the restaurant. Liqu was thirty years old, and he inherited some of the business from his father. Because he already knew how to run a business system, it continued to work with or without his input. His wife was a dentist in San Salvador, and a Hindu convert.

They both wanted to show me an odd land formation. The night before, I'd mentioned something about chasing the trail of strange glyphs, ancient civilizations, and the Mayans, and the both of them got excited about it. They said they had an interesting place on their property, and an American archaeologist studied it in the 1980's. Because of the civil war and the lack of interest from North America, no foreigner returned to the site, until I arrived.

I trudged up the path with Liqu and Marcello, sampled the dry forest fruits, and looked at the crops they produced. Corn, massa, jacote, a type of cactus to braid rope with, cattle, the list went on and on. We arrived at one of the hill peaks, and looked across the landscape towards the volcano.

"A woman hiking in these hills claimed to have found a Buddha carved into the rocks here." Said Liqu. *"We have seen a few as well. Seems the Chinese were here long ago."* He added.

"There's a lot of stories of the lost fleet of Admiral Zheng He. Apparently, many of the ancient imperial Chinese records talk about land forms, plants, and animals that describe the Americas, including the Grand Canyon. Except this was about 100 years or more before Columbus."

In 1405, China's Emperor assigned a Muslim eunuch, the famous admiral Zheng He, to lead several expeditions abroad, to seek out new lands and races, and to establish Chinese influence and knowledge. At Admiral He's command was a vast fleet of enormous treasure ships, many times larger than any European wooden sailing vessel. Cheng's command included 314 ships in one expedition. Many of the ships were five times the size of Columbus's biggest ships. China's technology during that time was the best in the world, and the expeditions advanced Chinese science and technology greatly.

The funny thing was that unlike the Europeans, the admiral gave more than he received. There was no real economic purpose, and it was only to expand their knowledge, and to get the outside Islamic, and barbaric world to acknowledge China as the supreme power of the time. I imagined an African warlord in South Africa, and this giant fleet of enormous ships, some which looked like an aircraft carrier with sails, bristling with Chinese sailors and marines, and armed with rockets and cannons, landing on his shores.

After the expeditions, the new emperor was deposed, and the bureaucrats determined that it was too expensive, wasteful, and there were barbarians in the western borders to take care of. Subsequently, they had the records burned and the ships destroyed. No ship with more than one mast was allowed. Had China chosen to take the step further, and kept up their explorations, the world might be using mandarin as the diplomatic language today. They already knew most of the known world, not to mention bits here and there of landing in the Americas.

But that was just one instance. Another instance was of a Buddhist monk's travel story, the monk and missionary Hu-shen. He traveled with a group of monks on a Chinese trade ship that took the North Pacific gyre, a combination of winds and currents that work clockwise through the northern Pacific, past Japan, the Aleutian islands, and along the western coast of North America. He wrote of his accounts, which were recorded 499 AD, and detailed an enormous canyon, what appear to be a type of cactus that the Hopi, Navajo, and Aztec's used for water, timber, rope, and wine, and a Mesoamerican culture called the Itzi, who influenced the Mayans. The first mention in the West of this discovery was by a French scholar named Deguignes in 1761, and then by Dr. Carl Friedrich Neumann in 1841, and then by Charles Godfrey Leland in 1875, who translated the Neumann's work from German into English.

Today, all we have are the fragments describing California's coast, the Grand Canyon, cacti, ancient Chinese imperial maps of Africa with Chinese lettering dotting the hinterlands long before European exploration of that continent, Chinese writing on Mayan artifacts, the remains of giant treasure fleets in ancient shipyards in China, African and other random peoples in other continents with Chinese genes, and an assortment of stories about carved Buddhas in the Central American mountain sides.

The great admiral retired, is still fondly remembered in China, and commemorated in his hometown. One of my co-workers at the hospital was from his town. Due to his Muslim roots, he was especially remembered for his religious tolerance and impartiality. He made sure to pay tribute to all the deities where ever he landed. No one deity or name went without him paying homage.

We finally got to the site. It was a large land petroglyph, carved into the rock, and it was similar to the Inca and Tiwanakan styled shrines I saw near Cuzco and Tiwanaku. It was carved into a large, in ground, rock, using a groove the weaved in and out like a wave form. There was another, anthropomorphically carved rock that bore similarities to the headstone I found near Macchu Picchu.

"What else did you find here?"

"A strange vase." Said Marcello.

"A strange vase?"

"Yes. I will show it to you when we get back."

Liqu waited for us. Marcello was in his teens, thin, brown, and he bubbled with energy. Like me, he was eager to figure out some of the strange mysteries in the area. We came back to the house, and I took a look at the vase. It looked like it belonged to Tiwanaku, Bolivia. It definitely did not look Incan, or for that matter, Mayan. What was a Tiwanakan styled vase, doing so far north? I took some pictures for Christian to analyze. But archeology wasn't the real reason for my presence.

Tito came up to me again, when we examined the vase, he started making spiral movements with his hands.

"Has he ever done that before? Making spirals with his hands like that?" I asked Jose.

"No, never. I've never seen him do that. Actually, he didn't start doing that until you came."

"Really. I need to sit down with him then."

Later that evening Liqu showed me some books on spirituality that he and his father possessed. One book was an old, Spanish book printed in the early 20th century. As I read it, I noticed its similarities to the sutras of India. It described various dimensions, dimensional bodies, vibrational forms, and about how love was actually an energy form. It talked about the existence, within the human being, of eight different forms of bodies, corresponding with a dimensional frequency. It also went in depth into the structure of energy, the spirit, and one's purpose in life. Jose kept it in a safe spot away from Tito.

"Where did you get this book?" I asked Liqu.

"Ah, it was passed down from generation to generation. My grandfather found it. The men of our family are unique in what we are searching for. Do you like it?"

"Yes! It's a very good book! A lot of this stuff sounds like quantum and hyper-dimensional physics! Back then, they could only describe it, but now we have the math to do it. This is amazing stuff!"

"Well, you do know the Hindus knew about this for a long time." He replied.

"True, but still, the fact that the author knew and wrote it down accurately is amazing. Can you make a copy for me?"

"Sure bro. Hey man, you're like family here, it's no problem. You know, it's good that my father met you. He's wondered about this stuff for the

longest time."

Through the day, I mulled over my reasons for ending up in Comedor Lafuente. More precisely, I ruminated the purpose for the sequence of events that led me to this family, and I concluded that I was there to meet Tito. Those spiral symbols he kept making, were the symbols I'd been tracking since I started my entire journey. Tito knew something, something that at the moment, I didn't understand. Yet, I'd been preparing myself with the journey to find out what it was. There's an old saying that when the student is ready, then the teacher will appear. And Tito appeared.

****

Early the next morning, Tito woke me up, and sat down outside on the worn, sturdy, wooden picnic benches. It was a cool morning, and a breeze rustled the branches of mango trees and coconut palms. Jose walked about the grounds directing some exterminators, who were there to spray the area for cockroaches. The cafe staff hurried by and looked at us curiously. I went and finished my breakfast, and sat down with him. He had a stack of paper, a pen, and a newspaper. Class was about to begin.

Tito started drawing, mumbling, and pointing his fingers in several directions, making "manh" sounds with an intention that sounded important. He then pulled out a picture in the newspaper, and then started drawing on it, as he continued to make the sounds, pointed his fingers, made movements with them, and then he drew. After a couple of times, I noticed something peculiar.

There was a pattern, and it consisted of a picture, drawing, and then a motion. Each time, it was a picture, drawing, and then motion. He appeared to use a picture to express an emotion, a drawing to express an action, and then a body motion to show it in real life. Each time it was the same. I noticed that he used spirals and straight lines frequently. But it was still too confusing. I didn't have a Rosetta stone. I needed a breakthrough, or at least some idea of how to understand him.

Later that afternoon, in our second session, Tito started flipping through my notebook, and he came across a page where I drew a design for a solar sail space ship. It was a science fiction doodle, and it was one of my fantasies, to travel in a ship using the wind, whether it was on earth or in the stars. As soon as Tito saw the picture, he grabbed a large piece of paper, and drew the Milky Way Galaxy. It was the first time in our session that he actually drew something intelligible. As I observed him, he pointed to a distant corner of the galaxy, pointed at me, the surroundings, and then he pointed at it.

"We're here..." I replied. He was accurate, that I was certain. The galaxy he drew looked like some of the old star charts I used to study when I worked at the Franklin Institute Science Museum during my high school years. There was an observatory where I gave tours to visitors to look through the telescope. The Solar System was on a distant arm of the galaxy, near the edge. He pointed to the arm, and made a dot. I looked at him, suspiciously this time. No, it couldn't be, could it? Was Tito one of those special children that Sheryl, months earlier in Cuzco, Peru, speculated were incarnating to help the planet?

"So, where do you come from?" I asked him, seriously this time.

His whole face immediately brightened. He knew exactly what I was talking about, and smiled broadly. He pointed to a spot opposite of where the earth was, and then to himself. He then drew a picture of what he looked like in that sector, which was near the galactic core.

"Uh huh." I said as I nodded my head. Then he made a motion, which I learned earlier as his way of saying, "beautiful women, hot babes." He moved his hands up and cupped them in front of his chest in a sign of breasts, and then puckered his lips. Then he made a sly smile on his face. He pointed to a corner of the galaxy that was a quarter of the way around from the earth. He then pointed at me, and made a movement motion, as if to say, *"you have to go here!"* I laughed, and gave him a thumbs up.

He nodded his head, and started to look serious. He pulled out a picture of Che Guevara from the local newspaper, pointed at me, and then to the picture. He drew a line, which looked like a path. At that moment, I had an epiphany. Tito's language consisted of pictures which had a cultural or emotional relevance. His lines indicated actions that related to the picture. His motions and expressions indicated directions, opinions, and emotions. All through the afternoon, I watched as he drew his pictures, maps, spirals, and lines. In it all, I began to realize what he was trying to teach me. At that particular moment with Che Guevara's photo, he said that I was thinking and becoming revolutionary, or more precisely, changing; the lines indicated the becoming part, and his expressions illustrated that I was to become a person who embraced and evangelized change - or revolution.

Tito had a definite grasp on time. On top of the Galaxy, he drew two lines forming four quadrants. He took a picture out of the newspaper which had Israeli soldiers destroying some Palestinian homes, and pointed to a quadrant. He then pointed at us, and then back at the same quadrant.

"We...are... in a period of war?" I asked him, by making a motion that looked like I was holding a gun. He nodded yes. He then pulled out a picture of a smiling little girl, and pointed to the next quadrant.

"And...this indicates that we are close to a period of peace, happiness?" Which I illustrated by smiling, putting my hand on my heart, and then sitting back calmly. He nodded again. He then pointed at us, and drew a dot on the galaxy that was close to entering the quadrant of peace. He drew a spiral on top of the whole thing. It was the same direction as the spin of the galaxy's arms. He made a movement with his fingers, and pointed to his wrist.

"OK. We are in the time of war and destruction, but we are near the time of peace in galactic time, correct?" Again, he nodded yes, but then he stopped. He flipped through the pages, and pulled out the symbol of nuclear energy. He looked at me, smiled, giggled, and then drew a big round of circles on the quadrant of war.

"We're going to destroy ourselves?" I made a motion of an explosion. He shook his head. No. He started drawing two spirals, opposite of each other, and a line connecting the two. I practically jumped out of my chair. It was the same symbol from the circle of stones at the sacred site near Cuzco, where I was practically wiped off the map on top of an Andean mountain! I could barely contain myself. Tito motioned for me to sit down.

He started drawing what looked like rectangles at each of the end points, and made a door opening motion.

"Doorways." I said. He nodded, and giggled that maniacal laugh even more. I drew a stick figure of a human, and then, to my amazement, he made a walking motion of the man from one spiral to the next. He pointed to the galaxy and it's time quadrants.

"A doorway is opening that allows us to travel?" I made a motion with my hand like an airplane. Tito stopped, and looked at me, with this big grin on his face. I said something that was my eureka moment, and to him, was as familiar as his room. He pointed at the nuclear symbol again. Wait a minute. My mind buzzed. A nuclear reaction produced new elements. For billions

of years, stars spewed out elements from their nuclear fires. Stars transform things into other things. Then my mind lit up.

"Transformation." I slowly said, as I made a drawing of something changing into something else. I looked at him as he slowly looked at me again, smiling as broadly as ever, and nodded his head.

He laughed. "Ha Ha!"

****

I spent the night mulling over what Tito taught me. By now, I was getting the rudiments of his language, and his family was getting curious as to why I spent so much time with him. I wanted to pick his mind some more.

I sat down for my lesson the next morning. So far, his message was that the planet earth, and in fact the entire solar system was in an arm of the galaxy that was transiting through a sector where conflict occurred. However, we're near the next galactic quadrant, where there would be a time of peace. He superimposed a clock on top of the galaxy, where the galaxy itself was turned into the clock's sectors. Then he divided the clock into 4 quadrants. 12, 3, 6, and 9 were the points to enter the next quadrant. Imagine that between 12 and 3 is the time of conflict, 3 and 6 a time of peace, 6 and 9 is the time of conflict, and 9 and 12 is the time of peace. As the galaxy rotates, the sections of the galaxy, like our earth, passes through different sections of time. Those sections, have an effect on us. What amazed me was his command of the sections, and their cyclical nature. Even more baffling even more was that he understood the structure of the galaxy, its rotation, and that he knew that certain sections of the galaxy undergo energetic changes.

Tito started drawing his new symbols. They were three circles, and then he drew a circle of dots around them. Puzzled, I looked at him. He drew them again. He made a three sign with his fingers at me.

"Three."

He drew a lot of dots again. "Particles?" I asked. He nodded his head, and then shook his head. He looked up at the sun, and I noticed that he squinted in the rays. Again, he drew the three circles, and then the dots around it.

"Photons?"

Tito's face brightened, as he made a funny gesture back up at the sun. He made a spiral from the sun downwards. *"Energy... spirals down... to...*

308

three... spheres... dimensions... that... we exist... in..." I said as I began to decipher his drawings, pictures, and movements. He stopped and looked at me, and laughed that "ha ha!" laugh of his. He did it again, and this time, pointed at me, and shot his hand straight up into the sky.

"And then we return back." He shook his head.

"Wait a minute... We return back? Don't you mean energy returns back?"

He drew his line again, circling everything, which indicated, *"No. We are energy. We all return back."* He drew his circles again, with the energy around it. He then pointed at me.

"And we exist here in three dimensions."

Then he drew four circles, and no energy points around it, and then a line leading to it. He pointed at the nuclear symbol again.

"And we're transforming into 4 dimensions."

I took a deep breath. Now it was my turn to talk to him in his language. I started drawing his symbols, and talking to him at the same time, while referring to his pictures in the newspaper.

"OK. Let's see if I understand. We are nearing the end of the quadrant of war... We are close to entering the quadrant of peace. We are in a world where everything exists energetically in 3 dimensions. We are currently, because the galaxy is now moving to another quadrant, transitioning to a higher energy level of 4 dimensions. But in order to do that, it means that we have to transform ourselves. In order to transform ourselves requires conflict - a catalyst - to aid that transformation. When we have completed the transformation, we have traveled into a new dimension, and a new world. By learning what we need to learn here, we will return. because we are energy. Right?"

At that point, he did something I never saw before. He became very solemn, and made a triangle with his thumbs and his forefingers. He touched my forehead with them, and then brought it down to his chest. He then made a hand position that looked like the Buddhist prayer position, with two hands straight up at the solar plexus. He looked at me, and this time, he didn't smile. He simply picked up his things, and walked away. My lesson was over. I blinked in astonishment. Something inside of me spoke.

"Surprised?"

"Amazed is more like it. I think he just gave me the key. To everything."

"David... your journey has just begun."

****

The day I left El Comedor Fuente, I felt a pang of sadness. The family hid Tito, because they knew that I had to leave that day. The day before, I taught Marcello, Tito's younger brother, how to read and interpret Tito's language. I explained to the family how Tito spoke, and my astonishment at their child's ability and knowledge. They were surprised, and wanted to learn more, so I showed them the rudiments of Tito's language. We spent the day and night at the beach, and then back in their home as Tito lectured us in some of the nuances of his language.

I made contact with a being from another world, who chose to incarnate here as a human being. His mission was to show his family unconditional love. Then along that path, he taught a wayward traveler something wonderful and magical. People with Down's Syndrome, particularly the more intense variety, die young. Tito was halfway through his lifespan, at the middle age of 17 years. That made his lessons much more precious.

I don't know how I managed to leave that morning. First, we had breakfast, and the mood was somber, yet Tito was happy. After we ate, and took a picture, Marcello distracted Tito, as I said my thanks and departed.

As I cycled down the desolate highway, I thought about everything Tito told me, and connected the dots.

In the last half of the 1990's, across the solar system, massive changes were recorded by NASA. Among the most peculiar was the sudden global warming of Mars. It's polar caps were receding faster than when records were first kept. The Sun was peaking in solar cycles and sun spot cycles never seen in recorded history, whether written on paper or in tree cores, coral reef cores, and Antarctic ice samples. Of course, given the observational age of humanity, that would be two to three hundred years at most. But there were other strange changes.

Pluto was growing an atmosphere, despite its distance in the icy fringes of the solar system. Venus started glowing in the dark. The Earth is experiencing temperature increases that out pace anything in the planetary record. The record goes back about 5000 years or more, from core samples of trees, arctic and Antarctic samples, coral samples, and other methods of reading climates of the past.

All over the solar system, one planet after another was changing, in a way that centuries of observation never recorded.

Was all of this just a cycle that we never knew about? Or was it a cycle predicted in ages past? From the "Rapture" of the Bible, to the Kali Yuga of the Vedas, every single scripture of religious or spiritual significance, spoke of a time when humanity, and the planet, would come of age.

Humanity, in all of its history, has a rich tradition and culture of prophecy. In modern times, we forgot the ancient words and sooth sayer's messages. We managed to land on the moon, send machines to far flung corners of our solar system, exploit the powers of the atom, and create a culture of material excess. We turned a culture that once revered a supreme power, into a culture that said that we were the supreme power.

In the process, we lost touch. Sure, we repetitively and blindly went to church, mosque, temples, shrines, and synagogues. Despite their anti-religious nature, scientific materialism, darwinism, creationism, atheism, new ageisms, and other such ism's were really just religions in themselves anyway. In one way or another, we gravitated to some form of worship that would supposedly fill a void in our lives so full of accomplishments and material excess. In that process, we divorced ourselves from the planet. We were destroying Gaia, her great and rich biology, her life support systems, and her inhabitants, which included us. We were destroying the planet which made our temporary existence to make religion, wage war, sing songs, and make love, bearable. In arrogance and disdain, we said, "We are not of the World. WE ARE the World."

By doing those things, we lost touch with what the purpose of being human really meant. That purpose was passed down to us in every culture, and in every language. No religion or spirituality had dominance in its message. That purpose was embedded in our prophecies.

Every prophecy spoke of a time when all would return to a maker, a god, an energy form, or a oneness of all things. But in order to make the return, we would be tested. Some writings perverted the old prophecies, speaking of hell and damnation. Others preserved them in their entirety, such as the Hopi, Incas, Mayas, and Hindus. They spoke of a point when all must evolve to a higher form, regardless of race, creed, or faith. Each one of these ancient foresights gives a purpose and many paths to a single destination. The destination was being human.

Tito's view was that as the sun rises and sets, so must humanity. We can't stop the sun from rising and setting. Nor could we stop the path of our solar system into this new and energized region of the galaxy. Yet, during the path of the sun, we can do many things. A farmer gets up, sows his seeds, and tills the soil. A bicycle maker begins work on a frame. A writer crafts his words, and finishes a poem. These little processes are what make the difference in our lives. When the sun sets, the farmer harvests his crops. A bicycle maker finishes a masterpiece for a racer to test his speed on. A lover finishes a poem to set a flame to the heart. Of course, these are positive examples. Negative examples are just as valid under the sun, because the sun shines equally on them as well.

When the sun sets, the finished work, in mind, heart, and body, through the experience, was what mattered. During that work, we'd encounter all kinds of trials and tests. The farmer pulls weeds. A craftsman cuts his hand. The poet gets writer's block. The better quality experiences came from the negative. We like to call negative things evil or wickedness. Yet, to focus on the wickedness of the act divorces you from truly learning. A killer provides a true test of the victim to learn forgiveness. A thief would truly teach another of the folly of materialism. The negative is a catalyst. The positive learns to experience and understand from the lessons of the catalyst. In order to have the good, you must have the bad. They go hand in hand, because without each other, there wouldn't be spiritual and emotional awakening. I found it interesting that the greatest, most beautiful things were born in the fires of agony, anger, and hate. My parents found love precious in the Vietnam War, which raged around them and killed so many of their loved ones. Jose found True Love in the chaos, anger, and madness of a Down Syndrome inflicted child.

As with all things, eventually the sun must set, and each person must go to sleep. This is the natural rhythm. Awakening, doing, thinking, experiencing, and sleeping. Birth, life, and death. How we choose to take on the challenges while awake was what mattered, because in the end, we all go back to sleep, both saint and sinner, wise and foolish, lover and hater. We all came from one source. Eventually, we go back to that source.

Tito's message astonished and humbled me, especially in the time period we were entering. This great age humanity is full of chaos, war, turmoil, and despair. Yet the ancient seers looked upon this period with awe and wonder. They would have wished to live in these times, and they probably are. These times are remarkable, because they truly are fertile conditions for any person to experience enormous spiritual and emotional awakening. Now we can give ourselves to aid others, to experience the wonders of the human emotion and spirit, and in that experience, to return to the source from which we came.

Tito and his family gave me one other gift before I left. It was a gift whose magnificence far surpassed the incredible message that Tito had given me. It was the gift of True Love.

As I bicycled into the sunset, I felt my heart quiver on that last gift. I found a very special kind of magic, a magic of True Love, in the middle of the desert. I discovered True Love that I never imagined I would experience. I observed Jose watch and hold his son, Tito, and how he looked into the eyes of his son with such enormous compassion, with an affection that blossomed like flowers in the dry sands of the desert. I was overwhelmed, because they truly were perfection. No religion, no spirituality, no story of miracles, no hallowed faith could hold a candle to what I saw. I saw the source of all of us. Truly, I witnessed God itself.

The simple act of a father who learned to love his son, despite the obstacles was the true miracle. I hoped, and wished that even for a moment, to feel from within the love that Jose had for Tito. That was the greatest gift that Tito and Jose had given me.

****

"HONK! HONK!"

"David!" I heard him yell out at me. I watched as he pulled the car up in front of me. It was Ricardo, Tito's uncle

"Ricardo, how are you?"

Ricardo was a Salvadorian immigrant who regularly traveled in between Virginia and El Salvador. In the States, he had a bathroom and general home remodeling company, and he employed many latin immigrants, and aided them in settling down.

"You know man, I got to the restaurant, and Jose told me that you left. So, I said, 'sheet man! He left already?!', so I got into da car, and said, 'I'm gonna find him, and hey look man! I found you!'"

"You did a good job on that one."

313

"You know man, I wanted to talk to you, so why don't I give you a lift?"

I was roasting in the Salvadorian sun. It was noon, and typically, around this time, I'd find a mango tree or some shade to take a nap in. The ascent into the mountains combined with the heat was punishing.

"Sure!"

We then strapped my bike to his car, after I unloaded the bags and stuffed them inside. I got in, and sat next to the hired nanny, while his pregnant wife sat in front of me.

"Hello! How are you?" I said.

"Hello! We are fine." They timidly replied. We drove off.

"You know Dave, it's great that you got to meet Jose. Before, you couldn't have paid him to even come over and say hello. Man, I remember when he used to sit with a pistol in one hand, and a shotgun in the other."

"Looks like he changed a lot."

"Oh man, you wouldn't believe how much he's changed. Anyway man, I wanted to like, catch up with you. I had a lot to talk about, you know, about some of that crazy shit you were showing us, about Tiwanaku, Atlantis, and all. You know man?"

"Ha ha! Well, what'd you think about the book that I showed you?"

"You know man, here in Central America, we have the Aztecs in the north, the Mayans around here, and the Incans down in the south. My people know man, that the Incas were coming up through Central America, and they were damn strong. The Aztecs in the north were also really strong. But the Mayans, they were damn smart man. They were like, the diplomatic country between the two Empires."

"That would explain that Tiwanakan style vase Marcello found on his land."

We talked for a while as he drove me up towards San Salvador. One interesting point we got into was about Carlos Castaneda. Ricardo was more inclined to the spirituality, as opposed to dogma, much like Jose.

"You know man, one thing you have to do when you get to Mexico, is you should read about Carlos Castaneda. I mean, all that eastern spiritual tradition stuff, like Buddhism, Taoism, here the indigenous people have it too. He talks about how he meets a master, I mean a real master, a shaman, in the desert, and the master shows him the way to the truth. First they use drugs to induce a trance, but then the master, Don Juan, he teaches that the truth is found by pure introspection. It's some good stuff, man."

"Carlos Castaneda. I've heard of that guy."

"Yeah man, he's a good guy you know? But here in Central America, South America, we all have that tradition in our blood, of the shaman. It's like the tradition of the guru in India and Asia. I mean, man, I once paid a thousand dollars to see a lecture with Deepak Chopra. So, you know, I know about this stuff. Every time I come back to El Salvador, I have some books with me to show Jose and his family. Stuff like the Hebrew code, Conversations with God, good stuff man!"

Ricardo was my kind of guy. Although he came from a catholic country, his mind was open to the possibilities. It's not easy meeting people like that in general.

"So man, you are a vegetarian. Does that make me a bad person?"

I looked at him. "What? No! I'm a vegetarian because I need to tune my body in a way that's like an instrument. Especially when you go exploring ancient energy mysteries, you need to be in tune. But at the same time, I need people like you, you guys are like the audience that hears the musician play the instrument. So no, you're not a bad person if you eat meat! I'm not a good person just because I'm a vegetarian. It's just that for this energy stuff, my body has to vibe in the right way, otherwise, I can't play."

"OK Man, I feel a lot better about that."

We stopped at one of the ramps that went into San Salvador, got out, and untied my bike.

"Thanks Ricardo! I really appreciate your generosity. If there's anyway I can make it up to you and your family..."

"No sweat man! My pleasure. Hey man, a tip for you. If you ever need a safe place to sleep for the night, go to a gas station. You can setup your tent, they'll take care of you, and in the morning, they'll give you a cup of coffee to send you on your way."

After that I waved good bye and headed into and around San Salvador. I wasn't interested in staying in San Salvador. It was reputed to be a crime ridden and nasty place to go, so I went to the satellite city of Santa Tecla. Santa Tecla was higher up in elevation, and cooler in climate. All I needed to do was find a place to stay.

Being an ignorant foreigner, I asked around if there were any hostels to stay in. Everyone, as always in Latin America, regardless if they knew or not, most of the time not, pointed me to "Just across the street around there."

Then I saw it. A sign! It was a tiny sign on an electrical post that said "Hotelito Guerero." I'd never heard of that as a term for a hostel before. I went up to the receptionist.

"I'd like a room for the night" I asked.

"For the entire night?" She looked at me, hiked up an eyebrow, and said, *"You're a good one, eh?"*

"Yes, for the entire night."

I was a good one?

"Wait here please." She jumped off her stool and ran inside to talk to the management. That was strange. Usually it was normal to ask for a room for the night, right? A mustachioed man came walking out of the doorway. He addressed me in English.

"Hello friend, you want a room for the night?"

"Yes."

"Ok then." He looked at the receptionist and said, *"just bill him for 12 hours."*

Payment for 12 hours? That was new to me. I followed the receptionist into the hotelito to my room, and we walked inside. There was a photocopied piece of paper on the wall that said, "3 hours for $2". Three hours for two dollars? That was a strange thing to put in the room. Who would want to rent a room for three hours for two bucks? I did some mental mathematics, and asked the girl, *"since I am staying the whole night, can I get a discount?"*

"Sure sure! We already figured that out for you. I just need to clean your place for you. It's ah, pretty nasty in here."

I looked at the sheet on the bed. It had a small, red, dried bloody stain.

"Oh." I muttered to myself. I let the girl put a new sheet on the bed.

I sat down on the bed, and took off my biking clothes. It was depressing to think about sex, and not be with Claudia. I laid down on the bed, stared at the ceiling fan, and took a long nap.

I stayed in Santa Tecla for a few days, walked around town, resupplied, and caught up on the news. I'd been away from civilization for a while, and I wanted to enjoy it before taking off for my next destination.

That destination was the brilliant, mysterious, and incredibly ancient Mayan Empire. The Mayan Empire endured for twice as long as the Roman Empire. Its calendar system, and mathematics were unrivaled with much of the world, except for maybe China and India. Once, they had vast libraries with records of their culture and people. Unfortunately, the Spanish, with their Catholic zeal, proclaimed the libraries to be works of the devil, and they burned them all, in an effort to subjugate and convert the native peoples. Only three books survived. Still, the Mayans accomplishments weren't shabby for a group of people whom most Americans called illegal immigrants. At least the murdering Spanish weren't able to destroy their ancient cities, many of which were saved by the jungles.

I pedaled hard on the road heading towards Santa Ana, and for Ahuachapan. I knew I was about to enter an ancient empire when I started hearing names that didn't sound Spanish. I stopped to get some water at a gas station. I drank the tap water wherever I went. Most guide books said not too, but it's not really due to poor sanitation standards. Almost all tap water was chlorinated. The real issue was that the bugs were a bit different. After Peru, I never ever had another case of diarrhea. It really was a matter of adapting.

One of the interesting features I saw on the Salvadorian highway was how bicycle friendly they were. I passed by several enormous signs that stated, "Please be aware of the bicyclists", or, "Please Respect the Bicyclists". As I rode by them, I fell in love with El Salvador. I've never seen so much respect for people on a bicycle.

To look at the bicycle, is to feel both a sense of nostalgia, and love for something elegant and beautiful in its simplicity and grace. The bicycle is a poem in motion. When you're on it, you've become it. When you ride it, you're not so much riding it, as it's transporting you into a magical wonderland, where all your senses are alive. The wind, the rain, the sun, the sky, the sounds, and the smells, they are you and you are they. Suddenly, you're not in a body anymore. You're everything and nothing at the same time. No other vehicle can do the same thing for you. A motorcycle is too loud. A car puts you in a box with what looks like televisions on all sides. But a bicycle, is truly a work of magic and art.

The bicycle returns you to who you are, in elegance and grace. The daily cycles, of sunrise, noon, and sunset, all of these celestial rhythms become your body's rhythms. When traveling on the bicycle, you've become the planet itself, as the stars streak by above your head, or as the moon rises. All of us have a certain rhythm about our lives. Day in and day out, we live, subconsciously according to our customs and cultures. Yet to reunite with the rhythm of Gaia herself, the planet, the stars, and the sun, you've once again become part of the whole. It created us, and It's where we'll return. By traveling on the bicycle, I became part of that rhythm. I became the Sun. I became the Moon. I became the great sky streaking above. I became Gaia herself.

Of course, the other beauty of the bicycle is how it's a passport into people's hearts. At noon, I stood on the side of the road, harvesting ripe, orange, soft, mangoes from the trees. I sat down to eat, and ten minutes into my meal, a police truck, white with worn blue stripes, an old Toyota pickup, pulled up in front of me, with several mestizo, Salvadorian policemen, who were heavily armed with assault rifles and submachine guns. They looked at me and smiled. I smiled and waved back to them. Two of them got out of the truck and walked over to me. I felt no fear as I smiled.

"Hey buddy, what're you doing here?" One guy asked.

"I'm having lunch!" I smiled back. He looked at my bike.

"Whoah! You came here on that? Where did you start from?"

"Peru." He looked at me in astonishment.

"Where did you go through?"

"Peru, Bolivia, Panama, Costa Rica, all the way to your beautiful country."

"Whoah man, that's great!... Get in the car." He said in a rather urgent manner.

"What?"

"Get in the car, right now. We'll put your bike in for you."

"OK."

I wasn't going to argue with heavily armed men. I got in the car and looked at their faces. They reached out to shake my hand. One of them spoke up as we started off with my bike in the back of the truck.

"There was a murder about a mile up and we're chasing two bandits. We saw you on the side of the road, and we don't want you to get hurt. We'll take you about 4 miles away from the site, just to make you don't run into them. By the way, it's very brave of you to bicycle through all these countries, and especially ours. So many people think our country is so dangerous and full of war."

I was stunned at the preconception. *"What?! This country has some of the friendliest people I have ever met in my life!"*

"I know man, but, you know. You are very blessed, man." He replied.

"Well, when I get back, I want to make sure everyone knows about the beauty of your country and people." They dropped me off up the road, next to a road side stand, and I waved them goodbye.

****

When I arrived in Ahuachapan, after a stop in the central square, I went to the archaeological site, which was the first ancient, Mayan temple that stood as the southwestern gateway to the Mayan Empire. I wasn't impressed. It looked like a large, 75 foot by 75 foot, squat stack of concrete blocks, in a step pyramid fashion, that some modern artist made while having a hangover, instead of the magnificent pyramid that I expected it to be. I walked around the top and then down the solid, limestone stairs. I imagined myself as the barbarian at the gate, with hopes that I would impregnate the glorious cities.

Instead, I was myself, a rogue in smelly lycra and spandex wandering amongst the ruins. I left Ahuachapan and walked onto the street. I caught the eye of an attractive girl selling food off her stand. She signaled me over to her stand, and soon I gulped down a couple liters of juice, some fried plantains, and a few vegetarian tamales.

We started talking. I told her I was a biomedical engineer from the USA, and how I used to work in the bio-tech industry. She mentioned how she was familiar with bio-tech, and studied genetics at the university. We talked about DNA and DNA sequencing techniques. This wasn't a typical street conversation. The more we talked, the more I realized just how well educated she was, and how startling it was to see her selling food on the street.

She then introduced me to mother and sister. Her mom, a teacher, and sister, a lawyer, and herself, a biologist, were all graduates of the university. When I asked them about the problems of El Salvador's economy, her mother said,

"David, people here are well educated. The educational system here is better than that of the USA. The only problem is the lack of capital. The salvadoreños are hard working, and educated, but we don't have any money."

"Did you like Ahuachapan?" The girl asked.

"Yes, I liked it a lot." I lied.

"Really? I think it's a boring site. Well, that's the way I thought of it until my father started investigating the ruins. He found a lot of strange

things there." I was caught off guard with her statement.

"Your father..."

"Was an archaeologist. He's dead now."

"I'm sorry."

"Don't be. That was a long time ago. Would you like to come inside? I can show you some of the things that he was studying."

She lead me into the house. On the outside, it was just a brown door on a nondescript building. Inside, the coolness of the brown tile floor relieved my body. The girl flicked on the switch, and in the lit walls were clippings of newspaper articles about new discoveries in Ahuachapan that linked to the Mayans, as well as some unique artifacts they discovered. In each article was the same man, her father.

Her father lead an international team of archaeologists in Ahuachapan until the day he died. After his death, all excavation ceased, and all that remained of his efforts was a humble museum, which his daughter lovingly maintained. I examined the things he retrieved: arrowheads made of obsidian, spearheads of limestone, pottery, and the odd skull were among the artifacts.

"Here David, this arrowhead is for you." She said as she handed me an obsidian point. I felt it's tip, and shaved my finger tip on the razor like edge.

"It's for good luck."

"Thank you." I replied.

"No, thank you. It's been so long since I've shown anyone this place. You're my first guest in a long time. It's been quiet here." She said as she looked at the floor.

"Well, I'm honored." I said as I lifted her chin.

After kisses and a goodbye to the family, I hopped back on my bicycle, and headed north towards Guatemala.

I cycled down the road, past groves of mango trees, people on their bicycles, old 1970's era buses, and make shift stands of wood and plastic, selling food and drinks. Soon, it was six in the evening, and I started my search for a place to pitch my tent. Silly me. I'd forgotten that this was El Salvador. As I went up the highway, a man jumped in front of my bicycle.

The sides of the road were cut into the hillside, and the sides were steep. The man ran along one of the sides as he yelled, *"Hey friend!"*, and then he ran down a steep dirt road that cut through the side, and jumped in front of me. He was thin, with sandy brown hair, and a grin on his face. He didn't look mestizo or indigenous, and he appeared almost German looking.

"Where are you going?" He asked.

"I'm going to Guatemala."

"It's 6PM friend, it's late!"

"Oh, then, do you know if there's a place where I can camp?"

"Why do you need to camp? Come over here! You can stay with us!" He smiled. I couldn't refuse. I stopped and watched as the man's sons came running down the side of the road. One of them was a thin, short, brown kid with a bright smile, which shone like a flash of white across the earthen tones of his skin. He had short cropped hair, and held a soccer ball under his arm.

"Hey Gringo! Hey, wait, you're no gringo. Are you Japanese?" He smiled.

"No, not Japanese. Vietnamese." I replied.

"You're not Japanese? Vietnamese? Like in Rambo?" The boy asked curiously, as he gave me a thumbs up. I laughed. I nodded.

"You look Japanese. Follow me, friend." Said the boy.

I followed the kid and his father up the dirt road to their home. In front, near the road, was a tamale and drink stand. The home, or to be more accurate, the family compound, sat amongst mango trees, palm fronds, coconut, and jacote trees. It was made of mud adobe and cinder blocks, with a rusting tin roof, and it looked like a squatter residence.

"Here here! Put your bike here!" The son motioned to me. He watched me lay the bike on the wall, and touched the bright yellow panniers.

"You travel in this?" He looked at me incredulously.

"Yes." I smiled.

"Really? Don't you get tired?"

"Well, I'm probably not tired because I want to play futbol with you and your brother." I replied back. He grinned.

"Futbol? Let me go get my friends!" He said. He ran off as a middle aged man came out to greet me. The man had a broad grin on his face, short, dark hair that rested on his head, a slightly balding hairline, a long sleeve, white shirt, and a baggy set of dark slacks. He also looked like the other man's older brother, but with a bigger nose.

"Hello hello! So you're the traveler! Are you Japanese?" He asked.

321

"No, my parents are from Vietnam, and I was born in the USA."

"You're not Japanese? You're Vietnamese? You look Japanese. So you're from the USA? Where abouts?"

"Philadelphia."

"Ahh, Philadelphia! A lot of black people there. You're also from Philadelphia?" He looked at me confused.

Of course I was sure I was from Philadelphia. I was born there.

"Philadelphia has a lot of Vietnamese and Chinese there too."

"Ahh. No Japanese?"

"Yes, Japanese are there too."

"OK. Permit me to show you around."

He led me to another house, built in the same fashion as the first one. Bits of straw stuck out of the rough material, and they used two by fours for the window frames. In front of the compound was a latrine, where they received water. Water came twice a week, if they were lucky. A wire from the telephone pole across the road led to their home, into an embedded electrical meter set inside a rough, adobe wall.

The men, both the gentleman who jumped in front of me and the other in baggy slacks were both light skinned. Their spouses were the opposite, with dark native, mesquite features. Their children were mestizo, and looked more like their mothers than their fathers.

The gentleman's name was Victor Hernandez. He graduated from college with a bachelor's in management. As I walked around his home, I saw the photos of his graduation, and his diploma, which he earnestly presented to me to prove that he wasn't just a bum.

Many Salvadorians were well educated, yet, education wasn't the complete solution to everything. Victor was unemployed for a year and a half, and to survive with some semblance of dignity, they squatted on land before claiming a home of their own. Victor gave me a plastic chair to sit down on, before sitting down himself.

"Do you like music?" He asked me.

"Sure, I do."

He played some popular latin tunes, and danced while sitting down for ten minutes, simultaneously switching between tunes. Finally, we went back out to have dinner. Victor's son saw and ran to me.

"Where were you? We wanted to play futbol with you!" He said.

"I know, but your father wanted to show me around."

"Oh OK. Well, maybe tomorrow then."

"What would you like for dinner?" Asked Victor.

"Well, anything you can make that doesn't have meat or fish. Or chicken. I'm vegetarian."

"You don't eat meat?"

"No."

"Wow, but you're really strong to bicycle all the way through the country!"

I asked them if I could take a bath, taking care to be sensitive about the water situation.

"You're lucky! We get a lot of water today! Of course you can take a bath! Please! Besides, I'm sure you don't want to stink up the table for dinner. It would ruin appetites."

I walked into the latrine, and noticed a lot of large, plastic containers, some full of water, and others partially filled. After I bathed, I refilled a few containers for them, before getting dressed in my semi formal attire, which was starting to look thread bare. They prepared a lot of food, evidently they were excited at having an unusual guest. There was steamed corn, cheese, bean tamales, bread, butter, mangos, bananas, beans, fried plantains, and their special fresco, a refreshment they sold at their road side stand. I was overwhelmed at the amount of food they prepared, and I felt guilty, due to their level of poverty. Here, they were rich in other things, which they generously shared. As we ate, and laughed, I cracked my jokes, and they commented on riding a bike.

"When you have children, David, they will be born with wheels." Said Victor.

"Well, that's if sitting on my crotch all day hasn't effected my plumbing! I definitely want to have children one day."

"I ride a bike too!" Exclaimed the uncle, the man who jumped in front of me on the street.

"Let's go for a race!"

"But I'm not dressed in lycra like you my friend! I couldn't go half as fast as you."

"It's not the lycra! It's how hard you can ride!"

"Woo! Ride hard like you all day? No no, I'm not like that. I ride to get

to work. What you do, I don't know how to define it. Ah yes. You ride for pleasure."

"Pleasure?! Pleasure? You're kidding me right? Some days, yes, it's pleasant to ride, but on others, my knees sometimes want to fall off. And forget making love to a woman that night, if you ride too hard that day. But then again, I enjoy it that way. It's sort of masochistic."

"Masochistic? You mean macho, right? I couldn't be macho enough to ride like you do."

As we ate, a friend of the family, Pablo, came over. We greeted each other, and sat down to eat. All through the night, came questions, stories, and laughter.

"How did you get so good at Spanish? Many people study it for years, and they can't speak half as well as you. And you only learned it in what, about a month? That's amazing! I have a few gringo friends, and they studied through the university, yet they cannot hold a decent conversation."

"Ahh, well, it's all about motivation. Do you remember how you talked about me being fast in lycra? A woman in Bolivia thought I was trying to be fast on her"

I recounted my story of how I was dropped like a rock when I thought the word "mentiroso" was a beautiful word, and how I proclaimed myself to be the biggest "mentiroso" in the world.

The family rolled with laughter on the benches.

"So can we trust you? Ah ha ha!!" Pablo guffawed.

"Did you see her again afterwards?" Asked the uncle.

"Did you at least get any? Ya gotta get something for all that effort buddy!" Exclaimed Victor.

"Victor! Can't you see that we're in front of the children?" Said the mother.

The kids giggled in delight.

"Love, I know, but he's a good looking guy, so he must be getting women, eh David?"

"Uh, I have a girlfriend, who I'm very loyal too." I stated.

"Oh ho ho! Really?! Even after seeing the Salvadorian women here? Come on David! She's over there, and you're over here. And so are the Salvadorian women. You know what they say right? Two at a distance makes four! Or more if you like. Your girlfriend, she's Latina, right?"

"Yes, Bolivian."

"Well, tell, me aren't the women here gorgeous though? Come on take a look at my wife."

I watched his wife glare at her husband and shake her head.

"Well? Aren't they?" He insisted.

I smiled. *"Salvadorian women are beautiful, and if I didn't have a girl-friend, I'd definitely get a girlfriend here."*

"David, so do you know martial arts?" Asked Pablo.

"Yeah! Are you Bruce Lee's brother? You look like him. Can you show us some moves?" Asked the little boy.

"I know just a few." I lied.

"Show us!!"

"Yeah, do it to my uncle!" The little boy pointed to his uncle, *"he knows how to handle it! He knows some moves too!"*

I looked around.

"Please!"

"Oh, OK OK."

I got up, and walked over with the uncle. I showed them a few of my Kung Fu techniques, which consisted of grappling, joint locks, and throws. Half the time the poor guy was either on my back, or being supported by my arm from falling onto the ground.

"Wow! That was cool!" Exclaimed the little boy.

"I guess you didn't any problems with bandits, eh?" Smiled Victor.

We sat down and conversed some more.

"So what do you think of El Salvador?" Asked Pablo.

"I love your country! In the USA, most people think of El Salvador as a third world country in a civil war. They think about drugs and illegal immigrants. Everyone told me to stay away from El Salvador, except for the ones who took the time to go through it. The ones who went through, they're like me. So, I came, and the people are the nicest, friendliest, most hospital people I've met yet!"

Everyone looked and smiled as I raved about their country, but soon it was my turn to ask them questions.

"As I was riding through, I saw a US army base in San Miguel. What is the US military doing here? I thought El Salvador was an independent country."

I just opened a can of worms.

"David, Central America is a plantation of the USA. We are essentially slaves to the gringos." Said the cop.

"What do you mean slaves?"

"For example, you are Vietnamese, right? Many Salvadorians fought in Vietnam as conscripts of the USA. Each Latin American state has a pact with the USA that when the USA goes to war, each of us must send a contingent of our troops whether we like it or not."

"How can they force you to send troops without your permission?"

"Because some time ago, through agreements with your banks and other organizations, in order for us to take loans out to help our country, we had to agree to that condition. Many of the conditions are destructive to our societies, but especially terrible are the ones that demand our people to fight abroad for the USA. We Latin Americans often form the front lines for your wars. In return, if they stay alive, the soldiers receive a visa to live in the US."

"And the slave part?"

"Oh, that one is easy. We have to open our markets completely, as well as our farms. We are not allowed to subsidize our industries and farmers. This is a hypocrisy of your country, because most of your farms are paid for by your government. When they bring their products here, they dump it here to destroy our farms. When we try to restrict trade because of this, they in turn apply pressure on us through the loans. We've paid the loan off, but we are still paying. We've paid off that debt several times. When our industries go bankrupt, or our farms are destroyed, we become dependent on the US for food, for products, and on their industries, so they open up factories here for the cheap labor, pay below subsistence level, and then move off whenever prices go up. We are left with no infrastructure, and a lot of debt."

Victor decided to pipe in.

"The sad irony, is that we want to live and prosper as well, so we send family members to the US to work, and send home money. If you think about it, do we really have a choice? We can either live poor, and not be able to provide for our families, or we can have someone go and help all of us. That is why you have the illegal immigration problem. It's not because of your borders. It's the results of those policies and agreements."

"How do you know all of this?"

"I've studied this when I had so much trouble looking for work. I couldn't understand it. I worked hard for my degree, only to see many people like me with no opportunities, no work, and very little hope. If you think about it, if these policies did not exist, El Salvador would still have its economy, we would have jobs, and you wouldn't have illegal immigration. People don't migrate just for the sake of it. They often migrate just to help their own families. Right now, I have a son and his wife working in the US, to send us money. He recently became injured, and hasn't been able to send money home."

Most of El Salvador's economy came from families working in the US and sending money home. Very little of it actually came from their own economic production.

"Is he there illegally?"

"Ah ha ha! What is illegal and legal? Legal is when the white man goes to your country. Illegal is when anyone just a shade darker goes to your country. Look David, most of the Mexicans are native Americans. True native Americans. They lived in those areas of the USA for millennia before the white man. Yet now, when they move about in what is still the land of their ancestors, they are called "illegals." Isn't this obscene? And when the gringo goes in killing everyone off in genocide, what he does is "legal." Did you ever see the native American committing genocide against the gringos? No! The fools invited them into their own homes! Tell me David, what is illegal and legal? Shouldn't we really be saying what is just and unjust? Or moral and immoral? Think about what happened to your ancestors, in their country fighting for just a piece of self dignity against the French and the Americans. When they fought back for their lives, for the right not to be dogs in their own country, what they did was 'illegal.'"

I thought about that one.

"How did your son get to the USA? It is far from here through Mexico."

"He went through a Coyote."

"A Coyote?"

"Yes, a coyote. Several families will put up some money to send a member or two to work in the US. Their hope is that the ones in the US will be able to make back the cost of the coyote by working and sending money home."

"How much is it?"

327

"4500 US dollars."

"What?! How can you afford that in these conditions?"

"Many families will pool their money in the hopes that 1 or 2 will get through, send money home, eventually establish themselves, and then get the rest of the family through."

"Does it work?"

"Not all the time. Many die in the deserts. Many are raped, tortured, and then killed. Some are robbed, or beaten. Left to die. Their bodies litter the deserts of Mexico and the US. Many of us do this in desperation."

"What is the average Salvadorians living needs per month?"

"$100"

"And what is the average salary?"

"$14 most places."

"How much do you make, David, as an engineer?"

This was always a sensitive question. The fact is, even the poorest American was far better off than 90% of the world's population.

"I make enough to live. The US is also a very expensive place to live."

"Then you should live here!" Smiled the little boy.

I smiled back, *"that's not a bad idea."*

I asked them about all of the Japanese and Taiwanese volunteer projects, and the lack of US volunteer projects that I saw during my ride.

"Where are the American volunteer projects?"

"Oh, we have American volunteer projects!" Said the little boy. He made a motion with his arms as if holding a rifle, as well as a grimace. *"They donate guns!"* He said as he made shooting noises. I was aghast at the boy's response. Victor spoke up.

"You know over in that town David?", he said as he pointed west, *"the Japanese are building us a geothermal electrical reactor, to use the volcano's heat to give power to the locals. This is their donation to us. We are not required to pay a cent. They don't obligate us to anything, and their works are mostly, at least as far as we can tell, unconditional. The Americans are not like that. Every donation has a price on its head. Even if we don't want the donation, they will still force it on us. The Japanese don't force anything onto us."*

Whether it was altruistic or not, the long legacy of soft diplomacy by the Japanese and the Taiwanese was effective. It had already captured the hearts and minds of many Latin Americans. We continued to talk through the night until 2 AM. Then I was ready to crash. The next morning, I woke up to the crowing of the rooster. I got up, and the whole family was already up.

We walked across the road to the soccer field, and then up the hill to watch the sunrise. The air was warm. It had a light, moist flavor to it, with a touch of tropical flowers. I watched as the sun lit the sky up in a warm, bluish red hue. We took some pictures, and then headed back.

I cleaned myself, and got my bicycle ready, as the family prepared a breakfast, Salvadorian style, of tamales, beans, rice, eggs, and fruit.

The grandmother, the family matriarch, came out and sat down with me. I noticed the family watch her suspiciously. She was dressed for Sunday mass, as was her family. She was quiet as I ate. I talked to the boys about soccer, and who their favorite players were. Then, as I finished, she spoke.

"David, I want you to know something. We are very poor here. And you came to stay here. I want you to pay 10 dollars for the night." She certainly was blunt.

Suddenly, the boys, the father, the mother, and the other family members got into a fight with the grandmother.

"He's our guest!"

"We invited him over!"

"You shouldn't charge a guest, that isn't right!"

"How can you do this?"

"That's not very catholic!"

"Don't pay David!"

"Yes, don't pay her! That's not right!"

I looked as they fought, unsure of what to do. So I pulled out my money pouch. Victor stopped me.

"No David, don't do this. You are our guest." Said Victor. I looked at everyone around me. I had to do something, as the argument intensified.

"I am not paying you. This is the only way for me to say thanks for inviting me over. It's not like a charge for a hotel, or a room, or for a dinner at a restaurant. This is what I have to say thank you. In my culture, we have a custom, called lucky money. We give money as a gift. Will you accept it this way?"

They looked at each other. It wasn't customary to use money as a way to say thanks. Then again, for the grandmother, that was thanks enough. She snatched the money out of my hands, and deftly put it in her pocketbook. Victor sighed.

"David, as long as that is the intention, then that it is alright with us. It's alright with grandmother after all." Said the uncle.

"I guess that settles it!" I said with a grin, *"I have to go now. Thank you so much for letting me stay over."*

"No David, Thank you. We love talking to people like you. The children enjoyed it as well."

"Yeah, well, I didn't get to play soccer with them."

"Will you come back David?" Asked the little boy.

"Please?" Asked another one.

"Yeah please? We'll play soccer with you, that's for sure."

"Will you come here to live?"

"I'll stop by again someday." I said.

I walked onto the road, and mounted the bike. My muscles were fresh, and the cool, crisp, moist, morning air had an energizing feel to it. I was only 10 miles from the border of Guatemala, which was a new country, land, and people. I waved to the children as they ran along side the road to wave goodbye.

Figure 23.1: A sign for a joint Japan El Salvador project.

Figure 23.2: Tito makes some friends at the beach.

Figure 23.3: The strange pottery at Comedor Lafuente. I sent photos of the vase to Christian, in La Paz, Bolivia, who showed the photos to an archaeological expert in the Tiwanaku museum. We didn't tell the expert where the vase came from, but the expert, after thoroughly examining the photos, stated it was Tiwanakan in origin. When we revealed that I found the vase in El Salvador, he retracted his statements.

Figure 23.4: El Salvador really respects its cyclists.

Chapter 24

Guatemala

The beginning of the Guatemalan southwestern mountains greeted me as I came out of the dry, scrub brush jungles of the Pacific Coast, and headed inland. It'd been months since I ascended mountains. I looked ahead of me and saw a brown and green, forested hill, with a black, two lane road, recently tarmacked, rise into the blue sky. The road climbed skyward, and all I could see of its end, was a distant peak.

"Nothing I can't handle." I said to myself. I switched gears, and pedaled up. I imagined there would be a nice surprise at the top, like a beautiful view, or a road side stand with water, juice, or even watermelons. In Nicaragua, I stopped by a family stand, selling watermelons on the road, bought five of them, and devoured every single one. Each one was the size of a volleyball. It was the most refreshing meal I had in months. I pedaled up the mountain and dreamed about the succulent, pink, moist, sweet flesh of the melon, dripping with a liquid that would sate my thirst.

As I approached the peak of the second mountain, my thirst and hunger intensified, as did my mental wanderings into food, dishes, and drinks. My legs were on fire, and I felt the fatigue. I stopped to rest, stood up, and balanced the bike between my legs. I laid my chest on the handle bar, and quietly controlled my breathing. My hard breaths started to calm down. It was silent, so silent, that I could almost hear a butterfly land on a leaf.

Suddenly, I heard a crack in the air, and a whistling noise in front of my face. My head popped up, and my hair stood on end. I immediately recognized the sound. An animal like instinct exploded in me, and took over my body. The next thing I knew, I mounted my bike and pedaled with an almost inhuman force, as my body screamed to get out of there quick. Once I reached the peak, I continued to pedal the way down, as fast as I could go.

I reached the bottom, and came to a stop to catch my breath. My heart was pounding. Someone took a pot shot at me! Completely alert, I looked around me and listened. I heard bird songs in the trees, and then I started to calm down. I realized that the speed down the mountain took me about two miles away from where the shot happened. I needed more distance to even begin to feel safe again, so I quickly resumed cycling. As I biked, I searched for a gas station. No way in hell was I going to take a chance on the side of the road

As I traveled through two more mountains, I heard another sound. Bang! Whistle! Pop! When I heard the "bang", I dropped my bike and dove into the side of the road. I breathed a sigh of relief, when I saw little clouds in the sky. They were bottle rockets.

It was getting close to six in the evening. I stopped, and ate dinner in a small, crude, adobe road side café, and asked the lady if she knew of a place where I could pitch a tent. She thought it was ridiculous for me to pitch a tent on the side of the road, and said I should get a hotel somewhere. I didn't have that kind of time. It was almost twilight, and the last thing I wanted was to ride at night, especially after getting shot at.

I looked at my map, and the town of Barbarena was a few miles away. I looked at the distance, and figured I'd need two hours to get there. Hopefully, since it was a population center, there'd be a gas station.

I cautiously biked through the night, and guarded against the sparse traffic. The moment I saw a Texaco sign, and I biked in. The eager station crew, fascinated, watched me enter.

"You've never had a cyclist stop by here before?" I asked.

"Like you? No. That's pretty cool what you're doing." Said one attendant. I asked for permission to camp, and they were excited that I wanted to stay the night. They helped me unload some of my gear. As I started to pitch my tent in the corner of the station, I saw a shadow in the station's light, as it walked over to me.

"Excuse me sir? I'd like to invite you to my home." Said the gentleman. He was a middle aged Guatemalan, with glasses, rather rotund, and dressed in a collared shirt and slacks.

"Oh! Well, as long as it doesn't inconvenience you." I replied.

"No, no inconvenience! I want to hear your story! You're my guest, and I'd like to have you over for dinner."

"OK. Thank you very much."

We loaded my bike onto his red, 1980's era Chevy pickup truck. He was driving with his wife, so I jumped in the back. I said thanks to the station crew. They seemed a little disappointed.

We drove for an hour, and were stuck in a traffic jam entering Guatemala City. I could feel the air temperature drop as we ascended the mountains. Finally, after a long ascent, we entered a private, gated suburb. As we drove through, I noticed the homes looked like the suburbs of Los Angeles.

The difference between rich and poor was dramatic. I went from biking alongside mud huts, into an upper middle class neighborhood. By now, I'd been invited by both classes. Curious, I wanted to learn more about the differences and similarities. We arrived at their home, which was a white, concrete, stuccoed, prefabricated home with a red clay tile roof. We took my bike out, and introduced ourselves to each other. The man's name was Fernando, and he was a Guatemalan businessman who ran a coffee export company. He introduced me to his wife, daughter, and son, who was also an avid cyclist. His son presented a Specialized carbon frame bicycle, one of the company's early attempts at carbon frames, He also ran a motocross shop in Guatemala City.

"You traveled on this? How far did you go?" He asked.

"My computer died after about 2000 kilometers, so I have no idea."

"You went from where to where?" I listed the country names.

"Incredible! That's amazing! You must be in incredible shape to do that!"

"No, you don't have to be. You just need to get up every day, get on the bike, and enjoy the ride. It's nothing special."

"You weren't afraid of bandits?"

"I actually wanted to ask you about that. You know where your father picked me up? Before that on the second mountain, I heard something like a bullet go by me!"

"I'm not surprised. People are still messed up from the war. A lot of people died, and it was terrible. A lot of people have weapons here."

I put my things in their guest room, took a shower, and washed my clothes. We sat down to a modern, glass, and dark wooden table, and I looked around the room. It was well decorated and furnished. Fernando's wife made me some vegetarian dishes, fried eggs, and bread.

"I've heard about this place through other travelers. Lake Atitlan." I said, as I pointed to it.

"Well, it is nice, but you should see Antigua first," said the mother, *"it's an old colonial city, but many Mayans live around the area."*

"Check out the blue river over here!" Exclaimed the daughter, pointing east, *"it's beautiful, with animals you've never seen nor heard of."*

"But beware this place," said the father, as he pointed at a dot on Atitlan – Panajachel, *"this is gringo land."*

"Here on the west coast, is the Pacific mountains, and they're rugged." Said the mother as she pointed west.

"In the north here, the mountains descend into jungle and cloud forest." Said the father, as he pointed to the north regions of the country.

"Here, in Guatemala City, you are in the population, industrial, govern-ment, and business center of the country. It's also central to most of these locations." Said the father, as he pointed to it, and traced the lines of the roads north, south, east, and west.

"Do you have plans to go to Tikal?" Asked the mother, as she pointed to it.

"No, is it beautiful?" I asked. She went to her bookshelf, and removed a book with photos of enormous pyramids. A shiver went down my spine as I looked at the pyramid of the Jaguar.

"This is a sacred place. Tikal. You must go. Of all the places to go to, in the land of the Mayas, Tikal is one of the most spectacular," she said, *"but you must be careful, bandits sometimes roam the outer extremes of the park."*

"But be very careful here." Said the father, as he pointed at the lone road entering Belize.

"Last week, two Mennonites were murdered there." He said.

I looked at the lone road. It was the only road into Belize.

"Many bandits, drug runners, military men, illegal loggers, and ex right wing militias still roam this area." He said as he pointed at the Peten area.

I looked at the map, the family, and then smiled. This country had it all. It had a population that was mostly indigenous, which still retained its ancient cultures. It had ancient ruins, ancient mysteries, diverse ecologies, and it was dangerous. Adventure isn't adventure without an element of danger.

"I love your country already. Even though I was shot at while entering, I'm already looking forward to it." The family burst out in laughter.

After we ate, Fernando and I talked about family, while his family went to bed. We talked about how my parents escaped from Vietnam in 1975. He told me about the articles in the Guatemalan newspapers about the cruelty of the French during the colonization, and then later about the ruthlessness of the Americans. Fernando was well educated. He said that what the Vietnamese endured was similar to what many of the Guatemalans endured during the right wing regime.

"Did you ever take sides in that war?" I asked.

"David, we're like most people. We simply want to live peaceful lives, see our children get an education, and to prosper. In a war, taking sides is an excuse. The true nature of life in war is survival, nothing more, even for those who took sides."

"At least the war is over," I said, *"what's it like now? Is there still a lot of animosity, or is it like Vietnam, where people are friends again?"*

"It's a little bit of both. Like Vietnam, we've been reconstructing ourselves, and most people try not to hold grudges. But the murderers in the government have mostly gotten away with just a slap on the wrist. Many of them have connections to the American CIA, and we think that is why."

"What was the cause of the war?"

"The cause? The cause was like most of the civil wars that happened in Central America. In each country, the people elected a government that they chose, whether it was good or bad. Or, the majority of the people held a political orientation where the established powers would lose, so the establishment called the USA. The USA is like the ultimate mercenary. It really doesn't care about the politics. It just cares about money, and the USA's business is war. Any place that has a war, or wherever they can create a war, is where they'll make their money."

"Well, the war is over now. At least you're an independent country, right?"

"We're a colony," he bluntly said, *"the USA leans on all the Central American States to gain critical votes in their favor in the UN. Why do you think certain unjust resolutions pass in the UN? It's not because we want*

it too. We are forced to. They bribe our officials, and put up politicians that will represent their interests. We have a democracy in name only. And, we are at their mercy through trade and loans. We have almost no trading rights, and they dictate all of the terms. It's colonization, but covertly. The funny thing is, everyone knows they are doing it, but there is little that we can do about it."

"You know the other day, I stayed with a very poor family, and asked them the same questions. I would think that your family would be considered the upper crust, the ones who would benefit the most, and yet your feelings are the same way." I said.

"One thing you have to realize is that colonization is colonization, rich or poor. Just because you're rich doesn't mean you will benefit, especially when the gringo holds himself to be superior to you. Sure, maybe for a little while you may feel like a privileged child. But that's all you'll ever be with the gringo."

We talked about his coffee export business, and about globalization. He told me that the biggest exporters of coffee in the world were Brazil, Colombia, Vietnam, and then Guatemala. He also added that Vietnam was about to overtake Colombia as the 2nd largest producer of coffee. Coffee was the world's second largest commodity after oil.

"Has globalization benefited you?"

"More or less. I have access to a wider market, but then the entire world is involved, so there's an oversupply of coffee. When that happens, I have a harder time finding buyers for coffee at our prices, which are already low. Then we go out of business, and without a market, the farmers go out of business, and then we all suffer. In addition, these trade agreements we sign with the USA are not designed for free trade."

"How so?"

"The problem with these agreements is that we cannot compete with tax subsidized farms and corporations. Our government doesn't subsidize many of the farmers here. In the US, the taxes subsidize the corporate farms. They have essentially no startup costs. With no startup costs, and no loans to pay, they've already won. Then, they flood the markets with their product at prices below our prices. For me, as a business man, this cuts profits, which means less money to operate my business. With lower profits, I'm unable to purchase and export coffee from the local farmers at the farmer's prices.

When I'm unable to do that, the farmers lose money, and then they go out of business. When they go out of business, I lose suppliers, and this causes problems in finding a consistent supplier. Or the coffee plantation becomes a slave shop just to survive. It's like that already. It's a whole chain. Business people on the wrong side get destroyed by those agreements. But I believe this is effecting the small farmer in the USA as well, no?"

"Yes, it is. The worse part is that these corporate farms use genetically modified food."

"Ah, we've already been invaded by that. Even though we may protest, the power of the corporations, through the US government and its agreements forced us into using the genetically modified food."

"Can the farmers choose not use the seed stock? Can't they just boycott it?"

"Then they'll dump their food here at below market prices to put the local farmers out of business. According to the agreements, we have to accept the food, otherwise they will file a suit with the World Trade Organization. The WTO is intimate with the International Monetary Fund, and with the banks who provide loans. Consequently, there's a lot of unemployment, which supplies labor at a lower price."

"How do you feel about this?"

"I run a business to make money, and to fairly employ others so they can live and prosper. Any business must profit, and it must pay its workers fairly to keep them working. If the employees have to work for unfair wages, then the work quality suffers, and the business suffers. I can understand that, because I wouldn't work for someone who was unfair to me. But fairness is not what the gringos want. The gringos want the best quality, but at a slave's price. You cannot have both."

It was the same story, but from a different class of people, and from a different perspective. From what I'd listened to across Latin America, the message was the same. All across these countries, the people were getting sick of the "Free Market", because it wasn't about free markets. From Argentina, Bolivia, El Salvador, to Guatemala, it was about access to resources and labor at slave prices. It was about inequitable positions, and the virtual enslavement of an entire group of people, to produce at the least cost possible, and force them to buy overpriced products from the company store. There was no "Free Market". How could it be free when the American tax payer subsidized the corporations?

This feeling of anger, the pulse that I felt across Latin America, was a reaction to the corporatization of the government at the people's expense. In a truly free and unfettered market, the Guatemalans would benefit the most, due to their lower living costs, which translated into lower cost of labor. People could still get by decently at a decent wage in Guatemala, but it would come at the expense of the ridiculous profit projections of Wall Street and commodity traders. In fact, when I thought about it, the so called "capitalism" that Americans used was a lot more like a corporate socialist operation. It was hard to fit it into any kind of category that I could understand. It certainly wasn't capitalism, and it definitely wasn't free market. Yet, American style "capitalism" was branded as free market, and the backlash against the USA's hypocrisy smoldered across Latin America.

"What about finding export partners in other countries? Is their anyway to get another market?"

"Well, with China entering the WTO, there is hope and fear. I would like to sell coffee to them."

"Problem is, they drink mostly tea. They're not like the Vietnamese. I drink a kind of coffee called Café Saigon. It'll probably take some time, before the Chinese adopt the coffee habit. Hey, if you ever need someone to import coffee, let me know."

He smiled at that.

****

Guatemala City was in the high mountains, so to get anywhere, I had to go down hill, and then back up again. The road to Antigua spiraled down the side of a mountain, and I cruised down the relatively smooth road into the colonial town. My bike started to rattle as the road changed from tarmac and concrete, into cobblestones.

The houses were low, one story homes, and made of adobe. It was mid-morning, and I cycled by cars and horse drawn carts. I cycled by passersby, and overheard their conversations. They didn't speak Spanish, and the languages didn't sound like Quechua or Aymara. 1950's era yellow school buses rumbled by, and kicked up clouds of white dust in their wake. They had steel racks welded on top, and they were loaded with large, woven sacks. Packed inside were people, and occasionally, a chicken or two, sometimes a goat. The squeaking sounds of rusted hinges hurt my ears, as an old, 1980's Toyota truck rolled by. In the back, the odor of decaying chicken meat wafted into my nose. I rode into the central plaza, and dismounted. My hands shook from the vibration of the cobblestones, as I walked down the streets looking for a hostel.

I found a hostel three blocks from the plaza, near the market, that had a fold up sign outside, and a deal with breakfast included. In the evening, and I walked around the plaza, and stopped in a sandwich café. I sat down to eat when suddenly, about fifteen Korean students stepped in. Antigua is one of the world centers for learning the Spanish language. The other place was Bogota, Colombia. Surprisingly, learning Spanish in Spain wasn't on the list, said the owner of the shop. The owner was a young woman, separated with a child, who studied at the local college.

The next afternoon, I checked out of the hostel, and biked northwest, to the Mayan city of Tecpan. As I slowly pedaled up the mountain, I frequently rested to watch the cotton like clouds float around the mountain sides. The road turned into dirt, and it cut a deep ravine into the mountain side.

As I ascended, I frequently looked at the ground directly in front of me. The ground was dark brown, and as the sun poked through the late afternoon clouds, it took on a darker hue. I turned around a corner, and noticed a wetness that coated the dirt and dust. I looked up to see some flies buzzing around. I looked back at the ground as I pedaled. The ground was dark, and it seemed soaked. It hadn't rained in the area for several weeks, and I knew how precious water was. Then the color began to change into a deep, dark, red.

I shivered, as my hairs stood on end. My mouth was dry, open, and my breathing quickened. My stomach turned. Dead, hacked opened, mutilated, and gutted bodies of dogs, at least eight or nine of them laid on the road, and their guts were all over the place. The blood was still warm and flowing. I began to get sick, and my mind was numb.

"Calm down. Calm down. Get the fuck out of there. Get the fuck out of here. Calm down, *Calm down.* Get the fuck out of there, Get the fuck out of here. Calm down. Calm down!" I repeated to myself as I pushed the bike up. My blood ran cold, and I shivered. I got off the bike and ran with it. I turned back, I turned forward, I looked side to side. There was no one. Silence. As the sun set, the dark shadows of the bodies grew, and the shadow's tips masked and deepened the blood's color. They made everything dark, wet, and frighteningly disturbing. I felt like throwing up. I just wanted to get to Tecpan.

By six in the evening, as the sun set, I finally entered Tecpan, and checked into the first hostel along the way. As I sat in my room, I thought about war's effects on the human psyche. I remembered the stories of the Vietnam War that my parents told me when I was a kid. I remembered how my mother told me how she had to pick up the pieces of her uncle, who was blown up by a land mine, and put them in a plastic bag for cremation. I remembered how my father told me about the fields of dead bodies, from human to animal, that he walked through while growing up. I got a taste of my parent's experiences, and all I wanted to do was cry.

It was night time, and the high mountain air chilled my body. I was up 1000 meters in altitude. I wandered the streets looking for a café, and noticed how similar Tecpan appeared to Peru. The people were a reddish brown tint, the women wore clothing that was rainbow colored, and most everyone greeted me with a smile. My nose dripped; I a light nasal infection. In the café, after I ate, one of the girls gave me a pot of boiling water, some eucalyptus oil, and a towel. I steamed my face and nostrils in the cafe. When I returned, and went to sleep, the woman's warning, and the memory of the dead dogs haunted me.

The next morning, I awoke to a commotion outside my window. In the square, just beyond my room's 3rd floor window, people played a soccer match in the middle of the market. The men were dressed in red and blue, and they played amongst the bright blue tarps that hung over the market stalls in the bright, high mountain sun. I slowly packed my things, and grabbed a breakfast of fruit and bread.

I cycled to the Iximche complex, which was a cluster of pyramids from the Western fringes of the Mayan Empire. Long ago, the city supported about twenty five to thirty thousand people. The city complex was full of square, step style pyramids. I hiked up one of them, and sat down next to a four hundred year old tree that grew out its base. In the clear sunlight, my mind began to wander. I thought about the bodies, the ruins, and about war. And then I remembered the people who I met along the way: Fernando and his family, the people at the gas station, the sandwich shop owner, even though the war effected them, they got on with their lives. I didn't want to think about the past day's events too much.

The next day, I coasted down the mountain, and watched the high, cold, mountain slopes change into warm, emerald colored forests. The sky painted a broad swath of orange, red and yellow across the pale blue evening. I headed to Solola, the first town before the resort village of Panajachel, on a quiet road with little traffic. As I cruised down the road, the forest sped in a green blur on both sides. I listened to the chirping of strange birds, as I continued onto Panajachel's muddy, dirt road.

Panajachel looked like a poorer version of Atlantic City's boardwalk. Open air tourist shops hawked trinkets and souvenirs. Restaurants and cafes lined the one street town on both sides. Like other tourist traps, there were multiple souvenir shops, all selling the same thing, at mostly the same price. There were bright lights everywhere and almost no locals, except for the ones running the shops. At one outdoor café, I heard two aged German women complaining about the poor service in English.

The next morning, I hopped a boat, and crossed the lake to the far shores of San Pedro. Panajachel had a number of tourists and backpackers, but there was also a large, local Mayan population who lived in small villages dotting the shores.

I landed at the dock, and checked into a hostel on the waterfront. It was just six dollars a night, and it was clean and bright. As I lugged my equipment upstairs, I noticed a tiny five fingered seedling pop out between the cracks of concrete. Marijuana. It looked like a backpacker accidentally spilled their seed there. I dumped my things on the floor, lay down on the bed, and took a nap.

****

In a tense moment of concentration, I eyed my opponents across from me in the dimming light of the evening. I glanced into their steely, dark brown eyes, focused and lit with what they were doing. Both of them looked at me with laser beams of concentration. I furrowed my brow, and squinted back at them with defiance. Only one would win tonight.

It was my turn. I looked up at the two. Their dark red features were taut, and their eyebrows measured me in the moment. Their faces were grim. The air was silent between us, and even the sand outside made a sound as it settled. I took a deep breath, cocked my finger back, and then fired.

KLAK! *"I won!"* The little Mayan boy yelled as he threw his hands up in the air. I looked in disbelief as the marble I hit rolled out of bounds. The other boy gave a congratulatory pat on the kid's back, as I wiped the sweat off my brow. I lost, sighed, and smiled as I shook the kid's hands. They asked me to come back and play the next day. I smiled, and said that I'd consider it.

I got up, wiped the dust off my pants, and got ready to finish my stroll through the Mayan Village of San Juan.

San Juan is above the backpacker town, which rested on the shores. It was a steep quarter mile hike up the sides of the sunken, water filled bowl that made Lake Atitlan. The homes, made of gray adobe or brick, were covered with green plastic or tin corrugated roofing. Roosters crowed, and chickens pecked in the dust, as little children ran about. Many families sat in their porches, or sat inside watching a soccer game on TV.

I walked down the sandy path between the houses, and watched the sunset glow in the distance. It bathed everything with warm, red and yellow tones. A cool, moist, breeze blew a refreshing scent from the lake. Mayan women, dressed in soft rainbow colored clothing, carried their children home, while the men, usually dressed in long pants, a t-shirt, and a baseball cap, headed home after work. Work consisted of a job in construction, tourism, or basic services.

I rounded a corner in the soft dust, in a narrow alleyway, and came to a small open field full of sand. Four boys and an adult were dribbling a soccer ball between them. I walked up to the field.

"Can I play?" I asked.

"Sure!" The group replied.

I took off my shoes and got onto the court. The sand was soft between my toes, and it held the dust down. One of the boys passed the ball to me. I dribbled and passed it to the other kid, as the adult came up to defend. The boy deftly passed the ball to me as I passed it to the first kid. He shot the ball, which was blocked by the opposing team. We played for almost an hour, and the field's lights gave us some illumination.

"Do you usually meet here to play?" I asked.

"Yes, we do. Every Saturday evening."

"OK, I'll try to make it again."

I hiked down the hillside steps back to my hostel. Backpackers rarely hiked up the slopes to the village, which probably explained why the locals were so open. Locals can get really jaded with travelers. The hardened ones rarely dealt with them as humans; usually a traveler was just an income source. For the backpackers, the locals were at best part of the service and the scene.

I hiked down the cobblestone road, down the steep slope to my hostel, and grabbed some groceries in the local market. While cooking dinner, I met a Canadian girl, Chiba, who joined me in the kitchen. Later, while sitting on the porch overlooking the waters of the lake, we enjoyed a meal of spicy stir fried vegetables, and macaroni salad. The lake's water sparkled, and a moist wind touched our faces as we swapped stories about our backgrounds. Chiba's father, a Japanese man, rescued her mother, a French woman, in Afghanistan from some kidnappers in the early 1970's.

"So how did your dad rescue your mom?"

"The kidnappers put a sack over her, and pulled her into the car. As they started to accelerate, my dad jumped on the car. The tried to turn and shake him off, but he hung on. The Afghani police saw the car with a man hanging to the top, so they rushed to blockade the car's escape. They stopped the car."

"And that was the first time your mom and dad met?"

"Yup."

"I'll bet the rest of their relationship wasn't as wild as that first date."

Chiba smiled. "It's like any other relationship with its ups and downs."

"Where'd they get married? In Japan or France?"

"They decided to move to Canada after traveling some more together."

"So what was your mom's first impression of your Dad?"

"Well, he was the first person she saw when they took off the sack, so imagine a lanky, dusty, dirty, bruised, and wild haired Japanese guy saying, 'Are you OK?' Then my mom grabbed him and kissed him."

"That's a gutsy Dad. So how do they feel about you traveling alone?"

"My mom said, don't get kidnapped, and if I do, make sure I'm with a Japanese guy to rescue me."

"And your Dad?"

"Don't get kidnapped unless you want to get married."

"Isn't that the same thing?" We laughed.

The next day, while cooking lunch, I met the owner of the hostel, a pregnant Mayan woman with three kids. She wore a traditional Mayan dress, and eyeglasses. Her husband was busy building another hostel, and I was curious. With all the development going on, were the Mayan people concerned about their environment?

It was a question I was hesitant to ask, because it was so arrogant. The West, in the last 400 years cut down 90% of their own forests, polluted most of it's own lakes and rivers, and scoured the land and sea in the name of economic progress. On top of that, the West enslaved and brutally oppressed other countries and peoples to exploit and use their resources during the colonial period, up to the present day.

Just recently, in the last fifty years have the poor and undeveloped countries decided to follow the West's model to foster their own economies, but they had to get rid of the colonial presence first. Before that, their environmental destruction was on too small a scale to effect their surroundings. Most of their forests were still in tact until about forty to fifty years ago. Now, as they make an effort to match the West, the West told them not to in the name of "environmentalism" and "preservation". To me, this felt like oppression and subjugation under another name.

"Environment is a bad word to use," she said, "a better word is our land, our holy grounds, the lands of our ancestors. Only a gringo uses 'environment', because they see it as separate from themselves, as something to admire, like a statue. Where I live, that which feeds me and my family, provides clothes, water, food, and shelter, this is not the function of a statue. This land and life is my body, my soul, and my spirit."

"I've never heard it like that before."

"Are you so sure? You said that your mother's village and farm lands in Vietnam are centuries old. Surely, people who are able to sustain themselves for so long in one place would have a true relationship with the soil, air, and the forests. David, let me give you an example of how we Maya do things around here. All around Atitlan, there is a major water shortage, yet the villages have banded together, and agreed not to take water from the lake, or to empty sewage into it. To do so would destroy the beauty and life that brings in the tourists and money. Instead, we dig wells, and sewage is piped away into septic tanks."

"Did the government help?"

"They are too corrupt. Those Ladinos couldn't even clean their own city.

348

No, this is our initiative. We are from here, we Mayans grew up here, and we will die here. We want to serve this lake, so that she may serve us for generations of our families. Our lake is our spirit, and our body. You must nourish the spirit and the body for it to nourish you."

"What about the new developments along the lake with all of the new hotels they're building. Aren't you afraid that's going to add more pollution?"

She smiled as she asked, *"how much pollution does New Jersey produce and dump into its ocean and rivers?"*

"A lot. I know. Americans have no right to talk about pollution."

"Or the Europeans, they also claim environmental leadership, but they were the colonizers, and they took our lands for their own use. Even the Japanese are polluters, but they don't go around telling us what to do and what not to do. David, as people with families, we have to take care of our children. This land is also our family member. What is pollution? What is it when you go to the bathroom? Is that pollution or is that something your ancestors put back into the rice fields? Pollution is a part of us as well. You will always have pollution, because pollution is your brother, but it is your duty to transform your brother."

The next few days, before heading back to Antigua, I bicycled around the slopes of the lake. I passed by high, misty, mountain villages, hidden amongst the dark green of the forests, while an azure lake sparkled like gemstones, and clouds cast dark shadows onto the water's surface.

Figure 24.1: The ruins of the city Iximche.

Figure 24.2: Coasting down the mountainside towards Lake Atitlan in the evening sunset.

Chapter 25

The Journey to El Mirador

It took the better part of the day to climb the high mountain slopes on the way back to Antigua. Along the way, I stopped inside a small roadside café for lunch, and next to me was a white, middle aged, man. His graying beard hid his face, but it was well trimmed, and his brown hair was combed back. He observed through plastic rimmed glasses, as I laid my bike against a table.

"Not the typical way to get home is it?"

"No, it isn't. Are you a traveler here too?" I asked.

"No, no, I'm an ex hippie turned capitalist."

"A what? A hippie turned capitalist? Isn't that an oxymoron?"

"Yup."

"So what do you do?"

"We make designer clothes, which we design in the states, and then we use the Guatemalans for their cheap labor, and then sell the clothes in the states."

"And you were an ex hippie? That doesn't sound very left leaning."

"I have to be honest about this, otherwise I wouldn't be able to do business. I'd rather be honest about what we're doing, rather than be a damn hypocrite like a lot of our countrymen. Sometimes this side of the business can be really depressing, so I do some volunteer work to help out down here."

We talked some more about my journey. He asked me how my mother felt about my trip. I told him that she wasn't too happy with my decision. He wasn't surprised. As if to remind me for my mother, he said to make sure I gave her a call.

I arrived in Antigua that evening, and checked into another hostel. After some rest, and food, I went to the central plaza, browsed in a bookstore, and drank some fresh coffee. Later that night, I returned to my hostel. In the courtyard, I had tea with a Swedish man studying Spanish with his instructor, an older Guatemalan man with an old, worn, leather cowboy hat. The lines on his face made him look 40 years old.

The Guatemalan was a ladino, a creole, descended from the Spanish, but he identified himself with the Mayans, and the rest of indigenous Latin America, since he grew up amongst them in the country. He was especially conscious about what the USA and Europe did to all of Latin America, and we spent part of the night talking about Guatemala's history with US colonialism and neocolonialism. He educated me about the United Fruit company, an American corporation, and their fruit plantations, which essentially enslaved the local indigenous population long after slavery was abolished in the US. He told me the long list of atrocities, leading right up to Guatemala's civil war, and the US's role in aiding and abetting the right wing paramilitary death squads.

"David, you need to read 'The Open Veins of Latin America' to understand us. When I read the book, I simply confirmed all that I've seen, and I've seen a lot. I was so angry at the son of a bitch USA."

He made two obscene gestures with both hands in the air.

"If you want to understand why Colombians would want to kidnap a white gringo, and not you, read that book. If you want to understand why the socialist movements are still so strong in Latin America, then read that book. The West has been fucking us for a long time. They've done that to everyone for a long time. But one day, God will bring balance. September 11th was just the start."

When he said those words, I could feel the anger well out from him. He wasn't alone in Latin America with those views. I looked at the Swede, and noticed he was a little uncomfortable. He asked me what the conversation was all about.

"How long have you been studying Spanish?"

"One week."

"You never took it before?"

"No."

"It's alright, we're just, ah, talking about sports rivalries, you know, like football?" I lied.

"Oh, that was it?"

"Uh huh."

I patted him on the back and smiled, as I said, "you know how football fans can be."

I winked at the Guatemalan. The Guatemalan smiled back. "Yah, I know." Replied the Swede with a smile, who seemed more comfortable. He enthusiastically started talking about the upcoming World Cup.

I spent one more day in Antigua before meeting up with John and Grits in the central plaza. When I arrived at the plaza, I saw John and Grits sitting on the bench. John sported his usual 5 o'clock shadow, and he had a lit cigarette in his mouth. He was casually dressed in cargo pants and a green, open collared shirt. Grits had a cloth rimmed hat on, an Abe Lincoln beard, and he was dressed in a Hawaiian shirt.

"Hello John, it's been a while."

"What's up man. Didn't think you'd make it."

"Well, considering the bang of an entry I got entering this country, it's been one adventure after another. I got to relax at Atitlan."

"Oh, this is Grits." John said as he introduced me.

"Hello. Nice to meet ya, Dave." Said Grits.

"Nice to meet you." Grits had a soft southern accent.

"Well, I'm all set. When do we go?" I said.

"That's all your stuff?" John said as he pointed at my bike.

"Yup."

"Damn. How much does that thing weigh?"

"About 100 pounds total, I think, when I'm loaded with water. The bike does all the work though, I just pedal the thing."

"That's work too."

We took a "chicken bus" back to Guatemala city, a white, beaten up 1970's US school bus that had steel racks welded onto the top. We crammed into the bus, taking care to make sure our belongings were secure. A short while later, we were in Guatemala City, and took a taxi to the Guatemalan Office of the Peace Corps, the largest Peace Corps office in the world. Inside, I sat down and chatted with some of the volunteers.

"Are you a volunteer?" Asked one girl.

"Nah, just a bicycle traveler." I replied.

"Ever considered it?" She replied.

"Don't!" Said Joseph, a blonde, long haired guy who opened up a recently delivered package of books.

"Huh?" I replied.

"Seriously man, think really hard before you consider volunteering for the Peace Corps."

"Say what? I love what you guys do. I've been thinking about joining for quite a while. I've always wanted to do international volunteer work."

"Well, you don't have to go through the Peace Corps to do that. Really man, it ain't all it's cracked up to be. Yes! My permaculture books are in!"

I read the titles as he pulled out book after book: "Chicken Tractor","Human Manure","Biodiesel from Garbage Scraps","Straw Bale Building", "How to make Tofu." In total, Joe pulled out 20 books.

"I finally have my reference library!" He grinned.

"You actually do that permaculture stuff?" I asked.

"Hell yeah man. Out here, it's normal life to live like this. We have to find ways to help the Guatemalans without wrecking everything man. Whoah dude! How to grind soybeans into diesel fuel!"

Soybeans into diesel fuel? I definitely could hang with this group. John walked into the room with Grits, and three other volunteers.

"Interesting bunch you guys have here." I said.

"That's the Peace Corps for you. Hey, we have to get ready to go. We're going to see a movie, and then head out to buy supplies. Then we're off." Replied John.

"Good deal. I'm all set. Let's go."

Together with John, from Indiana, Grits, from North Carolina, Mike from Massachusetts, Scott from northwest New Jersey, and Erin, an Oklahoman, we took off to watch a movie in a mega-cinema complex, in suburban Guatemala City. Then we picked up supplies in the supermarket nearby.

I loaded up on an assortment of iron rations: twenty five packs of mashed fried beans, fifteen packs of ramen instant noodles, three packs of burrito bread, one jar of ketchup, one jar of peanut butter, one jar of jam, hot sauce, some dried fruit, pop tarts, berry flavored fruit juice powder, and coffee. After loading everything into our bags back at the central office, we took an overnight bus from the station at 10 PM.

At 3 AM, I awoke from my fitful sleep as a customs officer poked me in the shoulder, *"passports please."*

I handed him my passport, and eyed him carefully. It took him several minutes before he finally gave it back. I already was forewarned about the corruption of the Guatemalan police.

"Do you have any fruit on you?" He asked.

"No, I ate it all."

Guatemala kept a check point on the lone highway to the Peten for fresh produce. The country was rich in its geography and biodiversity, and its richness made it in danger of biological contamination within its own borders.

We arrived in Flores at 6 AM, and waited at the stop to meet another volunteer. I went to pick up a machete in the local market. The machete was the standard tool for the average Guatemalan and Peace Corps worker. It's used to dig, cut, slice food, cut down trees, and for all sorts of construction work. It was also a deterrent to thieves and criminals, although it was used by both. As I looked at the selection, men walked by with their machetes in leather scabbards attached to their waists. They occasionally decorated the scabbard with a tassel, artwork, or colored paint. I picked up a large machete. John showed me his after examining the blade.

"You'll need to sharpen the blade like this." He said, as I felt the edge of his blade.

"A machete is very useful," said Mike in his faint New England accent, as he adjusted his New York Yankees baseball cap, "you can use it for everything. I sometimes use it to hammer stuff in, and you're definitely gonna need it for this trip."

"Yeah, we're going bushwhacking." Piped Grits.

"For real? We're headed to frontier country, like the wild west?" I asked.

"You said it." said Scott. Scott was about five foot eleven, and was the tallest of the group. He had an odd stare as he talked. I kept looking to where his eyes pointed to, until I saw that one eye was off center from the other one.

"We're gonna chop our way through the jungle, man." Scott exclaimed.

"You'll need it for defense too. Where we're going is really dangerous." said John.

I took a look at our group. John was the de-facto leader. He planned and organized the expedition. Grits sported a bandanna, and like John, was in his early 30's, and honed from rough work out in the Guatemalan countryside. Mike had a narrow face and a thin build, and Erin was Oklahoman. Whenever Erin spoke, his powerful Oklahoman accent seemed to slur his words. I could never make out what he said. Finally, we started speaking to each other in Spanish.

Erin was a mestizo of Russian and native American descent. With pale red burnt skin, and a shock of red hair, with native American eyes and cheekbones, Erin stood out. He grabbed my hat, and started examining it.

"That's a good hat. Where did you get it?"

"Bolivia. It's made of llama wool."

"Cool." he said as he continued to examine it. His accented Spanish was strong, but at least it was understandable.

We were six American, five white and one Asian, men, about to explore a fascinating, remote, and dangerous region of the Yucatan Peninsula, the Peten. The Peten jungle covers the upper right hand corner of Guatemala, all the way to Mexico. It's a dense and almost impenetrable jungle that spans an area comparable to Pennsylvania. It was the ancient homeland of the Maya, and the Center of the fabulous Mayan Empire. Lost cities littered the forest, and many of them still eluded explorers.

The Peten is home to deadly snakes, like the Fer De Lance, which killed as quickly as a cobra. There were boa constrictors, alligators, crocodiles, and peccaries, a species of wild boar that roamed in packs and were famous for shredding people to pieces. Jaguars roamed the jungle, while monkeys and bats inhabited the jungle canopy. During the rainy season there were mosquitoes, insects, ants, and other creepy critters. Malaria and yellow fever were still persistent problems.

We didn't fear any of these. What we feared, was the most dangerous animal in the entire Peten - man. The Peten was a hive of villainy, full of drug runners, armed bandits, mercenaries, marijuana growers keen to protect their crop, illegal loggers, squatters, settlers, oil explorers, and criminals of all types. It was the scene of many violent crimes, and a place to bury the evidence. About a year ago, according to John, a Peace Corps worker and his Canadian Peace Corps girl friend went for a hike in the Peten. A group of armed bandits tied him to a tree while they gang raped the girl in front of him.

"Make sure you sharpen that thing," John said, "you might need to use it for things other than chopping bushes."

"Will we have an armed guard?" I asked.

"Probably not, he could hold all of us up," replied John, "we'll be armed only with machetes. That should be enough."

"Besides, whose gonna mess with six guys armed with machetes?" Asked Scott.

"Hey, where's my machete?" I asked, when I reached to grab it, only to find it missing. I looked up and saw Erin playing duelist with it. Machetes factored into the Guatemalan machismo, and the longer machetes were used in duels for honor.

We waited at the bus stop in Flores in the harsh morning sunlight, as white dust flew around us. It was mid morning, and the glare off the pale mud adobe homes was blinding as we waited for another volunteer, Dan. Off in the distance, I could see part of the jungle in the horizon. Finally, a blonde, curly haired, lanky guy with sunglasses came riding in on a mountain bike.

"What's up guys!" Dan said, in a laid back California accent.

"Not much. Just waiting for you." Replied John.

I reassembled my gear, and Dan took a glance at my bike.

"Come a long way huh?" He asked.

"Yeah, you could say that."

He straddled his bike and gave us a look over. "You guys are ready for the big expedition huh? And you decided to join with these guys?"

"Yup. It sounded like fun." I replied.

"I'll bet. Well, grab your gear."

We followed Dan back to his place in Flores. It was an apartment building built far off the main road. It was a bright pink edifice, three stories tall, and it stood out like a tower among storied, mud brick, adobe shacks.

We hiked up the stairs to the third floor, and entered a modern, fully furnished room. The beige tile kept the floor cool, and I sat down on a bean bag as we unloaded our things.

"OK guys, dump your shit here." Said Dan as he poured some water in several ceramic cups. He handed me a cup, as I asked, "how long have you been in the Peace Corps?"

He took a sip, "three years, My first two years was in Mali, Africa."

"Three? How was Mali?"

"Gorgeous. Lots of desert."

"Good experience?"

"Yup." He took another long sip.

"Hey guys, let's go visit Linda, she's in the downstairs apartment." Said John.

We entered Linda's quarters. She sat in her kitchen, and worked on her laptop. A case full of books was on the wall, and the room was decorated with a minimum of necessities. Linda, a New Yorker, was a white, professional, woman in her thirties, with short cropped blond hair.

"Can I check my email real quick?" Asked John.

"Sure."

Linda looked me over, and asked, "you're new. Did you just arrive with the other new volunteers?"

"Oh no, I'm not Peace Corps. I'm just a vagrant traveler."

"Hm, now this is a motley crew. So you decided to join these guys for their adventure?"

"Yes. You know, for the frontier country, you volunteers have a pretty good life out here." I said as I looked around.

"It's funny you said that. When I left for the Peace Corps, I was under the impression that I'd have to make do in tough conditions. But, as you can see, I have everything - Internet, even cable TV."

"Not everyone has it like this. These are city volunteers. You should talk to country volunteers. Like us." Said Grits.

"I don't have electricity." Said Scott.

"Or proper toilets." Said Mike.

"Dang man I don't even have a basic clean water supply out where ah am." Said Erin.

"What did you say, Erin?" Asked John jokingly.

Erin shot back, "shuddup man."

"Alright guys, get your stuff repacked. We leave at 2 PM." Said John as he sent off his last email.

"Nice meeting you, Linda." I said as I shook her hand.

"Likewise. Have fun guys. Try not to get killed."

We repacked our things, and stashed the rest in Dan's apartment. We took only the essentials. I packed two of my panniers with two sets of cloths, food, water, and survival equipment. I saddled up my bike while the rest finished packing their backpacks. The bus station was a large gravel lot, and it was full of rusting, white, miniature versions of chicken buses. The dust flew around us in white clouds as we boarded. As we left the lot and followed a one lane road into the jungle, I watched as the homes changed from mud adobe with tin roofs into mud homes thatched with palm leaves. The road soon gave way to rough dirt and ravines, and soon there were no homes at all as we traveled several hours into the jungle. Despite the jolting ride, I dozed off.

I suddenly awoke when the bus stopped in a small logging camp. I looked around, inside of the bus. For the last four hours, it was just the six of us. Everyone left where there was civilization. I stepped out of the bus and stretched my cramped muscles, as I watched the dust settle. In the distance were three small huts, and a large open field which bordered the jungle. Chickens and roosters scratched about in the dust as the mid afternoon sun cooked us. The air was hot and dry, and I took a drink from my canteen. Waves of heat rippled up from the field. I watched the jungle horizon dance through the vibrating air.

I looked at the clearing. It looked like a small airfield for single engine aircraft, since there was a flat, long strip that ran to the edge, before it was swallowed by jungle.

We grabbed our gear as the driver lifted it off the top of the bus. John and Grits talked to the owners of the house, which was a general store, about a guide. They talked for what seemed to be hours. I sat on a bench with Erin, lazily sharpening my machete with his whetstone. John and Grits finally came out of the store.

"Alright guys. We've got a guide, but he won't be here until tonight." Said John.

"And we have food." Added Scott.

A middle aged woman, plump, brown, with a crinkled smile and nose came out. She wore a worn out, red sun dress, smiled at us, and waved for us to come in. We followed her to the back of the general store, and exited into a makeshift restaurant, shielded on all sides in mosquito netting. The tables and benches were rough planks, and we sat down to fresh salsa, chips, burritos, and tortillas.

Later, in the evening's dry heat, I listened as John and Grits negotiated with the owners of the huts. Loggers picked up supplies in the store, before heading out to remote areas of the jungle, but for a general store, it was sparse in its wares. As the sun set, we set up camp. Scott and I shared my tent, while Erin and Mike shared the other one. John and Grits strung up their hammocks, and we fell asleep to the sound of a blaring, televised soccer game.

At 6AM I woke up, washed up, and packed the tent. As we cleaned up camp, a small brown man with a mustache came towards us, leading a mule with two saddlebags.

"Guys, this is Jose. He's a champino and our guide." Said Grits.

"Hello Jose," we said as we shook hands. *"Meet Palomo, the mule,"* he replied, pointing to the mule's gray, mottled skin. Palomo snorted as Jose introduced him, and turned his head away. Jose unwrapped the hitch to the saddle bags, and lowered them. Inside were two twenty five liter containers, full of water, and we added a backpack to each saddle bag. It took two people to get bags back on Palomo, but he didn't seem to react to the increased weight.

"Alright guys, it's fifty dollars per person." Said John. We pulled out our cash and handed it over. Jose spent a few minutes to count the money, before finally nodding his head to go.

I pulled out my bike, and loaded my saddle bags when I noticed that the shop owners and Jose were looking at me. Finally, the shop owner spoke up.

"You don't want to go out there with the bike."

"You'll never make it through." Jose added.

"What? What do you mean?" I asked.

"You won't make it with the bike." The shop owner repeated.

"I don't understand, how come I can't go with the bike?"

"You won't make it," said the owner, *"we had two other cyclists like you come out here a while ago. They left with their bikes, and then came back. They didn't make it through. They left their bikes here and went back in again."*

"Why? Is it the jungle? The brush? There's no trail?"

"You won't make it with the bike," the owner simply said as he turned around and went back into the store.

I looked at Grits.

"I won't make it? What's out there?"

"I don't know." I looked at John and then Grits.

"Well, I'm definitely not leaving it here." I said, as visions of my bike getting heisted appeared in my mind. There were no metal poles and no secure spots that made me feel safe for locking my bike. Leaving it there would be too tempting a target for theft.

"The hell with that. I'm taking my bike with me." I defiantly said.

"I don't know why they said that to you. It can't be that bad. That's a mountain bike." Said John.

"Yeah, I wouldn't worry about it," Grits said.

We started on our way, and after about a hundred feet into the road, I decided to mount and ride my bike past the group. Suddenly, Palomo reared up on his hind legs in a defensive stance, as Jose, taken by surprise, ran around to calm the mule down. I stopped and dismounted the bike as I watched Palomo try to turn around and run. Jose grabbed the rope and tugged her down. Finally, Palomo calmed down and stopped moving, but then he jumped up again as I walked to the back of the line. *"Shit!"* Said Jose as Palomo tried to run in a circle.

"I'd better stick to the rear." I said.

"Good idea," said John.

We crossed over the air field through some brush over a worn out logging road, up a small embankment and then onto a trail. The trail was sandy and we walked for about four miles before we entered a jungle canopy at 9AM. As we hiked, the trail became rougher, and pushing the bike became difficult. Then, we stepped through what appeared to be a dried up marsh. There were enormous cracks and fissures in the ground, and they formed deep canyons in the clay. Sometime the cracks were wider then part of the wheel's curve, which made it tough to push through.

As we hiked, the trail became increasingly difficult, as I strained to push the bike through. After a half mile of pushing, straining, and pulling the bike across what seemed like an endless valley of cracks and holes in the ground, I began to feel the ache in my arms.

"In the rainy season, this place is an ocean of mud," said Jose. When it was dry, it was a cracked and fissured jungle landscape, which made it impossible for wheeled vehicles to penetrate. That explained the difficulties in penetrating the Peten. When Jose said ocean, he meant it. At one point, I grunted aloud in anger and frustration. I cursed myself for being so block headed, as my body wore on, pushing and pulling my bike, all twenty five pounds of it plus another forty pounds of bags, water, food, and gear, for the next three hours. I wiped the stream of sweat from my brow with my

bandanna. At least we were under the canopy, so there was no direct sunlight, but the heat cooked everything underneath at 90 degrees or more.

Between the sweat and the overwork of my body, I realized that I put myself into unnecessary danger with the bike. I burned up large amounts of energy, and the water loss could become life threatening if I didn't replace it. Due to the conditions, we had a limited amount of fresh water on us. It was the dry season, the only season that made the jungle passable, but the season also made the jungle drier than a desert. Still, I felt safe, since I had a water filter on me.

I trudged on, and despite the rigors of the trail, I still observed the jungle. It was an endless green and brown wall. Sometimes, in a beam of sunlight the leaves would shimmer. I listened for animals, birds, or monkeys, but the jungle held its silence.

By 11:30 AM, we called a lunch break, and under the cool shade of some trees, I collapsed on the ground, opened up my canteen, and drank. My arms were sore. The rest of the group sat down in the shade on a pile of leaves, and pulled out our food. Our iron rations were mashed beans, tortilla bread, and some hot sauce.

Suddenly, out of the wilderness came a European couple, gaunt, perspiring, and they had a haggard look on their faces. The man's blond hair was soaked, and the woman's shirt was saturated in perspiration. Behind them came two mules with saddle bags, and a dark reddish brown Mayan boy astride one of them with his arms wrapped around an empty canteen. Their guide walked alongside the mules.

The man looked at us with eyes that seem exasperated, even desperate. His accent was Germanic.

"All of you are here to go to El Mirador?" He asked us.

"Yeah." Said John.

"There's a real water problem out there! When we're done, Lonely Planet will no longer be in business! We're going to make sure of that!" He said as the blond, German woman nodded her head in agreement. I looked at the two of them dressed in khaki shorts, sandals, and short shirts. They certainly looked somewhat fashionable in the middle of nowhere. In contrast, all of us were in pants, except for John, and we wore either short sleeved shirts or long shirts. We had bandannas, hats for the sun, and machetes. They didn't.

"Water problem?" I asked.

"Yes! Lonely Planet did not tell us that there would be no water! Wait till they hear from us! We'll make sure they'll no longer be in business. Where are all of you from by the way?"

"USA." We replied.

"Well, be careful! And be careful of the natives! They will take your water!"

I glanced at the Mayan boy. He didn't look too happy himself.

"We paid $350 each for this trip! Can you believe that?" He shrieked. I looked at the mules. They had two mules, they paid that much money and they were still that unprepared?

"Well, we better get going." Said John.

"We're not far from the town are we?" Asked the German guy.

"No, it's just up ahead. It's probably about eight or nine miles." Replied Grits.

"Good!"

We joked about the Europeans after they left, and then pushed on, and at 2 PM, we called a break, and dropped the mule's saddle bags to grab some water from the backpacks. One of the containers went down with a loud "THUD". Jose and Scott grabbed the burlap sack, and after we retrieved the containers, we put the saddlebags back on the mule.

We started hiking again for about fifteen minutes when from behind, I noticed that the right saddle bag, the one that hit the ground hard, developed a wet spot. It started to drip profusely. Our water!

"What's that wet spot?" I said as I pointed to the corner of the saddle bag. John took a glance.

"Ah shit!"

We quickly pulled the container out, and flipped it up. There was an indentation in the corner, and a crack. The water level was lower, and eighth of our water was lost.

"Shit." Said Mike. I pulled out my bottle. I always kept a length of duct tape wrapped around it for emergencies.

"Can we patch it up with this?" I asked as I handed it to Grits.

"Yeah, that might work." He said.

Between the seven of us and the mule, we had about fifty liters of water riding in those two containers, and a few liters in our own stashes. Now, we were down about five or six liters, and we were still at least another day's journey from El Mirador. Grits patched up the container, and remounted it with the hole facing up. It would still leak, but as long as it stayed upright, we'd still have some water. We didn't have enough for the entire journey, and we needed the pond at the midway point, if it existed, to resupply. If not, then the expedition would have to retreat.

Water was the last thing on my mind as we hiked along the narrow trail. My arms were exhausted, and I felt them start to give at 4PM. I endured a course of roots and giant cracks in the ground, and my bike felt like it was 150 pounds. The sweat on my brow dripped into my eyes and my frustration mounted. I badly wanted to stick my saddle bags on the mule, and at one point, I asked Jose if I could.

"No, it's too much weight for the mule."

"OK." I quickly conceded. The last thing I wanted to do was be a burden on the group. Finally, late in the afternoon, I broke down in frustration. "Fuck!" I muttered as I stopped in my tracks. My arms were throbbing from six hours of lifting, pushing, dragging, and balancing a heavily laden bicycle through cracked and fissured jungle floor. We were walking through an area where roots from rubber trees and other jungle giants blocked and made for hellish, unmovable, obstacles on the ground.

I was in hell. The rest of the group stopped. I hoped that I wouldn't have to put it in words. I didn't. John was the first to offer. I shouldered his backpack as he started to push the bike. After thirty minutes, his hands were throbbing, and we switched back. Later, Scott offered to push, but he didn't have to push for long. We came to a clearing in the jungle, and before us was a small pond. On the embankment next to the pond was a lean to shelter made of broad, green leaves, and two mestizo men underneath. Puffs of smoke came out from the shelter.

"We're here!" yelled John. I collapsed against the tree, and sat down, resting my arms. I'd had enough.

****

We shook hands with Don Marco, the occupant of the lean to shelter. Don Marco was clean shaven, dark brown, and he had a distinct voice and laugh. He was dressed neatly in a collared, short sleeve shirt, dark slacks, and sandals. He sat down on a makeshift stool made of logs and lit a hand rolled cigarette. He put one hand down on a table made out of small logs and twine. Neatly wrapped stacks of bright green, chicle tree leaves were piled up next to his shelter. Don Marco was one of the few hunter gatherers who still eked out a living in the Peten, and he became a relic when the rest of his tribe settled down as farmhands or as low paid employees in the cities. He gathered the products of the chicle tree for markets in the American and Japanese gum industries. He made about thirty five Quetzales, or five dollars a day for his work. He lived off the jungle, and hunted peccaries, monkeys, and pheasants. He often traded his chicle goods for either money, or living staples like sugar, coffee, and salt.

Making a living this way did not help his social life. Few women would stand living in these conditions out in the Peten, especially when city or town life was more appealing. Still, I had to ask.

"So what do you do when you need a woman out here?"

"What, whores?"

"No, women."

"No, Whores!" Laughed Scott.

"Ah, whores or women, they're both too much trouble. I'll never under-stand women. Don't want to. I can't understand how someone can take hot boiling wax, pour it on the upper thigh, rip the hair out by the roots, and still be afraid of a spider."

Don Marco took another drag from his cigarette.

"So tell me my new friends, what brings you to this corner of the world? Obviously not women."

"Adventure. We want to see El Mirador." I replied.

"Ahh, El Mirador. A beautiful place. It's a long way off. At least another day's journey."

"How long have you been working out here?" I asked.

"I don't know. That's a good question. Years, decades, I learned the trade from my father."

"Are their others like you?"

"No, few of us continue to live this way. Many have gone to the cities and haciendas, seeking work."

"So why didn't you go?"

"What, why didn't I go to work as a slave? No my friend, here, I am still free. I am no slave, I am a man here."

I went down to the banks of the pond in my bicycle shorts to take a bath. Erin had just walked out of the water. John watched us as I went in.

"Dude, that is the nastiest fucking water I've ever seen. Do you know what's in there?" John asked.

"No, and I don't want to know. I just need to wash off." I replied.

I walked in the water until it came up to my waist, and smelled the pungent, sulfuric odor of a stagnant pond. I moved to a section where it smelled fresher, and a swarm of silver fish swam around my legs. They started nipping at me. "Yipes!" I yelled. They were eating me alive.

Immediately, I plunged into the water and swam out to the middle, where it was cooler, deeper, and fresher smelling. As I swam, I noticed there was no bottom in such a small pond, which was odd, especially since it was the dry season. What could've made the pond deeper? This was an established camp, and I doubted Don Marco would've maintained it.

I swam back to shore, borrowed Don Marco's large pot, dipped it in the water, and went behind my tent to take a sponge bath. It was refreshing, and wonderfully therapeutic. But I smelled like a combination of pond sulfur and soap.

Scott cooked spaghetti on his MSR gas stove. I grabbed my filter and the pot, and scooped some more water to refill our water supplies. Mike finished making a large pot of coffee, and we drank the bitter liquid.

While we sat around the stove relaxing and enjoying the the coffee, we heard a whinnying sound, and four horses came in with two men. We watched as the men led the horses to the pond. The horses promptly peed and defecated into the water. I stared as the horse dung dropped with loud, splashing noises into the spot where I recently retrieved water. The horses began to drink, as more dung fell in. One man opened his zipper and peed in the water.

Mike and I looked at each other, and then we looked back at the horses and the man, who closed his fly, bent down to wash his hands, and turned around to smile at us. We looked at the cups of coffee we drank, and then at Scott, who was busy cooking, and completely oblivious. We stared at the boiling pot of water which he'd just added spaghetti too. I looked at the filtered water in my bottles. Was the brown tint from the iodine filter? We looked at each other again, with sour looks on our faces.

"Well, at least we have water filters." I said. Mike's face didn't improve.

"And iodine. We have lots of iodine." I said. Again, Mike's face didn't move at all. He just stared blankly. Finally, he opened up his mouth.

"That... was just nasty!"

"It could be worse." I said.

"Man, we are drinking water that those horses shat in. Worse? Whaddaya mean, worse? What's worse than that?" Said Mike.

"Ah, it's all good man." Said Scott, as he stared into the boiling pot.

"How so? Those horses just took a roaring shit into the water we have to drink, eat, and bathe in!"

"I dunno man, but it's all good. We're alive, we've got good coffee, and good food coming up. Besides, we boiled the water. It's not as if you're gonna die or anything."

"That's just gross. I ain't going in that water, you can't pay me to go in there. I think you'll die just going in."

A thought nagged me. "You guys happen to have anti parasite drugs on you?" I asked.

"No." They both said.

"OK." I dove into my tent, and checked my first aid kit for metrodizole, a powerful anti parasite drug. It was there. I pulled out a tablet, and swallowed it.

As night fell, we ate spaghetti, and told crude jokes around the campfire. John excused himself after eating, "I'm going for a walk guys," he said as he grabbed his machete, and disappeared into the darkness. Scott told a crude joke to Don Marco. Don Marco burst out laughing, when – suddenly - John yelled out, "Dave! Guys, come look at this!"

We ran to him at the water's edge, where he shone a flashlight into the water. I then discovered just who it was that kept the pond deep, as I saw two eyes above the waterline blink. We were about seven meters from the eyes. It was a crocodile, and if I took the distance from the eyes at seven meters and brought them close to me, the distance between the eyes would have been nine inches wide, which made for a two and a half foot snout, and a six foot long crocodile, without including the tail.

Next morning, I got out of my tent. No one woke up, and no one was around. I ran for my bike, unlocked it from the tree, and quickly walked it to the back of the campsite. I walked around a grove of trees until I found a spot that was completely isolated and out of sight. I locked the bike down, and buried it under some dried leaves. I stuck in a stick to remember where it was. I walked back to the entrance, and suddenly felt my abdomen growl, and tighten up.

"Perfect!" I said to myself. In the middle of the entrance, out of view, I squatted and defecated. My poop made a steaming, fetid obstacle to anyone who'd walk into the grove. After five minutes of re-fertilizing the jungle floor, I cleaned myself up, and headed back to the tent. Scott was already up and brewing coffee. Everyone else was still asleep.

"Morning." I said.

"Morning to you. I heard ya rustling out there man, good thing too, cause I wanted to get up early. Wanna share the wealth? Coffee always tastes good when you're trekking."

"Sure thing, man."

It was strong coffee. I pulled the large half empty water container up, and with the large pot, scooped up some water from the deep end of the pond to filter it.

I figured we used about five liters of water a day per person. The two large containers held a total of fifty liters, and the rest of us had two to four liters per person. We had just enough for dietary water consumption. For seven people, we needed 105 liters. We carried seventy five liters on us. We also had filters and iodine, but the unknown was if there was any water near El Mirador. We'd have to locate another twenty five liters in our expedition.

As I started to refill my canteen, I felt the pump handle get harder to move. I checked it for debris, washed it off, and got ready to go.

I walked to the group with my two saddle bags.

"No bike?" asked Grits.

"Where's the bike?" Asked John.

"Hell no! I stashed it away in a safe place under some leaves. It's well hidden and well guarded."

"You sure that's a good idea?" Asked John.

"Yeah, I think it'll be fine. It's better than hauling it with us. Besides, I don't want you guys to suffer with me. I'll help carry the packs."

Jose put my bags in the saddle bags with the water containers. I shouldered one of the backpacks, while Mike shouldered the other one.

"OK! I hope it'll still be there when we get back!" Said John.

"I hope so too." I replied.

"Alright men, its bushwhacking time!" Said Scott.

We pulled out our machetes, and hiked to an open valley. We took a break in a crude hut, and then walked around the rim of the valley. Mike and I were in front, hacking and slashing any overgrown bush in our way. Soon, we entered the deep jungle, as we watched an odd raccoon like animal run in front of us. Later, we saw a flock of pheasant flee ahead of us, while in the treetops, I saw an animal dart in the branches. At first, I thought it was a squirrel, until it hooted at me. It was a troop of monkeys. The forest canopy shaded the ground, and enormous trees appeared and then disappeared into the forest. The underbrush was thick, on the sides, and Mike and I were busy cutting our path.

We hiked and hacked the rest of the morning. After a lunch break, John spread out the Guatemalan government supplied topographical maps. We were still five or six hours from El Mirador. After lunch, we continued our hike.

We started up a steep hill. Dense jungle brush and trees surrounded us. The leaves were large and glossy, and leaf litter piled up around the trunks. I felt relieved that I didn't bring my bike as we hiked up. Suddenly, Jose's hand shot up, and he called out to us, *"stop here!"*

We stopped and watched as Jose tied up Palomo to a tree. He pulled out his machete, and walked through a crowd of brush that was in the way of the trail. We unsheathed our machetes. The air's silence made every move sound like a crash. My ears focused on the sound of our breathing. After a few tense minutes, Jose came back and motioned for us to follow him. We hiked to a part of the trail that was cut into the hill. I looked at the trees growing on the mounds next to us.

"Here." He said, as he pointed to a mound with a straight deep cut into it. There was a trench cut into the mound.

"What the. . . " I muttered.

"Thieves." he replied, and pulled out an ancient, Mayan, pottery shard.

"Oh shit." Said John. We started looking around, at the mound, and at the shard. We were standing on the remains of an ancient, Mayan pyramid.

"Is this on the map?" I whispered.

"No." Said John.

We walked into a "lost", Mayan city.

We explored the mounds. It was one of three forested mounds on top of the hill, and everything was covered in trees and brush. I looked down the side of the steep hill, only to realize that it wasn't a hill, but a high pyramid completely engulfed in the jungle.

"Dude, I'll bet all the hills in the Peten are Mayan Cities." Said John.

They were right. Other than the geographically anomalous hills, the Peten was flat. I crawled into the freshly cut trench and peered into a small tunnel. It wasn't deep, and the bandits seemed to be after clay artifacts.

On the black market, a Mayan pottery piece could fetch a handsome price, and this fueled an active black market of archaeological treasures. The Guatemalan government tried their best to clamp down on the illicit trade, but it was difficult when all a bandit had to do was bribe a custom's official. The buyers were almost always westerners, from Europe and North America.

After about a half hour exploring the site, we continued on our way to El Mirador. The trail got rougher the closer we were to El Mirador. My hands throbbed from slashing the brush. The dense jungle floor was covered in leaves. Filtered sunlight reflected of the vibrant, dark green leaves.

"Ah shit! Fucking bugs!" Yelled John, as he clawed his legs. The insects swarmed through in some areas, but they generally didn't bite. There were plants where whole swarms of insects climbed on top of each other, creating a swarm of black husks and wiggling legs. Another strange, raccoon animal appeared in front of us and trotted to the other side of the trail. He didn't seem alarmed at seeing us. Above our heads, spider monkeys peered down at us, twisting their heads around to observe us. Multicolored pheasants flapped overhead, disturbed by our noise. Jose smiled as he watched them, and massaged his stomach. "Jose eats pheasants." Said Scott.

The air was still and quiet, except for the crunching of dry leaves underneath our boots. Amazingly, the area appeared to be virgin, ancient forest. Rubber trees, with multiple trunks, reached gracefully into the sky, while chicle trees dropped their small, round, tan, fruit that were no bigger than a plum. Jose cut a few, which I ate. No one else had a taste for them. They were sweet, like a persimmon, but they left a chalky residue on the teeth.

It was late afternoon, and I looked up to see swarms of bats over our heads. They were large, fruit bats, prowling the jungle for fruits and insects. After a few more hours, in the early evening, we walked into a giant, sun drenched field. The curtain of the forest withdrew, and revealed a field bigger than three football fields, and at each of the four corners, was an enormous hill. Two of the hills cast great shadows onto the field.

I looked at the field, and saw a small shack in the distance, and some free ranging chickens. We sat down on a bench, and took a long drink from our water. Our water prospects were poor. There wasn't any fresh water nearby, and we were short twenty five liters. But I didn't care. No one did. We were in a place that few people in the world had ever seen. We were in the biggest city of the Mayan Empire, El Mirador!

****

We set up camp, and celebrated with lots of ramen noodles, burritos, mixed fruit juice, and with Erin's bottle of "El Amigo Viejo." I looked at John's leg. It was swelling with angry red welts and scratch marks. A large bump developed on his forehead. For the last two days, he constantly scratched his legs, and resorted to slapping dry dust on them.

"Why don't you wear long pants?" I asked.

"It's too goddamn hot."

I pulled my long sleeved, cotton shirt on, and put on my gloves. Oddly enough, because of the dry season and the intense heat, there were no mosquitoes. I drank some juice that I mixed from an orange packet. We spent the night telling jokes over the campfire before retiring to bed.

As I went back to my tent. Inside, I opened a packaged cleaning pad, and wiped myself down before dozing off. Scott came in moments later, and fell asleep quickly. The odors of our sticking arm pits, feet, and the noxious sweet smell of the pad suffocated me. I opened the door for some fresh air. Since there were no mosquitoes, I left the tent completely open. As I listened to the night sounds of the jungle, I heard Erin retire into his tent. Then, I heard something.

"Ugh... man..gotta git me...some more o' that old friend." The alcohol slowed and slurred his speech down enough for me to understand what he was saying. I heard the sound of a cap pulled off a bottle.

"Glug," went the sound of a drunk man getting drunker. He seemed to drink for an hour. Then, it was quiet. Suddenly, he coughed, and then came a distinctive sound of hands making a desperate attempt for the tent zipper. The zipper quickly slid open, and suddenly came a mad dash of footsteps when he immediately let out another cough.

"Hugh hugh... Bleah." The sound of a thick liquid dropped onto the floor punctured my ears, as I heard a wet splashing against the tent. A powerful scent of alcohol induced vomit filled the air. I looked in the direction of the pyramids, and thought, "Gods, please don't punish us for our misdemeanors."

A gentle breeze pushed the smell into the tent. Combined with the odor of Scott's fetid armpits, and the sickly sweet aroma of the cleaning pads, our sweat and stinking feet, it overpowered me. I got up and walked towards the bench next to the fire. I passed by a pale, prostrate form on the ground, who continued to cough next to a large puddle that reflected the star light. He was breathing, and slowly got up as I squatted to help him.

"You alright man?" I asked.

"Huh? Yeah. I think I had too much," He replied.

Erin went back to his tent, and I continued to the bench. I sat down, and watched the glowing embers. Everyone else was asleep, except for Jose. He poked a stick into the coals.

"Hello Jose."

"Hello. No sleep for you?" He asked.

"Me? No, not until that smell disappears."

"Hahaha! Disgusting isn't it? That's alright. Old Friend always does that to a man."

"It's that strong?"

"Oh yes, you could run a car off of it. That will clean his system out."

"Yeah, not to mention most of his brain cells."

I waited for an hour, until the smell died out before going back to sleep. I left the flap on the tent open, to let the breeze in.

At 3 AM, a flapping sound against the tent woke me up. I poked my head out of the tent, and looked around. There was nothing there, and no sound. I looked up at the sky. A multitude of tiny lights glimmered. I was so groggy that I collapsed back on my foam pad, and fell asleep.

A short while later, the flapping against the tent woke me up again. I felt dizzy as I got up. I looked out the tent again, and again, there was no sound, except for the occasional snore. Groggy, I looked around. In a fit of exhaustion, I collapsed on my pad. The next morning, Scott tapped the tent to wake me up. It was mid morning.

"Hey man, you're gonna miss the tour! Can't miss the tour man!" He said. "Huh?" I woke up, and changed into my long pants. I got out, and walked to the fire, where the group stood around Palomo. I walked up to them and looked at what they were staring at. Red blood drops stained the ground. I followed the red drops up to Palomo. A large stream of dark red blood coated Palomo's neck and leg.

"Vampire bat." Said Grits. That flapping sound! I quickly grabbed my neck and felt it. There were no holes.

"Damn things can be rabid," Said John. I looked at the mule and blood. That could've been me.

"Well guys, let's eat, and then have a look around." Said Scott.

After breakfast, we followed Jose to the first pyramid, and ascended. The pyramid was enormous. It had a width of two city blocks. We followed Jose up to the top, which was about fifteen stories high, not including the three smaller pyramids at the top. Along the way, I spotted an ancient stone with a spiral. I did a double take, and stopped. I pointed to the stone, and said, "hey Grits. That's the symbol I've been following through out my journey." Grits took a long look at it.

"Yeah, I'm familiar with that." He said.

"You are?"

"Yeah. I'll tell you later."

We continued up the pyramid to the top, where there were three smaller pyramids. I followed Scott and Mike up one, while John, Grits, and Erin went up the other two. At the top, we looked in the four directions. We were surrounded by a vast ocean of green trees, as large white and gray cloud puffs cast dark shadows directly underneath them across the Peten. We could see for hundreds of miles in every single direction.

"Holy." I said.

"Ain't it great?" Said Scott.

Mike put his hands on his hips, and for the first time during the trip, he had an enormous grin on his face. He breathed a sigh, and said, "look at that. Miles and miles of nothing."

Suddenly, we heard a crashing sound in the distance. Mike's smile disappeared as quickly as it came. It was a giant tree that some loggers must've cut.

We stood in silence, as the wind whispered. Far below us, as we gazed at the ground, a troop of monkeys traveled along the canopy top, and leapt from tree to tree towards the east. A flock of multi colored birds flew above the trees in formation, as their plumage shone in the sunlight. In the distance was another anomalous, forested hill, that jutted skywards, and surrounding it was low, flat land. In each of the four cardinal directions was a large island hill.

"More undiscovered cities?" I asked as Grits arrived onto the peak.

"Yeah, we saw a few in our direction too."

The mounds rose out of the flat plain like a breast, and many of them weren't marked on any of John's Guatemalan government topographical maps. We took some pictures and followed Jose through a large part of the city. There were stellae, which were statues carved out of limestone rock, half buried ball courts, square domiciles overgrown with trees, and many pyramids. There were structures that looked like the basement of an apartment block, and squat, step pyramids with trees growing in them. The complex covered at least one square mile.

"I wonder what New York will look like in 1000 years." I said.

"Probably like this." Said Grits.

We ate lunch at noon, and then had a siesta. During the siesta, I inspected the two large water containers. They were almost empty. My own bottles were almost empty, and I had one small reserve bottle left. Almost everyone was out of water. While we toured the complex, we kept our eyes open for water, but there wasn't a single pond, lake, stream, brook, swamp, marsh - not even a puddle. The complete lack of mosquitoes made sense. I gazed at the shed on the far side of the field.

"Hey John, we should check out the shed over there. There might be some water." I said. John, Mike, and I walked to the shed, and opened the door. It was full of garbage and some shelves with black containers similar to the water containers we used.

"Anything?" I asked John as he shook them.

"Yes!" he said, as he hauled out a full twenty five liter container. He opened it up and sniffed it. The liquid was dark.

"Well, it's not gas." He said. We suspended the container by the handle on a long pole, and John and I carried it back to our camp on our shoulders.

"We found water!" Announced Mike.

We opened it up and inspected it. It was dark, muddy, slimy, swamp water that sat there for months, but it was still water. Mike and I grabbed our pumps, and started the laborious task of filtering it. We all took turns, but when it was my turn, the pump was too difficult to operate. I opened it up, and tried to dump out some of the debris. I reassembled it, and started filtering again. The clean water container was only half full of our filtered water. Suddenly, the handle stopped moving.

"Aw come on. . ." I said as I pressed. I pressed harder, and then a little too hard. It broke with a loud, "crack", and the pump blew apart at the threads. The cap was shattered in two.

"Shit." I cursed. John came over to inspect the pump, and looked into the muddy container. "Time for plan B." He said, as he pulled out a bandanna. I made a makeshift funnel from a water bottle by cutting it in two. The top part served as the funnel. We put the bandanna into the funnel, and poured the water into the clean container. Then we dropped some iodine tablets in. The water was dark brown and slimy, but it was drinkable. I mixed some fruit juice in, which helped to change the taste.

Later in the evening, I climbed up the biggest pyramid to see the sunset. Scott was already up there, watching the red skyline.

"Don't mind me." I said as I sat down and put my jacket over my head.

"No problem."

I started to meditate on top of the pyramid. I wasn't sure why I did that, but as I went inside, I felt like I was trying to tap into something. This was an ancient capital city in one of the most opulent and impressive civilizations on the planet, and I wanted to see if I could feel something. I wanted to feel if the place was still alive, if maybe it held a spark like the mountain in Peru where Marco and I almost lost our lives.

The place was dead. It was empty of life and spirit. It was nothing more than a hollow shell, and it'd been that way for a long time. The city was just a skeleton of its former self. After twenty minutes, I uncovered my head and let the wind soothe my face. I opened my eyes, and looked across the horizon.

Later that evening, while eating dinner, I talked to Scott about his experiences in the Peace Corps. Scott was a country volunteer, and he worked without running water, heat, or electricity. He went to bed when his candle burned out, and woke up at dawn. He'd seen a lot of situations with the champinos, as the locals called themselves, and how they endured poverty and hardship. I asked him about the forest logging.

"I ain't gonna argue with a man whose got a family to feed. I had some champinos ask me that. Know what I said? I said cut down that forest! You've got three kids to feed, and the government isn't going to help you, man! What can he do? Only people in the states are so out there to save the forest. Cut it down and plant some corn."

"I agree with you. I just hope they don't do cattle ranching, because that destroys the land even faster."

"I hear you man. That cattle bullshit just screws everything up. Besides, that meat gets shipped into either the cities or to the States. Same with the wood they cut."

Most of the deforestation was to create pasture land for cattle. Most of the lumber harvested was sold to American lumber companies. We talked about his efforts in the back country to help the locals with their economic development, sanitation, and basic services such as education and health care. Their efforts were noble, and what the volunteers learned about themselves and their own country was startling. But the next day, when we returned to the chicle camp, I learned the most startling reason for the existence of the Peace Corps.

That night I slept with the screen door up. Unfortunately, I had a rough time sleeping. I woke up six times to the crowing of a rooster. The next morning, I woke up and I was very irritated.

"Agh!" I yelled as I chased the rooster around the campsite with a stick. Erin and Mike looked on with weary eyes. "Vegetarianism be damned!" I said to myself as I chased him, "I didn't do a thing to you and you kept me up all freaking night!" I finally stopped when I realized I that I needed my energy.

"Agh ha ha ha!" Yelled John as he chased another one and playfully swung at it with his machete. He took a look at Jose and laughed. With his bald head and five o'clock shadow, he made me think of an insane asylum escapee. I rubbed my face and felt the sharp bristles of my beard.

We cleaned up camp, burnt the garbage, buried Erin's puke, and waved good bye to El Mirador. The hike back was quiet, except when I asked John for a sip of his water, which I helped to filter. He yelled at me for it. Several days with a shortage of water, bug bites, and lack of sleep stressed everyone. I took it in stride. Jose took us on a different return route, and after several miles, we found a marsh nearby another chicle camp. We filtered the water through our bandannas, treated it with iodine, and refilled our bottles. Scott and Erin, however, were sick of the taste of iodine.

"Gimme some of that sweet ass pond water!" They both smiled as they drank the water straight from the marsh. I guess it was fine for them, since they had access to health facilities with the Peace Corps. I didn't, and the last thing I wanted was a protozoan making my internal plumbing jump through the hoops. I opened up an iodine tablet, put it in my bottle, mixed in some tangerine juice powder, and drank. The water oozed down my throat, as the wet slime clung to my tongue and mouth.

On the way back, I talked with Grits about the spiral.

"Dave, what's so special about that symbol?" The way he asked hinted at a deeper understanding. I told him about the sacred, forbidden site in Peruvian mountain, the enormous stones at Tiwanaku, and the Nazca glyph with the spiral. I told him about the strange energy form that scanned Marco and I in the mountain, and the odd light behind the escarpment. John listened as we conversed. He knew my story. I told him about my hunt for clues in the Mayan Empire, and about what Tito told me. Grits was remarkably astute.

We talked more about the Mayans who Grits worked with, and about 2012. We also talked about the Tao Te Ching pentagrams, and how they represented the amino acids and structure of DNA. Grits affirmed that many ancient cultures already had knowledge of DNA. John also had some information.

"Dave, there's a book you should get. It's about how every indigenous tribe in South and Central America already knew about the DNA helix for thousands of year. I think it's called the 'Cosmic Serpent'. Anyway, what it said was that the shamans, when they go into a trance, they meet these deities who tell them the knowledge about plants, herbs, food, and sacred wisdom. It still baffles the West how these 'primitive' tribes could possess knowledge of DNA, not to mention their vast knowledge about medicinal plants and uses. But DNA, holy shit, you need microscopes to find that, and they didn't even have that. Every single one of these cultures saw the intertwining of serpents that represented DNA."

"Cool. Get high, then get smart."

"Exactly." Replied John.

It made me curious about how the shamans discovered the medicinal qualities of thousands of plants for so many ailments. The western scientist often claimed that it was through centuries of deaths and experiences with the plants that the knowledge was handed down generation after generation. That would work, as long as there was writing to record the results.

The problem was that the natives didn't have a hand writing system. Also, the Indian tribes were small groups of people completely dependent on each other in family oriented relationships. If a family member died due to a shaman's science experiment gone wrong, then the communal trust was broken. That would put a halt to any more "experiments" on a plant, and many of the plants had many different effects.

The shaman's themselves always said that their Gods taught them the ways of the rain forest plants, about the secrets of life, and about the thousands upon thousands of plants and treatments. There was no written library, yet somehow, the shaman's knowledge was vast. Much of that knowledge was derived from the data they collected, while in trances from the mind altering plants that the shaman's consumed when they wanted to communicate with their Gods.

"How do you know about the symbol Grits?"

"I built a structure of that spiral into the construction of my house."

"Why did you do that?"

"I had reasons that were architectural and artistic, but there's also a strange property about that symbol. So I wanted to incorporate it into my home."

"Strange property?"

"Yeah, I can't quite put my finger on it. But it is special."

We finally arrived back at Don Marco's camp, and he greeted us. I ran to find my bike, hopped over my booby trap, and found the stick. I uncovered my bike, and walked back to the camp. John saw me coming back with the bike.

"Man, I was afraid something was gonna happen to your bike."

"Yeah, I was too." I said.

I boiled some water to take a bath, and then boiled some more to refill my water containers. We cooked and our remaining rations. That evening, as we sat around the fire, I listened to each member talk about his grievances with the Peace Corps. Nobody was perfect, and the Peace Corps certainly wasn't a perfect organization, but John's comments took me by surprise.

"It pisses me off with some of the kinds of people we get in the Peace

Corps. We've been getting some real cases lately. They're either party types who think the Peace Corps is some kind of two year party, or they're dope heads. I mean, look, you come into the Peace Corps for these reasons." John noted the numbers with his fingers.

"One, you come here to work. You're supposed to work not goof off all the time. Two, you're supposed to help people, that's what we're here for. Three, the Peace Corps is here to show that white people are good people."

The Peace Corps is here to show that white people are good people? I became cynical as the grievance session continued. John picked a tick off his skin, looked at me and said, "man, I sure am glad I'm not a darkie like you. I wouldn't be able to see my bites."

"Yeah, I'm the token of the group!" I said as I waved my arms.

"Well, actually, in this country, we're the minority." Said Mike.

"We?" I replied.

"Yes. Us. All six of us."

I looked at John, and said, "that's why I love traveling. When I'm in the USA, I'm never considered an American, even though I was born there. But when I'm traveling, and I meet Americans, they always consider me as an American." John looked back at me with a sad, pained look on his face, and said, "that, is truly awful."

****

The next morning, we gave Don Marco all of our coffee, sugar, salt, pasta, and I gave him my machete. I did not look forward to the hike. At least I knew what to expect, and I pushed myself through six hours of hell. Because we finished our food supply, and chose to carry our water in small containers, we were considerably lighter. We reached the logging camp, and grabbed some food and clean, slime and iodine free, water.

"Where's the bus?" Asked Mike.

"There's no bus for another two days." Said John.

We walked up to the road, sat against an empty logging truck, and waited. An hour became three as we patiently waited for a vehicle. We were napping when out from the jungle came a flatbed, eighteen wheeler, loaded with four foot thick, logs.

"Hey buddy!" yelled Scott as he waved. John ran and flagged the truck to a stop, and then jumped on the driver's side stair platform, and talked to

the driver. The driver nodded his head.

"We're outta here!" yelled John. We tossed our bags in between the logs, and stacked my bike on top. Then we straddled the top log. The driver revved up his engine, and drove us for a two hour, bumpy ride. Along the way, as we drove down a turn in the road, we spotted some giant six foot thick, logs that'd been dumped on the side of the road by an illegal logger. Each log was worth about 500 to 1000 dollars. Illegal logging was lucrative for the average guatemalan, and most of these logs were destined for markets in the USA, to supply home improvement chains. Very little of the harvested lumber was ever used internally in Guatemalan homes, which was apparent, as the rich homes were made of concrete and the poor homes were made of mud adobe. Almost no significant amount of timber was involved in the construction.

As we bumped and jostled down the road, we ducked the low hanging branches that swung at our heads. My left side itched, and I opened up my shirt to see a bright red rash that covered my entire left side. The driver dropped us off, on a paved road, and we hitched a ride in an old Toyota truck to Flores.

We arrived at Dan's place, picked up our gear, and then walked to the neighboring town of Santa Elena, where we stayed at another volunteer's home on the lake. We slept on the balcony, and awoke to the sunrise over the lake. We then registered in a hostel, and went out to party that night in a carnival in the frontier. We picked up Guatemalan women using Scott's whistling technique, danced to Norteño music, did wrestling with some kids in an outdoor wrestling ring, and sampled some of the frontier festivities.

Later we had dinner with another volunteer, Pete, that turned into yet another rant session about the Peace Corps. Pete was a middle aged professional from New York, who had a mustache, eyeglasses, and a severe angst against the Peace Corps bureaucracy.

"You know," I said, "after listening to you and the fellas here, I'm really surprised. I've always wanted to do volunteer work internationally in the Peace Corps. I mean, you guys just made it sound like a den of bureaucratic incompetence and ineffectiveness."

"Well, it's like any other federal agency. I had to get through a ton of red tape to get something done, and on top of that, they were spending money to fly me to Washington, for alcohol counseling every other weekend. And

I only drank once a week! Dave, you have to understand, there's a real lack of leadership, clear goals, and the bureaucracy is tedious."

"So for a guy like me who likes to get to the point, what do I do? I still want to do volunteer work."

"There's a good book called Alternatives to the Peace Corps, or you can form your own effort. I've met a lot of people who've done that."

We talked some more about his adventure into an obscure Mayan ruin, where in a fresco inside the ruin, he saw pictures of Mayans dragging crying angels in chains. I made a note of it to explore in some future date. The next day, our group disbanded. We had a great time, but it was time for me to go. I spent one more night in Santa Elena, to enjoy the delicate rhythms of marimba music in the central plaza before biking on the lonesome jungle road to Tikal.

It took a day to reach Tikal. I registered for a two day stay, and biked to the campgrounds next to the pyramids.

Tikal and El Mirador were different in climate. The land was moist, and the mosquitoes swarmed around me in the evening. I wore a head net as I finished cooking the last of my ramen noodles, and slapped the mosquitoes off my exposed hands. A Canadian couple set up camp next to me.

We exchanged travel stories and adventures. They were wrapping up a long trip that started in northern Mexico. I took a much needed shower, and then went to sleep.

At three in the morning, I stirred awake to the roar of howler monkeys in the distance. It sounded like a man inhaling and expanding his mouth a the same time, and it boomed like thunder through my tent and ear drums. I sat straight up, naked in my tent.

"Hwaa Hwaa Hwaa Hwaa!" I listened to the echoes of the monkeys. How primal it felt! It felt so powerful, savage, so... I looked at the glowing hands of my watch. It felt so late, and I wanted to get up at 4AM to ascend the biggest pyramid in Tikal to watch the sunrise.

I quickly got up to my alarm. There was no howler monkey roars, and all I heard were jungle insects. I looked at my watch, and then got dressed. I grabbed my cameras, and got out of the tent. The air was cool and moist, and the crickets were still serenading. Quickly, I donned my hat, and jogged across the camp, the road, past the visitor's center, and then onto the jungle trail. I followed the trail past the pyramids of the jaguar and the leopard.

381

They looked like square, dark mountains in the courtyard at night, and they cast haunting shadows.

I walked by, looked, and turned around as I walked backward. They rose out of the darkness like thrones to lost gods. I walked by shadowy, dead temples in the darkness, and put aside my questions regarding the priceless cultural treasurers that thousands labored and toiled to create. A shiver went up my spine as I jogged silently to the enormous, fifteen story pyramid.

I grabbed the wooden pole that formed the sides of the ladder, and quickly ascended. With little effort, I propelled myself to the top of the pyramid. There, alone, I sat down, and set up my cameras. The land began to lighten, and black became blue black, to dark blue.

I heard some people climb up, and soon the Canadian couple was there. Later, a pair of French came up, and then a German, an Israeli, and another Canadian. I greeted each one in silence; we were silent, as we anticipated the moment of truth. The crickets and night insects began the prelude to the symphony. Like violins, they brought a flourish of ambiance and sweetness in their rhythmic song. The parakeets and other exotic birds warmed up, and brought their lilting hymns and warbles, chirps and tunes, and created a dance of high notes, full of sharps and flats. In this orchestration, the howler monkeys in unison boomed their rhythmic cries across the horizon, calling forth the sun.

Soon, we saw the sky glow. It became pink, and then light blue with pink, and slowly, from the veil of gray clouds, I watched as the sun's light struck the two pyramids in the courtyard that I passed just a few hours ago. Their peaks drew shadows, as their fronts glowed in the sun.

I sat on the pyramid, as I looked at the great city of Tikal. This was just a skeleton, and nothing more. Its cultural treasures were lost to the colonization. I clutched my knees as I thought to myself about how the universe operated.

For the rest of the day, I explored pyramids, temples, and ball courts. I saw ruins of apartments, palaces, and homes. There were stately stellae, giant carved circular slabs of stone, and courtyards. I walked in peace through the temple complex. So many pyramids, and so many temples were here! On top of each pyramid was a room that was the size of a large janitorial closet. Given the large number of pyramids, it didn't make sense to buy the theory that these were for kings, or even sacrificial chambers. There was an older theory that made more sense to me. The tops of the pyramids had a spiritual role, but that was all I knew.

Figure 25.1: A logging camp serves as our base camp.

Figure 25.2: Don Marco ponders the meaning of life.

Figure 25.3: Mike and John observe the horses drinking after the horses defecated in the water.

Figure 25.4: I peer into a well excavated looting tunnel.

Figure 25.5: A pyramid peaks out from the jungle.

Figure 25.6: John secures my bike onto a logging truck.

Figure 25.7: I'm going shotgun on top of a logging truck through the jungle!

Figure 25.8: Tikal emerges in the morning mists.

Figure 25.9: Temple I.

Figure 25.10: Rubber trees still growing out of the ancient ruins of Tikal.

Chapter 26

Belize

I left Tikal, and biked a hundred kilometers until a friendly horseman, Francisco, let me set up camp at his family's hut. I slept with the pigs, and listened to them grunt and snore through the night. I was grateful for his family's hospitality, since this was a dangerous road. Despite the dangers, there was low traffic, and the road seemed relatively safe, until I rode around a curve.

The shade of the jungle canopy cast distorted shadows on the white, dusty, unpaved road as I biked. The day was overcast, and I was the only road into Belize. I remembered the warning to me about how two Mennonites were killed just a month ago, and I kept my wits about me. What would I do if someone pointed another gun at me?

As I rode around, I saw a field where several brigades of brown men, in military buzzed hair cuts, jogged in unison. I was close to the Guatemalan-Belizean border. I continued biking until I came alongside a large military outpost. I stopped, pulled out my map, and looked for a landmark symbol, but the post was nowhere on the map. Out of the corner of my eye, I noticed a young soldier raise his M-16 rifle towards me. I immediately realized my mistake of stopping and looking at the map, and he didn't look friendly.

Quickly, I yelled, *"hey buddy! I'm lost. I'm trying to get to Belize. Do you know the way?"* It was a dumb question, since this was the only road, but the sentence just came out of my mouth. He stopped in his tracks as if he was confounded, re-shouldered his rifle, and then pointed down the road.

"This way."

"Thanks man! You don't know how lost I was! I'd been lost for a day. Say, what's you're name?"

"Luis."

"David. Nice to meet you."

I walked up to him, and we shook hands.

"OK, I'd better get moving. I don't want you to get in trouble. Thanks again."

Quickly, I biked down the road. Before I left the proximity, I turned and waved back to Luis. He waved back. As soon as the installation was out of sight, I was once again in the silence of the jungle. No one followed me, and I wiped my brow.

I kept biking until the road became tarmac at the bottom of the hill. Soon, the familiar site of a border entry gate appeared, as well as a customs office. I pulled out my passport, and opened it up. It was full of stamps and stickers. I walked into the custom's building, and got my papers in order. After my exit and entry stamps, the Belizean custom's officer asked me as I went out the door,

"Sir! Where are you going? Where are you staying?"

"I don't know. How big is Belize? Is it a big country?"

"You can cross our country in two hours by car."

"You're kidding me!"

"No. It's a small country."

"Well, I guess I'll find a hotel or hostel along the way."

"Sir, we need to know what hotel you'll be staying in."

"Um, he's coming with me," interrupted a man in his late twenty's. He looked vaguely Arabic, and I looked at him in surprise.

"OK." Said the official.

"Come with me." The man said.

I followed him outside.

"Hey, thanks for the help." I said.

"It's not a problem." He replied in a British accent, and added, "you're a bicycle traveler, and so am I. I'm your comrade. My name is Rudolfo Juan."

I shook his hand. He got into a taxi in the parking lot, and said, "just follow me." It was a short distance into the next town, and we passed by several shops: Wen's hardware, Yao's groceries, and Tsu's convenience store.

Panama was loaded with Chinese Panamanians, Costa Rica had a long history of Chinese ticans, and so did the Honduras.

I followed the taxi up the hill to Rudolfo's shop. "Wait here." He said as he unloaded his supplies. He went back into the taxi and left. We were in front of the police station, so I set my bike up against the yellow wall of Rudolfo's trading post. A black officer came out, smiled at me, pointed at my bike, and nodded his head in surprise. I grinned, and nodded, "yes". He did a double take. Rudolfo came out of the shop.

"Come in!" Rudolfo said. I walked into a well supplied general store, and watched as he excitedly opened the doors. There were shadows on the floor, and the smell of old and new wood mixed with adobe and concrete tickled my nose. Rudolfo started opening his shelves as a tall, south Asian man with a baseball cap, and long hair walked in.

"Hey mon! Rudolfo! Whatcha be doin here deese days?"

"Hey Sanjeev! Good mon! Just da usual tings. I prally be workin, mon."

"Hello." I said as I extended my hand. He shook it warmly.

"How are you, mon? Where you be from?"

"The US."

"USA?"

"Yeah."

He mulled for a moment. "I be tinking you from here mon. Or Japanese." I smiled and said, "no man. Vietnamese. And are there a lot of Indians like you here? I miss good Indian food." Rudolfo burst out laughing.

"Ah no, mon. Sanjeev is one of the few south Asians here."

Sanjeev smiled, and said, "if you want to meet south Asians, Trinidad and Tobago, Suriname, and Guyana is where you should be goin. Well gentlemen, I haveta go now." Sanjeev left the store, and I watched Rudolfo pull up a tray of eggs.

"Need any help?" I asked.

"No, I'm good. So tell me, where did you travel?" I noticed Rudolfo spoke British English again. I told him my list of countries.

"And you Rudolfo? You said you were also a bicycle traveler. Where have you gone?"

"I went through every single country in South and Central America in two years on the bicycle."

"Holy crap!"

393

"No, crap is not holy, but it works well as fertilizer here. And yes, I did have a few situations where your expletive would've worked well, but nothing terrible. I'm sure you've had your share."

"You went through every single country?"

"I went through every single one. Some I went through twice."

"How was Colombia?" I remembered the Japanese cyclists in Peru, who'd gone through Colombia.

"It was great, I didn't have any problems. Why didn't you go through?"

"I had to be in Costa Rica to keep a promise to two friends."

"Well, the next time you get a chance, go to Colombia. It's wonderful there."

"That's what everyone tells me! Nice, friendly people. Beautiful country, and lots of untouched places. Did you have problems with the FARC?" The FARC were the national socialist party, the guerrilla rebels who were part of the forty year civil war.

"No. They only want Americans. You don't look like typical American, so you won't have a problem. They thought I was a Brazilian."

That was why the Japanese cyclists didn't have any problems. It always surprised me how my ethnic appearance was now my advantage. I'd gone from a lifetime of being singled out negatively for my race, to being seen in a positive or neutral manner. During my voyage through Latin America, I discovered my American-ness with the Americans, t and for everyone else, I was either a curious Japanese traveler, or a potential local. Why that never happened in the States always bothered me, but not anymore. It gave me access to places that were forbidden to westerners. It allowed me to hear the unfettered truths and opinions from the hearts and minds of the locals. Even stranger still, that which made me different at home, made me a part of the local society in foreign lands. More people started coming into the shop.

"David, have you been to the ruins of Xunantunich?"

"No, but I've been to Tikal. Where's Xunantunich?"

"Just down the road. Why don't you go visit those ruins, and then come back at noon. I'll take you to my home."

I left and walked down the hill, crossed the road, and headed to the Mopan River. At the river bank was a large boat with a hand cranked cable system. I boarded, and the operator started moving the ferry across the waters. After a mile hike, and payment for my ticket, I scaled the ruins of

Xunantunich, the second highest pyramid in the Belizean area. Despite the beauty of the intricate friezes, and the pyramid, and the fact that it was carved from solid stone, I had enough of ruins.

I quietly walked among the ramparts, and enjoyed the scenery, of a polished white pyramid against the brilliant green of the jungle forest. I looked at one frieze, and the weather worn edges of the carving. I explored for two hours, and soaked up the intricate artwork of the carvings. Tikal was impressive, but Xunantunich was artistically expressive. Here, I could see the artists most detailed work, his emotions, his cultural richness, and his heritage in the carvings of the faces, pictographs, and geometric patterns in the frieze.

Yet like the other ancient sites I'd visited, it was still a ruin, a place that once teemed with people. It took people to make it alive, and to give an energetic, living, vibrancy. People made life worth living for, and this place was devoid of it.

I walked back to Rudolfo's shop. He was closing and locking up for lunch.

"Alright then! Let's go."

I followed him for six miles down the road to his family's farm. The Juan family farm was nestled in a cleared area at the edge of the Peten jungle. It stood on top of a hill with a river on the slopes below. Several small cabins dotted the landscape, while across the farm, several cows grazed. Two dogs eagerly ran out from the one story ranch styled home to greet me, as well as a short, white lady, Rudolfo's mom, who was Irish, and an expatriate living in Belize.

"David, you can stay in one of the cabins down there. You're our guest. When you're done unpacking your things, please come and join us for lunch."

"Thank you for your hospitality. Please let me know if I can do anything for you," I replied.

I took a cabin facing out to the river, and stepped up to the porch. Before going inside, I sat on the porch, cross legged, and looked over the grassy plain towards the forest and the river. My journey was ending. I could feel it, but I also knew in my heart that the last ten months was just the first step I'd taken into a world I'd never imagined before. I unpacked my things, showered, and hiked up the hill to the Juan family home.

****

Belize is a country about the size of New Jersey, with a population of just 200,000 people, most of whom reside in Belize City, and a few more in Belmopan. The rest are scattered in the countryside's villages and settlements. There are three main highways, if a two lane road could be considered a highway. The biggest event in Belize was the agricultural trade show, and it drew people from all four corners to exhibit their wares, produce, and products. Daniel Juan, the youngest brother, invited me to come see the show. I met him the night before, when I dined with his family. Daniel was a local school teacher, and he noticed me eating a plate of pure vegetables, and asked, "are you vegetarian?"

"Yes."

"How come?"

"I'm Buddhist, and it's part of my spiritual beliefs."

"Oh."

"I had two friends from Malaysia at my school who were Buddhist. We got one of them to covert." Said his mother. The whole family was Catholic. I looked at his plate. It was just a steak and some rice.

"Well, you're not the only one with an out of place diet here. People think I'm odd, because I eat just beef, rice, and milk." Said Daniel.

"Why do you eat like that?"

"Because everything else is so saturated with chemicals, pesticides, and fertilizers. My beef is from cows that eat just grass. My rice, I grow my own. And I squeeze my own milk."

He passed a glass of fresh milk to me that he'd just squeezed that morning. I sipped it, and it didn't taste like store bought milk in the States.

"That's really sweet!"

"Yes, it's completely organic. Have you ever had rain water?"

"No."

"Try some."

I sipped some of the water in a glass. It was also sweet, and refreshing. There wasn't a hint of chlorine, metals, or any other chemicals.

"There's no pollution here, so the water from the sky is pure. It even makes you feel better. Thank goodness Belize is hundreds of miles from any kind of polluting industry."

I asked Daniel and his mother about the military facility I'd seen the other day before entering Belize, and told them the story about the soldier.

"I checked my map, but it's nowhere on there."

"David, Guatemala has wanted Belize for decades. This used to be the British Honduras before it became independent Belize. Belize never was part of Guatemala, even in their old maps. What's going on is the USA and Israel have been funneling arms to the Guatemalans, and supporting them in their territorial claims. War is their business after all. The British have opposed this, and they've been able to force Guatemala from that position. But even now, the Guatemalans send in landless people to settle on the land. When we try to enforce the borders and move the people off, they agitate a conflict, which gives them an excuse to use armed force. This has been going on for a while. Whenever that happens, the British sends a small force here to help."

"Why is the US supporting the Guatemalans?"

"Where ever there's a war, the US is there. You saw the M-16. Who makes those? They supported the right wing death squads during the civil war in Guatemala, and they supported the massacres, and honestly, I've lost any interest in what motivates the US in its actions. Did you hear about that trade war the US had with Europe over bananas?" Mrs. Juan asked.

"Yes, I did read about it. Europe has a quota from Africa, the Carribbean, and some South American countries."

"Well, central to it is our country, Belize. Because we used to be a British colony, we had favored trade status with Britain for bananas. Dole fruit didn't like that, so they had your government spark a trade war to make the British drop the quota. Britain refused, so that's why your government enacted tariffs on several European goods. They're such bitter losers; it was a big fuss over a few bananas."

"Well, the Dole fruit company has huge influence in the government. Bob Dole ran for president."

"Dole isn't the only one. Who really runs your government anyway?" Mrs Juan asked.

It was a question that we'd answer the next day. The next morning, we went to the fair, but not before I grabbed a glass of Daniel's fresh milk.

"So you've become a fan of that milk now?" He smiled.

"Yes. I need to keep a cow around at home. I just have to figure out what to do with all that cow manure."

We arrived at the fair in time to see the livestock competition for the best

397

breed. Daniel's father, a Lebanese Mexican man, was eager to present his bull. The agricultural fair was the place where the entire country got to know everyone. There were blacks, Hispanics, Asians, and a few whites, talking, eating, and enjoying themselves. I watched a table where a Chinese man, his family, and his wife, a black Belizean woman, and her family, sat down to eat. Elsewhere, kids from the local schools were a mix of Hispanic, Chinese, black, and white, played on the fair ground amusements. Everyone spoke a laid back Belizean creole, and everybody knew everybody.

I walked to an exhibit of a sugar cane processing plant which used it's own organic waste to produce the energy needed to run the facility. It was the new wave in sustainable industry. A white man came out to explain the plant to me, while an Asian man asked about venture opportunities in the project. Elsewhere, a Hispanic lady was hawking building products while her Chinese husband played with their children. Another Chinese woman and a black woman were handing out flier's. A black policeman patrolled the grounds giving information to people who asked. Daniel and I sampled some of Marie Sharp's famous hot sauce, and I tried some fried dough. I looked at Daniel, and said, "Daniel, tell me about your country. Are there a lot of class problems here?"

"No, almost everyone would be considered middle class here. It's not like Latin America, where the top 5% owns 95% of the country's resources. We'd be considered poor in terms of capital to the US, but in living standard, we are very much a middle class majority."

"What about racial problems?"

"Racial problems are everywhere, since that's part of human nature. But here, it's not institutionalized, which would give racism legitimacy, and everybody participates in their civic duty here. Here, everybody's voice is important, since we're such a small country. Our president was a Palestinian émigré, as an example, we've had black city counselors, Asian officials and cabinet members, and Hispanic officials. Here, we make everyone feel like an important part of our society."

We watched as the Asian man's Asian-Hispanic boy ran between us after his little sister.

"And it seems that racial mixing is also normal here, like in Latin America. But this is an anglo society, isn't it?"

"No, not really. Our culture is much more inclusive here. We have to recognize that in a country as small as ours, if we don't work together, then our country would not function, and that would put us at the mercy of Guatemala, or worse, the USA. So, it's out of necessity."

"We're like this because we're descended from pirates. In fact, we were the first foreign democracy in this hemisphere, if you leave out the Indian nations."

"Pirates?"

"Yes. The pirates were an egalitarian meritocracy. That is where our culture comes from. Everyone functioned with a purpose, and decisions were put to the vote. Belize used to be a safe haven for pirates."

"That would make your country's democracy older than the US, since pirates were around raiding the Spanish before the US ever was settled."

"Yes, and unlike the US, we're not a representative democracy. We don't use your electoral college system. Here, everyone's vote counts, and everyone matters."

"I wonder why I never heard about your country being among the first democracies."

"What do you expect from a bunch of gringos?"

"Good point. It's funny. Greece wasn't the first democracy in history. India had the first democratic republics almost two to three hundred years before Greece, in the Republics of Vaishali, but you never hear of anyone giving the Indians any credit. So your government institutions aren't afraid of mob rule?"

"Not at all. Have you noticed in your travels how some country's democracies didn't work?"

"Yes. Bolivia's was the worse. Nothing got done, nothing functioned, and the country was constantly paralyzed with protests and blockades about the fact that their country did not function." I said.

"Did you ever wonder why that happens?"

"Yes, I did. And it's interesting how many people down there told me that even though Pinochet was bloody and terrible, he brought order, cleaned out corruption, and made things work. Fujimori was considered authoritarian, but for once the Peruvian government got rid of terrorism, roads were actually built, taxes were paid, and the country stabilized. Things got stable enough to actually build a functioning economy and society."

"Do you notice David, that what you just said outlines the first prerequisite for a democracy?"

"What, order? A bloody dictatorship? Authoritarian power?"

"No. Stability to build a majority middle class. Even your countries founders were largely land owning elites or middle class. Not only that, but you need an educated middle class. Those two dictators functioned to bring order and stability to develop a middle class. Here in Belize, the middle class make up the majority, and everyone gets access to education. There's another component to have a functioning democracy."

"And that is?"

"A free and unfettered media. Freedom of speech, but from multiple sources. You must have a majority of people who are educated enough to comprehend the issues at hand, but more importantly, who have something to lose. You need to have a multiple sourced media that can present the issues on all sides. You need to have both for a democracy to function, because if not, a democracy will not work."

"So let's say you just have a large middle class, but a controlled media." I said.

"Then you have a public that makes poor decisions."

"And a poor majority but a free media?"

"Then you will have a country where everyone votes to do something, anything to help themselves economically, even if it means losing their democracy and freedoms. They will elect people who they feel are strong, will improve their lives, and will stop threats to them."

"And a poor majority and a controlled media?"

"North Korea, or any other dictatorship."

"You just described the state of most of today's democracies Daniel."

"What do you think your country is, David?"

"A large middle class that's poorly educated, with a controlled media."

"Now you know why your country made such grievous actions on the world, and continues to do so."

"So what do you think about capitalism?" I asked.

"Capitalism is better than most other economic systems out there, but capitalism has its limits. Communism ran up against the laws of the marketplace. Capitalism will run up against the laws of Nature, or it will create social disorder where people revolt against it when inequality becomes too great. Chile was a fascist dictatorship, but they were the most capitalistic country of all Latin America. So, you don't need a democracy, which is government system, for capitalism, which is an economic system, to flourish. Those two are fundamentally different. I'm sure you noticed that China already figured that out."

"That's funny that you said that. Right now, in the US, we've fully corporatized our government. Mussolini said that fascism is simply just the corporatization of government."

"Yes, and your media is owned by the corporations. Which is why we Belizeans bristle every time you Americans come telling us what to do. Your country isn't even a democracy."

"Well, we at least look like one."

"But you certainly don't act like one. And your country supports the worst despots, including Pinochet, and your policies have destroyed too many innocent people and lives. What you sow, is what you reap."

I was quiet. I knew what he was alluding too. We continued to explore the fair grounds, and met some of his colleagues and neighbors. A sheepherder from New Zealand, a Taiwanese rancher, a black fruit jam maker, and a Hispanic fair organizer. There were no stereotypical roles, no preconceived stereotypes, no tokenism, no notions, and not a single accent. Everyone sounded creolish in their speech. For a country founded by egalitarian pirates, it was only natural that their society and culture of the Jolly Rogers would continue to thrive and flourish.

****

The night was a warm tranquility of rich black across the sky, and millions of pale diamonds flickering in the moist, warm touch of a cool spring breeze. Crickets resonated while an occasional howl from a dog would break the calm night.

It started innocently, with me discussing more about democracy with Mr. Juan. Mr. Juan was a tall, overweight man with thick arms and legs from daily work with cows. He also radiated a geniality which instantly put me at ease. Brown skinned with an Arabic nose, Mr. Juan spoke in a slow, languid creole that disguised a razor sharp mind.

After dinner, we went to the porch. I sat down on a lawn chair while Mr. Juan rocked himself in his hammock. Dominic Juan, an environmental monitor, sat down on a stool while Mrs. Juan sat on a chair working on her knitting. Santiago leaned on the porch, as he bundled his long hair into a pony tail. Santiago was a rancher.

"So now you know what it's like to live in a poor country, eh?" Said Santiago.

"Poor? Everyone here seems to have land to live on."

"Poor compared to your country."

"I guess in terms of capital and money, yes. But in living standards, it's equal, well, that's what I've observed so far. I may earn more than people here, but then I have to pay more to live, and I don't live on much. It doesn't look like Latin America here in terms of inequality among the classes. Everyone here seems to have some food, land, and something to do."

"Not everything is cut and dried David," Said Mrs. Juan.

"How so?"

"Well Belize has its share of social problems too. There's no health care, so I get a long line at my health clinic." Mrs. Juan ran a free medical clinic for the Catholic Church.

"And we do have our share of corruption as well." Said Dominic.

"Well, I didn't say Belize was paradise. But it's far better off than a lot of other places I've been to."

"So what do you think of our greatest event in Belize, David?" Asked Mr. Juan.

"The fair? It was amazing! I saw some aquaculture projects, and sustainable industry displays. The aquaculture stuff interests me because I've seen some research at NASA regarding it."

"How do you know about NASA?" Asked Santiago.

"I used to work on a rocket project with my University and NASA."

"About that NASA aquaculture project you were talking about, we know the scientist. He's a Belizean. You'd be surprised David, many Belizeans are well educated." Said Mr. Juan.

"I believe it. I've seen more hope here for the future than anywhere else."

"Do you honestly believe that Americans landed on the moon?" Asked Santiago.

"Yes."

"How do you know?"

"What do you mean how do I know?"

"How can you be so sure that the Americans landed on the moon? What evidence do you have?"

"We have rocks, equipment, stuff we've left there."

"Really? How can you prove it?"

"Well, there's a reflector up there you can aim a laser off of." He still didn't believe me.

"And I got to see some of the moon rocks at a museum where I worked."

"Come on David. How is it even possible for man to walk on the moon? Let alone land there?" Asked Santiago, who seemed agitated at my response.

"Well, you work out the math and the physics, test out the equipment, and then go. We've been going there for quite a while. You can see the experiments they've run with that laser and the reflector." Santiago didn't say anything, and he still seemed incredulous. I shrugged my arms.

"I don't know what else to tell you, except that we've left a lot of equipment up there and we blew a ton of money on those missions. I know what I believe, and so do you. So, until you come to the US and see what they did to go up, nothing I say is going to convince you."

Santiago didn't talk to me for the rest of the night. Before I left the Juan residence, I wanted to talk to Rudolfo about his adventures. After several days, we got together in the family restaurant.

Rudolfo originally started his journey in Brazil, and pedaled through Argentina, Paraguay, Chile, Bolivia, Peru, Colombia, Ecuador, Suriname, Guyana, Panama, and all of Central America for two years before he arrived back home. He worked for a year and a half in the UK, saving up for his journey, and he worked for 6 months in Argentina to finance the rest of his trip.

We talked through the night, traded stories, looked at his slides, my photos, and as fellow bicycle nomads, told each other about the hairy and the hoary of the journey.

"So what's next Rudolfo?"

"Africa. That continent is enormous. And you?"

"The World. Or maybe I'd finish South America."

"Oh, did you run into four Japanese cyclists?"

"I met two of in Peru."

"Well, these four were Yoshi, Kenji, Hikaru, and Guy."

"Oh yes! Kenji was the one with the mustache. I think he went to Colombia to stay with his Colombian girlfriend."

"Ha ha! I guess Yoshi continued?"

"Dunno. They said they'd gone around the world three times."

"Four."

"Four times?!"

"Yes. I saw Yoshi's speedometer."

"It didn't break?"

"No. It's made in Japan."

"They went around the world four times?"

"It took them five years."

"That's a long time."

"Yes it is. Yoshi said he had a borderline obsessive compulsive wanderlust disorder."

"I think we both have that."

"Yes, that appears to be the case."

The next day, I bid my farewell to the Juans. It was time to go. I pedaled down the road, and through a thundering downpour. It felt wonderful to have the rain cleanse my sweat as I biked. I swam through a land rich in deep green, savanna, and the edges of the Peten jungle lined the road. This was untouched and untamed country; it was the stuff of pioneers. Most of the people who settled in Belize were pioneers, but unlike the legendary violence of the wild west, Belize was a laid back nation. I stopped by a small, crude café on the side of the road. An attractive, black, Belizean woman came out, and I asked her for a plate of rice and beans, fried plantains, cheese, and some salad.

"How long have gone suh?" She smiled as she asked.

"A long way. I started in Peru."

Her eyes opened in shock.

"My dat's fah. Well, welcome to my country, suh. I do hope you have a good time. We're much safer then Latin America."

"I've heard a lot about that. It's laid back here."

She looked at the bicycle, shook her head, and said, "amazing."

****

"Uno!" Yelled Kerry, as he slapped down his card on the table. I looked in disbelief at Kerry, then to Mimi, his older sister, and then to Lisa, the youngest. They too were blinking in disbelief.

"How? That's the 15th time?!" I said in shock.

"Hahaha!" He laughed.

"He's cheating!" Cried out Lisa, "lemme see those cards!" She said as she tried to grab them.

"Kerry, how… dat's not possible, mon!" Said Mimi as she also tried to make a grab for the deck.

As they started arguing, I sat back and looked around the Jou residence. It was a combination of wooden palm board slats, corrugated aluminum roofing, bamboo and concrete struts, steel poles, cement blocks, and some thatch. Inside the living room, the walls were lined with book cases full of taiwanese language texts, magazines, and reference books. It was electrified, with a large kitchen that also looked like a workshop, and an outdoor thatched car port. These were the pioneers. Like the settlers of the American West and their sod roofed homes, the Jou's made good use of local materials to construct their comfortable home.

Their home sat on top of four acres of land, in Tea Kettle Village, a tiny settlement far off the main road. Although it was common to find Asian Belizeans, Tea Kettle Village was populated by some uncommon Asians. They were a tribe of indigenous Taiwanese, whose pacific islander roots were more Polynesian, but that itself wasn't uncommon. What was uncommon was this particular tribe was once a tribe of head hunters. Mrs. Jou was the daughter of the village chieftain. Her husband, Mr. Jou, was an ethnic Han Chinese from the mainland, who later escaped to Taiwan at a young age.

Lisa showed me a black and white photo of her grandfather, which included some family "heirlooms", shrunken human heads that were passed down from ancient times. Unfortunately, when the tribe moved to Belize, they weren't permitted to take their prized possessions along.

"So what are your people going to do now for fun? Just play heads up?" I teased. Mimi laughed.

"No mon, now we're still deciding."

"Dinner time everyone!" Yelled Mrs. Jou, adding, "David! I cooked a lot of food for you, so you better eat up! You're too thin!" Mimi looked at me, and said, "actually, we just decided what we're going to do, mon." As her teeth flashed in a wide, and evil grin.

"Ha ha ha! We're having David for dinner, mon. Uh, I mean, we're having David over for dinner." Laughed Kerry.

"I think Dave's scared now." Said Lisa.

Mr. Jou walked into the room, a ladle in hand, and with a light smile.

"David, mon, time for some good home cooked Chinese food. You're Chinese right, mon?"

"Part Chinese, on my Dad's side."

"Good good. We have good hot sauce for you."

"The poor ting! He seriously tinks we going to eat'im." Said Mimi.

"Well, gee! First your mom wants to fatten me up, then Kerry talks about having me for dinner, and then your dad even recommends hot sauce! Well, I'm lean meat, so you're gonna have a healthy meal."

We laughed as we sat down at the dinner table in the kitchen. They bowed their heads down as Mr. and Mrs. Jou recited grace. I bowed in respect, and said a few words when it was my turn. Then it was time to eat.

I poked my chopsticks into the steaming fried noodle dish. On the table was an assortment of dishes, expertly prepared by Mrs. Jou over the propane and wood stove. There was moo shoo tofu, and lightly fried Chinese cabbage, bok choy, and noodles for me. There was rice and beans, with Cantonese pork, fried chicken with Marie's Sharp's hot sauce in a Schezuan mix, some noodle soup, radishes, a side of fried plantains, and jack fruit. I chowed down the plantains with gusto.

Every culture has some kind of exchange, and no one is ever truly independent of each other. The food showed how culture adapted and blended in with the local food. In Asian culture, food is where culture begins, spreads, and passes down to later generations. As always, the cuisine adopted and later re-expressed itself in new dishes and styles of the new land. Mrs. Jou's cooking was quintessentially Chinese creole. The vegetables, meats, and most of the ingredients were grown in the fertile Belizean soil, harvested by the Taiwanese, Hispanic, and black farmers and ranchers, all of whom were Belizean, and then re-expressed as the blending of Chinese, Hispanic, and Belizean dishes.

After dinner, we sat back, and drank tea and orange juice, while Kerry sighed deeply with satisfaction.

"Dave, you've only been here for one day. We want you to stay a week."

Said Lisa.

"Yes, you're invited to Lisa's graduation." Said Mimi, and then added, "now, after graduation is when we will perform our tribal customs."

"Yah mon." Said Kerry. He belched.

"And don't forget, we'd like you to teach a class about some of your travels." Said Kerry.

"Sure! I'd love to!" I replied.

"Well, let me show you your room."

We walked outside to another one story building. Suddenly, from out of the twilight, charged a huge, snarling, muscular dog out of the dark dog house that sat on the corner of a homemade basketball court. A chain abruptly stopped it short. It was a big Rottweiler. I could see its fangs glisten in the twilight, as its powerful jaws snapped at me. Behind it was a thick chain that clanged.

Kerry walked over to the dog, where it immediately calmed down. "It's OK, she's chained up. That's Lady by the way."

"That's Lady? She's one mean looking bit... I mean mother of a dog."

"Yeah. We use her as our guard dog."

We walked into the one story shed. Inside was a cot with a mosquito net.

"This is your room, and here are some mosquito incense coils. We got these shipped in from Taiwan." He said as he lit a coil.

"Is this your guest house?"

"Yeah mon. We had a Salvadorian here two weeks ago."

"Why was a Salvadorian here?"

"He was an illegal immigrant who had no place to go, no money, and no food. So we took him in to help him out. We do that a lot."

We walked out of the shed, and Lady watched me. She dashed out at me, but the chain's length yanked her back. She barked and snarled as we walked out of sight, and then she calmed down. We walked towards the back of the property, where, hidden amongst the palm and banana trees, was an old dilapidated wooden house full of old tools, bicycles, and assorted stuff.

"This was our first house. The new one we built is much better. This is the toilet." He said as he pointed to the wooden outhouse. "It's a Belizean style toilet." He said as he showed me the toilet paper. After a shit and a shower, I laid down in the cot in exhaustion.

****

407

After teaching a basic class on geography, some archeology, and basic expeditions at the Christian Academy, where Kerry and Mimi taught class, I spent the next day in the house reading and writing. Mr Jou went to work in Belize, where he worked as an electrician. Mrs. Jou ran a shop in Belize City. Lisa was at graduation practice and theater dance practice, and Kerry and Mimi were preparing student transcripts at the academy. The house was empty. As I wrote, I realized I'd left my notebook in my room, which was across the yard.

Now, during the week, I walked by the snarling, snapping, drooling, and badly behaved Lady. I always made sure that I was beyond the reach of her chain. Every time I passed by, she dashed out of the dog house, and immediately her chain stopped her midair, which caused her saliva drops to spray in all directions. It reminded me of an old Looney Tunes cartoon. By the third day, I started saying, "Hello Lady!", and when she rushed out at the end of her chain, I said, "how are you today Lady? What, the chain is keeping you from eating me alive? Pobrecita perra, that's alright. Kerry will feed you and then you'll forget about me." And then I'd smile at her while she furiously barked and strained against the chain.

On this day, I walked out from the kitchen, which had an enormous open door, and as I started walking to the shed, Lady came out. She started her dash, and I suddenly noticed that her chain was off the post.

I screamed as I made a mad a dash to the house door. I grabbed the door open, ran in, and then I ran into the shower room, where I closed both doors on both ends, sealing myself in. Outside, I could hear the dog's barking stop, and then a low growling. I waited for fifteen minutes. Quietly, I opened the door, and I didn't hear a sound. I tiptoed to the door, and looked out through the screen. Lady walked back to her dog house, and the moment I looked out the door, she saw me, and dashed at me again. I ran back to the shower room, and waited for an hour until the Jou's got home.

"Dave?"

"Dave!"

"Where's Dave?"

"I'm in the shower room!" I yelled out.

"What are you doing in there?" Asked a surprised Lisa.

"Lady! Her chain was off!" I said.

Lisa looked puzzled, and then she suddenly realized what I was talking about.

"Oh no! Kerry!"

"Let me go and see." Said Kerry. He went outside, and chained Lady back up. When he came back, I recounted the story.

"I don't know how the chain came off, but you're OK. Sorry about that." We all laughed about the incident. Mrs. Jou came in and saw us laughing. She looked me up and down.

"David! You're so pale! And just yesterday you were a nice brown like us. What happened?" Asked Mrs. Jou. I told her the story, and then she laughed. Later that evening, I attended Lisa's graduation and celebration.

On Saturday, I took a bus with Mr. Jou from Belmopan to Belize City. Mr Jou was finishing up some electrical work on a hotel in the city, and I took a ferry out to San Pedro. I spent the day snorkeling in the barrier reef. There, I chased color changing cuttle fish, and was mesmerized at the schools of fish, ray, and anemones. It was a riot of color, and I followed the fish until I got sea sick. On the docks, I watched an enormous ray swim in and bask between the pilings. The next day, it was time to go.

"Your family is wonderful, and I'm going to remember all of you for as long as I live. I'm going to miss you, Kerry, Mimi, and Lisa, for being such a fun bunch. Mrs. Jou, thanks to you and your food, I felt so much at home. Thanks Mr. Jou for showing me around. And thank you, all of you, for not eating me." We burst out in laughter.

"Will you come back?"

"One day. One day I will."

****

I biked up the steep hill overlooking a large ranch. There was a sign on the ranch with Chinese language on it, and then in English, "Yu's Ranch" printed below. It was misty in the valley below, as several cows grazed in the field. I left Tea Kettle Village two days ago, and met Jackie, a Taiwanese Belizean who was with Becky, his girl at a general farm store. I stayed with his family for the night, since I biked through some torrential rains. His family was very Taiwanese, and considered me crazy for taking on such a journey. For Jackie, I was a potent symbol of rebellion, and we talked about my travels.

I left the next day from their home and pedaled north to Mexico. I decided to bypass Belize City by taking a back country route north east, where I met Robert, a black Belizean fruit wine maker, and camped on his farm for the night.

"Have you ever had other bicycle travelers come through here?" I asked him.

"Yes, but no Americans like you. Japanese and Canadians, we got many, and we let them camp on our farm."

I shared dinner and breakfast with his family, and before I left, we took some pictures of me holding his wine for an advertisement. From there, I headed north. For most of the day, I kept biking, since the clouds covered up the sun, and the rain kept me cool. On average, I typically did eighty to ninety kilometers. That day, I did about a hundred and ten. Along the way, I spotted orange markers for a fiber optic line.

My trip was coming to an end. I knew I couldn't continue once I reached Mexico. June was just a week away, I was low on money, and severely lovesick for Claudia. I wanted to go back to Bolivia. All during my journey, we kept emailing each other, and when I could, I called. It was heart breaking to be so far away from her, but my wanderlust was too powerful. I also wanted to see Kendra, and find out how she felt about the picture.

"Hey! Hey you, mon!" A shout came out from the side of the road.

"Huh?"

"Over here mon! Over here!"

A half naked, black, Belizean man came out from the road side stand, waving his hands. He had a wide grin, and his teeth glowed in the glare of the sun. He was thin, but well muscled from hard farm work.

"Wouldya like sumfin to eat mon?" He said.

"Do you have jackfruit?" I asked.

He held up the large, green, spikey fruit.

"That's it! How much?"

"Four belizean dollars my friend. But please, stay and eat. I will cut it for you."

I walked into the shade of the stand, and looked at the wall behind him. As he cut the fruit, I saw a Koran, a Bible, a Talmud, a Baghavad Gita, a Buddhist Sutra, and several books on philosophy and Buddhism. We introduced ourselves. His name was Ibrahim.

410

"You know my friend," he said as he cut the fruit, "it is no coincidence that you've appeared today."

"Well, there's no such thing as a coincidence." I said.

"Bingo" he said as he gave me a heaping plate of the fruit's white flesh with a fork, and I started to eat. The sweet succulent juice flowed onto my tongue, and I relished the treat after such a long ride.

"I'm sure you've journeyed far and wide my friend, but did you ever ask yourself why you journey?"

"For adventure and exploration?"

"Oh, it goes much deeper than that. I can sense that in you. It's something you can't put into words."

"Good one." I said as I ate another piece of fruit.

"I've read many books. You can see them in back of me. I've thought for a very long time about being alive in this world. And I learned something, today, that I would like you to take back to your people."

"What's that?"

"Tell them this. It is the statement they must understand if they seek the answer. They must know, that the 'I' did not know."

"The 'I' did not know? Is that like I don't know?"

"In one way yes, but in others, no. What is the 'I', David?"

"Me, oh wait. It's my ego."

"And what is the ego?"

"The role I play in this world."

"Good. What else can the 'I' be?"

"My soul."

"Very good. Which is it then?"

"The ego, because the soul is all knowing."

"Good. Why would the 'I' not know? Have you ever thought about that?"

"It's the ego, and the ego is easily taken by its own pride, so it stays forever ignorant."

"David, in our earthly form, do you see this as your true-self?"

"No, because the soul, or the spirit within is the true-self."

"Then why is it that almost all of humanity has forgotten that?"

I paused before replying. "I see what you mean."

411

"Remember, the 'I' did not know, remember that message, and you will see that we exist to find the 'you' behind the 'I'."

Figure 26.1: I rest in a brief haven in the wilds of the Peten Jungle on the way to Belize. Course, that means sleeping with the pigs.

Figure 26.2: Me (upper left) and the Jou family.

Maps

Figure 26.3: Peru

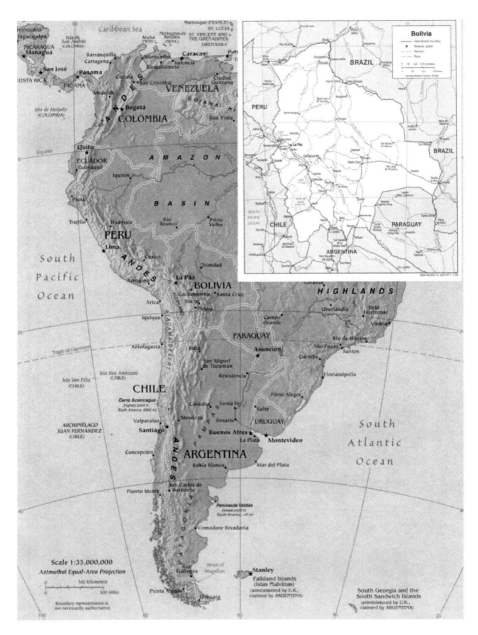

Figure 26.4: Bolivia

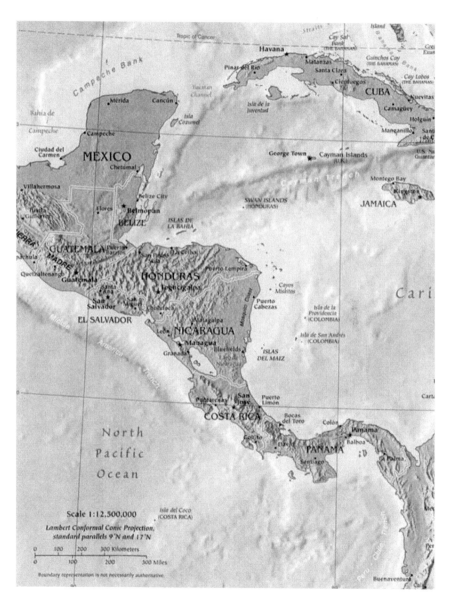

Figure 26.5: Central America

Afterword and Acknowledgments

Making a decision to publish a book is a lot like deciding to get married or to have a child. Up front, it sounds like a wonderful endeavor. There's fortune and glory. There's the pride in seeing your work in print. There's the endless possibilities that could happen from publishing a book.

It's all bunk. It's long nights, often for months and years, of staring at the computer screen until your eyes ache and your butt goes numb. Then you stand up and feel a rush of dizzying blood go through your head, feel like you're going to faint, lean over the computer and ask yourself, "why the hell am I doing this?"

Why indeed. In a lot of ways, despite the book's documenting and memorializing of my expedition, it's really a tribute to the marginalized peoples in the Western Hemisphere. They have earned much, from what they endured and accomplished in ancient times all the way to the present. They're the forgotten ones in world history. In addition to the past injustices that have gone without resolution, it's further injustice for us to be ignorant of their achievements, hopes, and aspirations.

But making a tribute is also like trying to buy a gift for your significant other. You rarely, if ever, get what they really want. Sometimes you'll get lucky, and they'll love your gift. More often, doubts linger inside. I hope this book gets halfway there in that regard, and if it does, I can sleep well at night.

Writing, despite it's solitary image of a person hunched over a typewriter, is still a team effort. So thanks to my editor Owen P. Langston for taking the time to edit, clean up, focus, and critique the book. Thanks to Andy and

Judy Shaw for reading and critiquing the preface and afterword sections. It's also hard to write a book if you're cooking, cleaning, maintaining, and doing chores all the time, so thanks to my family for their general support, and for putting up with my antics. Thanks to Elizabeth Shaw for supporting me through the publishing phase of the book. For a first time author, it's helpful to know other authors who've walked through the publishing gauntlet, and made their dreams real, so thanks to fellow writers Starr Kirkland and Cesar Alejandro Becerra for their advice and encouragement. Thanks to Anthony Khan for taking the photo of the coral reef in the caves of Isla de Pescado in the Salar. Thanks to Xavier Amaru Ruiz Garcia for teaching me more about the amazing mathematics of Tiwanaku and its advanced computer algorithms towards prime number theory and cosmology. Thanks to the folks involved in the Free Software Foundation and in Open Source Software, since this book was written in Open Office Writer, corrected with ispell, and then formatted and typeset in Lyx and Latex. Graphics were done in Gimp, Imagemagick, and Scribus. If it weren't for you folks, I'd have a hell of a time trying to make this book look professional.

Planning, executing, and surviving a major expedition is always a team effort. I don't know how else to thank the countless people who've helped, guided, protected, and assisted me in my explorations, but I'm going to try, so here goes: Marco Vidal and Ernesto Huaman for guiding me through Cusco, Sonia Suarez and her family for their hospitality, the 2001-2002 Peace Corps staff in Bolivia and Guatemala (you guys rock!), Chyang and Claudia Hwang, Christian Olivo, Elsa Quiroga, Roberto and Marco, Fernando Bonafe, Ted and Megan Friedenson, the Betancourt family, Jose, Liqu, Tito, Marcello and family, Don Carlos, the Jou family, and the Juan family. You folks didn't just help me in myriad ways, but you've also helped keep me humble in understanding just how much of a team effort an expedition is. Finally, I especially want to thank all the people of Peru, Bolivia, and Central America who helped, protected, and guided me during my expedition. This book is dedicated to you.

Finally, as with any quest or adventure, it never truly ends. You can learn more about my adventures at my website, http://davesnewadventure.com. My latest adventure is the cross country expedition through the backwoods of the Amazon, all the way across 3,700 miles of South America during 2007. Yes, it's connected to the ending of my romance. Yes, it's another crazy, death defying, exploration adventure. And yes, I did it almost completely on the bicycle, and this time, no one tried to keep me from crossing the Andes. Come to think of it, I'm surprised I survived that expedition too!

About the Author

David Nghiem is an adventurer, explorer, writer, and analyst. He's appeared in various Latin American programs and talk shows on television, radio, and print, speaking about his adventures and investigations. He's also been published in the Philadelphia Inquirer, and various internet publications.

David is also a biomedical engineer, speaker, and science teacher. His current project is on the advanced mathematics of Tiwanaku, an ancient ruin of the Aymaran peoples in Bolivia. Past projects include the design and fabrication of technologies for zero gravity suits, which involved the MIT's Aerospace and Astronautical Engineering department and the Boston University Neuromuscular Research Center, and as the co-founder and project coordinator of SPECTRE, a sounding rocket project designed and built as a collaboration of the Boston University Space Physics Lab, the Electrical-Computer Engineering Department, and NASA, which was launched on 14 June 2000.

You can read more about his latest adventure, "Sun Drenched on Two Wheels" in his website, http://davesnewadventure.com. David spends time between his residence in the USA, and in interesting places around the world investigating mysteries and learning about people.

List of Figures

LaVergne, TN USA
18 June 2010
186541LV00002B/1/P